WHITE
FRIGHT

ALSO BY JANE DAILEY

Building the American Republic, Volume 2:
A Narrative History from 1877

The Age of Jim Crow:
A Norton Documentary History

Before Jim Crow:
The Politics of Race in Postemancipation Virginia

WHITE FRIGHT

THE SEXUAL PANIC AT
THE HEART OF AMERICA'S
RACIST HISTORY

JANE DAILEY

BASIC BOOKS
NEW YORK

Basic Books
Hachette Book Group
1290 Avenue of the Americas, New York, NY 10104
www.basicbooks.com

Printed in the United States of America

First Edition: November 2020

Published by Basic Books, an imprint of Perseus Books, LLC, a subsidiary of Hachette Book Group, Inc. The Basic Books name and logo is a trademark of the Hachette Book Group.

The Hachette Speakers Bureau provides a wide range of authors for speaking events. To find out more, go to www.hachettespeakersbureau.com or call (866) 376-6591.

The publisher is not responsible for websites (or their content) that are not owned by the publisher.

Print book interior design by Six Red Marbles

Library of Congress Cataloging-in-Publication Data
Names: Dailey, Jane Elizabeth, 1963– author.
Title: White fright : the sexual panic at the heart of America's racist history / Jane Dailey.
Description: First edition. | New York : Basic Books, [2020] | Includes bibliographical
    references and index.
Identifiers: LCCN 2020019694 | ISBN 9781541646551 (hardcover) |
    ISBN 9781541646544 (ebook)
Subjects: LCSH: Miscegenation—Southern States—History—20th century. |
    Interracial marriage—Southern States—History—20th century. | African
    Americans—Sexual behavior—Public opinion. | African Americans—Southern
    States—Social conditions. | Whites—Southern States—Attitudes. | White
    supremacy movements—United States—History—20th century. | African
    Americans—Civil rights—Southern States—History—20th century. | Civil rights
    movements—Southern States—History—20th century. | Southern States—
    Race relations. | Southern States—Social conditions.
Classification: LCC E185.62 .D25 2020 | DDC 306.84/509750904—dc23
LC record available at https://lccn.loc.gov/2020019694

ISBNs: 978-1-5416-4655-1 (hardcover), 978-1-5416-4654-4 (ebook)

LSC-C

1 2020

Contents

Introduction

ORIGINS OF WHITE FRIGHT

A NATIVE OF INDIANA, Emily Reed had been living in Alabama only a few months when she faced a momentous decision. She had taken a job as director of the Alabama Public Library Service Division—not the sort of position that captured headlines. That changed when the Montgomery chapter of the prosegregation White Citizens' Council demanded that she ban a children's book, Garth Williams's *The Rabbits' Wedding*, from libraries throughout the state. The book—which told the story of the marriage of a little black bunny to a little white bunny—was attacked by segregationists for promoting interracial marriage.

The notion of an outright ban of *The Rabbits' Wedding* rubbed Miss Reed the wrong way. In an effort to mollify the enraged Alabamans without banning the book, she ordered it stowed on her department's reserve shelves. Her decision pleased neither the Citizens' Council, the Alabama state government, nor the author, who was appalled by the action and insisted that his book had no political significance. "I was completely unaware," he announced, "that animals with white fur, such as white polar bears and white dogs and white rabbits, were considered blood relations of white human beings." In a parting shot at Alabama, soon to be identified in the popular mind with fire hoses and snarling police dogs, Williams declared that the book was not written for adults, and that they would not understand it, "because it is only about a soft, furry love and has no hidden messages of hate."[1]

(Undaunted, Reed later included on a state-recommended list of notable books Martin Luther King Jr.'s book *Stride Toward Freedom*, an account of the 1956 Montgomery Bus Boycott, during which the successful efforts of local African Americans to desegregate the municipal buses sparked a robust civil rights movement as well as savage white resistance.) Reed's latest provocation inspired the state legislature to conflate genealogy and culture, and demand that the state library chief be a native of the state and a graduate of the University of Alabama or Auburn University.

A stranger to Alabama's racial politics, Emily Reed was surprised by the reaction to *The Rabbits' Wedding*. More astute—or at least more experienced—students of Southern social relations would not have been. The racially segregated and suffocating world of Jim Crow, which lasted from roughly 1890 until the 1960s, was rooted in fears of interracial sex and racial reproduction. When *The Rabbits' Wedding* was banned in 1959, marriage across the color line was prohibited in twenty-nine states, including Alabama and Reed's home state of Indiana. Most of those laws remained on the books until 1967, when the United States Supreme Court declared them unconstitutional in the case of *Loving v. Virginia*. Throughout this era, the politics, social relations, and laws of the South reflected and reproduced white fears of interracial sex and marriage.

As early as the abolition of slavery in 1865, advocates for African American equality understood that racially restrictive sex and marriage laws, and the state-enforced regime of racial identification that those laws made possible, lay at the heart of the segregated system they struggled to overthrow. In 1905, the sociologist, journalist, and activist W. E. B. Du Bois wrote the right to "associate with those who wish to associate with me" into the pledge of the Niagara Movement, the predecessor to the National Association for the Advancement of Colored People (NAACP). After the NAACP was formed in 1909, its first national lobbying victory was to convince Congress not to pass a racially restrictive marriage law for the District of Columbia. In the 1920s and 1930s, the Communist Party of the United States and Communist-affiliated organizations called for complete social equality and the repeal of state antimiscegenation laws. During and immediately after World War II, Christian interracial associations like the Federal Council of Churches joined secular radicals in this call. In the 1950s and 1960s, new organizations such as the Southern Christian Leadership Council (SCLC) and the Student Nonviolent Coordinating Committee (SNCC) also embraced this position on sex and marriage even as they focused primarily on issues of education, voting, and housing.

Given the centrality of racially restrictive sex and marriage laws to the creation and maintenance of white supremacy, one would expect their reversal to have been a top priority for advocates of African American equality. But for all the advocacy and lobbying against these laws, there was never a mass movement to overturn them. When the Supreme Court finally ruled in *Loving v. Virginia* that laws forbidding Americans to marry across the color line violated the Fourteenth Amendment, the case was argued by representatives of the American Civil Liberties Union (ACLU), not the NAACP.

For more than a century, between emancipation and 1967, African American rights were closely bound, both in law and in the white imagination, to the question of interracial sex and marriage. At every stage of the struggle for civil rights, sex played a central role, even when its significance was left unspoken. Overcoming the conflation of sexual and civil rights was a project of decades and arguably the greatest challenge champions of Black equality faced.

INTERRACIAL MARRIAGE WAS regulated in America for more than three hundred years. In the beginning, in the colonies of Maryland and Virginia, freeborn English men and women were permitted to marry

Africans and the indigenous people Europeans called Indians. But laws governing interracial sex and marriage emerged only a few years after the first contact between Africans and Europeans in America and played an essential role in establishing stable categories of Blackness and whiteness, and therefore stable categories of slave and free.

The sexual activity of white men with Black women, mainly between masters and slaves, produced most of the mixed-race population in the South. The majority of these encounters were almost certainly coerced, either through force or through more subtle invocations of the vast disparity of power between the partners. The children born of such unions were enslaved, as their legal status followed that of their mother. As time went on, liaisons between white women and colored men, tolerated as recently as the seventeenth century, presented a social dilemma insofar as the mixed-race children of white women were free, and undermined efforts to link freedom and racial identity.

In an attempt to solder status to race once and for all, Southern states passed new laws in the eighteenth century that prohibited marriages between whites and Blacks and also punished people who engaged in interracial adultery. The first legal ban on interracial marriage was a 1705 Virginia act, which also defined who was nonwhite.

These laws did not mean that white and Black Americans stopped having sex with each other. Although white men crossed the racial boundary in search of sex more often than white women did, even white women's interracial sexual liaisons went uncensored more than might be expected. Sex between Black men and white women seems to have been tolerated unless and until such unions produced mixed-race children. Dorothea Bourne, for example, could probably have indefinitely sustained her long-standing adulterous affair with a neighbor's slave had she not borne his child. The arrival of a suspiciously dark baby cast Dorothea's much older husband, Lewis, in the public role of cuckold, and he filed for divorce in 1824.

Prosecutions under the anti-intermarriage statutes often turned on complex questions of racial identity. A court could rule that a marriage was illegal only once the racial identities of the spouses could be established at law. Miscegenation as transgression depended on the establishment of clear legal boundaries to transgress. Yet miscegenation as historical fact undercut those very boundaries. Because miscegenation threatened to undermine any system of straightforward racial classification, it became a problem for the Southern social and labor system, which depended more and more on clear distinctions between white and nonwhite.

Mixed-race families nonetheless flourished without much incident from the eighteenth century until well into the nineteenth, though public opinion was by then hardening against interracial sex and marriage.[2] Antebellum state legislatures wrote laws defining racial categories for the purpose of marriage, outlining people's marital possibilities according to the various numerical degrees of Blackness. Depending on the state and the decade, people who were more than half Black, one-fourth Black, one-eighth Black, one-sixteenth Black, or even one-thirty-second Black could not marry anyone defined as white under the law. In 1850, the US Census introduced a new racial category of "mulatto" and concluded that 11 percent of the nation's African Americans were mixed race.[3] Most of this population was enslaved, but an unknown number of mixed-race Americans lived as free men and women, many of them "passing" across a color barrier that was more akin to a barbed-wire fence than a wall.[4]

Arguments about interracial sex and marriage became highly politicized in the late 1850s, following the birth of the Republican Party in 1856. In the 1858 Illinois senatorial campaign, Republican Abraham Lincoln was confronted by Democrats hoisting a banner depicting a Black man, a white woman, and an interracial child. Democrat Stephen A. Douglas accused Lincoln of supporting Black-white "social equality," a charge Lincoln rebutted, proclaiming that he did not favor "the social and political equality of the white and black races." Lincoln emphatically denied any support of interracial marriage, and he pledged to uphold Illinois's law forbidding interracial sex and marriage. Six years later, in the 1864 presidential election, Democrats portrayed President Lincoln and other Republicans as champions of "miscegenation," a term a pair of Democratic political operatives coined to describe the amalgamation of the races through sex across the color line.

This fixation on interracial sex was a new development. Before the Civil War, white slaveholders who reveled in their sexual domination of slave women had not concerned themselves with maintaining white "racial purity." Nor did they worry about Black men, slave or free, raping white women. They were more concerned, in fact, with the possibility that white women might desire and pursue slave men, as Dorothea Bourne did.[5] As the historian Eugene Genovese wrote more than forty years ago, the "titillating and violence-provoking theory of the superpotency of that black superpenis, while whispered about for several centuries, did not become an obsession in the South until after emancipation."[6] White anxiety about African American sexual prowess and Black men's desirability to white women emerged alongside the enfranchisement of African American men during Reconstruction.

Starting with the first congressional debates over the Reconstruction amendments to the Constitution, opponents of African American equality began to link sexual and political rights, arguing that emancipation and, especially, the enfranchisement of Black men would inevitably lead to interracial sex, marriage, and children. As one Southerner laid it out, "Do away with the social and political distinctions now existing, and you immediately turn all the blacks and mulattoes into citizens, co-governors, and acquaintances: and acquaintances…are the raw material from which are *manufactured friends, husbands, and wives.* The man whom you associate with is next invited to your house, and the man whom you invited to your house is the possible husband of your daughter, whether he be black or white." This fixation on interracial sex—or, in the language of the postemancipation South, miscegenation and amalgamation—was not only an individual reality but became a powerful political disposition crafted in opposition to African American liberty and political power after the Civil War.

Champions of Black voting (especially if Black men voted Republican) insisted that clear lines could be drawn between political and what became known as "social" rights. "It is fright that makes you mistake a ballot for a billet-doux" (love letter), Republican William "Pig Iron" Kelley teased the Democrats in 1868. "It cannot be possible that any man of common sense can bring himself to believe that marriages between any persons, much less between white and colored people, will take place because a colored man is allowed to drop a little bit of paper into a box."

But many white men believed exactly this, and after emancipation in 1865, "white supremacy" acquired both new meaning and, for white Southerners, new urgency. As practiced by those dedicated to the proposition, "white supremacy" was both a social argument and a political program designed to reestablish white men's social and political dominance after the war and Reconstruction. Forged out of the catastrophic Confederate loss, the new, supposedly "solid" white-supremacist South of the turn of the twentieth century was not the immediate outcome of the war but the product of forty years of violence, voting fraud, and mass disenfranchisement.

What became known as the Jim Crow South, after a minstrel character and dance, was founded on two interrelated lies: on the supposed political incapacity and unworthiness of African American men, and on their inborn tendency to sexual predation and fixation on white women. This false narrative of African American civic incompetence and sexual rapaciousness arose alongside Black electoral success and participation in governance.

These myths did not preempt Black empowerment. White Southern men had already experienced the effectiveness of African American participation in governance after emancipation by the time these stories began to spread. During Reconstruction, Black men held political office in every state of the former Confederacy. Twenty-two African Americans were elected to Congress between 1870 and 1900, including two US senators, both from Mississippi. More than one hundred Black men won election or appointment to posts with jurisdiction over entire states, and almost eight hundred served in state legislatures. A much larger number held public office at the local level.[7] The argument that Black men were inherently unfit to participate in democratic rule came *in response* to their electoral potency, not as an effort to prevent it.

Across the South, but especially in the Upper South, freed Blacks and Republican or dissident Democratic whites combined, usually in support of fiscal policies that would deliver public services for everyone, such as schools and hospitals. These interracial coalition parties did surprisingly well in a political region where partisan divides were expected to parallel the color line, and they contributed to the volatility of late nineteenth-century Southern politics. The success of each of these factions depended on the ballots of African Americans, who voted in most places throughout the late nineteenth century.

Black-white political fusion galvanized elite white Southerners, whose power was threatened by this development, to use every weapon at their disposal to end the danger of biracial opposition parties. Building on grids of kinship and political patronage, and fired up by the experience of military defeat, white men across the South reacted to the political mobilization of Black men with unprecedented violence. Functioning effectively as the paramilitary arm of the Democratic Party, the Ku Klux Klan and other allied groups organized in the late 1860s and early 1870s to destroy the political infrastructure of Black life. Reconstruction was experienced as an organized brawl in many states as the Democrats captured control of state governments through a combination of intimidation, electoral fraud, and violence, including indiscriminate massacres of Black men, women, and children, and political assassination. White Republicans who allied with Black men were also targets. In one incident in Louisiana in 1876, armed white supremacists executed six white Republican officeholders. That same year in Mississippi, White League units murdered some three hundred African Americans.[8]

Both elements of white Democrats' justification for Jim Crow— Black incompetence and interracial sexual designs—were necessary components of their region-wide campaign to enhance their own power at the expense of all others. By the dawn of the twentieth century, white supremacists had stripped Black men, and a majority of Southern white men as well, of political power, justifying their actions through a new political discourse about racial purity and sexual danger. African Americans, particularly Black men, were left in the position of fighting a powerful and perilous new representation of themselves.

ALTHOUGH SOME SLAVES gained their freedom by escaping during the war and some by joining the Union army, most slaves were emancipated through a series of statutes passed by Congress between 1862 and 1865, and, finally, through the Thirteenth Amendment to the Constitution (ratified in 1866). The new amendment declared, "Neither slavery nor involuntary servitude, except as punishment for a crime whereof the party shall have been duly convicted, shall exist in the United States, or any place subject to their jurisdiction." An enabling clause endowed Congress with the authority to enact "appropriate legislation" to enforce the amendment.[9]

The Thirteenth Amendment did more than abolish slavery—though how much more was subject to debate. By failing to define the terms of the amendment, its authors invited a conversation about its attributes and about the meaning of emancipation, freedom, and equality. African Americans considered everything that constrained life on the basis of race part of the definition of slavery. Rather than define "freedom" in abstract terms vulnerable to constriction, African Americans and some white abolitionists spoke concretely of what might be termed "not-slavery." As an assembly of Alabama freedmen put it as early as 1865, "We claim exactly *the same rights, privileges and immunities as are enjoyed by white men*, because the law no longer knows white or black, but simply men."

First and foremost, not-slavery meant self-sovereignty and recognition of one's humanity, by oneself and others. Slavery robbed people of personal autonomy. Emancipation, in theory, restored it. Free people moved about the land and lived where they chose. Free people were protected from assault to their persons: whipping, branding, rape, mutilation, forced labor, kidnapping, murder.[10] Free people formed lasting human bonds within the institution of marriage if they chose. Free people governed their domestic households, including their children and, if husbands, their wives. Free people were welcome in the common spaces of the public sphere: schools and libraries, theaters and parks, places of public accommodation and refreshment. Free people had access to all the rights other people enjoyed, including rights to property and contract and the right to join in the common project of democratic governance. The most obvious means of participating in the governance of the people was by voting. As Frederick Douglass, the premier African American leader, argued in May 1865, less than a month after the Confederate surrender at Appomattox, "Slavery is not abolished until the black man has the ballot."[11]

Whereas African Americans considered the Thirteenth Amendment to contain within it the necessary attributes of freedom, whites in Congress were embroiled in a heated effort to define and enumerate the rights of free people. When all-white Southern legislatures passed laws in late 1865 known as the Black Codes, which severely restricted African American movement, freedom of association, and employment, Congress was obliged to expand on its understanding of abolition. The task fell to Illinois senator Lyman Trumbull, who had drafted the Thirteenth Amendment. Elected to the Senate by the Illinois legislature in 1855 over, among other candidates, Abraham Lincoln, Trumbull was one of the first Republicans to see emancipation as a war goal. Responding both to white persecution of the freedpeople and to the demands of Southern Blacks for "a republican form of government" (i.e., one that included them), Trumbull drafted the Civil Rights Act of 1866. This act was designed to enforce congressional Republicans' understanding of the freedom promised to slaves by the Thirteenth Amendment, and it guaranteed African Americans the "full and equal benefit of all laws and proceedings for the security of person and property as is enjoyed by white citizens."

When doubts arose about the constitutionality of the 1866 act, Republicans enacted the Fourteenth Amendment, which embraced African Americans as citizens, guaranteeing "due process of law," "equal protection of the laws," and "the privileges or immunities of citizenship" to all persons. It also incented white Southerners to permit Black suffrage by reducing the congressional representation of any state that denied the vote to male citizens aged twenty-one or older.

Although the Fourteenth Amendment eventually became the most powerful constitutional tool for the protection of minority rights, in the short term it failed to guarantee the political participation of Black men. In 1868, the Georgia legislature dealt with the election of African American representatives by expelling them, prompting Congress to draft its third and final Reconstruction amendment. The Fifteenth Amendment (1870) prohibited any state to deny any citizen the right to vote on "account of race." The amendment was silent about the right to hold office and did not forbid other suffrage restrictions such as literacy tests and poll taxes. Yet despite its limitations, the Fifteenth Amendment enshrined in the nation's fundamental law the principle that no citizen may, on account of race, be denied the right, as its Senate sponsor William Stewart put it, "to protect his own liberty" through participation in governance.[12]

THOUGH MARRIAGE WAS not expressly mentioned in the Civil Rights Act of 1866, the act provided that all "citizens, of every race and color,...shall have the same right...to make and enforce contracts... as is enjoyed by white citizens." Whether interracial marriage was a "contract" within the meaning of this guarantee was a matter of sharp debate during Reconstruction.[13] Indeed, President Andrew Johnson vetoed the 1866 act on the grounds that it might be construed to forbid laws against interracial marriage. "I do not say that this bill repeals State laws on the subject of marriage between the two races," Johnson explained, but he worried that if it allowed "Congress [to] abrogate all State laws of discrimination between the two races in the matter of real estate, or suits, and of contracts generally," could it not "repeal the State laws as to the contract of marriage between the two races?"[14] The act was passed over Johnson's veto, but the effect of the law on interracial marriages remained obscure.

Marriage had always been regulated exclusively by the states. In addition to incorporating traditional limitations on polygamy, consanguinity, and age of consent, many state legislatures in the nineteenth century prohibited interracial marriage. These laws, of course, restricted the liberty of whites as well as Blacks, however porous the legal definition of each category might be. After the Civil War, Alabama, Arkansas, Delaware, Florida, Georgia, Louisiana, Mississippi, Missouri, North Carolina, South Carolina, Tennessee, Texas, Virginia, and Wyoming all enacted or reenacted antimiscegenation laws. Moreover, Alabama, Florida, Kentucky, Missouri, North Carolina, and Wyoming went even further, passing laws prohibiting interracial sex.[15] Nevertheless, under interracial Republican rule during Reconstruction, seven of eleven states of the former Confederacy *repealed* their antimiscegenation laws or declared them unconstitutional.[16] Given the prominence of Black men in these political coalitions, it was not paranoid of white Southerners to fear that African American men empowered with the vote would wield it against other race-based laws.

During the early postwar era, Radical Republicans tried to carve space for Black political participation by pushing vexing questions of social relationships to the margins. Drawing a sharp boundary between the public world of men and the private world of families, Republican politicians staked the future of interracial democracy on their ability to detach interracial marriage from the bundle of rights otherwise belonging to the freedpeople. White supporters of civil rights went out of their way to explain that they had no intention of outlawing antimiscegenation laws, and that, indeed, new legislation protecting African Americans' civil rights had *nothing* to do with marriage.

When asked during debate on the Civil Rights Act whether a Black man had a civil right to marry a white woman, Lyman Trumbull replied that the law's chief object was "to secure the same civil rights and subject to the same punishment persons of all races and colors." How "does this interfere with [a state law] preventing marriages between whites and blacks?" Trumbull asked. "[The law] forbidding marriages between whites and blacks operates alike on both races. This bill does not interfere with it. If the negro is denied the right to marry a white person, the white person is equally denied the right to marry the negro. I see no discrimination against either in this respect that does not apply to both."[17]

Congressional Democrats rejected this concept of segmented rights and forged a link between sexual and political rights, warning that giving Black men the vote would lead inevitably to interracial marriage and the leveling of all social distinctions. Insisted Kentucky senator Garrett Davis, "The races are either equal or unequal….If they are equal, they not only have the right to vote, but they have the right to be eligible to all offices; they not only have the right to civil protection and to enjoy all civil rights, but they are entitled also to all political and social rights."[18]

Republicans did their best to unlock the logic that underlay this Democratic vision—that there was an inexorable progression from citizens to cogovernors to acquaintances to family—but doing so proved both difficult and frustrating. During congressional debate over Black suffrage, a Pennsylvania Republican accused the Democrats of injecting the miscegenation issue into every discussion: "Let our sensitive friends compose their nerves and try to tell us how a little enlargement of the elective franchise…will result in marriage between the two races."[19] "Social" rights such as marriage, argued the Republicans, were separable from political or civil rights such as voting; indeed, legal prohibitions on interracial sex and marriage could serve as the barrier between an integrated masculine public sphere and a private sphere where racial separation still applied.

In the short term, separating marriage rights from suffrage and creating a category of "social" rights that would both uphold and demarcate political rights helped create space for African American political power and facilitated interracial democracy in the South. But from the perspective of African American equality, there were two unfortunate effects to this strategy. First, African Americans' political allies rejected freedom of marriage as a right. Second, when congressional Republicans denied that marriage was a contract like any other, they opened the door to Democratic arguments that the institution of marriage fell exclusively under the jurisdiction of the states. Indiana, a nonslave state with a white-supremacist outlook, set the example in 1871. In *State of Indiana v. Gibson*, the Indiana Supreme Court ruled that marriage "is more than a mere contract. It is a public institution established by God himself....The right, in the states, to regulate and control, to guard, protect, and preserve this God-given, civilizing, and Christianizing institution is of inestimable importance, and cannot be surrendered."[20]

Southern state courts were only too happy to follow the lead of this nominally Northern state. Within a few years, all the Southern states whose Reconstruction legislatures had repealed their antimiscegenation laws reinstated them. Five states wrote bans on interracial marriage into new state constitutions, and others increased the criminal penalties for violation of this law.[21]

An 1881 miscegenation case in Alabama went even further. Tony Pace, an African American man, and Mary Cox, a white woman, were not married (which was a felony in Alabama), but they cohabited. In *Pace and Cox v. State*, the Alabama Supreme Court adopted the argument offered in defense of the Civil Rights Act of 1866 by Senator Trumbull to find antimiscegenation laws in accord with the Constitution. There was no discrimination in the antimiscegenation statute, declared the court, because "the punishment of each offending party, white and black, is precisely the same." Two years later, in *Pace v. Alabama*, the United States Supreme Court agreed.[22] This remained the law until 1964, when the Supreme Court in *McLaughlin v. Florida* struck down Florida's law against interracial cohabitation—but not its law against interracial marriage—as unconstitutional.[23]

While these issues were being established in the courts, white supremacists sexualized ever greater portions of public space. They received considerable help from the courts, many of which internalized the notion that "social amalgamation leads to illicit intercourse which leads to intermarriage."[24] Limits on freedom of sex and marriage justified limitations on other forms of social contact believed to lead to sex and marriage. Public schools, hospitals, trains, streetcars, restaurants, theaters—the list goes on—were segregated through the extension and application of this sexual logic. Out of this web of social regulation the Jim Crow South was born.[25]

Yet the process was not quite as easy as white supremacists imagined it would be. Southern Democrats were confronted repeatedly by interracial political challenges to white-supremacist unity. North Carolina, for example, developed a robust tradition of African American voting and Black-white political cooperation. Having been voted out of power by an alliance of Black Republicans and white Populists in the mid-1890s, North Carolina Democrats turned the 1898 state election into a referendum on white supremacy. Equating the participation of Black men as voters and officeholders with the complete oppression of whites, Democratic newspapers complained in bold letters of "NEGRO DOMINATION" in public life. More ominously, they reported a nonexistent epidemic of Black-on-white rape, which they connected to Black political power and a related desire for "social" equality. Handbills spread the message in cartoon form for the illiterate: one showed James H. Young, a Black politician from Raleigh, lurking in a white woman's bedroom.[26]

A few weeks before the election, the editor of the *Wilmington Record*, North Carolina's only Black daily newspaper, responded to white men's apparent sexual worries. Alexander Manly was the mixed-race son of Charles Manly, a former North Carolina governor, and his slave. On the topic of interracial sex, Alex Manly wrote:

Our experience among poor white people in the country teaches us that women of that race are not any more particular in the matter of clandestine meetings with colored men than the white men with colored women....Every Negro lynched is called "a Big Burly Black Brute," when, in fact, many of those who have thus been dealt with had white men for their fathers, and were not only not "black and burly," but were sufficiently attractive for white girls of culture and refinement to fall in love with them.[27]

The possibility of white women's desire for Black men was so threatening to the social myths white supremacists held dear that this kind of speech could not be countenanced. White supremacy depended on a lot of things to work, but at the level of racial reproduction it insisted on white women cooperating in their role as the guardians and repositories of white racial purity. In this role, white women would not—could not—engage in voluntary sexual intercourse with Black men. Under the new conditions of the Jim Crow South, the space for white women's sexual desire constricted almost as quickly as Black men's political power.

Alexander Manly's editorial inflamed North Carolina whites, allowing the Democrats to cast the election in terms of race and manhood. Across the state, white men who had cooperated previously with African Americans abandoned their former allies and voted Democratic. Victory in the election, however, was not enough. Even after the election, Wilmington, North Carolina's largest city, retained its biracial municipal government, which included three Black aldermen, a number of Black policemen, two all-Black fire companies, and John Dancy, the customs collector, who represented the federal government at the city's port, its center of trade. In the days following the election, illegal Democratic militias patrolled Wilmington's streets, seized public buildings, and forced the city council to resign. A mob burned Alex Manly's press to the ground, causing him to flee to the North. The armed white men then turned on the Black community, killing at least fourteen people and expelling hundreds more, who melted into the nearby forest with whatever property they could carry.[28]

Despite their victory in North Carolina and in Wilmington, Southern Democrats realized that they could not rely forever on terrorism to destroy their political opponents. Hoping to legitimate their rule rather than operate outside the law through violence and fraud, Southern Democrats looked for more legal, and lasting, means to disenfranchise the competition. "There must be devised some legal defensible substitute for the abhorrent and evil methods on which white supremacy lies," one Mississippi newspaper put it unselfconsciously.[29]

The Fifteenth Amendment forbade voter discrimination on the basis of race, color, or previous condition, yet outside those broad guidelines, each state could define its electorate on its own terms. Beginning with Mississippi in 1890, all eleven states of the former Confederacy rewrote their constitutions to adopt poll taxes, literary tests, and other devices calculated to eliminate the votes of Black men and their white political allies.[30]

The catastrophic consequences of disenfranchisement for Southern Blacks cannot be overstated. In the 1880s, more than two-thirds of adult Southern males voted. That proportion rose to nearly three-quarters in the 1890s in states that had not yet limited the franchise. By the early 1900s, fewer than one man in three, white or Black, voted in the South.[31] As intended, voting restrictions had a hugely disproportionate effect on African Americans. If Black men could not vote, they could not be elected to office; if they could not be elected to office, they could not shape or administer the laws that governed them. Sixty-four African Americans sat in Mississippi's state legislature in 1873; none did after 1895.

Although many Southern whites were disenfranchised alongside their Black neighbors, and the South as a whole suffered from the creation of an uncompetitive one-party political system, African Americans paid by far the greatest price. Stripped of the vote, Black Southerners lost what little political leverage they had just when they needed it to fend off the codification of Jim Crow.

TO TRULY UNDERSTAND the story of the African American freedom struggle, we must consider the central role played by issues of sex and marriage, and particularly interracial sex and marriage. Equally or per-haps more importantly, we must also take into account the sustained resistance to Black rights. The civil rights movement was articulated against a white opposition that was explicitly and thoroughly sexu-alized. Understanding why that was, and how civil rights activists navigated this position, is crucial to a broader understanding of racial politics in America.

One

FIGHTING FOR JUSTICE

W HEN IN 1896 the Supreme Court, in a seven-to-one decision in *Plessy v. Ferguson*, upheld a Louisiana law requiring all railway companies operating within the state to provide "equal but separate accommodations for the white, and colored races," Justice John Marshall Harlan's dissent leveled the most odious insult at the majority opinion that he could think of. "In my opinion," the former Kentucky slaveowner and Unionist declared, "the judgment this day rendered will, in time, prove to be quite as pernicious as the decision made by this tribunal in the *Dred Scott Case*."[1]

Dred Scott v. Sandford (1857) had denied the possibility of African American citizenship and declared infamously that the Black man had no rights "which the white man was bound to respect." That notorious decision was overridden first by the war and then by the Thirteenth, Fourteenth, and Fifteenth Amendments to the Constitution. Harlan considered Louisiana's separate but equal law to be at odds with the Fourteenth Amendment—whose object, Justice Henry Billings Brown had conceded in the majority opinion in *Plessy*, "was undoubtedly to enforce the absolute equality of the two races before the law."

In response, Harlan argued that "separate but equal" was "inconsistent with the personal liberty of citizens, white and black,…and hostile to both the spirit and letter of the constitution of the United States." Certain that the purpose of the Louisiana statute was to "defeat legitimate results of the war, under the pretense of recognizing equality of rights," Harlan predicted that the statute's affirmation by the court would "keep alive a conflict of races, the continuance of which must do harm to all concerned."[2]

Justice Harlan's colleagues on the court could not have disagreed more. In their view, the Louisiana separate-carriage law had nothing to do with the Fourteenth Amendment. The equal protection clause "could not have been intended to abolish distinctions based upon color, or to enforce social, as distinguished from political, equality, or a commingling of the two races upon terms unsatisfactory to either." Laws requiring segregation by race did not, they insisted, "necessarily imply the inferiority of either race to the other, and have been generally, if not universally, recognized as within the competency of the state legislatures."

In a fateful link, Justice Brown gave two examples of legally imposed segregation common across the nation: segregated public schools and racially restrictive marriage laws. Admitting that antimiscegenation laws "may be said in a technical sense to interfere with the freedom of contract," he noted nonetheless that such statutes were universally accepted as a reasonable exercise of the police power of the state "for the preservation of the public peace and good order" in such areas as health, safety, and morals. Gauged by this standard, Brown concluded, "We cannot say that a law which authorizes or even requires the separation of the two races in public conveyances is unreasonable, or more obnoxious to the fourteenth amendment than the acts of congress requiring separate schools for colored children in the District of Columbia…or the corresponding acts of state legislatures."[3]

In his dissent, which followed the logic and language of Albion Tourgée, the lead lawyer for the plaintiffs, Justice Harlan ridiculed the majority, "who affect to be disturbed at the possibility that the integrity of the white race may be corrupted, or that its supremacy will be imperiled, by contact on public highways with black people," but he did not expressly address the root fear that lay behind nearly every invocation of the "social equality" argument by whites in the postemancipation period: interracial sex. As the Pennsylvania Supreme Court had already observed, integrated rail carriages would promote "promiscuous sitting," which could only lead to "illicit intercourse" and facilitate "intermarriage."[4]

The *Plessy* decision raised more questions than it answered. What were the "political" rights protected by the Fourteenth Amendment? What were the "social" rights beyond the scope of the Constitution? In the short term, at least, the list of political rights looked exceedingly brief, while the list of social rights grew ever longer. Louisiana's separate-car rule metastasized and spread to other regions and areas of life. In 1904, the state of Kentucky passed a segregated education bill that forced Berea College, founded on the former estate of the abolitionist Cassius M. Clay to "promote the cause of Christ" by educating "all youths of good moral character," to close its doors to Black students. When Berea College sued, the trial court upheld the statute and opined that "no well-informed person in any section of the country will now deny the position of the Southern people that 'segregation in school, church and society is in the interest of racial integrity, and racial progress.'" The Kentucky Court of Appeals, invoking a higher authority, asserted a correspondence of the law of Kentucky with that of God: "The natural law which forbids their intermarriage, and that social amalgamation which leads to a corruption of the races, is as clearly divine as that which imparted to them different natures.... From social amalgamation it is but a step to illicit intercourse, and but another to intermarriage."[5] When the Supreme Court of the United States upheld the Kentucky statute, the lesson was clear: because the right to prohibit miscegenation had been established, "to prohibit joint education is not much more of a step," as the *Harvard Law Review* put it.[6]

IN THE SPRING of 1914, Louisville, Kentucky, followed the lead of other border-state cities in passing a residential segregation ordinance. Designed to "prevent conflict and ill-feeling between the white and colored races," the ordinance provided that Blacks could not occupy a residence on a white-majority block, or vice versa.[7] As a response to the northward migration of Southern Blacks, residential segregation laws were necessary, according to the Kentucky appeals court, "to prevent the mixing of the races in cross breeding."[8] Or, as the attorneys for Louisville put it to the Supreme Court, "It is shown by philosophy, experience and legal decisions, to say nothing of Divine Writ, that... the races of the earth shall preserve their racial integrity by living socially by themselves."[9] In addition to aggravating African Americans, such sentiments so alarmed the original custodians of Divine Writ that Louisville officials had to reassure local Jews that they would not be next.[10]

Residential segregation laws turned out to be an excellent recruitment tool for the NAACP, which was founded in 1909, launched a branch in Louisville specifically to fight the municipal law. NAACP founding president Moorfield Storey, a prominent white Boston attorney and past president of the American Bar Association, built a case against the restrictions in Louisville squarely on the question of property rights. He took it all the way to the Supreme Court. It was only the second case of the NAACP's to reach that level.[11]

The case was a success. In *Buchanan v. Warley* (1917), the Supreme Court concluded that Louisville's residential segregation law was intended to maintain racial purity and protect the value of property owned by whites. Although recognizing that there was a public interest in controlling certain uses of property (as when, for example, a municipality regulated a stable or a saloon in the interest of public safety and health), Justice William R. Day concluded that there was no constitutionally legitimate justification for residential segregation, and insisted that this "drastic measure" was "based wholly upon color; simply that, and nothing more."[12]

Invoking the Fourteenth Amendment, Day observed that the original purpose of the amendment had been "to expand federal protection to the recently emancipated race from unfriendly and discriminatory legislation by the States." Citing the underutilized Civil Rights Acts of 1866 and 1870, which granted all persons the same rights to purchase or sell property and to make and enforce contracts, Justice Day noted that the two laws concerned not mere "social rights" of association, but "those fundamental rights in property which it was intended to secure upon the same terms to citizens of every race and color." Recognizing that "there exists a serious and difficult problem arising from a feeling of race hostility which the law is powerless to control," Day concluded that "depriving citizens of their constitutional rights and privileges" was not a permissible way to further the cause of racial comity. Explicitly rejecting Louisville's suggestion that residential segregation laws were of a piece with antimiscegenation laws, which were accepted by all as a legitimate police power of the state because both prohibited "the amalgamation of the races," Day, speaking for a unanimous court, rejected the ordinance as violating the "fundamental law" of the Fourteenth Amendment.[13] Norfolk's Black newspaper the *New Journal and Guide* acknowledged the importance of the decision, remarking that "never before in the history of the Supreme Court has that tribunal reached a unanimous decision upon any question upholding the rights of the Negro."[14]

The decision in *Buchanan* did not end residential discrimination or segregation by race. What was formally forbidden could, the *Richmond News Leader* reassured its white readers, still be maintained "by custom, if not by law."[15] Neighborhood residential covenants—through which property holders circumscribed their own property rights voluntarily—passed constitutional muster, at least for the moment.

One of the lessons of *Buchanan* was that although the state could constitutionally impose segregation, there were limits. Rights of property, for example, could trump the presumptive power of the state to regulate social relations between the races. *Buchanan* revealed that the miscegenation analogy could be broken, or at least rendered ineffective, by a sufficiently strong counterclaim.

At least one longtime defender of African American equality, who was nonetheless not immune to contemporary constructions of racial difference and hierarchy, was heartened by the transformation in arguments to justify social segregation. In 1913, Moorfield Storey wrote to William Monroe Trotter, Boston's crusading Black journalist and head of the National Equal Rights League, that fifty years earlier white men insisted that Blacks were "and always must remain hewers of wood and drawers of water because they are incapable of anything else." But "the cry now," Storey continued, "is that there is danger of racial equality, that colored men will sit at the table with white men and may marry white men's daughters. This is not the fear of an inferior race; it is the fear that a race, though inferior, is proving its right to equality. The very arguments of those who would discriminate against you are admissions of your ability to rise, and of the fact that you have risen and are rising."

IN HIS INFAMOUS *Dred Scott* decision in 1857, Chief Justice Roger A. Taney had emphasized the degraded status of free Blacks in America in order to deny them citizenship rights. To this end, Justice Taney had pointed to two facts: Blacks were forbidden from marrying whites, and Black men were excluded from serving in state militias. After quoting a number of state antimiscegenation laws, Taney turned to white-only state militias. Why, he asked, were African American men not permitted to share in one of the highest duties of the citizen? The answer, he explained, was obvious. "He is not, by the institutions and laws of the State, numbered among its people. He forms no part of the sovereignty of the State, and is not therefore called on to uphold and defend it."

Taney concluded, "Nothing could more strongly mark the repudiation of the African race."[16]

The connection between bearing arms in defense of a community and being vested with full rights within it is ancient and enduring. As Justice Taney noted, the issues had been linked in America since the nation's founding. Members of a community are expected to defend it; by the same token, those who defend the people may expect whatever rights are enjoyed by the people. Forty years after *Dred Scott*, African Americans rushed to enlist in the Spanish-American War, hoping that fighting for Cuban liberation might gain them freedom at home. But white Southerners, who were overrepresented in the military, blocked every effort to train Black volunteers as combat troops. African American leaders, disappointed that Black military service in Cuba and the Philippines had not undermined Jim Crow, saw the advent of another war in 1914 as a further opportunity to promote civil equality. This time would be different.[17]

For Europe, World War I was an epic disaster that destroyed a generation and inaugurated an era of impoverishment and political revolution.[18] The United States, peopled as it was with immigrants from both sides of the European conflict, remained neutral for the first three years. President Woodrow Wilson, elected in 1912 and reelected as a peace candidate in 1916, reluctantly asked Congress for a declaration of war against Germany in April 1917. The president framed American entry into the European war as a crusade to redeem the Old World from its own most corrupt impulses. It was a "war to end war," in which America sought a "peace without victory."[19]

Wilson's idealism appealed to many African American leaders, who embraced the "war for democracy" rhetoric in the hope of challenging racial discrimination and second-class citizenship at home. The white-supremacist system that the Wilson administration had supported by segregating government offices and replacing the nation's few African American foreign emissaries with white men seemed suddenly vulnerable. W. E. B. Du Bois, who edited the NAACP newspaper, *The Crisis*, allowed himself to hope that the tide was finally turning. In December 1917 he wrote, "From now on we may expect to see the walls of prejudice gradually crumble before the onslaught of common sense and social progress." Setting aside the disappointments of the Spanish-American War, Du Bois advised Blacks to "forget our special grievances" and "close ranks" behind the war effort.[20]

Shipped off to Europe under strict Jim Crow conditions (separate and inferior bunks and mess, and Southern social conventions), most Black fighting men in WWI served with two units in France, the 92nd and 93rd Infantry Divisions. Undertrained and suffering from grave morale problems caused, in good measure, by the widespread belief among white commanders that Black soldiers were "naturally cowardly" and "hopelessly inferior," the 92nd did not, on the whole, distinguish itself in battle.[21] The 93rd was a different story. Composed of four infantry regiments attached to French divisions and unhampered by white American officers, the 93rd fought well. Indeed, three of its regiments were awarded the Croix de Guerre (war cross) by a grateful French government.[22]

African Americans had hoped that their participation in the Great War would cement their claim to equal status at home. Instead, Black soldiers were so vilified at the time, and so slandered afterward, that the NAACP commissioned Du Bois to write a history of Black men in the war and called for a congressional investigation into the performance of Black troops and white discrimination in the Armed Forces.[23]

The belief that it was official US policy to discredit the efforts of the colored troops in France was widespread across Afro-America. Arriving in France in the spring of 1919, Du Bois was appalled at the easy racism that pervaded the American army. White officers and enlisted men spoke freely and disparagingly about their "nigger" troops. The few Black officers who were commissioned were undertrained and then declared incompetent, Jim Crowed in places of accommodation and amusement, and denied the respect that accompanied their rank by white men who refused to salute a Black man in uniform. Black troops were undersupplied and overdisciplined, and on occasion were shot and killed by their own officers in battle.[24]

Segregated barracks, degraded working conditions, endless use of racial epithets by white soldiers and officers: these things rankled. But nothing enraged Du Bois more than the charge of Black sexual predation of white women. Hearing that General Charles C. Ballou, the commanding officer of the 92nd Division, had referred offhandedly to the men under his charge as "the rapist division," Du Bois wrote to the mayors of twenty-one French towns and villages where Black soldiers had been stationed. No serious instances of misconduct were reported. Examining the records of the 92nd, both Du Bois and Robert R. Moton, Booker T. Washington's successor at Tuskegee Institute, found only one Black soldier convicted of rape. That private's execution by hanging was filmed by the division's official photographer, who had passed up the chance the day before to document the presentation of the Distinguished Service Cross to two members of the Black 368th Infantry.[25]

Although the American Expeditionary Force had crossed the Atlantic to fight the Central Powers, the American higher-ups devoted considerable time and energy to regulating interactions between African American soldiers and French soldiers and civilians, particularly women. As the Black troops moved toward the Vosges in August 1918, the French army, tutored by its American comrades in arms, issued a document titled "Confidential: Au sujet des Troupes Noires Americaines" ("Confidential: On the Subject of Black American Troops"). Intended for French officers but issued with American support and authority, the report was designed to instruct the French in correct race behavior. Alarmed by French "familiarity and indulgence" toward Black soldiers, the Americans wished to draw attention to a few unhappy facts about the Black man. He was, according to the report, "an inferior being" whose "vices," particularly rape, were a "constant menace" to white Americans, who were forced to "repress them sternly."

Such vices would only be encouraged by intimacy with French officers, who were instructed not to shake hands or eat with the Black

Americans, or to "talk or meet with them outside of the requirements of military service." When it became clear that French men and women were unmoved by the AEF's remedial course in white supremacy, Brigadier General James B. Erwin took the burden of protecting white racial purity on his own shoulders. In orders issued in Vienne in December 1918, Erwin explained that a principal duty of the white officers of the 92nd was to prevent their Black soldiers "from addressing or holding conversations with the women inhabitants of the town."[26]

This was one order that did not have to be repeated before it was implemented. As a young British author observed, "The fact is simply that the Negro walking with a white woman is to the southern American White as a red rag to a bull."[27] According to Du Bois, a Black officer, "a high-minded gentleman, graduate and Phi Beta Kappa man of a leading American institution," was court-martialed and sent to a labor battalion for "keeping company with a perfectly respectable girl of a family of standing."[28]

Strolling through Vannes one night, Lieutenant Charles Hamilton Houston, the future architect of the NAACP's school-desegregation litigation, was drawn into a dispute with two white captains after their French dates had deserted them and had found refuge in the arms of another Black lieutenant. In the space of a moment, the four officers were surrounded by a crowd of white enlisted men screaming at the "niggers" and calling for a lynching on the grounds that "it was time to put a few in their places, otherwise the United States would not be a safe place to live."[29] Houston and his companions were saved from this fate by the timely intervention of the captain of the American military police, but these were exactly the sort of "French-women-ruined niggers" that worried Mississippi senator James K. Vardaman about Black veterans who would expect interracial relations at home after intimacy with white women abroad.[30]

AFRICAN AMERICAN TROOPS returned to an America that was anxious, jumpy, and dry: Prohibition had been adopted by constitutional amendment in 1920. Democracy was not immediately forthcoming. Black veterans who believed they had earned some status and respect because of their military service found themselves returning to a country even more obsessed with racial identity and its markers than before. Laws of racial identity designed to protect white racial purity and social and political dominance blossomed across the landscape.

African American organizations surged after the armistice. NAACP membership exploded nationwide, but especially in the South. Black workers joined whatever unions, such as the United Mine Workers, would accept them. The Universal Negro Improvement Association (UNIA), founded in New York by Jamaican immigrant Marcus Garvey, called on Blacks to present a united front against the "white devils" who robbed African Americans of their citizenship rights and dignity.

Members of these organizations met fierce repression. John Shillady, the white executive secretary of the NAACP from 1918 to 1920, was beaten practically to death in broad daylight in Austin, Texas. In Phillips County, Arkansas, Black sharecroppers and tenant farmers, tired of being fleeced by white landlords, organized the interracial Progressive Farmers and Household Union of America—and were promptly attacked for their audacity. In September 1919, six hundred federal troops helped whites in Phillips County "round up and disarm" suspected revolutionaries. An unknown number of blacks died at their hands; the army admitted to killing "about twenty negroes" for refusing to halt when ordered. One hundred twenty-two Black men were indicted, seventy-three of them for murder. Twelve received death sentences. The NAACP appealed the verdict, and in 1923 the Supreme Court ruled in *Moore v. Dempsey* that the trials had been "dominated by a mob," thus depriving the accused of their Fourteenth Amendment right to due process.[31]

The Phillips County bloodshed capped a summer of racial violence so extreme that NAACP leader James Weldon Johnson dubbed it the "Red Summer."[32] In the first year following the war, more than seventy African Americans were lynched, many of them after having been tortured and mutilated.[33] Scores of race riots, including in Chicago and St. Louis, left untold numbers dead, wounded, and homeless—and the victims were not all Black. African American soldiers returned home ready to fire back. Indeed, observers at the time considered Black self-defense a watershed in American race relations.

White Southern advocates of segregation often argued that it was designed to prevent the violence that was generated by interactions between white and Black men on public transportation and in other public arenas. Likewise, laws of racial identity were intended to dissolve any ambiguity about where anyone belonged.

Two

PROTECTING "RACIAL PURITY"

O N AUGUST 11, 1921, Edwin Stephenson, a Methodist minister, shot and killed Father James Coyle on the rectory porch of St. Paul's Catholic Church in Birmingham, Alabama. Earlier that day, Father Coyle had presided over the marriage of Stephenson's eighteen-year-old daughter, Ruth, to native Puerto Rican Pedro Gussman, a forty-two-year-old wallpaper hanger. Independent-minded Ruth had been interested in Catholicism since adolescence; Coyle had baptized her into the church some months before her marriage. When word of the wedding reached Ruth's father, he grabbed his gun and headed for St. Paul's.

Because Coyle had been unarmed, Stephenson's legal team needed to come up with a more plausible explanation for the violence than self-defense. It did. Lead lawyer Hugo L. Black argued that Stephenson had acted in a state of temporary insanity brought on by the marriage of his daughter to a "negro."

Pedro Gussman's identity as a Negro came as news to him. Prior to the trial, he had always been regarded as white. He was listed as white in the 1920 US census, and he lived in white boarding houses.

He dated white women. He was registered to vote. Had Gussman been considered nonwhite, he and Ruth could not have acquired a marriage license, because marriage across the color line was strictly forbidden in Alabama. "No one has ever questioned my color until I became mixed up in this case," he complained.[1]

By transforming Pedro Gussman from a tanned Puerto Rican into a "negro," Hugo Black offered the jury, composed exclusively of white men, a credible basis on which to find Edwin Stephenson temporarily insane. Father Coyle had seduced Ruth Stephenson away from the true faith and her father's rightful rule and married her to a man whose religion and color marked him as inferior. Any self-respecting white man would blow a fuse under such circumstances. The jury voted to acquit. Hugo Black's reputation grew. He joined the local chapter of the Ku Klux Klan, which, reflecting anti-Catholic animus as much as horror at alleged miscegenation, paid Stephenson's legal fees.

Formally reconstituted at Stone Mountain, Georgia, in 1915 by white men inspired by the heroic portrayal of the Reconstruction-era Klan in the film *Birth of a Nation*, the second Klan was not the province of the rural South. The resurgent KKK was strongest in the West and Midwest, and as common in urban areas as in rural ones. The 1920s Klan was rooted in WWI vigilance committees that policed the speech and actions of opponents of the war, and it is more accurately grouped with other postwar organizations like the American Legion than it is with its Reconstruction antecedent. Two factors distinguished the modern Klan from other fraternal organizations of the postwar era, however: its use of violence and its political influence. Klan-backed candidates won office at every level of government in the 1920s. Six states sent candidates endorsed by the Klan to the United States Senate. Edwin Stephenson's lawyer, Hugo Black, was one of them.

Hugo Black's strategic redefinition of Pedro Gussman from Puerto Rican into "negro" cast Ruth Stephenson as unknowing (because no white woman would ever knowingly associate with a nonwhite man) and her father as heroic. It is unsurprising that the jury rewarded

Edwin Stephenson's violent defense of white racial purity and opposition to interracial marriage. Yet Black's defense of Stephenson was risky insofar as it underscored the plasticity of racial categorization and subverted notions of stable racial identity. Racial identity implicitly became an *argument*, something to be litigated. Inside the courtroom, Gussman's new identity as nonwhite exonerated Father Coyle's killer and jump-started Hugo Black's political career. Yet outside the courtroom, Pedro was a white man married to a white woman, as attested by the marriage license.[2]

Compared to most people who underwent involuntary "racial reassignment," as the *Richmond News Leader* put it in 1926, Pedro Gussman got off easy.[3] In the antebellum South, having one's racial identity altered could mean the difference between a life of slavery and one of freedom. In the postemancipation and Jim Crow South, the same process could affirm or unravel a marriage, establish or destroy the legitimacy of children, and uphold or alter lines of inheritance. Being redefined racially threw into doubt the racial status of one's children and grandchildren, the lives they led, and their future prospects. In Gussman's case, no one seems to have challenged his claims to whiteness after the trial. Indeed, in 1930, seven years after he and Ruth divorced, Gussman married yet another white woman.

Despite endless efforts to define it, racial identity was not fixed in the Jim Crow era. Edwin Stephenson benefited from the flexibility of the white racial regime; Pedro Gussman was not harmed. The turn-of-the-century rhetoric of blood purity, with its mathematical tables to assist racial assignation and deny hybridity, nevertheless reflected an increasingly mobile and fluid racial environment.

People concerned with protecting "blood purity" were often also preoccupied with the phenomenon of "passing," which seemed to explode after World War I. The large decline of persons in the "mulatto" category in the 1920 census (compared with ten years earlier) and the lack of a corresponding increase on the Black side of the color line struck fear into the hearts of white supremacists that mulattoes were "fad[ing] into the great white multitude." A 1924 article in *Opportunity*, the magazine of the National Urban League, adopted the white-supremacist point of view and spoke menacingly of "the deliberate annihilation of ethnic affiliation when physical appearance does not proclaim it."[4] In 1926, Urban League leader Elmer A. Carter wrote of the "synchronous but more subtle migration" of passing that accompanied the broader postwar movement from South to North of African Americans, who crossed both geographical boundaries and legal boundaries in their movement from "Black" to "white."[5]

Northern states without laws of racial identity or racially restrictive marriage laws posed particular problems for self-appointed guardians of the color line. On the one hand, the North's racially permissive society allowed fair-skinned African Americans to pass permanently or situationally, donning and shedding racial identities with ease. That same society could allow nominally "white" people to confound racial categories by insisting on their identity as African American, as the NAACP's blond, blue-eyed executive secretary Walter White did. In the North and much of the West, people considered Black elsewhere could marry whites, whatever their genealogy. It is impossible to tell how many people passed over the years. But whites in the 1920s worried to the point of paranoia that their race was being "infiltrated" with inferior blood. Virginian Walter Plecker, a leader in the Anglo-Saxon movement, lamented that "many thousands of white Negroes…were quietly and persistently passing over the line."[6] *Opportunity* magazine characterized the "subtle migration" of passing as "the most ambitious offensive ever launched by the sons of Ham."[7]

IN 1924, QUESTIONS of genealogy, of lineage, upended a society marriage in New York. That year, Philip Rhinelander discovered that his son had married a working woman of unclear racial identity. Rather than take the Alabama track and murder the county clerk who had married the couple, Philip Rhinelander's lawyers removed the groom, twenty-two-year-old Leonard Rhinelander, from his honeymoon. His father then bullied Leonard into filing for annulment of the marriage on the grounds that the bride, the former Alice Jones, had deceived her husband into believing that she stemmed entirely from the white race when it appeared that she had some quotient of "Negro blood" through her supposedly mixed-race father, George. Alice, her husband's suit argued, had not been candid in outlining her genealogy; namely, she had not revealed that her father, an Englishman who described his family as coming from "the West Indies," was categorized as "colored" on his American naturalization papers.[8] In the eyes of the Rhinelanders, this lack of candor constituted fraud; the marriage was therefore null and void.[9]

The 1925 Rhinelander trial was a sensation, carried on the front pages of newspapers across the country. The popular allure was twofold: in addition to the question of racial identity, the class gulf between Leonard and Alice was seemingly impassible. Philip Rhinelander's fortune, gained through his family's 250-year-old shipping business and supplemented by large landholdings in Manhattan, was estimated at $3 million. His son Leonard's was considered to be about $400,000 at the time of the trial. The family was counted among Caroline Astor's original list of the "400" society families in New York.[10] Alice worked, among other things, as a housecleaner.

Interracial marriage was legal in the state of New York. There was never any question of the validity of the union. The case turned on questions of racial knowledge: Had Alice deceived Leonard as to her race? Or did he know of her heritage and dismiss its importance? How possible was it to discern Alice's racial background? The challenge was whether separating white from nonwhite was feasible in a world of racial hybridity, one marked by waves of anonymous humanity rolling from South to North in the Great Migration.

The Rhinelander case was about knowledge, about recognition, about the capacity of white elites to recognize nonwhites even when they presented themselves as white. Antimiscegenation laws theoretically protected white "racial integrity" (as it was becoming known), but in places like New York, which lacked any such statutes, what was to protect whiteness? The vigilance of white men and their capacity to recognize race and thus protect the precious commodity of whiteness were all that stood between increasing numbers of mixed-race people and white racial purity.[11]

The jury looked to two bodies of evidence to establish Alice Jones Rhinelander's racial identity and to address the question of fraud. First, they looked to the Jones family. The family, with whom Leonard had spent so much time (even living with them after the wedding, while the newlyweds' apartment was being readied), made no efforts to portray itself as "white," despite the undisputed white racial identity of Alice's mother, Elizabeth. Alice confounded racial assessors: her birth certificate and a New York state census identified her as mulatto; her marriage certificate listed her as white. Alice seems to have passed situationally in public spaces like hotels and restaurants when being Black was awkward or inconvenient. Alice's darker sister, Emily, identified as Negro; Emily's husband considered himself a Black man.

The key question for the jury was whether Alice's Blackness was written somewhere on her body. Leonard and Alice's all-but-pornographic correspondence was read in court. The love letters detailed, among other things, Leonard's felonious practice of cunnilingus. Lovers who had experienced such intimacy should recognize each other. In a dramatic and sensational move, the jury asked Alice to partially disrobe, so that they could see her back and legs. Alice complied with this degrading request in the judge's chambers, cleared of all but judge, jury, and Leonard. The white men of the jury declared Alice mixed race. Given their physical intimacy, the jury determined, Leonard Rhinelander should have been able to "read" Alice's body as easily as the jurors, who promptly found that Alice had not committed fraud. Leonard was sent by his father to Las Vegas to obtain a divorce.[12]

Digesting the case, the Urban League's magazine, *Opportunity*, concluded that one "important angle of the Rhinelander annulment suit which no amount of clever editorial skirting, or summary disgust, or pity for the self-inflicted smirch upon the blazing escutcheon of a proud old family can overshadow" was the underlying premise of the trial: that even in the absence of antimiscegenation laws, marriage with nonwhites constituted a "complete and defiling impurity."[13]

The Rhinelander case demonstrated to white supremacists the importance of having clear, narrow definitions of whiteness. In the early twentieth-century South, definitions of whiteness grew narrower and narrower, although no state was as stringent as Virginia. Virginia's 1924 Act for the Preservation of Racial Integrity provided that any trace of nonwhite ancestry (the infamous "one drop" rule) defined someone as ineligible to marry anyone defined by law as white. The act was the project of Walter A. Plecker, the state's first Registrar of Vital Statistics and a leader in the Anglo-Saxon Club. The 1924 law alarmed the so-called First Families of Virginia, many of whom traced their ancestry to the seventeenth-century union between Pocahontas and colonial leader John Rolfe. Under the new law's stringent definition of whiteness, these leading families were poised to pass from white to "colored." What became known as the "Pocahontas exception" transformed the Powhatan princess into an honorary white woman, pacifying US Senator Harry Byrd and the rest of the town-and-country set. Criticizing the Virginia law, John Powell, founder of the Anglo-Saxon Clubs of America, complained that "Indians are springing up all over the state as if by spontaneous generation."[14]

WHITES UNIFORMLY DEFENDED antimiscegenation laws as necessary to protect the "purity" and the "integrity" of "white blood" and the "white race" (often, in the 1920s, rendered as "Anglo-Saxon" or "Nordic"). These arguments, which were often bolstered with appeals to divine authority, were already prevalent at the end of the nineteenth century, but the emphasis on racial purity gained steam in the first decades of the twentieth century, buttressed by the twin pillars of eugenics and nativism.

In the 1920s, many Americans embraced the popular doctrine of eugenics, which fused Charles Darwin's theory of evolution with Swiss botanist Gregor Mendel's research in plant heredity to take the first shaky scientific steps toward genetic science. Eugenicists claimed that "unfit human traits" such as "feeblemindedness, epilepsy, criminality, insanity, alcoholism, pauperism" ran in families and were inherited "in exactly the same way as color in guinea pigs." These traits were disproportionately associated, scientists insisted, with the "lesser races."

As states shored up their legal definitions of whiteness, groups like the Anglo-Saxon Club urged immigration restriction. They hoped to limit the dilution of the "Anglo-Saxon race" by inferior Asian, African, and Eastern European bloodlines, arguing that "the idea of the great American melting pot, into which one can put the refuse of three continents and draw out good, sound American citizens…is simply and perilously false."[15]

Middle-class whites had been sounding alarms about "race suicide" since Teddy Roosevelt's day, when it was first argued that the "wrong" people were having too many babies and the "right" sort were having too few. In addition to stemming the flow of immigrants into the United States, eugenicists in the 1920s advocated involuntary sterilization and selective breeding for human improvement. Contests to recognize "Fitter Families" and "Better Babies" sprang up across the country (in Kansas, the competition was held in the "human stock" section of the state fair). Eugenicists spanned the political spectrum from white supremacists to socialists like Margaret Sanger. Usually they were political and social progressives who saw the quest for a better gene pool as compatible with their broader dream of human advancement through public policy grounded in scientific methods.

Eugenicists' chief interest was to protect and improve the white race through state action. Antimiscegenation laws were justified with this goal in mind: they uniformly forbade marriage between whites and members of "other races," including Africans, Mongolians, Chinese, Japanese, Malayans, American Indians, Asiatic Indians, Hindus, Koreans, Mestizos—the list goes on. Buttressed by the work of Earnest Sevier Cox (*White America*, 1923), Madison Grant (*The Passing of the*

Great Race, or the Racial Basis of European History, 1916), and Lothrop Stoddard (*The Rising Tide of Color: The Threat Against White World-Supremacy*, 1920, and *The Revolt Against Civilization: The Menace of the Under-Man*, 1922), American eugenicists disputed the conclusions of cultural anthropologists and sociologists, which stressed environmental factors in human development. The eugenicists dismissed the environmentalists as "sentimental" and, often, Jewish.

America's anti-immigrant stance protected more than white men's jobs and political power; it protected their blood. Restrictive immigration policies were part of a broader governmental effort to preserve white racial fitness and hierarchy, as exhorted by prominent eugenicists such as Charles B. Davenport, who insisted that states "take positive measures to increase the density of socially desirable traits in the next generation—by education, segregation, sterilization, and by keeping out immigrants who belong to defective strains."[16]

In 1924, Congress passed the National Immigration Act, also known as the Quota Act. The act ended nearly all Asian immigration, and set quotas for other nations based on the percentage of immigrants from that nation already present in the US population in the 1890 census (the last census before the great wave of immigration from southern and eastern Europe). The flood of postwar immigration was reduced to a trickle.

State antimiscegenation laws were paired with compulsory sterilization acts and were reflected in other national immigration legislation. The 1922 Cable Act, for example, stripped American women of their citizenship if they married Asian men.[17] Repeated efforts to eliminate interracial marriage through constitutional amendment failed, but they reflected ongoing white concern about the social and biological consequences of interracial sex.[18] Such laws were touted by eugenicists, who proclaimed that the white race was superior physically and mentally to all other races, and warned that intermarriage by whites with "inferior" races resulted in "a lessening of physical vitality and mentality in their offspring."

39

Restrictive immigration policy was not enough for eugenicists, however. They warned that people with unwholesome genes were rapidly proliferating and urged policymakers to take steps to limit their procreation. By 1929, thirty states had passed compulsory sterilization laws for individuals whose sterilization was considered to be "in the interest of the mental, moral, or physical improvement of the patient or inmate or for the public good." By the mid-1930s, approximately twenty thousand individuals had been sterilized under these laws.[19] Eugenicists argued that there was a high correlation between "feeblemindedness" and "sexual delinquents" such as prostitutes, Peeping Toms, homosexuals, and sexually active unmarried women. In California, which led the nation in forced sterilization, three out of four sterilized women had been judged "sexually delinquent," which usually meant that they had engaged in sex outside of marriage prior to their institutional commitment.[20]

By the 1930s, Southern eugenicists and garden-variety white supremacists had created a vast bureaucratic apparatus designed to keep everybody where they belonged. Bureaus of vital statistics registered births, marriages, and deaths, and classified and cross-checked people according to race. Traditionally associated with a deep antistatism, the South created the most complex state bureaucracy in the nation in order to keep segregation up to date.

But even this system was not impregnable. Problems of classification bled easily into problems of control. Antimiscegenation laws were the lodestar of segregation because without controls on sex, racial classification became impossibly complicated. Sex across racial boundaries undercut all forms of racial differentiation based on genealogy. The point of segregation was to keep nonwhite people in their separate and inferior places. To do that, the state had to be able to tell who was who.

State governments had three good chances to place people racially: at birth, at marriage, and when a child began school. The rest of the Jim Crow segregation system depended on the state's getting the moment of classification right. What really protected segregation and the white race, what made each seem secure and unchangeable, were the state-sponsored moments in which a person was defined as either white or nonwhite, with all the privileges (or disabilities) carried by either classification.

These rigid lines were called into question by activists, however. When W. E. B. Du Bois agreed to debate prominent eugenicist Theodore Lothrop Stoddard on the race question in Chicago in 1929, he mischievously offered to argue both sides when Stoddard was late. Du Bois reminded the audience that he was not only "gladly…the representative of the Negro race," but was "equally" capable of being "a representative of the Nordic race."[21]

Du Bois spoke first in the debate and went immediately to the heart of the issue of American race politics. White Americans insisted that restrictions on interracial marriage were necessary to protect "purity of blood." It was, he judged, too late for that. Appropriating the language of white supremacy for his own purposes, Du Bois argued that it was the Nordics (whites) whose sexual conduct had produced mixed races. They had overrun the earth and "spread their bastards to every corner of land and sea." Americans were already mixed blood. There was no "pure" blood to protect with antimiscegenation laws. As the audience in the cavernous Chicago Coliseum bellowed its approval, the editor of *The Crisis* shouted, "Who in Hell asked to marry your daughters?"

The meaning of African American equality, Du Bois insisted, began with politics: African Americans "demand a voice in their own government; the organization of industry for the benefit of colored workers and not merely for white owners and masters; they demand education on the broadest and highest lines and they demand as human beings social contact with other human beings on a basis of perfect equality."[22] This was not a message white eugenicists and their sympathizers wanted to hear.

Three

THE UNITED STATES OF
LYNCHERDOM

J IM CROW had been built on the foundation of antimiscegenation
laws in the late nineteenth century. Those laws now defined the
South's segregated, stratified society, and rising anxiety over sex made
them impregnable. Fear of miscegenation assumed a new centrality in
the ideology that Southern whites developed to justify segregation and
reinforced race-based inequities of power. The centrality of miscegenation as a root fear for whites meant that every campaign for Black civil
rights was liable to get bogged down in sexualized race rhetoric.

The fear of miscegenation could be raised to counter any reform
effort. This was particularly true for integrated associations such as the
Commission on Interracial Cooperation (CIC), which was founded in
the wake of the race riots following the end of World War I. Facing
militant white supremacists, the CIC hoped initially to avoid questions
of sex by excluding women from the organization. Just as white supremacists found it imperative to focus on perceived threats to white racial
purity in their battle against race reformers, civil rights workers found it
strategically necessary to avoid questioning laws against miscegenation.

Yet the interracial reform movement was bound up with the question of sex from the start, because both women's and men's organizations focused on what seemed to be the greatest problem of the day: lynching, a phenomenon inextricably linked to the question of interracial sex. Racial reform organizations denounced both lynching and the sexual double standard that allowed white men their relationships with Black women while Black men lost their lives over mere breeches in racial etiquette with white women. As Methodist reform leader Carrie Parks Johnson thundered before the men of the CIC, "The race problem can never be solved as long as the white man goes unpunished, and loses no social standing, while the Negro is burned at the stake."[1]

Between 1877 and 1950, 4,084 Black men and women were lynched in the American South.[2] It is difficult, without seeming voyeuristic, to represent in any adequate way the barbarity of a mob lynching—a phenomenon that became more and more barbaric over time. In 1929, after a harrowing experience of undercover investigative journalism in which he passed as white, NAACP executive director Walter White concluded that the "harsher methods" used in lynchings, by which he meant torture and burning at the stake in front of thousands of spectators, had not been adopted until the early twentieth century.[3]

The social purpose of lynching was not difficult to discern. After a victim was burned to death before a large crowd in 1902, Andrew Sledd, a professor of Latin at Emory College in Atlanta, explained in a fiery article in the *Atlantic Monthly* that the object of such "savagery" was to "teach the negro the lesson of abject and eternal servility, [to] burn into his quivering flesh the consciousness that he has not, cannot have, the rights of a free citizen or even of a fellow human creature."[4]

For the purposes of definition, a lynching was carried out by three or more people acting together. The deadliest period of lynching, 1880–1919, saw an average of two to three lynchings per week, nationally. White Americans in the early twentieth century learned not to pay too much attention to news of a lynching; collectively, their attitudes progressed rapidly from horror to outrage to indifference. Walter White remarked in his 1929 account of lynching, full-frontally titled *Rope and Faggot*, "An uncomfortably large percentage of Americans can read in their newspapers of the slow roasting alive of a human being in Mississippi and turn, promptly and with little thought, to the comic strip or sporting page."[5]

In public discourse, lynching was linked to Black men's rape of white women. The pioneering research of African American journalist Ida B. Wells in the late nineteenth century, however, showed that less than a third of Black men lynched were even *accused* of assaulting white women, much less convicted. Southern whites didn't care; they sanctioned lynching as an appropriate punishment for a crime that could barely be named. South Carolina populist leader Ben Tillman caught the mood of the white South when he declared on the floor of the United States Senate in 1907, "I have three daughters, but so help me God, I had rather find either one of them killed by a tiger or a bear and gather up her bones and bury them, conscious that she had died in the purity of her maidenhood, than to have her crawl to me and tell me the horrid story that she had been robbed of the jewel of her womanhood by a black fiend." Walter White concluded that consensual sex and "alleged sex crimes have served as the great bulwark of the lyncher."[6]

A sharp increase in lynchings during WWI prompted the NAACP to mount an all-out effort to pass a federal antilynching law. Although the vast majority of lynchings occurred south of the Mason-Dixon Line, the North was not immune. In Duluth, Minnesota, where US Steel imported Southern Blacks as cheap labor during WWI, a white mob numbering in the thousands hung from lampposts three young Black circus workers accused of raping a white woman.[7]

Because racially discriminatory action by public officials violates the Constitution, the NAACP sought to enlist federal authority to punish state and local officials who failed to protect individuals from lynch mobs. In 1920, more than half the victims of that year's fifty-five recorded lynchings had been taken from officers of the law, lending credence to the NAACP's argument that local and state authorities were complicit in mob violence.

In 1921, the House of Representatives voted to enact the Dyer Anti-lynching Bill, which adopted the NAACP's approach. The legislation, which was introduced by Missouri congressman Leonidas Dyer, targeted local sheriffs who failed to stop mob action. Southerners howled about federal usurpation of state authority and denounced the proposed law as a "bill to encourage rape."[8] Although the Dyer Bill squeaked through the Republican-dominated House, it was filibustered by Democrats in the Senate. While the bill languished, three Black men were burned alive in the town square of Kirvin, Texas, and fifteen-year old Charlie Atkins was tortured and roasted "over a slow fire" before a mob of two thousand in Davisboro, Georgia. The bill died in the Senate.

In January 1919, a small group of white Southern moderates met in Atlanta to organize an interracial reform association in the hope of redefining the "place" of African Americans in Southern life—what became the Commission for Interracial Cooperation. The CIC was led by Will W. Alexander, a young Methodist minister whose interest in racial reform led him from the clergy to the YMCA and, later, to the New Deal and the Federal Council of Churches (FCC).

The race riots that greeted Black veterans in 1919 and the national revival of the Ku Klux Klan in the 1920s led the CIC to focus on racial violence. Like the YMCA (and the YWCA), the new organization was interracial but sex-segregated. Organizing white and Black men together was one thing; admitting women of either race was another. Bringing "white women and colored men into interrelationships that symbolize equality" would lead inevitably to charges of fostering "social intermingling," miscegenation, and intermarriage. Reformist men warned that white women were "the Hindenburg line" in race relations; mingling white women with Black male CIC members would open a Pandora's box of race taboos and preclude an open discussion of lynching, tied as it was to questions of white women's sexuality.[9]

Shut out from the CIC, white and Black women of the YWCA and various Protestant missionary societies founded their own organizations and predicted the failure of the men's-only groups. "The men might as well hang their harps on a willow tree," announced Carrie Parks Johnson, one of two white women who attended the first integrated National Association of Colored Women meeting in 1920, "as to try to settle the race problem in the South without the aid of the Southern white woman."[10]

CIC men who were concerned that women would be too timid to discuss so explosive a topic as lynching and the sexual anxiety that supposedly underlay it need not have worried. In a 1920 speech to the male members of the CIC, Johnson, the head of the Committee on Woman's Work, addressed the miscegenation issue straightforwardly: "If any black man publicly advocated the amalgamation of the white and colored races by marriage, he would be, if not burned at the stake, hung in effigy."[11]

Just as white supremacists found it imperative to focus on perceived threats to white racial purity in their battle against race reformers, those race reformers and, later, civil rights workers found it strategically necessary to downplay issues of miscegenation. And yet the interracial reform movement was bound up with the question of interracial sex from the first, because both women's and men's organizations focused on what seemed to be the greatest problem of the day: lynching, which was rhetorically, if not factually, linked to the question of interracial sex.[12]

Reformers had their own explanations for why white Southern men had become convinced that Black men were out to rape their wives and daughters. Lillian Smith, an early crusader for civil rights, an author, a playwright, and the publisher of the quarterly magazine *South Today*, shared her thinking on this question in her 1949 book *Killers of the Dream*. Smith blamed both lynching and white paranoia about miscegenation on what she called the "race-sex-sin spiral." The source of this vortex lay in white men's sexual exploitation of Black women during slavery. "The more trails the white man made to back-yard cabins," Smith explained, "the higher he raised his white wife on her pedestal when he returned to the big house." She continued:

The higher the pedestal, the less he enjoyed her whom he had put there, for statues after all are only nice things to look at....Then came a time, though it was decades later, when man's suspicion of white woman began to pull the spiral higher and higher. It was of course inevitable for him to suspect her of the sins he had committed so pleasantly and often. *What if*, he whispered, and the words were never finished. *What if....* Too often white woman could only smile bleakly in reply to the unasked question. But white man mistook this empty smile for one of cryptic satisfaction and in jealous panic began to project his own sins on to the Negro male. And when he did that, a madness seized our people.[13]

This, of course, is not a sufficient explanation. W. J. Cash, author of *The Mind of the South* (1941), conceded that the chance of a white Southern woman being raped by a Black man was less than the chance that she would be struck by lightning.[14] And most white women who engaged in intimate relations with Black men did so of their own resolve, as Ida Wells remarked. "White men lynch the offending Afro-American not because he is a despoiler of virtue," she wrote, "but because he succumbs to the smiles of white women."[15] But this was not something that could be said openly in the turn-of-the-century South without penalty—indeed, Wells was banished from the South shortly after saying so.

As both Cash and Smith perceived, white women personified the South itself—its mind, its essence, its timeless continuity. White supremacists equated any attack on white womanhood with an attack on the South, and vice versa. As Cash put it in *The Mind of the South*, any assault on the segregated South would be felt as an assault on white women, and "the South would inevitably translate its whole battle into terms of her defense."[16] "Protecting" white womanhood was the lynchpin of an ideology, and not just a rhetorical stance. This ideology came under severe pressure when two white working girls sneaking a ride on a freight train strained the reciprocal relationship between white male guardians and vulnerable white females to the breaking point.

ON MARCH 25, 1931, a fight on a freight train traveling south from Chattanooga, Tennessee, between two groups of teenage boys, one white and one Black, ended with the Blacks on top and the whites thrown off. The white boys complained at the first stop they stumbled into, and a posse stopped the train at Paint Rock, Alabama. As the men rounded up the nine Black youths, who ranged in age from thirteen to nineteen, they discovered two white women as well.

The women, dressed in men's overalls, had hopped a ride on the train like the boys. Victoria Price, who at twenty-one had already been married and divorced three times, worried that by traveling with seventeen-year-old Ruby Bates she might be violating the Mann Act, which prohibited transportation of girls or women across state lines for "immoral purposes." (The law had originally targeted world heavy-weight champion boxer Jack Johnson, who dared to cross state lines with his legal, white wife.) Whether on her own initiative or prompted by the local sheriff, Price charged that both she and Ruby had been raped by the Black youths, who were promptly arrested. Sixteen days later, all nine had been tried and found guilty. All but the youngest were sentenced to die in the electric chair. When the NAACP declined to intervene in this legal lynching for public opinion reasons, the Communist-led International Labor Defense (ILD) entered the fray and turned the case into a liberal cause celebre. The decade-long saga of the Scottsboro Boys had begun.[17]

If not for the efforts of local antilynching activists and the intervention of the National Guard to prevent mob violence in Scottsboro, the saga may not have happened at all. It wasn't easy: if ever there was a crime that called for a lynching, the gang rape of two defenseless white women by, as one headline screamed, "NINE BURLY NEGROES," was it.[18]

The facts that emerged cast the events on the train in a new light. Over the course of three series of trials between 1931 and 1937, neither the judges nor many onlookers believed the stories told by Price and Bates, who tried to drape themselves with the mantle of pure, white,

Southern womanhood. *This* wasn't easy either. After the women's personal histories were poked into, there was little debate about their lives or, indeed, their characters. Ruby Bates had once been arrested for hugging a Black man in public, and Price and Bates were known in their neighborhoods as willing to sell sex for money to supplement their meager wages at the mills in which they labored.[19]

Central to the defense was the shocking claim that there were white women in the South, including Ruby Bates and Victoria Price, who had consensual sex with Black men. Responding to this assertion, Jessie Daniel Ames, the leader of the Association of Southern Women for the Prevention of Lynching (ASWPL), was forced to conclude that Southern white women often covered up the tracks of their own interracial affairs by crying rape. The judge in the second Scottsboro case, William W. Callahan, was himself immune to such revelations. His charge to the jury included the information that when a white woman had intercourse with a Black man, the presumption must be that she was raped. The trial put that presumption to the test by questioning whether the umbrella of sacred Southern womanhood could cover prostitutes, and asserting that there were white women who engaged in consensual sex across the color line. Bates's and Price's personal histories were clear, and they probably had not differentiated between Blacks and whites as sexual partners. In other circumstances—if they had been arrested for prostitution, for example—Bates and Price would have been prime candidates for sterilization. Instead, in this instance, they became the limit test of white chivalry: Could they, too, be brought under the umbrella of "protection"?

THIS WAS, IT must be said, not the NAACP's finest hour. The organization hesitated to become associated with a presumably hopeless sex case involving uneducated Black laborers. Into the void rushed the International Labor Defense, the legal arm of the Communist Party, which white Southerners, tutored by the *Atlanta Constitution*, associated with interracial rape, intermarriage, and promiscuity. The "crime at Scottsboro"—as the ILD described it—provided the basis for a campaign of mass action. The governor of Alabama was besieged with clemency petitions from around the world. Communist Party USA (CPUSA) organizers convinced African Americans all over the North that the party was not simply the most militant force for racial justice in the nation, but the most effective.[20] After all, while the NAACP had dithered, the CPUSA had acted.

Fourteen years before Scottsboro, at the Sixth Communist Party Congress in 1917, party leaders had characterized Southern Blacks as an oppressed nation deserving of liberation and self-determination, akin to the ethnic-minority states carved out of postwar Europe. Even so, recruitment efforts yielded a meager crop: there was not more than a handful of African American communists in the United States before the mid-1920s. Nonetheless, their existence generated considerable white anxiety about Black reds. That tiny cohort gathered in 1924, at a national All-Race Assembly in Chicago. Dubbed the "Negro Sanhedrin" after the supreme council of the biblical Israelites, the assembly brought together more than sixty-one African American organizations and was the first event in which Black communists (all five of them) participated openly. Kelly Miller, a professor at Howard University, was elected chairman. He was flanked by NAACP executive secretary James Weldon Johnson and Cecil Briggs, the fiery leader of the African Blood Brotherhood, who dismissed red-baiting racists and instructed, "Don't mind being called 'Bolsheviki' by the same people who call you 'nigger.'" Despite its promise, the Sanhedrin accomplished little, "save to expose class differences among African Americans."[21]

In the fall of 1925, the African Negro Labor Congress (ANLC), the official Black communist organization in the United States, sponsored a national conference in Chicago. Before a small crowd that included only three Black Southerners, the ANLC called for desegregation of public places, residential housing, and the army and navy, along with free speech and jury service for African Americans. Explosively, the delegates endorsed "full social equality" and demanded repeal of antimiscegenation laws. By 1928, these demands had been incorporated into Moscow's Negro Policy, which demanded absolute equality between individuals in all social situations. Whereas the American South legislated racial inequality and policed the color line with all the power of the state, in the Soviet Union, racism, or "social poison," was officially illegal.

While the GOP segregated Black delegates to its national convention behind chicken wire in 1928, the CPUSA nominated for vice president a Black man, James Ford, whose grandfather had been lynched for "being fresh to a white woman." In an obvious act of provocation, the party also nominated a Black man for governor of Alabama.[22] Always a presence but rarely a player, communists' efforts won the party more gratitude than votes.

In the 1920s and early 1930s, communists encouraged friendship, love, and marriage between whites and Blacks. "Social equality" remained the central slogan of the CPUSA to rally the Black masses, despite Moscow's efforts to focus on Black self-determination and nationhood. In 1930, after a dramatic but failed strike in the cotton mills of North Carolina, the communists denounced white terrorism and proposed the death penalty for "Negro lynching." Communist antilynching meetings drew healthy audiences in the South in that year. Organizing around issues like lynching invited Southern African Americans into the party, and American communist leaders declared "War against White Chauvinism."[23]

Despite the NAACP's hesitation to take on the Scottsboro case and the association of social equality with the communists, the association had, in fact, held that position all along. In 1920, W. E. B. Du Bois explained in a *Crisis* article that when the NAACP was organized in 1909, "it seemed to us that the subject of 'social equality' between races was not one that we need touch officially whatever our private opinions might be. We announced clearly our object as being the political and civil rights of Negroes and this seemed to us a sufficiently clear explanation for our work." Nonetheless, he continued, no matter what stand the NAACP took on any issue, the organization was constantly accused of advocating "social equality."[24]

Now was the moment to clarify the organization's position supporting full equality. Such a statement, Du Bois hurried to add, "does not imply any change of attitude on our part; it simply means a clear and formal expression on matters which hitherto we have mistakenly assumed were unimportant in their relation to our main work." Any attempt to deny social equality—meaning the moral, mental, and physical fitness to associate freely with one's fellow men and women—by law or custom constituted "a blow at humanity, religion and democracy." *The Crisis*, he concluded, advised against racial intermarriage because of social prejudices, but it defended "the absolute legal right of such marriage," and regarded freedom of voluntary association as "the most fundamental right of a human being."[25]

The Scottsboro cases "disrupted the long-standing political usefulness of southern white women's purported [sexual] purity." At the outset of the trials, the white women of the ASWPL, although unalterably opposed to lynching, accepted the conventional Southern assumption that any sex between a white woman and a Black man was ipso facto rape. But they were disturbed by Price's and Bates's shifting stories, and by Bates's flat-out recantation of the rape accusations. Few white women had ever considered the possibility that behind many lynchings lay interracial affairs or other acts of consensual sex across the color line. Was it possible that white women cried rape when none occurred? One Alabama woman described herself as "amazed beyond expression" by the "real facts," which, if known, "could never be explained."[26]

Within ten days of their indictment by the grand jury in Scottsboro, all nine of the Scottsboro Boys were tried and found guilty. Eight of the nine were sentenced to death; thirteen-year old Roy Wright received a life sentence. The convictions were appealed and resulted in a milestone Supreme Court case, *Powell v. Alabama* (1932), in which the majority held that the defendants were denied the right to counsel in violation of their Fourteenth Amendment right to due process of law.

A later appeal resulted in *Norris v. Alabama* (1935), in which the court decided that the exclusion of African Americans from the local juror rolls denied the defendants the right of equal protection of the law.[27] These decisions did not free the nine. After the four youngest served six years in prison, the charges against them were dropped in 1938. Of the others, four were paroled during and immediately after WWII, and one escaped.

Represented by the communists, the Scottsboro defendants were not communists themselves. The defendant in another noteworthy trial was. In 1932, Angelo Herndon, a nineteen-year-old Black labor organizer in Atlanta, was arrested on a charge of fomenting insurrection for possessing communist literature that called for the creation of an independent Black nation. Like the Scottsboro Boys, Herndon was represented by ILD lawyers, who lost the case but kept their client off of death row. As with Scottsboro, the Angelo Herndon trial, in Georgia, generated a landmark US Supreme Court decision, in which the court held that Herndon's actions did not pose a "clear and present danger" to the government, and that therefore his conviction under an antebellum anti-insurrection statute designed to prevent slave uprisings violated the First Amendment.[28]

From his perch in Cambridge, Massachusetts, Harvard law professor and free-speech scholar Zechariah Chafee ruminated about insurrection. Simply advocating the overthrow of the government was not illegal. But what if "insurrection" had a broader definition? Herndon's lawyer Ben Davis insisted that lynching—including the lynching that occurred in courtrooms across the South—was insurrection.[29] White Southerners considered Black voting and other political action insurrectionary. They were right insofar as Black political power, including the sort of demonstrations that Angelo Herndon led as a communist, was aimed straight at Jim Crow. But advocacy without action was not itself revolutionary.

"My guess is that the men concerned in this prosecution were not worried in the slightest about any plotted insurrection or the possibility of a new Liberia between the Tennessee Valley Authority and the Gulf of Mexico," Chafee wrote. "But they were worried, I suspect, about something else that Herndon really wanted—his demand for equal rights for Negroes. If he got going with that, there was a clear and present danger of racial friction and isolated acts of violence by individuals on both sides." Yet, he continued, states could hardly "indict a man for seeking to put the Fifteenth Amendment into wider effect. And the advocacy of other kinds of racial equality, even of intermarriage, is not, I assume, a serious crime in Georgia, if it be a crime at all." The Georgia officials who prosecuted Angelo Herndon were not afraid that the United States Constitution was in danger of being overthrown, Chafee concluded. They were worried that it might be enforced.[30]

Four

"NOBODY IS ASKING FOR
SOCIAL EQUALITY"

IN THE LATE SUMMER of 1938, Mark Ethridge, an outspoken foe of lynching, a progressive journalist, and a leading "southern white man of good will," delivered a speech before the Fourth Southwide Conference on Education and Race Relations in which he said:

> I have nowhere mentioned the abolition of segregation or so-called "social equality," because I have nowhere found these steps to be among the Negro's aspirations. Upon the whole, he is as proud of his race as we are of ours....But even if these were his aspirations, I should consider him foolhardy if he pressed them, because, as friendly as I am, I would consider them against his own interests and against the general welfare and peace.

Quoting a CIC pamphlet, Ethridge explained that "what the Negro wants" was a reorientation of the horizontal race line along a vertical axis, "so that he may have on his side the rights and privileges to which he is entitled, just as the white man on his side enjoys the rights and privileges of American civilization."[1]

Ethridge's words were those of a man who felt the ground moving beneath his feet. Since the riotous summer of 1919, when significant numbers of white Americans arose to stamp out any hope of equality on the part of Black veterans of the Great War, moderate Southern whites like Mark Ethridge had worked shoulder to shoulder with African Americans in regional organizations dedicated to improving social and political conditions in the South. The fact that Ethridge now felt moved to warn those African Americans who were not asking for social equality that they should keep on not asking for it signaled a seismic shift.

The membership of organizations such as the CIC, the YMCA and YWCA, the ASWPL, and the Southern Conference on Human Welfare (SCHW) overlapped, as did many of their goals and ideological commitments.[2] All these groups functioned within the confines of the Jim Crow system throughout the 1930s, and all subscribed publicly to what might be termed the central myth of reformist Southern race politics: that Black Southerners, although unhappy with many of the more grievously discriminatory aspects of racial segregation, had no desire for social, or what was sometimes called "full," equality. In the language of the day, African Americans were "as proud of their racial integrity" as white people were of theirs. Rather than equal rights and integration, African Americans wanted equal rights within a world that would remain, in its most intimate spaces, segregated.

The insistence on a supposed Black dedication to "race purity" and a lack of interest on the part of the South's oppressed racial minority in "social equality" were preconditions for white action in the interest of Black civil rights in the 1930s, with the noteworthy exception of the Communist Party. Taking "the inequalities out of the bi-racial system" threatened neither Jim Crow nor white supremacy, white sociologist Guy B. Johnson explained at the CIC's annual meeting in 1935. Political equality did not lead to miscegenation. "The races," Johnson contended, "can go the whole way of political and civil equality without endangering their integrity."[3]

This understanding that "nobody is asking for social equality" served to balance claims for other, more obviously public, rights before WWII. "It is entirely possible for a southern white man to be uncompromisingly in favor of justice to the Negro and uncompromisingly against intermarriage," is how Richmond author and editor Virginius Dabney phrased it in 1933.[4] If Virginius Dabney and Guy Johnson and Mark Ethridge had not subscribed to the idea that African Americans rejected the possibility of social integration and complete equality, they could not have been reformers. The argument that even Black progressives drew the line at social equality made it possible for white progressives, most of whom believed quietly but steadfastly in white racial supremacy, to work for social and political changes that benefited Black Southerners without seeing those changes as endangering their own racial beliefs or privileges.

The argument that African Americans themselves rejected the possibility of equal sex and marriage rights with whites helped white and Black reformers make enormous strides in the pre-WWII South. Keeping sex out of the equation eased the way of the NAACP as it began its legal assault on Jim Crow education. Strategic avoidance of the sex issue also helped facilitate the organization of the SCHW, whose voting-rights campaign would meld with that of the NAACP and inform efforts to ensure the right to vote to all American citizens. In 1942, explicit denial that the federal Fair Employment Practices Committee (FEPC), which policed discriminatory employment practices in war industries, had any jurisdiction over private social relations was a crucial step in creating the possibility that the wartime economic boom might benefit African Americans without overturning social hierarchies.

For years, white Southern reformers had insisted on maintaining the core of Jim Crow: restrictive marriage laws and the social segregation that sustained them. Now, the myth of African American indifference to full equality became increasingly untenable, thanks in great measure to the experience of WWII and the unfolding discourse of universal human rights associated with the Allies. By the middle of WWII, even conservative Black Southern spokesmen denounced "compulsory segregation" and found it "unfortunate" that efforts to address social and economic injustice continued to be interpreted as "the predatory ambition of irresponsible Negroes to invade the privacy of family life."[5]

The Second World War is remembered as America's "good war," in which a reluctant United States unleashed its military and industrial might in the interest of democracy and human rights. That same war changed the course of American race politics. The fight against fascism substantially shifted the terms of the debate about white supremacy in America, as many of the assumptions that underlay America's racial regime were laid bare and challenged more forthrightly than they had been since Reconstruction. By the end of the war, leading African American institutions and individuals were all but unanimous in demanding economic opportunity, political equality, and the end of legal segregation in all its forms, including in sex and marriage.

THE SOUTH LOOKED to the massive war mobilization effort that began even before Pearl Harbor to lift the region finally out of the Great Depression. Most of the thirty-two million citizens of the eleven states of the former Confederacy (nine million of whom were Black) lived without electricity in 1940. Although the South benefited from New Deal legislation, the war—which was, in domestic policy terms, an enormous and unprecedented government-spending program—is what finally reversed decades of Southern economic stagnation. Southern Democrats who had stymied New Deal spending since 1938 leapt at the chance for federally funded infrastructure. Between 1940 and 1945, the federal government invested in excess of $10 billion in war industries and military installations in the South.[6]

It seemed a natural choice to turn the South into the nation's military training center. The region's land was cheap, its climate was warm, and, following Pearl Harbor, its congressional delegation was newly cooperative. The men who trained and were housed in the recently built military bases were, as often as not, white Southerners motivated by a combination of patriotism and want, trading in their denim overalls for khakis. Those who did not enlist right away often either found work in the defense industry—twenty-eight thousand men were employed in the aircraft plant at Marietta, Georgia, alone—or held one of the more than one million civilian jobs created in those years to support the region's burgeoning military-industrial complex.[7]

Still concentrated disproportionately in the South, Black Americans had suffered through the Great Depression with little in the way of government assistance. In the South, New Deal programs were almost without exception administered exclusively by white Southerners for the benefit of white Southerners. By late 1940, as President Roosevelt pledged the United States to become Great Britain's "arsenal of democracy" in its desperate war against Nazi Germany, African Americans wanted, and were willing to demand, their fair share of the bounty of any war. This was as true for Black women—who, by the war's end in 1945, constituted 60 percent of the one million African Americans who entered paid employment during the war years—as it was for Black men.[8] But with half of all defense industries excluding Blacks as a matter of course, finding and keeping a job was not easy. Even the wartime draft did not guarantee Black employment: the Army managed somehow not to call a single African American in the first selective service requisition after Pearl Harbor.[9]

Not one of the booming shipyards on the Gulf Coast employed even a single Black welder. Black workers wielded brooms, but not drills, in Detroit's aircraft factories. As long as there were still unemployed white men and women available, neither private nor government employers were going to voluntarily hire African Americans in anything other than a menial capacity. In response to the segregated military and war industry, Black Americans added a fifth freedom—freedom from segregation—to the four freedoms already denominated by President Roosevelt in 1941 (freedom of speech and religion, freedom from fear and poverty). The *Pittsburgh Courier* dubbed this binding of local and national interests the "Double V" campaign, for victory at home and abroad.

A. Philip Randolph, the powerful leader of the Brotherhood of Sleeping Car Porters, had spent the depression years arguing in favor of Black unity and organization. In a White House meeting on segregation in the armed forces in September 1940, President Roosevelt had outmaneuvered Randolph, NAACP executive director Walter White, and the National Urban League's T. Arnold Hill by seeming to commit to change but denying it later. Five months later, Randolph denounced the national defense as corrupted by "race prejudice, hatred, and discrimination" and called on Black America to "march 10,000 strong on Washington, D.C." to demand the "Right to Work and Fight for Our Country." Randolph's rhetoric and his goals for the march ballooned during the spring of 1941, until at last he had a clear vision of a hundred thousand Black Americans staging "an 'all-out' thundering march on Washington, ending in a monster huge demonstration at Lincoln's monument."[10]

Editorials and back-channel negotiations had their place in the Black freedom movement. But mass action enabled ordinary people to be seen and heard, to do something for themselves rather than rely on others. Randolph's proposed March on Washington would "shake up white America"; it would "shake up official Washington"; it would "gain respect for the Negro people." If anyone could pull off such an audacious plan, it was A. Philip Randolph. The date was set for July 1, 1941, and Randolph's team got to work. Recalled the Northern Black journalist Roi Ottley, "Buses were hired, special trains chartered," and Randolph's "efficient couriers—the Pullman porters—carried the word to Negro communities throughout the country."[11]

The March on Washington Movement alternately outraged and worried Franklin Roosevelt. Eleanor Roosevelt, sent by her husband to talk Randolph out of the march, was rebuffed. The president then charged New York mayor Fiorello LaGuardia with sorting things out, but his charms had no effect. After a face-off with Randolph at the

White House in mid-June, the president finally gave in. With less than a week to spare before the march, Roosevelt issued Executive Order 8802, which stipulated equal hiring practices in defense industries and government agencies but did not desegregate the armed forces. To administer the order, Roosevelt created the Fair Employment Practices Committee (FEPC), an interracial committee designed to investigate racial discrimination in war industries, and installed at its helm the moderate and well-connected Louisville journalist Mark Ethridge. Randolph called off the march.

Endowed with investigatory but not enforcement power, the FEPC illuminated but was unable to alter the racially stratified war economy. Originally housed in the Office of Production Management, the FEPC was abruptly transferred in July 1942 to the War Manpower Committee, which routinely overruled FEPC policy in the interest of keeping war production smoothly on-track.

The agency's chief weapon was moral suasion. This might have worked had employers had any scruples about their discriminatory hiring practices, or shared the same moral premises as the committee. Instead, leading Southern whites attended FEPC hearings as if summoned before the Grand Inquisitor. For white Southerners, the FEPC represented a clear federal response to Black political power, which was reason enough to despise it. Equally disturbing was Roosevelt's use of executive power to implement the meddlesome agency. No other federal agency, either during the war or after it, elicited such passionate support, on the one hand, and loathing, on the other. Roi Ottley reported that white Southerners regarded Executive Order 8802 as "the initial assault on [their] way of life."[12]

White Southerners, as we know, would travel a long way to defend that way of life, enunciating a white version of African Americans' Double V war aims. The mayor of Shreveport, Louisiana, considered the FEPC as great a threat to regional white supremacy as the Axis powers posed to the nation. Both should be resisted. "Of equal importance with winning the war," he declared, "is the necessity for keeping

Negroes out of skilled jobs." Alabama governor Frank Dixon turned down a federal defense contract rather than accept its nondiscrimination provision. Making the usual rhetorical leap from antidiscrimination in the public sphere to integration in private spaces, Dixon argued that desegregation would not stop at the workplace. "Under cover of this clause," he declared, the federal government would "break down the principle of segregation of races" in all spheres of Southern life. In public hearings in Birmingham in 1942, in which the governor was forced to answer questions posed by Black members of the commission, Dixon denounced the FEPC as a "kangaroo court obviously dedicated to the abolition of segregation."[13]

African American calls for equitable distribution of war work and participation in the war effort were promptly, and predictably, translated into sexual demands. Mississippi congressman John Rankin railed that the FEPC's goal was "to dictate to you who shall work in your factory, who shall work on your farm, who shall work in your office, who shall go to your schools, and who shall eat at your table, or intermarry with your children." A white correspondent with California governor Earl Warren was more succinct, writing that the FEPC acronym stood for "Fornicate Every Possible Caucasian."[14]

Georgia senator Richard Russell did not consider the FEPC a joking matter. "The FEPC," he insisted, "is the most sickening manifestation of the trend that is now in effect to force social equality and miscegenation of the white and Black races on the South." Virginia eugenicist Earnest Sevier Cox denounced "nuptial-couch race harmony" and wrote that miscegenation was a war aim. "If [miscegenation] is not disengaged from our war ideals, but left with them," he announced, "it could be truly said that if our soldiers, white and Black, return from the war and find that in their absence their sisters have not conceived a mulatto child they will feel that their sacrifices have been in vain."[15]

Mississippi senator Theodore Bilbo was even more explicit. Known as the "Prince of the Peckerwoods" (a dialect word for woodpeckers, considered a pest by farmers) for his robust representation of poor whites in northern Mississippi, Bilbo was usually a Roosevelt loyalist and strong supporter of New Deal programs as well as a strident exponent of white supremacy. Whereas Louisiana senator John Overton spoke broadly, insisting that the war would "bring not only political but social equality," Senator Bilbo connected the dots and lectured white Southerners that they should not forget that federal support for equality in one realm led irresistibly to demands for equality across the board. Framing his claims as broadly as possible and in terms that connected hiring and marital practices, Bilbo intoned, "Every Negro in America who is behind movements" like the March on Washington Movement or federal oversight of federal programs "dream[s] of equality and inter-marriage between whites and blacks."[16]

This leap in the imagination from nondiscriminatory hiring practices to enforced interracial sex and marriage flummoxed and frustrated supporters of African American rights. Poet Carl Sandburg, for one, complained about people who "have a standard question to ask as though you are floored and out of breath with nothing to say when this question hits you in the face. This question...runs like this: 'Would you want to marry a nigger? Would you like to have one of your daughters marry a nigger?' This is supposed to choke off any discussion" people might want to have about whether or not Blacks have a right "to any or all of the Four Freedoms."[17]

As the head of the FEPC, Mark Ethridge was awash in such rhetoric. Hoping to head off the likes of Dixon, Bilbo, and Russell, Ethridge explained in a statement at the 1942 Birmingham hearings that the FEPC's goal was not to dismantle segregation but to make it "as painless as possible"—to uphold segregation while trying, somehow, to address discrimination. Achieving even this modest goal required neutralizing the "social equality" question. There must be no talk of dissolving the sexual barrier between the races. In prepared remarks, Ethridge acknowledged and tried to allay white Southern fears that the FEPC intended to reorganize Southern social relations. He began by speaking to the white men and women in the room. "No white

Southerner," Ethridge asserted, "can logically challenge the statement that the colored man is entitled, as an American citizen, to full civil rights and to economic opportunity. Full civil rights," he continued, included "the right to vote, the right to justice in the courts, the right to share equitably in the tax burden and in the distribution of tax moneys for public health, for public education, for public improvements such as streets and sidewalks and parks." Economic opportunity embraced "the right to work according to one's own skill."[18]

Then, in a conscious effort to defuse the "social equality" question, Ethridge denied that the FEPC had any influence in the private sphere. Admitting that "individual members of the committee have their own ideas" about desegregation (indeed, Black committee members Earl Dickerson and Milton Webster showed no signs of bowing to Jim Crow conventions), he insisted that the committee "recognized that the President was not endeavoring, in Executive Order 8802, to write a social document....I believe it is perfectly apparent that Executive Order 8802 is a war order, and not a social document." Had this not been apparent, Ethridge added, he would not have agreed to serve on the committee, because he "would have considered a Federal fiat demanding, for instance, the abolition of social segregation against the general peace and welfare" and an inappropriate federal usurpation of state sovereignty over local affairs.

Turning his attention to the African Americans present and to the Black press and organizations monitoring the Birmingham hearings, Ethridge warned them not to press too far, too fast, in their urge toward equality. Then he spoke the words to which he would be forever tied in civil rights memory: "The Southern colored man...must recognize that there is no power in the world—not even in all the mechanized armies of the earth, Allied and Axis—which could now force the Southern white people to the abandonment of the principle of social segregation."

It is easy to read Mark Ethridge's comments in Birmingham as evidence of the inflexibility and virulent racism of white Southern liberals.

In the midst of a world war, the white Southern administrator of the first federal antidiscrimination program took the opportunity to articulate his region's commitment to Jim Crow in apocalyptic terms. What this perspective misses is Ethridge's redrawing of Jim Crow's territory, the narrowing of its realm. Standing stoutly on the rock of social segregation, Mark Ethridge conceded in principle almost everything else on the Black reform agenda.

But this was insufficient. Lectured by Ethridge, African Americans talked back. The CIC characterized the Black reaction to the speech as "vituperatively violent." The African American weekly paper the *Pittsburgh Courier* declared FEPC approval of segregation by a federal agency "a surrender to the Nazi racial theory."[19] Calling for Ethridge's resignation as head of the FEPC, the *Baltimore Afro-American* declared that the social equality question needed public airing, not repression. "The average Southern white…becomes so emotional and noisy" over the "social equality" question, the editors noted, "that we ought to talk about it a little. We begin by saying that the AFRO believes in social equality if it is anything other citizens have. We think we are entitled to all the public rights of citizens and therefore need no special arrangements made for us."[20]

Running down Ethridge's list of the rights of citizenship, the editors added marriage. "If intermarriage is social equality, we are for it. Free people choose their own life-time companions without any interference from the State." It was the editors' belief, in short, "that in every human relationship government can have but one standard—citizenship….The only spot reserved for social equality is in the home, or private club which requires no public license to operate." Mississippi's Prince of the Peckerwoods may have exaggerated the fantasy life of American Blacks—but his analysis of the trajectory of African American politics was on the mark.[21]

AFTER PEARL HARBOR, government military spending began, at last, to lift the American economy out of the depression that had plagued it for a decade.[22] A few goods were rationed—coffee, sugar, meat, tires, gasoline—but overall Americans had never had it so good. Indeed, the United States was the only nation that managed to build a war economy on top of a consumer economy during World War II.

America's allies experienced no such comfort. In Britain, personal consumption shrank by nearly a quarter, and rationing did not end until 1955. With the German Army deep in Soviet territory, the Russians were forced to fight from a diminishing economic base; every step west taken by the Red Army was underwritten by calamitous civilian sacrifices. Americans sacrificed at home, too, but on a completely incommensurate scale. With beef rationed, enterprising housewives searched for alternative sources of protein. "Peanut butter carrot loaf" was one mother's nutritious if much-maligned invention. Urged to supplement his diet with game, one food writer turned poetic: "Although it isn't / Our usual habit, / This year we're eating / The Easter Rabbit."[23]

Exhilarating as wartime was for many American civilians, others found little charm on the home front. High rents combined with housing shortages led to severe overcrowding in the United States, particularly in cities with concentrated war industries. The water pressure in Mobile, Alabama, home to several enormous shipbuilding enterprises, was so low that residents in an outlying suburb let their taps run all day to accumulate a bucket of water. Just going downtown in places like Oakland or Detroit required an aggressive single-mindedness of purpose. The Motor City alone squeezed in five hundred thousand Southern whites plus fifty thousand Southern Blacks between 1940 and 1943. The sidewalks in many cities were too crowded, the buses a disaster. There were too many kids and too few swings at the local playground.[24]

The mass migration of war workers led to the expansion of African American communities in cities that had had negligible numbers of Blacks before Pearl Harbor. The Black populations of Oakland, Los Angeles, and San Diego tripled. Seattle's Black population expanded tenfold, from four thousand to forty thousand. The Hispanic population swelled as well, as the bracero program, created by the federal government in 1942, imported Mexican farm workers to fill the agricultural jobs vacated by the new war workers.[25]

Disagreement about segregation exacerbated more general wartime aggravations, and the people who kept track of such things worried about the rising number of interracial altercations across America. The Social Science Institute at Fisk University counted 242 incidents of interracial rioting and violence during 1943.[26] The most exceptional and the most common violent outbursts concerned control over public space. Detroit, known as the Arsenal of Democracy for its massive war industry, witnessed both the mundane and the spectacular. In April 1943, more than a hundred Detroit teenagers of both races duked it out on a municipal playground. Three months later, on a hot summer day on Belle Isle, a spate of individual fights touched off four days of rioting in which twenty-five African Americans were killed by Detroit police officers.[27]

More common than either riots or playground fights were violent interactions between whites and Blacks on the nation's overcrowded municipal public transportation systems. Arguments about civil equality were frequently acted out by passengers swaying within a trolley or a sweltering subway car beneath the streets of America's cities. A good depiction of the mood comes from New York, where, according to writer James Baldwin, "six Negro girls...set upon a white girl in the subway because, as they all too accurately put it, she was stepping on their toes. Indeed she was," Baldwin concluded, "all over the nation."[28]

Racial battles over the control of public space *did* occur all over the nation. But nowhere were these interactions more inflammatory than on the streetcars and buses of the urban South, where Jim Crow was supposed to rule unchecked. Novelist Ralph Ellison described the Southern bus as "a contraption contrived by laying the South's social pyramid on its side, knocking out a few strategic holes, and rendering it vehicular through the addition of an engine, windows and wheels."[29] It was a vehicle that reinscribed and reinforced racial inequality with every trip. Because they required the intimate acting-out of the script of segregation that occurred on them, streetcars and buses were among the most loathed components of the Jim Crow South. Buses were particularly resented by Southern Black city dwellers, who had to either pay at the front and then run around the bus and enter from the rear, or worm their way through a white throng at the front to find a seat at the back. Whereas Black Southerners of means went to great trouble to avoid having to ride buses, that was not an option for most working-class African Americans, who depended on public transportation to get to work on time and who thus had little choice but to submit to the system's degrading protocol.

By 1942 there was no mistaking the new assertiveness of Black riders in the wartime South, particularly young Black men, who moved the "white" and "colored" dividers, refused to vacate seats when instructed to, and hung over white women, sharing their breath and body odor. Southern whites linked such behavior with the new opportunities the war and the FEPC brought to Black workers. In November 1942, a white Birmingham woman wrote to Alabama governor Frank Dixon to complain about overhearing Black men on a Birmingham bus ask white girls on dates. Dixon blamed it on the federal government and explained that "certain elements of the national administration" (also known as "northern fanatics at present connected with the national administration") were determined to "try to force a change in the social structure of the South."[30]

Also emphasizing the danger the FEPC posed to white supremacy, an official of the Virginia Electric and Power Company linked economic power with Black rejection of Jim Crow. There were fights on the buses and streetcars almost every day, he wrote, because "the Negro...is making good money now and feels that he is as good as the white man." As Black sociologist Charles S. Johnson explained, wartime conditions "tend[ed] to reduce the *customary* patterns of segregation to highly volatile issues of *personal* status in racial situations."[31]

Enormous structural transformations characterized the South after 1941: a new assertion of federal power in the form of regulatory agencies, Supreme Court decisions, and the presence of the military; a demographic shift from farm to city and beyond; economic reconfiguration that would remodel the Cotton Belt into the suburban Sun Belt. In this context, the maintenance of day-to-day customs of racial hierarchy became a key preoccupation for white Southerners determined to preserve the foundation of their congenial (to them) way of life. For the first time since the Jim Crow state had been solidified at the turn of the century, white Southerners were forced to personally defend their own privileged place in society.

One of the most effective arguments in persuading white Southerners of the necessity of state-mandated racial segregation had been the potential of the Jim Crow regime to curb violence in public spaces. The arrival of so many strangers of uncharted genealogy across the wartime South made it more important than ever to keep everybody in their allotted racial spaces, just as it made it much harder to do so. In the overcrowded conditions of the wartime South, segregation laws were often honored in the breach by whites, who used Black-only freight elevators at the backs of buildings and sat in seats reserved for "colored" on buses and streetcars, forcing Black riders to stand.[32] Light-skinned Northern Blacks who bunched in the "colored" section or stood rather than sat among whites confounded white drivers required by law to enforce Jim Crow, at gunpoint if necessary.

With so many people on the move during the war, bus and trolley riders were often unsure of the rules and could always plead ignorance of local custom, particularly in border cities like Nashville and Richmond. In 1942, Black poet and professor of literature Sterling Brown related a telling incident. "On a border city trolley," Brown reported, "a strapping white sailor, in a spic-and-span white suit, jumped up from the seat when an old Negro woman sat down beside him." The soldier stood scowling, looking around for support from his fellow white riders. "'Thank you, son,'" the Black woman said, settling in. "'But I didn't need the whole seat. I spread, but not that much.'"[33]

Stories of white/Black social inversion and African American assertion were not confined to the South. Race relations were more fluid in Los Angeles, which had its share of racial confrontations, violence, and rumors. In late 1944, J. F. Anderson informed California governor Earl Warren that "people tell me that in Los Angeles they [the Negroes] have what they call 'Shove Tuesday.' On that day the negro folks emphasize themselves in every way they can, even to shoving white folks off the sidewalk if they feel inclined to do so." The letter was accompanied by a newspaper clipping about a Black woman beating up a white woman in line at the county civic tax collector's office.[34]

Selective application by whites of the everyday rules of segregation and the confusion caused by lack of familiarity with Southern social practices by Northern soldiers created certain openings for African Americans. Blacks' subversion of the rules of Jim Crow transportation and their insistence that whites respect their own segregation rules were received in the South as part of African Americans' new "nationwide fight for full citizenship."[35]

It was in this context that Virginius Dabney, the progressive white editor of the *Richmond Times-Dispatch*, made a modest proposal. The city of Richmond should repeal its laws segregating streetcars and buses. Originally passed to lessen racial friction, the laws, Dabney argued, no longer worked and actually heightened racial tensions because of war-related overcrowding and attendant jostling for position. Under these circumstances, Dabney considered segregated public transportation counterproductive and a danger to the broader system of segregation, which he nevertheless still embraced.

Widely respected among Blacks for his editorials in the 1930s denouncing the Ku Klux Klan and lynching and decrying the miscarriage of justice at Scottsboro, Dabney's argument was entirely expedient, his goals ameliorative. As he explained to Louis Jaffe, the left-leaning editor of the white *Norfolk Virginian-Pilot*, he eschewed moral arguments against segregation because if it were true that segregation was undemocratic, as many argued, "it is just as logical to argue against it in the public schools, for instance." Dabney was willing to sacrifice segregated transportation as a practical measure to restore a degree of public decorum. An acute observer of human behavior, Dabney recognized that Black Richmonders had not internalized white norms of public deference. He also saw that when meeting the letter of the law meant aggressively pushing and shoving one's way to the back of the bus, that was what happened.[36]

Many white Richmonders seemed to agree with Dabney's piecemeal approach to reforming Jim Crow. Letters to the *Times-Dispatch* ran three to one in favor of his suggestion, and the Virginia League for the Repeal of the Segregation Laws was formed in Richmond in December 1943.[37]

Not everyone was convinced. Warren M. Goddard, an officer with the State Planters Bank and Trust Co. in Richmond, articulated precisely the slippery-slope argument that Dabney was trying to avoid in his correspondence with Louis Jaffe. Explaining that he had "some knowledge of negroes," Goddard expressed his concern "over the attitude and thinking of many of them at the present time, especially the younger generation."

This attitude and thinking took many forms, Goddard explained, "but there is only one goal—social equality. Many make no pretense of concealing it, in fact give free expression in words and actions. I feel…that if segregation on street cars and buses is abolished many negroes would construe it as a vindication and approval of their rudeness and openly hostile and unfriendly attitude." The banker concluded, "It would be an entering wedge, and they would be encouraged to extend the abandonment of segregation to the theatres, then the restaurants and hotels, then the schools, then the homes, and so on, ad finitum and ad naseum [*sic*]." The frustrated admonition of P. B. Young, editor of Norfolk's Black weekly *Journal and Guide*, that "the white South must come to realize that sober and sane attempts to correct basic injustices, to remove irritants, and to democratically spread civil rights are NOT disguised efforts to invade the privacy of family life" made little headway with the Warren Goddards of Virginia.[38]

Dabney's attempt at limited desegregation was soon dashed. Virginia governor Colgate Darden—described by a writer for the *Baltimore*

Afro-American as the only man he knew "who can pronounce 'Negro' with a small 'n'"—expressed his displeasure.[39] But Dabney's goal of preventing violence and shifting the defense of Jim Crow to those areas where he thought segregation mattered most, such as schools and the marital bed, remained.

AS VIRGINIUS DABNEY pursued his fruitless effort to rejigger the boundaries of segregation in the interest of social peace, renowned University of North Carolina sociologist Howard Odum noted in 1943 that his region was following "a new pro-South tempo, a solid South again highly motivated for self-defense." A prominent element of this wartime cultural jujitsu, Odum observed, was the circulation of stories concerning African Americans: what they had done, what they were doing, what they said they planned to do. Convinced that the South (by which he meant white Southerners) and the Negro (by which he meant African Americans everywhere) "faced their greatest crisis since the days of reconstruction," Odum collected the stories and published them in a 1943 book entitled *Race and Rumors of Race*.[40]

This was not the first time that white Southerners had expressed their anxiety about the enormous changes occurring in their daily lives, or their fear of potential change, through stories of troubling Black activities. Rumors of slave plots and insurrections were a common feature of life in the antebellum era, and anxious reports of anticipated Black assaults coursed regularly through the Reconstruction South, especially during moments of political and economic upheaval and perceptible African American influence.

Such moments often did produce explosions, but they were nearly always of the organized white-on-Black variety. This, too, was disruptive, however, and a principal rationale offered for African American disenfranchisement and segregation at the turn of the century was Jim Crow's capacity to reduce friction and deter violence. Odum's comparison of the mid-1940s with the Reconstruction era—a time when Black men voted and held office, labor relations were contested on a

contract-by-contract basis, and white Southerners complained endlessly of the erosion of African American deference—suggests the
depth of white Southern agitation about the disarray of the war years
and their apprehension concerning the rising expectations of African
Americans demonstrated by the Double V campaign.[41]

Odum divided the stories chronicled in *Race and Rumors of Race*
into three main categories that "recaptured the tensions of the past and
featured the very old threefold heart of the southern biracial culture."
The first represented whites' fear of social inversion, especially that they
would be unable to dominate African Americans after the war. The second concerned Black-on-white violence. The third consisted of stories
of "social equality," which asserted that predatory Black men were going
to steal white men's wives and daughters while the men were off at war.

The "Negro will take over" stories, reported Odum, "swept down
with renewed power as did the rumors that the whites would some day
work for the Negroes." One of the most common, and most colorful,
examples of such stories revolved around that nightmare of all bourgeois women, a sudden shortage of domestic labor. Black maids and
cooks, so the tale went, were plotting to coerce white women into their
own kitchens by abandoning their posts. As concerned with maintaining control over African American labor as their Reconstruction ancestors, who circulated stories in 1865 that the freedmen, influenced by
Union soldiers and advisers, would refuse to sign labor contracts, the
tellers of these tales were equally convinced that their workers were
influenced by powerful external allies.

The driving force behind this mass mutiny was, reputedly, the
president's crusading first lady. The domestic labor shortage was real
enough—African American women were as quick to seize war-related
job opportunities as Black men were, and those who did not recognized the increase in their own value. But the conviction that Eleanor
Roosevelt was somehow behind the supposed "Eleanor Clubs," where
African American women reputedly gathered and plotted to abandon
the kitchens of white women, reflected widespread fear of efforts to

organize labor and of mass action undertaken at the behest of outsiders. Eleanor Roosevelt's ability to stand in for all these fears left her a convenient scapegoat for the transformation of domestic relations in the wartime South. As Southern-born journalist Thomas Sancton noted wryly in 1943, "Mrs. Roosevelt is the most hated symbol of the white middle class since Harriet Beecher Stowe."[42] Yet the stories about the Eleanor Clubs were tame compared to some of the other rumors that circulated through the South during the war.

Another group of tales cataloged by Odum concerned alleged violent assaults on whites, often in the form of riots or uprisings, and the stockpiling of weapons such as ice picks, knives, and guns by Black Southerners. "I have heard rumors that the Negroes in several small South Georgia towns are buying all the ammunition, having secret meetings, and planning to revolt against the white people," reported one of Odum's sources. "They say the Negroes are going to demand equal rights with white people." Elsewhere the news was that "the police recently raided a Negro church in which was found an arsenal of firearms and ammunition to be used against the whites." Stories like these often resulted in preemptive violence directed at local Blacks believed to pose a danger to the local white community. Odum noted the gruesome details assiduously.[43]

Sandwiched in between these two compilations was a dangerous variation of the first group, grounded in the region's "sex-caste culture." These tales of "social equality," which broadcast Black men's intention to appropriate white Southern women while their husbands and brothers were away fighting the war, were the most numerous and the most inflammatory of the race rumors that circulated during World War II, and they prompted comment in the Black press as well as by Odum. "Though the villains in these phony fictions are always Negroes, the plot has variations," explained Edith Stern in *Negro Digest*:

> For instance, there is the "meat cleaver" story that circulated in at least nine cities. According to this fantasy, a Negro walked into a butcher

shop, rolled his eyes, and announced that now that the white men were all away at war, the Negroes would have all the white women. Where-upon the butcher seized his cleaver, and neatly sliced off the Negro's head. People in Rome, Georgia, heard that this happened in Savannah. Savannah heard it took place in Mobile. In Mobile, the locale was Memphis. And Memphis heard of its happening in Louisville, Kentucky.[44]

Numerous stories of Black Southerners' quest for social equality circulated throughout the South in the early 1940s and reinforced the general white Southern belief that African Americans cherished a secret desire for white women at all times, and, worse, that white women were not immune to the charms of Black men. Odum's sources documented extensive white fear of sexual and political displacement, reporting, for instance, that South Carolina Blacks had allegedly an-nounced that "after the war Negroes will marry white girls and run the country," and that a group of Black youths informed white inductees in uniform that "we will take care of all the white girls while you are gone." The most direct version of this type of story was represented by yet another Black South Carolinian, who reputedly saw his white soldier neighbors off with the following salute: "When you come back from the Army, I'll be your brother-in-law."[45]

Virginius Dabney, who had predicted unprecedented racial vi-olence should whites refuse to ease their segregationist expectations and Blacks their integrationist agitation, was aghast that Odum would publish such rumors in the explosive context of the war. "I think it is particularly important that it be made clear beyond any peradventure that irresponsible rumor-mongering is what you are talking about, and not actual statements of, or acts by, Negroes," Dabney wrote to Odum. "I feel that this is particularly important in the case of the various com-ments supposed to have been made by Negro men concerning white women. This sort of material is highly inflammatory as you know better than I, and it seems to me to be essential that you stress the thought that most of this chatter probably never was uttered by anybody."[46]

Compliantly, Odum explained in the book that his collection agents had emphasized repeatedly that the "rumors and irresponsible talk" they recorded were just that. Yet, he insisted, the stories' "number and variety" were "testimony as to the nature of their power....It was always hard to destroy their influence."[47]

It is difficult to gauge the significance of the race rumors that circulated throughout the South during WWII. Worried that the so-called Eleanor Clubs might be connected with alleged communist plans to "foment a 'black revolution' in the South," South Carolina governor Richard Manning Jefferies put his State Law Enforcement Division on the case. Constables found no evidence of a planned Black insurrection, but they did discover an abundance of white anxiety. A Beaufort officer unearthed no Eleanor Clubs, but he commented on the heightened level of white unease in his area. "There is too much talk about it among the white people," he reported. Whites were not calmed by a lack of local Black activity, either. White apprehension seemed to be "entirely about what is supposed to have happened elsewhere." Palpably rattled by the local white state of mind, the officer concluded, "The white people appear to be considerably disturbed."[48]

Five

WHAT THE NEGRO WANTS

Halfway through World War II, William Terry Couch, the director of the University of North Carolina Press, suggested to Howard University historian Rayford Logan that he assemble a collection of essays representing "the personal creed of 10 or 15 prominent Negroes," to be ambitiously titled *What the Negro Wants*. Barely thirty years old when he took over the press in 1932, Couch was by March 1943 a fully credentialed white Southern liberal. Left-leaning enough to have been tagged a "parlor Bolshevik" in the 1930s, an active participant in North Carolina interracial reform circles, and a founding member of the Southern Council on Human Welfare (SCHW), Couch's most lasting contribution to Southern race relations would prove to be his publishing record. Under his direction, the UNC Press (which has been described fairly as "the nearest thing the South had to a general-interest book publishing company") published a long list of books addressing various aspects of the South, including lynching and economic backwardness, as well as a significant number of titles by or about African Americans.[1]

An accomplished writer and social critic himself, Couch contributed an entry titled "The Negro in the South" to *Culture in the South*, a path-breaking survey, edited by Couch, of Southern society published in 1933. Appreciative of the unsparing portraits of the region emerging from a new generation of Southern writers such as William Faulkner, Robert Penn Warren, and Erskine Caldwell, Couch pushed his non-fiction authors to give up the safe ground of social science methodology, to rely less on statistics and more on description. His directions to H. C. Brearley, a sociologist who was writing a chapter on violence for *Culture in the South*, is instructive. "I should like especially to have a description of a mob," Couch wrote in 1932:

> How it gathers, becomes excited, starts a chase (possibly with dogs), gets on a trail, catches a Negro, and then proceeds to indulge in barbarous cruelty, pulling off toe and finger nails, cutting off toes and fingers by joints, pulling out chunks of flesh with corkscrews, and finally burning and shooting and gathering bones, teeth, or remnants of clothing as souvenirs. The cruelty of our mobs is, I believe, unique, and should be remarked upon in some detail.[2]

Bill Couch was not, generally speaking, inclined to flinch when confronted with the reality of the contemporary South. But as he discovered, some hard truths were more easily faced than others. First, he underestimated the radicalism of wartime African Americans, who were dedicated to full equality. Second, he failed to accurately gauge the belief systems of those Southerners who called themselves liberals. Despite white moderates' willingness to loosen the bonds of Jim Crow, they remained committed white supremacists. Swedish sociologist Gunnar Myrdal, who led a research and writing team of more than thirty Black and white scholars to produce the monumental *An American Dilemma: The Negro Problem and Modern Democracy*, remarked in 1944 on the incongruity of Southern whites who called themselves liberals while supporting racial hierarchy and segregation. "Southern liberalism is not liberalism as it is found elsewhere in America or the world," he concluded. "It is a unique species."[3] In his wartime book project, designed to reach white liberals, Couch collided with the limits of what those liberals could tolerate, even as he miscalculated the aims and desires of African Americans for the future.

INSPIRED BY A 1941 essay of the same title by poet Langston Hughes, Couch's intent in commissioning *What the Negro Wants* was to assess the state of American race relations, particularly in the South during the war, and to spark a lively discussion of the future of segregation. As he would later explain in his "Publisher's Preface" to the book, in which he assumed the role of Pontius Pilate to editor Rayford Logan's assembled high priests and elders, Couch pursued the volume in hopes of furthering discussion of how the white South could disentangle itself from the worst excesses of a social system that, he allowed, imposed "numerous unnecessary burdens" on its minority Black population.[4] The roster of contributors had been carefully curated to balance conservatives, moderates, and known rabble-rousers, in hopes of showing a breadth of opinion about solutions. When their essays arrived, Couch was appalled and Logan gratified by the result. The nearly unanimous opinion of the authors held that the Negro wanted absolute equality and an end to legal segregation in all areas of life.

The authors collected in *What the Negro Wants* included many of the leading voices of Afro-America. Most of the names remain familiar today. The NAACP's Roy Wilkins contributed an essay, as did W. E. B. Du Bois, Rayford Logan, A. Philip Randolph, and sociologist Gordon Blaine Hancock, who had convened the all-Black 1942 Southern Conference on Race Relations (also known as the Durham Conference) and whose equivocal stance on segregation was considered overly conservative by many Black leaders. The Congress of Industrial Organization's Willard S. Townsend and Doxey A. Wilkerson (the only open communist among the contributors) were balanced by the National Youth Administration's Mary McLeod Bethune and by educator Fredrick Douglass Patterson. Poets Leslie Pinckney Hill, Langston Hughes, and Sterling Brown added their voices, as did leading Howard University historian Charles H. Wesley and the *Pittsburgh Courier*'s inimitable iconoclast George S. Schuyler.

Included among the authors' combined credentials were six advanced degrees from Ivy League universities and one from the Royal Academy of Science, two Guggenheim Fellowships, and the SCHW's Thomas Jefferson award. The organizations represented included the CIO, the Communist Political Association, the YMCA, the American Friends Service Committee, the Southern Regional Council (SRC), the SCHW, the National Association of Colored Women, the Urban League, the National March on Washington Movement, the American Federation of Labor (AFL), and the NAACP. Together, the authors of *What the Negro Wants* had published in excess of thirty books and innumerable articles in national publications.[5]

Had they been brought together in a single room, tempers might have flared. There was bad blood between a number of the contributors, and at least one essay had been commissioned to explain what Logan considered the inadequacies of the Durham Conference. But from right to left, the contributors spoke against racial segregation with one voice. To Logan's demand for "First-Class Citizenship" was added "The Negro Wants Full Equality" (Wilkins), "The Negro Wants Full Participation in the American Democracy" (Patterson), "Count Us In" (Brown), and "'Certain Unalienable Rights'" (Bethune). George Schuyler's tart rearticulation of the book's organizing logic as "The Caucasian Problem" transposed the key, but not the leitmotiv, of the volume. As Logan recalled in 1969, "What disturbed Mr. Couch more than anything else, I believed then and now, was the virtual unanimity of the fourteen contributors in wanting equal rights for Negroes. This general agreement surprised and pleased me as much as it probably shocked Mr. Couch."[6]

To be sure, Black Americans had demanded "equal rights" before 1944. Frederick Douglass had shouted himself hoarse on the topic after the Civil War; Du Bois had done the same, as he put it in his essay for this volume, over "sixty years of purposive endeavor."[7] What was the 1905 Niagara Declaration if not a manifesto of full equality? Yet what had shocked Bill Couch and pleased Ray Logan in 1944 was the openness with which the contributing authors of *What the Negro Wants* addressed the fundamental question of sexual equality and intermarriage.

Of the fourteen essayists, half (Logan, Du Bois, Wesley, Patterson, Hancock, Brown, and Schuyler) called for the abolition of restrictive marriage laws. Three others spoke in code through references to "*absolute political and social equality*" (Wilkins), "the abrogation of every law which makes a distinction in treatment between citizens based on religion, creed, color or national origin" (Randolph), and calls for full "equality before the law" (Bethune).[8] Without demanding an end to what Schuyler referred to as "racial pollution laws barring marriage because of so-called race," Langston Hughes nonetheless noted that "Nobody as a rule sleeps with or eats with or dances with or marries anybody else except by mutual consent," and poked fun at the "ballot box to the bedroom" logic of Southern whites. "Millions of people of various races in New York, Chicago, and Seattle go to the same polls and vote without ever co-habiting together," he announced. Following on Hughes's heels, Sterling Brown ridiculed the notion that "crowded buses and street cars and cafeterias are marriage bureaus," approvingly quoted white Mississippian David Cohn's observation that the race problem in the South was "at bottom a blood or sexual question," and remarked finally that "Negroes have long recognized this as the hub of the argument opposing change in their status."[9]

Bill Couch had hoped to publish a thoughtful book with practical suggestions about how to make the postwar Jim Crow South more humane—the sort of book Virginius Dabney could recommend to the readers of the *Richmond Times-Dispatch*. *What the Negro Wants* was not that book.

Shell-shocked, Couch nonetheless sent the manuscript to readers for the press. O. J. Coffin, a journalism professor at UNC and considered a liberal, objected to the book on theological grounds, complaining that it advocated "overnight the re-ordering of His world."[10] N. C. New-bold, North Carolina's Superintendent of Public Instruction and a local leader in the interracial cooperation movement, favored publication but insisted that all references to interracial marriage be deleted. This suggestion was received unfavorably by Du Bois and Sterling Brown, who refused to change a word.

Suddenly unsure of his ability to comprehend, much less predict, what the Negro wanted, Couch wrote to Logan looking for solace, or at least affirmation. "For years I have been…telling people the Negro… is not interested in social equality," Couch complained. The fault lay, obviously, with the essayists and not with Couch. "The things Negroes are represented as wanting seem to me far removed from those they ought to want. Most of the things they are represented as wanting can be summarized in the phrase: complete abolition of segregation. If this is what the Negro wants, nothing could be clearer than what he needs, and needs most urgently, is to revise his wants." Until that happened, Couch could not—would not—publish this book.[11]

When Couch rescinded his offer of publication, Rayford Logan threatened to sue. Panicking slightly, Couch took his troubles to a trio of leading white liberals: Jackson Davis (an officer of the General Education Board, which was funded by the Rockefeller Foundation), Mark Ethridge (still resented among African Americans for his comments in Birmingham on social equality), and Virginius Dabney.

Cognizant of the explosive nature of the book, Davis and Ethridge nonetheless urged publication, as did Dabney, who alone seemed to understand how Couch had backed himself into such a corner. Couch's trouble, Dabney wrote, was that "you were under the delusion, when you arranged for this book, that the Negro does not want the abolition of segregation, establishment of complete social equality, etc." Dabney had thought the same in 1941. But his wartime experiences in Richmond, and his close reading of the Black press, particularly the *Baltimore Afro-American*, had taught him otherwise. The book should be published; the book would be published. But not without a disclaimer by Couch.[12]

W. T. COUCH's "Publisher's Preface" to *What the Negro Wants* might have been titled "True Confessions of a White Southern Liberal." Writing in the waning weeks of 1943, as the *Times* (London) reported soberly that "evidence from Berlin and Poland" gave the "bleakest possible picture" of the fate of European Jewry and warned that "the worst of Hitler's threats are being literally applied," Couch agonized that all theories of racial hierarchy were in danger of being completely discredited by the Nazis.[13] "Is there any sanity in the view now often stated that no one but a Fascist or Nazi can believe one people or race superior to another?" he asked. Explaining that he believed that the current condition of Black Americans was caused by their innate inferiority— whether racial, environmental, or some combination thereof he declined to say—Couch maintained nonetheless that "this inferiority could be overcome, and the prejudice resulting from it can be cured." Regretful of the more arbitrary and mean-spirited aspects of segregation, Couch agreed that many of the burdens white Southerners placed on the region's African American minority should be removed. But the Jim Crow barrier itself—by which Couch meant the antimiscegenation laws that were designed to guarantee and preserve racial identity and hence make segregation possible—must remain.[14]

Such a barrier could not be made completely effective, Couch acknowledged, "but the fact that some people may cross it in secret does not mean that the barrier ought to be torn down." Social and sexual segregation, he admitted, "may be a tremendous handicap on the Negro; but removing it would result in something worse." Sex remained the sticking point, and it should come as no surprise that Mark Ethridge was among the first to congratulate Couch on his introduction. "Your paper," Ethridge wrote privately, "pretty well presents my viewpoint." There was, nevertheless, disappointment, and a strong sense of an opportunity missed among those who had hoped for more. "The southern intellectuals are in a pretty sorry boat," Langston Hughes wrote to Rayford Logan in December 1943, as Logan negotiated with Couch over the future of the book. "Certainly they are crowding Hitler for elbow room."[15]

Hitler, however, was not the only problem—or even the main problem, as far as Couch was concerned. Of far greater import was the influence of contemporary American sociologists and anthropologists, who flipped Couch's claim that prejudice reflected inferiority and insisted instead that "the Negro is not inferior to the white man, that he only appears to be so, that his condition is wholly and completely a product of race prejudice, and the consequent disabilities inflicted on the Negro by the white man."

Since the early 1930s, Couch continued, numerous books, articles, and pamphlets had argued "that racial notions are responsible for Nazism, that race is a 'modern superstition,' a 'fallacy,' 'man's most dangerous myth,' that the concept of race has no scientific basis, that there is no scientific evidence of differences of ability among races, that mental tests have proved substantial equality, that custom, tradition, prejudice, rather than genuine differences in capacity are responsible for the status of the Negro in the South."[16]

Indeed, Columbia University anthropologists Ruth Benedict and Gene Weltfish coauthored a pamphlet, commissioned by the United Service Organization (USO) in 1943, that explained the common origins of humanity ("the peoples of the earth are one family"), noted that "any head can house a good brain," and, in an intentional provocation of the South, included a table showing that African Americans from the North outscored white Southerners from Mississippi, Arkansas, and Kentucky on the military intelligence test. The Army ordered fifty thousand copies of the pamphlet, titled *The Races of Mankind*, to be distributed among the troops before the chairman of the House Military Affairs Committee, a Kentuckian, found out and insisted it be withdrawn.[17]

The apogee of this trend had arrived at precisely the moment that Couch wrote his introduction to *What the Negro Wants*. Only months before, Swedish sociologist Gunnar Myrdal had published *An American*

Dilemma, which was the result of a monumental, and interracial, collaboration of scholars, including two of the contributors to *What the Negro Wants* and a number of Couch's friends and acquaintances in Chapel Hill.[18]

Invoking the notion that in a democracy the majority should control, and dismissing the guaranteed rights in the Constitution that are designed to override majority preferences, Couch seized the opportunity to attack the authors' argument "that the United States must either give up the 'American Creed' and go fascistic, or accept an equality which would permit amalgamation." The issues, ultimately, were sex and racial reproduction, which Couch considered tantamount to cultural reproduction. Lashing out at Myrdal for his cultural relativism and his refusal to take white Southerners' abhorrence of miscegenation seriously, Couch argued that the solution to the Southern race problem was not to be found in integration but in the ability of Negroes and whites to "remain racially separate and distinct and at the same time avoid inflicting disabilities on each other." Could not the white man, Couch asked, "separate cultural from biological integration, and help the Negro achieve the first and deny him the second?"

Continuing in his defense of "racial integrity," Couch attacked the premise of individual rights that underlay the critique of restrictive marriage laws in *What the Negro Wants* and that would, Couch anticipated correctly, support the postwar push for Black equality. Convinced that Myrdal and his team had seriously misapprehended "what such ideas as equality, freedom, democracy, human rights, have meant, and of what they can be made to mean," Couch posed a question. "Can biological integration be regarded as a right?" he asked. "What happens to the case for the Negro if it is tied up with things to which he not only has no right, but which, if granted, would destroy all rights"—by, presumably, dissolving the white civilization upon whose foundation liberal concepts of rights rested. "If any two people have a right to lead their own lives, certainly any two others or ten or twenty million have a right to opinions on what ought to be allowed and what forbidden."

Forgetting or dismissing the elaborate system of constitutional government designed to defeat majoritarian tyranny and preserve democratic governance, Couch placed his faith in the wisdom of the majority. "To say that the twenty million have no right to make and enforce decisions that they think necessary to the well-being of all is to say that society has no right to govern itself."

Couch continued:

> The assumption of a better, a more valid authority [than the will of the majority], one that can be understood and that ought to be accepted by all rational beings, one that speaks with the voice of reason and justice, is the only foundation for appeals against majority decisions. To say that two may be right and twenty million wrong is to say that there is a more valid authority, that it is the only trustworthy guide, and that all men ought to act in accord with it.

Couch concluded that the cultural relativists, to whose camp he assigned all who favored the abolition of segregation, had denied the existence of any authority beyond the protection of minority rights. In so doing, they had "destroyed the only possible basis for their arguments"—meaning that they could, and should, be dismissed.

Although he framed his preface as a response to *An American Dilemma*, Couch was arguing as well with his coauthors in *What the Negro Wants*, most notably with W. E. B. Du Bois. "Negro Freedom," as Du Bois explained in his essay "My Evolving Program for Negro Freedom," meant *"full economic, political and social equality with American citizens, in thought, expression and action, with no discrimination based on race or color."* Approaching the dread "social equality" question, he continued, "what does one mean by a demand for 'social equality'?" It was an unhappy phrase, he admitted, because of the ambiguity of both terms. But it could be interpreted to mean equal rights to private social intercourse (including friendships and marriage), equal access to public services (including residential neighborhoods, hotels, and restaurants), and freedom of choice in those arenas sheltered by the umbrella of "social uplift," by which Du Bois meant education, religion, science, and art.[19]

Insisting that "equality" meant "the right to select one's own mates and close companions," Du Bois conceded that "naturally, if an individual choice like intermarriage is proven to be a social injury, society must forbid it. It has been the contention of the white South," he continued, "that the social body always suffers from miscegenation, and that miscegenation is always possible where there is friendship and often where there is mere courtesy." Joining his voice to the sociologists and anthropologists denounced by Couch in his preface, Du Bois insisted that "modern science has effectively answered" this belief. "There is no scientific reason why there should not be intermarriage between two human beings who happen to be of different race or color."

Moving on from science to governance, Du Bois attacked the argument that the state had any legitimate interest in preventing interracial marriage. "The marriage of Frederick Douglass to a white woman did not injure society," he declared. "The mulatto descendants of Louise Dumas and the Marquis de la Pailleterie were a great gift to mankind. The determination of any white person not to have children with Negro, Chinese, or Irish blood is a desire which demands every respect," the defender of individual rights concluded. "In like manner, the tastes of others, no matter how few or many, who disagree, demand equal respect."[20] Declaring the issue of "theoretical rather than of practical moment," Du Bois minimized the odds of actual interracial marriages and interpreted the demand for repeal of antimiscegenation laws as designed to force "the admission...by whites that Negroes are human beings."

By 1944 Du Bois had been articulating this position for more than twenty years. Just a year previously, in a commencement address at Florida A&M College, he endorsed the full-equality agenda of the March on Washington Movement, which had pried the FEPC from a reluctant federal executive, and informed the students that the erasure of all legal restrictions based on race or color, including bans on interracial sex and marriage, was supported "not only by three million Northern Negroes but by the majority of the peoples of the world."[21] The possibility that Du Bois might be right about this latter point was already gnawing at white supremacists alarmed about the formation of the United Nations.

Reviewers and other readers had sharply varying reactions to *What the Negro Wants*. African American reviewers, predictably, raved about the collection and attacked the argument, common among Southern whites, that its views were unrepresentative. Cast a different net, the Hampton Institute's J. Saunders Redding advised readers of the *New Republic* in his review of the book. "Ask any expert—and any expert would be any literate Negro. Indeed, the validity of the book is derived from the undisputable fact that the editor might have chosen fourteen other contributors and achieved the same general result."[22]

White reviewers received *What the Negro Wants* with more equanimity than its publisher did, although they did not fail to note the call for social equality. In an evenhanded review published in the *New York Times Book Review*, William Shands Meacham, chairman of the Virginia State Board of Parole and a trustee of the Hampton Institute, stated forthrightly that "What the Negro wants is first-class American citizenship without any reservations." This included, Meacham explained, equal marriage rights. Although he understood the logical progression in the demand for full equality, Meacham worried about the effects of such a "frontal approach" for the amelioration of Southern race relations, which, he noted, "must count upon the support of the dominant race." "When a Negro leader implies that the breaking down of the legal barriers to mixed marriages is an essential part of the democratic process, he risks poisoning the atmosphere in which countless white Americans of good-will would like to eliminate needless differentials."[23]

By 1944, all hope of consensus between white and Black Southerners about the definition of needless versus necessary racial differentiation among citizens—about, in essence, the limits of equality—had vanished, a casualty of "the war against racism" (as J. Saunders Redding defined it). A clear answer had been provided by African Americans to the eternal white Southern question: "What does the Negro want?" Let all who would hear, hear, Redding advised. "The black South believes in equality now. The black South wants segregation laws abolished now. The black South wants an end now to the economic tyranny exercised over it. The white South would not know this if it could."[24]

THE TRUTH OF Redding's remark is underscored by the fact that even those few whites who were willing to advocate complete equality and the abolition of all segregation laws could only articulate that willingness on the grounds that sex with white women was not, in the end, what the Negro wanted. Although he argued in *An American Dilemma* that sex was "the principle around which the whole structure of segregation of the Negroes...[was] organized," Gunnar Myrdal nonetheless assured his readers that American Blacks wanted good jobs above all else, and that "the marriage matter, finally, is of rather distant and doubtful interest" to Black Americans. Eleanor Roosevelt—considered an over-the-top radical on the race question by rank-and-file white Southerners—equated opposition to racial intermarriage with Nazism, and argued that marriage was a question best left "to individuals to handle." At the same time, the First Lady addressed the root fear of Southern whites and dismissed it. "There is no more reason to expect that there will be more intermarriage" if "equality before the law [is] granted to all people in this country than will be if [that right is] withheld," she opined. "In fact, I think it probable that there would be less."[25]

Attacked by *What the Negro Wants* contributor Doxey Wilkerson as, in the words of historian David Levering Lewis, "the opiate of white liberals," this white utopian vision of equal rights unexercised was an extension of arguments offered during the war by reform-minded white supremacists. Alabama governor Chauncey Sparks, who considered himself an advocate of civil rights thanks to his support for Black suffrage and opposition to the poll tax, insisted that acceptance of the inviolability of segregation would allow a society "relieved of the boogey and fear of inter-racial marriages, of amalgamation of any kind, of social equality." Once the segregation question was off the table, the races would be able to cooperate to their mutual benefit.[26]

The power of the social equality argument was undeniable. A CIC statement from October 1943, "Is Social Equality a Red Herring?," considered the question. "The fear of 'social equality' stirs the emotions of white people. Even though editors may, and some do, insist that there is no such thing as 'social equality'; though they assert Southern Negroes do not want it; that the white South will never accept it, they seem unable to convince themselves of this. They continue to argue its non-existence." Whites' chronic insistence that they would lay down their lives to prevent the impossible straddled the sometimes porous barrier between politics and psychosis. "Why," asked the CIC, "if such a condition as 'social equality' does not exist—why, if neither Southern Negroes nor white people want it—why, if it is impossible and the South will not have it—do Southern editors and Governors write and talk about it as often as they do?"[27]

In 1944, white Mississippian David Cohn tried to parse the race issue for other Americans in an article written originally for the *Atlantic Monthly*, "How the South Feels About the Race Problem." Cohn began with three "candid acknowledgments" about the race problem in the South: first, that it was insoluble, in the sense that it was a complicated social problem and no "final solution can be found and the whole matter neatly disposed of." Second, Cohn asserted that "it is at bottom a blood or sexual question. The whites are determined that no white in their legal jurisdiction shall marry a Negro, and this is the law of all the southern states." Finally, he concluded, whites are "equally determined that white women shall not have physical relations with Negro men except, when discovered, upon pain of death or banishment inflicted upon one or both parties to the act."

Under these circumstances, Cohn wrote, "there can never be 'social equality' between the races. There cannot even be forms of physical propinquity"—such as sharing a train compartment or the soda-fountain counter at Woolworth's—"which smack of social equality. It is useless to tell Southerners that their fears are groundless; that Negroes say they do not want 'social equality' or intermarriage with whites," Cohn continued, appealing to the by-now tattered myth of Southern race politics. "Instinctively the Southerner argues that sex is at the core of life—that it is one of the most profound instincts or desires that animate the human body, and that it is capable of evoking primitive fears and demoniac passions. Southern whites, therefore, will not at any foreseeable time relax the taboos which keep the races separate. They fear and believe that once a small crack is made in the walls of social segregation, the walls will eventually be breached."[28]

Because it was condensed and reprinted in *Reader's Digest*, David Cohn's article reached many thousands of readers, who in turn shared their thoughts on the topic in letters to Cohn. Although some letter writers objected to the frankness of Cohn's remarks, others took up the position regarding Black equality articulated by the FEPC's Mark Ethridge in 1942. As "A Texan" wrote, "The Southerner is broadminded enough to see that intermingling with the Negro could result in inter-marriage. That is the main reason the Southern White man wants the Negro to keep his place, and we'll keep ours. We do, however, believe the Negro is entitled to civil rights." William J. Frazier Jr. agreed: "In our manner of doing, it will not be in our life time, nor our children's, but the negro will someday enjoy these freedoms *without intermarriage*." How, exactly, this limited equality was going to come about remained something of a mystery, and two students from the Florida State College for Women requested further advice. "For those of us who know how right you are," Vivian Thomas and Phyllis Freeman wrote, "won't you publish a follow-up of *How the South Feels* with an article about 'What the South can do, in spite of How the South Feels?'"[29]

There was no follow-up article. But the organization of a group of white Southerners, a group that included Mark Ethridge and Virginius Dabney, offers insight into what these leading white Southern men thought could be done about the race issue, in spite of how the white South felt about interracial sex and marriage. In March 1944 a new publication, *The Southern Frontier*, announced the creation of another Southern reform organization. Pledging to "try honestly and courageously to take the inequalities and inequities out of the biracial civilization of the South," the Southern Regional Council (SRC), formed in April 1943, dedicated itself to devoting its "very best statesmanship and untiring energy for the next twenty years to the realization of this goal." Thinking not in terms of months and years but rather in terms of "all the centuries that may lie ahead," the SRC sought to establish "a blue-print for the shape of things to come," a "more democratic, a more abundant South"; a South that subscribed, still, to the myth of Black rejection of "social equality."[30]

Those who advocated an immediate end to Jim Crow denounced the SRC right away. After all, the group addressed itself to "the inequalities which violate the law in letter and spirit," such as patently unequal "separate but equal" public schools, but not the segregation laws themselves. "Until [the SRC], or any similar group, comes clean on the question of segregation, I haven't much hope for it," wrote Margaret Anderson, the editor of *Common Ground*, to Virginius Dabney in January 1944. "I am convinced that the central drive in all our activity must be honest in its basic premise—that segregation is wrong; that we are on the way to right it, not merely to make it tolerable. I suppose I have in mind your proposal to outlaw Jim-Crow transportation in Richmond," Anderson mused. "For the specific proposal I was grateful and sent up many cheers; but by the reasons advanced for such a move, however sound an approach they made tactically, I was saddened as a human being."[31] Declining the invitation to join the SRC's board of directors, prominent white author Lillian Smith explained that she "would not feel comfortable as a member of any organization working for racial democracy that does not deem it important to take a firm and public stand in opposition to segregation and in defense of human equality."[32]

Black media response to the SRC was scorching. The *Pittsburgh Courier* disputed the SRC's insistence that segregation laws were "intended to minister to the welfare and integrity of both races," announcing that "it ought to be clear to everybody by this time that the segregation laws are intended to keep Negroes on an inferior plane as second-class citizens, and in that capacity it is clear that discrimination against them cannot be avoided."[33] What did the Negro want? *Courier* columnist Marjorie McKensie had addressed the question already in September 1943. The goal of Black Americans, she said simply, was to be accepted by white Americans as "workers, voters, and social beings."[34]

By 1945, African Americans were challenging Jim Crow at every level, demanding full equality, which included, as the authors of *What the Negro Wants* demonstrated, sexual freedom. The myth of Black disinterest in sexual equality, the comforting narrative white moderates told themselves in order to address some of Jim Crow's more glaring inequities, had collapsed. The political work done by recitation of that myth—Virginius Dabney's prewar insistence that one could believe simultaneously in Black enfranchisement and antimiscegenation laws—was upended by African Americans' determination to announce their historic demand for full equality, full stop.

Rather than cementing the bonds of progressive interracial alliance, the Second World War widened the distance between African Americans and many of their white Southern allies of the 1930s, exposing the sexual roots of accommodationist arguments. With the myth of Black accommodation to Jim Crow in tatters by the end of the war, sex became the problem around which the shattered fragments coalesced. What was to be done? The experience of world war—fought, according to the Axis, in the interest of racial and cultural hierarchy and, according to the Allies, to promote democracy and human equality—so radically altered the landscape of thinking about segregation that Mark Ethridge and others like him were pushed from left to right without ever altering their position. The ideological and political vertigo produced by this involuntary movement left reform-minded Southern whites apprehensive and off-balance. No longer able to dictate the content of "what the Negro wants" to African Americans, "white southern men of goodwill" like Mark Ethridge did not become overnight conservatives, but they moved from the front of the revolution in race relations to the rear just as the real battle was heating up.

Six

FIGHTING HITLER AND
JIM CROW

ACCORDING TO HIS former wife, Mamie Till-Mobley, trouble had
a way of finding Louis Till. Sometimes it came in the form of a
bad roll of the dice; sometimes it came from Mamie herself, who once
hurled a pot of boiling water on Louis after he had tried, she said, to
choke her. And sometimes this young man enamored of the "sweet
sport of boxing" found himself on the wrong side of a powerful right
hook or an unexpected uppercut. Most of the time, however, the young
boxer's troubles came courtesy of white men in authority, displeased
with his self-confidence.[1]

Only ten miles from Chicago, Argo, Illinois, might as well have
been in the Mississippi Delta. Home to Argo Corn Products, the small
town was populated extensively by African American migrants from
Mississippi. Unlike most of his neighbors, Louis Till had come to
Argo from New Madrid, Missouri. Though he had taken part in the
northern exodus like nearly everybody else, Louis Till was apparently
impatient with transplanted Southern social conventions.

On his first date with Mamie in 1940—they were both eighteen years old—Louis desegregated Argo's ice cream counter. Rather than having their food packaged to go, as was the local custom for African American patrons, Louis pointed his date in the direction of a window booth and settled in to enjoy his banana split. "What was he thinking?" Mamie wondered. "I realized he was new in town, but he was about to get us into some real trouble." Rushing over, the white proprietor announced that if the couple didn't leave Berg's Drugstore that second, he was going to call Mamie's mama, well-known to him as a local churchwoman. "Before I could say anything," Mamie recalled, "Louis stood, and he did it so slowly that he seemed to unfold right there, all five feet eleven inches of him, in a way that told Mr. Berg to back off. Louis never spoke a single word, but Mr. Berg left just as quickly as he had come out."

Trapped in a window booth at Berg's with Louis Till, Mamie began to worry about how she was going to explain this at home. But then she noticed something.

> Other black people on the street were passing by and doubling back to take a second look at us sitting in a window booth at Berg's. I'm sure they were as shocked as Mr. Berg had been. But then they started doing something I never would have expected. They began coming in, ordering something or other, and sitting at other booths to eat. Before long, it turned into a mob scene as word spread all over Argo that Louis and Mamie had integrated Berg's Drugstore. Everyone came in to be a part of it, I guess.

No civil rights activist, Mamie sat there miserably, just "looking through that window expecting to see Mama storming down that street to pull me out of that booth."

A tempestuous marriage followed, and it wasn't long before Mamie and the baby she had conceived on her honeymoon moved back home to live with her mother. Afraid of the man whose presence "made you feel secure to be with him and very uneasy if you were against him,"

Mamie obtained a protective order against Louis. But it did no good. Louis repeatedly confronted his estranged wife in the street, hoping they might reunite. In court, the judge, as Mamie put it, "was considerate enough to give Louis a choice: jail or the army." It was a fateful moment of decision. One imagines Louis Till weighing the alternatives with a boxer's poise and a gambler's sense of the odds.

Mamie saw Louis one more time after that, looking smart in his uniform after completing his basic training. He had showed up at the house and was warming to his old topic of getting back together when there was a knock at the door. "It was the military police. Louis had gone AWOL. I don't know what all they might have charged him with, but I know they threw him in the stockade before shipping him out."

Louis Till was not unique. His spontaneous desegregation of Berg's Drugstore was an extreme example of the rising militancy of African Americans during World War II, especially among young Black men. And the choice offered to Till by a Chicago judge was not unprecedented.[2] Although the particulars varied, as America tilted from depression into war, Till's story of migration, social confrontation, and the opportunity to invest his physical aggression with new meaning as a soldier was widespread. It would guide his generation in battle and offer a different lens as they looked anew at the trouble at home.

THE SUDDEN RISE to power of National Socialism in Germany after 1933 created ideological and rhetorical space for critics of American politics and society. Anxious not to offend the new German regime, both the American government and leading white American newspapers and magazines adopted a circumspect stance toward Nazi racism. But while the *New York Times* searched for a neutral tone to address the new German regime, and the *Christian Science Monitor* described life in Germany as "normal and serene," America's Black press made Nazi racial persecution a front-page story.[3] Although some white newspapers did note the erosion of Jewish civil rights in Germany, they did not acknowledge the obvious parallels between German *Rassenpolitik* and America's Jim Crow system, and they were uninterested in doing anything about what the *Philadelphia Tribune* (a Black paper) called "the Nazis zu Hause"—the Nazis at home.[4]

Black publications hammered home the point that "Nazi Prejudice Against Jews Is Like Dixie's."[5] W. E. B. Du Bois had reported from the 1936 Berlin Olympics via the *Pittsburgh Courier* that the Nazis had declared "world war on Jews"; the *Baltimore Afro-American* styled whites appealing the admission of a Black student to the University of Maryland law school as "American Nazis" and proclaimed them "Quite as Bestial as Their German Brothers."[6] Passage of the 1935 Nuremberg Laws regulating and restricting Jewish German life simplified efforts to make fascism synonymous with racism—and vice versa—and to tie democracy to nondiscrimination.[7] As J. A. Rogers put it in the *Pittsburgh Courier*, "What else are jim-crow laws but Fascist laws….It is difficult to believe that Hitler to save time did not copy them directly from the Southern statutes and from the unwritten laws of America against Negroes."[8]

In fact, Germany's new sterilization and immigration laws were based explicitly on American models. Hitler and other leading Nazis admired the United States' National Origins Act of 1924, a highly restrictive immigration law passed at the height of post-WWI nativist agitation and racial and religious bigotry. Reflecting decades of collaboration between German and American eugenicists, the 1933 German Law on Preventing Hereditarily Ill Progeny was strongly influenced by the sterilization laws of several American states.

Most useful of all to the Nazis were the American laws criminalizing interracial marriage. Eugenicists in many nations believed that marriage between "superior" and "inferior" races ought to be avoided, but legislative bans were rare. Even South Africa, which criminalized sexual activity between Europeans and non-Europeans in 1927, did not outlaw interracial marriage until 1949, as part of its post-WWII apartheid regime.[9] "It is in the criminalization of racially mixed marriage that we see the strongest signs of direct American influence on the Nuremberg laws," writes legal historian James Q. Whitman. "When the leading Nazi jurists assembled in early June 1934 to debate how to institutionalize racism in the new Third Reich, they began by asking how the Americans did it."[10]

Critics of American race politics continued to draw comparisons to Nazi Germany favorably as the Nazis became more brutally anti-Semitic. According to Howard University sociologist Kelly Miller, "In America the Negro is often lynched and burned at the stake, not so much for his crime, but on account of his color. The German people have not yet reached such depths of depravity nor reverted to such primitive barbarism."[11] In October 1939, a year after *Kristallnacht* and a month after Germany invaded Poland, William Z. Foster, chairman of the National Committee of the Communist Party, testified before the Dies Committee on Un-American Activities, saying, "I do not think you will find anywhere in the world a nationality so deeply oppressed as the colored group in America. They are worse off than the Jews under Hitler."[12]

With the United States still out of the war, even mainline groups like the NAACP made open efforts to link Nazi race policies and American segregation. *The Crisis* observed, "The only essential difference between a Nazi mob hunting down Jews in Central Europe and an American mob burning Black men at the stake in Mississippi is that one is actually encouraged by its national government and the other is merely tolerated." To the ideological right of the NAACP, the National Urban League editorialized in the April 1941 issue of its magazine, *Opportunity*, that "all over the world the color line is being erased as nations fight to preserve the democratic form of government—all over the world except in Hitler's Germany, Mussolini's Italy, and the United States of America."[13]

Those white Southerners who rejected the drawing of such equivalences but nonetheless denounced Hitler and argued for American intervention in Europe were lambasted as hypocrites. Even those who acknowledged parallels between the Jim Crow South and Nazi Germany nevertheless insisted on some fundamental differences between American democracy, however imperfectly realized, and National Socialism. "Hitler is anti-Christ, anti-individualistic, anti-American," sociologist Howard Odum lectured from his desk in Chapel Hill, appropriating language he had previously reserved for the Klan. "The fact that we ourselves in the South are fascistic and dogmatic has nothing to do with the logic of our believing in the principle of Americanism and fighting for it."[14]

In a 1937 article titled "Hitler Far Ahead of Simon Legree," W. E. B. Du Bois agreed with Odum. The attacks on Jews in Germany, Du Bois reported, were "more vicious than anything ever experienced in America. The treatment of the Negro here cannot be compared to the German situation." As he elaborated after a trip there, "There is a campaign of race prejudice carried on [in Germany], openly, continuously and determinedly against all non-Nordic races, but specifically against the Jews, which surpasses in vindictive cruelty and public insult anything I have ever seen; and I have seen much."[15]

In addition to noting the mounting repression of German Jews in all areas of life, America's Black press drew attention to three significant markers of degradation propounded by the Nazis during the 1930s: segregated public transportation, segregated schools, and restrictive marriage laws.[16] Segregated education and Jim Crow transportation were already high on the agenda of African American civil rights organizations by the mid-1930s, and the Nazis' embrace of them underscored the rightness of their cause. "The fact that Hitler has adopted the Jim Crow Car for Jews should be proof enough that it is malicious in intent and repressive in purpose," *Opportunity* editorialized in 1941.[17]

More than either racially exclusive schools or segregated streetcars, Germany's embrace of racially restrictive marriage laws revealed clearly the American influence on the Nuremberg Laws. In a 1936 article, Kelly Miller cited antimiscegenation laws as the centerpiece of the "striking analogy" between German and American race prejudice, and devoted two-thirds of his argument to this topic.[18] The Nazi embrace of antimiscegenation laws made it easier for critics of restrictive American marriage laws to portray them as undemocratic—as, indeed, integral to fascism.[19] Germans drew the same analogy for a contrasting purpose. In a 1937 article, the *Preussische Zeitung* chastised "liberal circles" that criticized anti-Jewish laws as an "intervention in human freedom" by pointing to the antimiscegenation laws of thirty American states.[20]

IT IS NOT surprising that questions of rights, and African American claims to them, grew sharper after 1939, as the United States gravitated toward the European war. The civic rights of male citizens have long been associated with potential military service. In his decision in *Dred Scott*, Chief Justice Roger Taney recognized this tradition by linking Black men's exclusion from militias to his contention that African Americans could not be citizens. This was why Black Northerners fought to fight during the Civil War.

The connection between military service and full citizenship remained common currency, even after the Fourteenth Amendment made all native-born Americans into citizens. This connection had prompted African American enlistment in the 1898 Spanish-American War and inspired Black leaders during WWI. Faced with the army's almost complete refusal to train Black soldiers for combat duty in WWI and the brutal repression of African American veterans, organizations emerged that were dedicated to expanding and protecting Black rights. As the prospect of a second world war moved from a possibility to a probability, Black leaders were determined that things would be different this time.

This was why Secretary of War Henry Stimson would have preferred that America fight the Second World War with an all-white Army and Navy backed up by all-Black service brigades. That this rational and efficient option was not, in the end, politically feasible was thanks to "the deliberate effort...on the part of certain radical leaders of the colored race to use the war for obtaining...race equality and interracial marriages."[21] Drawing the same connection between marriage and military service that Roger Taney had in *Dred Scott*, both Stimson and those he deemed "radical leaders of the colored race" realized that civil equality at home would depend, in great measure, on whether African Americans were trained as combat troops. For America's thirteen million Black men and women, *serving* their nation would not be enough: the campaign for equal rights could not be won by legions of heroic latrine diggers and gracious navy stewards. Black America needed its men to *fight*.

This was a lesson that had been learned painfully in 1917, when Black volunteers and draftees had been declared unfit for combat and relegated to labor battalions.[22] Out of some 350,000 African American soldiers who took part in the First World War, just 40,000 became combat troops—and this only because of the strenuous efforts of Black leaders. Looking back in 1940 on his previous wartime experience, NAACP legal strategist Charles Hamilton Houston was unsparing in his criticism of the nation his generation of Black leaders had served, and spoke to the ambivalence felt by many about encouraging their sons to don the uniform of the United States now. "I felt damned glad I had not lost my life fighting for this country."[23]

Black leaders launched their struggle for equal representation within the armed forces before the war had even begun. In 1938, as the actions of a remilitarized Germany and a suddenly imperialistic Italy increased the prospects of a general European crisis, a group of African American World War I officers headed by Howard University professor Rayford Logan formed the Committee for Participation of Negroes in the National Defense. The goal of the committee, as the *Baltimore Afro-American* explained two weeks after the German invasion of Poland in September 1939, was to stave off the "wholesale regimentation" of Black soldiers "to the service of supply" should the United States enter the war.[24]

The broader public became engaged in this campaign as well. In 1938, the American War Department found itself the recipient of a torrent of letters concerning Black soldiers as the result of a campaign begun by the *Pittsburgh Courier*. Trying to explain the depth of feeling among American Blacks on this issue, the editor of *The Crisis*, Roy Wilkins, wrote to Secretary of War Harry H. Woodring in 1940 that there was "no other single issue—except possibly lynching—upon which there is a unanimity of opinion among all classes in all sections of the country." In June 1940, Michigan state senator (and future United States congressman) Charles C. Diggs urged Black men to refuse to serve unless they were accepted for training in all branches of military service. George Rouzeau, a war correspondent for the *Pittsburgh Courier*, encouraged Black soldiers to "insist on combat duty," because, he asked rhetorically, "is it not true that only those who spill their blood are in a position to demand rights?" But it was Du Bois who best articulated what was at stake in the struggle for unrestricted participation in the armed forces. "This is no fight merely to wear a uniform. This is a struggle for status, a struggle to take democracy off of parchment and give it life."[25]

Leading race men made discrimination in the armed forces an issue in the 1940 presidential election. Spurred by the unrelenting campaign of the Black press, in the summer of 1940 Walter White, executive secretary of the NAACP and a frequent visitor to the Roosevelt White House, announced, "Any candidate for President meriting the colored support must stand first for elimination of the color line from the armed services."[26] The Republicans, looking to break the Democrats' seeming lock on the Black vote in the North, did not miss the hint and pledged in their platform to end racial discrimination in the civil service, the army and navy, and all other branches of the government. In August the *Pittsburgh Courier* endorsed Wendell Wilkie for president. The *Baltimore Afro-American*, which had not supported a Republican candidate for president since 1924, followed suit in October.[27]

Though he was in no danger of losing his position, the president was nonetheless troubled by the extent of Black criticism. Against the War Department's unbending position that "the Army is not a sociological laboratory," Roosevelt asked repeatedly what steps could be taken without actually ending segregation. The fact that the navy, the President's own branch of the service, was the racist outlier within the armed forces was inconvenient. Prodded by Roosevelt to "invent something that colored enlistees could do," the navy, which refused to enlist Black men in any position other than as messmen, answered that their policy was no more discriminatory than the general society's. Under pressure from both the president and the secretary of war, Secretary of the Navy Frank Knox abandoned lesser arguments and inverted African American linkage of military service and social inclusion. As long as "the white man refuses to admit the negro to intimate family relationships leading to marriage," declared Knox, the navy was under no compulsion to breach its own racial barriers of shipboard social intimacy.[28] Nevertheless, as a spokesman for the NAACP remarked, "If America wants the loyalty of [its] 12,000,000 colored citizens she had better wake up." Something had to be done.[29]

In late September 1940, Eleanor Roosevelt, at the behest of Walter White, arranged a meeting between her husband, representatives of the army and navy, and a delegation of Black leaders that included White, T. Arnold Hill (currently an advisor on Negro affairs for the National Youth Administration), and A. Philip Randolph, the formidable leader of the Brotherhood of Sleeping Car Porters. The Black leaders demanded nothing less than integration of the armed forces. Stonewalled at the meeting, they were subsequently embarrassed when the White House released a statement that upheld segregation. The statement attempted a compromise by allowing for expanded possibilities for African American service in all branches of the armed forces except the navy, which continued to insist that the only conceivable position for a Black man at sea was at a stove or behind a mop.[30]

The open racism of the navy (which refused even to allow a Black member of Harvard's lacrosse team on the field at Annapolis during the Harvard-Navy game in 1940) puts in perspective the initial reaction of some Black Americans to the fate of the Pacific Fleet at Pearl

Harbor.[31] *Afro-American* columnist Ralph Matthews did not apologize for what he presented as a generally muted response to the events of December 7, 1941. "The first reaction of black men when they learned our ships had been sunk was similar to what they would have felt at seeing a snooty jim-crow hotel collapse," Matthews explained. "A shrug of the shoulders and a 'so what?'"[32]

African American indifference to the conflicts raging in Europe and Asia posed challenges to both the American government and Black political leaders. After seven years of comparing Jim Crow to fascism, it was not immediately apparent to the Black public in December 1941 why they should now risk their lives fighting for a nation indifferent to its own core principles. Harry Carpenter of Philadelphia was arrested for treason when he remarked in public that the war was "a white man's war and it's no damn good." But the government was aware that, as journalist Dwight MacDonald pointed out, "You can't arrest thirteen million people." The New Jersey man who insisted that "the Constitution be enforced before a colored man faces the fighting nations" voiced the sentiments of many.[33]

Why not simply withhold support for the war while discrimination reigned in the armed forces? This was a serious argument, and some acted on it. John Hope Franklin, a Harvard-trained historian whose offer to place his intellectual talents in his nation's service was rejected because of his race, became convinced that "the United States did not need me, and did not deserve me." Franklin spent the war years "successfully and with malice aforethought outwitting my draft board and the entire Selective Service establishment."[34]

Aware of the existence of people like John Hope Franklin, the NAACP's official reaction to American entry into World War II acknowledged African American ambivalence toward fighting another European war when memories of the last war and its unfulfilled promise for American Blacks lingered so bitterly. "We all know that the attitude towards the colored people of the nations fighting Hitler, Mussolini and Hirohito leaves much to be desired," Executive Secretary Walter

White admitted. But he insisted that African Americans had special interests at stake in this war: "If Hitler wins, every single right we now possess and for which we have struggled here in America for more than three centuries will be instantaneously wiped out....If the allies win, we shall at least have the right to continue fighting for a share of democracy for ourselves." Urging Black Americans "to remember that the declarations of war do not lessen the obligation to preserve and extend civil liberties here while the fight is being made to restore freedom from dictatorship abroad," White added that African Americans must "continue to be the spearhead and the acid test of democracy in the United States."[35]

In the end, Black Americans committed to fight in WWII, as they had in WWI, out of a combination of patriotism and a commitment to the furtherance of civil rights. African American leaders saw the war as part of their own struggle to gain access to democracy and mold it to their liking. Determined not to let the opportunity of wartime change slip away, America's leading civil rights organizations exhorted, "Now is the time *not* to be silent about the breaches in democracy in our own land."[36] "There should be no illusions about the nature of this struggle," political scientist Ralph Bunche wrote in the summer of 1941. "The fight now is not to save democracy, for that which does not exist cannot be saved." Rather, the fight was "to maintain those conditions under which people may continue to strive for realization of the democratic ideals."[37]

These efforts to blend local and national interests into the so-called Double V campaign had, according to Black journalist Roi Ottley, the support of nearly every Black newspaper and pulpit.[38] Fed up with being chastised by Secretary of War Henry Stimson and other policy makers about putting their own interests ahead of those of the nation, even Mary Bethune, the venerable civil rights leader and director of the National Youth Administration, applauded the wartime race militancy of her fellow Black citizens. "We have grown tired of turning the other cheek," she declared in June 1942. "Both our cheeks are now so blistered they are too sensitive for further blows."[39]

Such sentiments informed the ongoing relationship between Black America and the federal government as the United States turned its massive human and industrial potential toward making war. The Black press, in particular, remained skeptical about America's wartime politics and strove unceasingly to keep the needs of the nation's largest racial minority center stage.[40] It also urged Black Americans to remember what had happened the last time America went to war. When Roosevelt's vice president, Henry Wallace, who stood far to the left of the president on the subject of African American rights, insisted in a speech on war aims before the Free World Association in New York in May 1942 that "the four freedoms must apply to all nations and all races," the *Afro-American* responded, "We Think He Includes Us, but We Thought Woodrow Wilson Did, Too."[41]

VICTORY AT HOME would require different tactics than those used abroad. The chief weapon was the vote. The Fifteenth Amendment forbade *denial* of the right to vote on the basis of race, color, or previous condition of servitude. But in practical effect this prohibition had only limited impact because states, especially in the South, found ways to circumvent it. The franchise was limited chiefly in two ways: through the use of highly restrictive primary elections, which in the one-party South determined all electoral outcomes, and through the use of poll taxes and literacy tests to drive away poor voters of both races. As a result, practically all Black Southerners, and many Southern whites as well, could not vote before World War II.

Poll taxes were extremely effective at limiting the electorate. Voters had to pay one or two dollars in cash months in advance of an election, and then produce the receipt at the polls. Making matters worse, poll taxes were often cumulative. To vote, one had to pay previously unpaid poll taxes as well as current ones. In most states, this rule applied to only two or three years, but in Alabama it accrued for as many as thirty-six years, and in Georgia it accrued for life, from the age of twenty-one.[42] In 1940, only 24 percent of adults voted in poll tax states, compared with 66 percent of adults in the rest of the country. That year, the National Committee to Abolish the Poll-Tax estimated that eleven million Southern voters were disenfranchised, 60 percent of whom were white.[43]

The poll tax also had a disproportionate impact on women in the perennially cash-poor South. As Alabama Democrat Virginia Durr recalled, "If a poor tenant farmer had scraped up a dollar and a half to pay his poll tax, he sure as hell wasn't going to pay a dollar and a half for his wife." In the 1930s, Durr spearheaded an effort by the Women's Division of the Democratic Party to abolish the poll tax so white women could vote.[44]

This campaign elicited some surprising responses. Senators and congressmen from the Deep South were "maniacal on the subject of sex," recalled Durr. The white men thought that "if anything happened to change the Southern system, the white women would just rush to get a black man." When she escorted a group of white Mississippi women dressed in hats and gloves to speak about removing the poll tax to their senator, James Eastland, "He jumped up. His face turned red. He's got these heavy jowls like a turkey and they began to turn purple. And he screamed out, 'I know what you women want—black men laying on you!'"[45]

African American voters (and the specter of sexually depraved white women) posed an obvious threat to white supremacy. Disenfranchisement had been essential to the construction of Jim Crow at the turn of the twentieth century, and its beneficiaries were not about to change the system. Politicians of every stripe understood that restrictive voting laws in the South ensured their own continuation in office and thus inflated their influence in national politics through the seniority system practiced by both houses of Congress. In 1943, representatives of poll tax states headed seventeen of forty-seven standing committees in the House of Representatives and ten of thirty-three in the Senate, or roughly 50 percent more than their representation in Congress would suggest.[46]

Because of their unity and their seniority, Southern congressmen could determine national legislative outcomes. Southern congressional bloc-voting effectively prevented the enactment of any laws that Southern representatives considered detrimental to their regional interests—such as antilynching legislation. "When Polltaxia is 'agin' a bill," investigative journalist Stetson Kennedy sighed, "the United States is often forced to do without it."[47]

The "white primary," like the poll tax, also sharply limited the franchise, perpetuated incumbency, and ensured white Southern seniority. Until 1941, state party primaries were not considered "elections" that implicated the right to vote. Because political parties defined themselves as private voluntary organizations that could limit their membership as they pleased, the Democratic Party was no more obligated by the Constitution to open its doors to African Americans than the Catholic Church was to admit Jews. This construction of the Democratic Party as a white men's club had profound political consequences. In most Southern states, the Democratic primary was the only election that mattered. For example, with only two exceptions, for more than seventy years in Texas, every Democratic nominee for office selected in the primary—from senator to governor to school superintendent to dogcatcher—won the general election.[48]

This method of limiting political participation to whites began to crumble in 1941, when the Supreme Court ruled that the primary and the general election were part of a single electoral process, and it collapsed entirely in 1944 when the court ruled eight to one in *Smith v. Allwright* that racially restricted primaries violated the Fifteenth Amendment.[49]

Reasoning that bad news is best delivered by a member of the family, Justice Stanley Reed, a border-state Democrat from Kentucky, wrote the opinion. But the lilting cadence of the bluegrass state could not disguise the threat *Smith v. Allwright* posed to white supremacy. As the *New York Times* editorialized approvingly, *Smith* put America "a little closer to a more perfect democracy, in which there will be but one class of citizens."[50] Luther Porter Jackson, the founder of the African American Virginia Voters' League, regarded this judicial victory as "the beginning of a complete revolution in our thinking on the right of suffrage." The NAACP's Thurgood Marshall, who argued *Smith* and who would argue the school desegregation cases before the Supreme Court a decade later, considered the white-primary decision his most important victory.[51]

It would take another twenty years, a mass movement, a federal voting rights act, and a constitutional amendment forbidding poll taxes before a majority of Black Southerners were able to exercise the right to vote without fearing for their lives and livelihoods. But in a context of heightened African American activism, the court's decision in *Smith v. Allwright* endorsed and enhanced Black power in a moment of national political transition.[52]

Smith v. Allwright was received favorably by many white Southerners. For the first time since Reconstruction, a substantial segment of the white population was willing to uncouple political rights from "social" rights, particularly where Black soldiers and veterans were concerned. The leading newspapers in Richmond, the former capital of the Confederacy, endorsed the *Smith* decision.[53] By the end of the war many Southern whites agreed with the sentiment that "men who faced bullets overseas deserve ballots at home," and that Black disenfranchisement reflected "the hateful ideologies" that the nation opposed in WWII.[54] These Southern whites recognized and supported the link between political power and military service that African Americans who were determined to overturn *Dred Scott* once and for all had invoked since the late 1930s. They rejected the old argument, as Langston Hughes put it, that "permitting Negroes to vote in the poll-tax states would immediately cause Whites and Negroes to rush to the altar."[55]

But however circumscribed, any weakening of Southern racial hierarchy was insupportable to stout defenders of Jim Crow. Mississippi senator James Eastland declared openly that white boys from Mississippi were "fighting to maintain white supremacy." When the hundreds of thousands of young white men from the South returned after the war "to take over," Eastland explained, they would "desire more than anything else to see the integrity of the social institutions of the South unimpaired." Substituting the Southern social system for the Constitution he had sworn to uphold, Eastland vowed to "protect and preserve white supremacy throughout eternity."[56] A disappointed *Pittsburgh Courier* concluded, "Our legislators have not yet learned the truth that you cannot have democracy and white supremacy at one and the same time."[57] But the *Courier* had it backward. White supremacists had drawn precisely the same conclusion from the war, and were determined to thwart one (democracy) to preserve the other (white supremacy).

IF LEADING WHITES were irritated by Black demands for equality, seeing them as untimely, many progressive white and Black commentators were disgusted by the reaction of white Southerners to the war, which seemed to be primarily to shore up the domestic racial caste system under wartime conditions and only secondarily to win the war.[58] According to reports filed in 1942 by field agents for the Bureau of Agricultural Economics, Southern whites refused to "go all out" in the war effort if "going all out may mean...a revolution in Southern...societal and racial relationships." Believing that they were fighting for things "as they have been in America" and haunted by "revolting visions of what the new society may be like," white Southerners often seemed to be fighting their own, separate war. "When you go South and hang around a while, asking questions and drinking beer and cokes with new-found friends, you get the uneasy feeling that the war the South is fighting isn't the same war that the rest of the country is fighting," reported white Northern journalist Victor Bernstein in September 1942.[59]

The campaign many white Southerners were most interested in pursuing was a rearguard action against African American efforts to erode Jim Crow. Chatting with the secretary of the chamber of commerce in

Birmingham, Alabama, Bernstein received a lecture on the looming dangers of social equality. "There's one thing you can put in your pipe and smoke," Bernstein was told. "There's no white man down here goin' to let his daughter sleep with a n—, or sit at the same table with a n—, or go walkin' with a n—. The war can go to hell, the world can go to hell, we can all be dead—but he ain't goin' to do it." Insisting that "nobody down South is asking for the colored man's right to sleep with a white woman," Bernstein dismissed the Alabaman's concern as "the artificially contrived bugaboo of almost every Southerner. You talk to him about giving the colored people a fair break with a job, or better housing, or better schools, and somehow the argument winds up with threatened rape and the sanctity of Southern womanhood."[60]

Yet with leading Black newspapers like the *Afro-American* now openly advocating intermarriage as "the quickest way to solve the racial problem," and NAACP assistant secretary Roy Wilkins's Bastille Day characterization of the war as a "social revolution" that demanded "absolute political and social equality" and rejection of the racial status quo, Southern whites were not wrong to interpret Black war aims as incompatible with their own.[61] Even if African Americans had been more reticent, Georgia author Lillian Smith's observation that "whenever, wherever race relations are discussed, sex moves arm in arm with the concept of segregation" remained accurate and to the point.[62]

The potential for both sex and integration loomed in a new wartime setting: United Service Organization (USO) canteens. The USO was established in February 1941 to provide safe settings in which to entertain soldiers. Civilian run and funded, the USO was staffed entirely by volunteers, most of whom were women, whose work consisted of socializing with soldiers far from home. Following local custom and the example of the military, most canteens were segregated by race.[63]

A significant exception to the pattern of segregated USOs was the legendary Stage Door Canteen in midtown Manhattan, where servicemen swung to the tunes of Benny Goodman, Tommy Dorsey, and Count Basie on a fully integrated basis. Making precisely the same link between civil rights and military service that Secretaries of War Woodring and Stimson had, writer Margaret Halsey, who managed the canteen, explained the Stage Door's operating principle: "a Negro serviceman who was good enough to die for a white girl was good enough to dance with her." It was the job of the volunteers to upset segregationist thinking on race and sex, particularly the seamless progression in the imagination from dancing to sex and marriage. It wasn't easy. As Halsey recalled:

> One of the most monotonous aspects of race relations in the United States is the blind acceptance—by otherwise sensible people—of any wild, half-baked, fragmentary, unsubstantiated or even patently absurd cock-and-bull story that comes along, provided it has to do with Negroes and sex....Nobody on God's green footstool could sell these people stock in a phony gold mine, but when the issue is sex and Negroes, they sit with their mouths open like fledgling birds and swallow whatever is dropped in.[64]

Educating these fledglings in racial camaraderie under arms was the task of the junior hostesses, young Black and white volunteers ranging in age from eighteen to twenty-five, who agreed to dance with any serviceman who asked. All the girls were taught, Halsey was at pains to explain, that "courtesy is not copulation." Known worldwide for its stance on nondiscrimination, the Stage Door attracted a self-selecting group of young women; the daughter of NAACP head Walter White worked there, for example.[65]

Even so, many of the white hostesses cherished prejudices that needed to be addressed. To this end, Halsey wrote and distributed a "Memo to Junior Hostesses" that outlined the canteen's policy on African Americans (which, she explained, was based on the Fourteenth and Fifteenth Amendments to the Constitution), and addressed frankly but with humor the root fear of white women asked to dance with Black men. "What worries you more [than how to make conversation with black GIs]," Halsey wrote, "is the fear of rape. You unconsciously, but very arrogantly, assume that no male Negro can so much as glance at you without wanting to get you with child. The truth is," the older woman informed the girls under her wing, "that while you are an extremely attractive group of young women, there isn't one single one of you who's *that* good."[66]

Halsey and her junior hostesses played one part in the broader campaign to widen the war aims to include democracy at home as well as abroad, and offered living proof that interracial civility need not lead to interracial concupiscence. The Stage Door Canteen entertained more than three million servicemen from all over the world over the course of four years. During that time there was reportedly only one major racial contretemps on the dance floor, when a white Marine tried to pull a Black sailor away from the sailor's white partner.

There was never, as Margaret Halsey put it dryly, an occasion for one of the white junior hostesses "to go home to Papa with an interracial baby wrapped up in an old plaid shawl." Mostly there were conversations between white Southern servicemen and the women about the color line and what it signified. There was not even all that much crossing of the line at the canteen: as Halsey recollected, the Black servicemen generally asked the Black junior hostesses to dance, and white GIs shied away from the African American girls. What America's Black men in arms liked, Halsey remarked, "was not dancing with white girls, per se. What they liked was being free to choose with whom they would dance."[67]

This freedom—to choose one's own social partners—had been at the core of African American politics for almost one hundred years. That enticing possibility was available to some Black soldiers serving their country. This reality made life dangerous for them all.

Seven

THE "SECOND FRONT"

THE POSSIBILITY THAT the war would bring African Americans social freedom beyond the Stage Door Canteen worried many white Southerners. Military mobilization had brought about markedly changed conditions already. Southern social conventions worked out painstakingly via elaborate municipal laws and local customs came under severe pressure as Southern towns were suddenly inundated with young men unprepared to accept local customs when it came to race. Many Southerners responded to the social dislocation by rearticulating their commitment to white supremacy.

As Northern Black recruits chafed against the strictures of segregation, military bases became a chief site for the violent reassertion of white supremacy.[1] Two army camp riots broke out within the three months following Pearl Harbor. By May 1942, fourteen Black men in uniform had been killed by civilian police in adjacent communities. At Fort Benning, Georgia, Private Felix Hall was found hanging from a tree, his arms and legs bound. Black soldiers stationed at Luke Field near Phoenix, Arizona, spent Thanksgiving Day 1942 in a deadly shoot-out with white military police (MP) from Pagago

Park, following an interaction between a (possibly drunken) Black soldier and a white woman in a local café. Three were killed and eleven wounded, and twenty-seven Black GIs faced courts-martial. The previous January, white MPs and civilian police wounded twenty-one Black soldiers and killed ten in a riot in Alexandria, Louisiana, that began when an MP slapped a Black soldier's girlfriend.[2]

Not all the violence occurred in the South, although white Southerners, particularly white military police, were often involved. Private James Greggs, a white Southern MP, shot and killed Private David Woods, a Black soldier from Chicago, outside a movie theater at Fort Dix, New Jersey, when Woods refused to go to the end of the line. It was the second fatal shooting of a Black soldier by a white MP at Fort Dix within five months, and the camp was spared a riot only by the concerted effort of its officers.[3]

All in all, wartime America saw six civilian race riots, more than twenty military riots and mutinies, and between forty and seventy-five lynchings. The Social Science Institute at Fisk University reported 242 racial battles in forty-seven cities; at least fifty Black soldiers were killed in race riots. As Howard Donovan Queen, a Black officer in the Regular Army who eventually rose to the rank of colonel, recalled years later, "The Negro soldier's first taste of warfare in World War II was on army posts right here in his own country."[4]

Much of the violence in and around Southern military bases was triggered by perceived competition over women. A riot at Camp Stewart, Georgia, was traced to a rumor that a Black soldier's wife from New York had come to see him, and that she was white. "How much was truth I really don't know," a Black GI recalled, "but it was enough to turn Stewart upside down."[5] No doubt hoping to limit the possibility of interracial tension among his troops, in January 1942 Captain A. D. Robbins of the 77th Anti-Aircraft Regiment defined interracial sex as synonymous with rape and therefore punishable by death under military law.

Denounced by the NAACP as "Funny War Order No. 1" and disavowed and revoked by the War Department, Robbins's order notably encompassed *all* interracial relationships, including those between white men and Black women, "whether voluntary or not."[6] Stories of Black soldiers intervening with whites in the interest of protecting Black women were common enough to have inspired the narrative of the origins of the Harlem riot of July 1943—which erupted after a white cop shot a Black soldier in uniform in the lobby of the Hotel Braddock following an argument over a Black woman. As novelist James Baldwin described it, "Rumor, immediately flowing to the streets outside, stated that the soldier had been shot in the back, an instantaneous and revealing invention, and that the soldier had died protecting a Negro woman." The facts, Baldwin noted, were rather different: the soldier had not been shot in the back and was not dead, and "the girl seems to have been as dubious a symbol of womanhood as her white counterpart in Georgia usually is."[7]

Harlem exploded all the same. As *The Crisis* explained:

Negro soldiers have been shot down by civilian police in Alexandria, La., in Little Rock, Ark., in Baltimore, Md., in Beaumont, Tex., and in a half dozen other places. They have been humiliated, manhandled, and beaten in countless instances. The Harlem mob knew all this. It hated all this. It could not reach the Arkansas cop who fired a full magazine of his revolver into the prone body of a Negro sergeant, or any of the others, so it tore up Harlem.[8]

All this was predictable—had, indeed, been predicted. Fifteen months before the Alexandria massacre, civilian aide to Secretary of War William Hastie, a former dean of Howard University Law School and later the first African American federal judge, had warned that "it is impossible to create a dual personality which will be on the one hand a fighting man toward the foreign enemy, and on the other, a craven who will accept treatment as less than a man at home."[9] Columnist Ralph Matthews of the *Baltimore Afro-American* was even blunter than Hastie. "America," Matthews charged, "is the only nation in the world which follows the policy of training its soldiers to be cowards."[10]

The cousin of NAACP legal department head Charles Hamilton Houston, Hastie had been foisted on a reluctant Henry Stimson by Supreme Court Justice Felix Frankfurter and President Roosevelt. Hastie resigned his position in January 1943 over the issue of segregated officer training in the Army Air Force and returned to his former role as an NAACP litigator. He helped defend Black members of the armed forces who got in trouble for asserting themselves, such as members of the 34th Seabee Battalion who went on a hunger strike in California over the "Hitlerite" activities of Southern-born white officers, and the one hundred African American officers who were arrested for refusing to sign a petition approving segregated club facilities for white and Black officers at Freeman Field, Indiana.[11]

Relayed home via letters and through the Black press, which increased its circulation by 40 percent during the war years, despite some base commanders' decision to ban Black newspapers, what happened on army and navy bases affected every Black neighborhood in America.[12] Conditions were so bad on what the *Afro-American* referred to as "Our Second Front" that African American parents breathed a sigh of relief when their sons finished basic training. As James Baldwin recalled:

> Perhaps the best way to sum all this up is to say that the people I knew felt, mainly, a peculiar kind of relief when they knew their boys were being shipped out of the south to do battle overseas. It was, perhaps, like feeling that the most dangerous part of a dangerous journey had been passed and that now, even if death should come, it would come with honor and without the complicity of their countrymen. Such a death would be, in short, a fact with which one could hope to live.[13]

UPHOLDING SEGREGATION AT home was one thing. Transporting it abroad was another. Preparing for the massive buildup of US troops in Britain in anticipation of a European invasion, Americans contemplated the difficulties of enforcing segregation in a society with no formal color bar, while British officials wrestled with the social implications of

America's Jim Crow army. Unsuccessful in their effort to limit the number of Black troops sent to England, members of Britain's government condemned the United States for exporting its internal race problem.

The great worry, of course, was that English women would fail to recognize the inferiority of African Americans, or as British Foreign Secretary Anthony Eden put it at a war cabinet meeting on July 21, 1942, "that certain sections of our people [might show] more effusiveness to the coloured people than the Americans would readily understand." At an unruly cabinet meeting the following October, where there was a "wild discussion" in which "everyone spoke at once," His Majesty's government ultimately decided to educate its troops in American race ideology without actually implementing segregation as British policy.[14]

Thought necessary to avoid the sort of deadly altercations among troops occurring in the States ("We don't want to see lynching begin in England," Eden's private secretary Oliver Harvey had noted in his diary), this program would also guard British reputation. Echoing Anthony Eden's concerns, Richard Law, a junior Foreign Office minister married to an American, explained to his colleagues that it was important that "[white] American troops should not go back to their homes with the view that we are a decadent and unspeakable race."[15]

Law's fears proved prescient. By February 1944, white and Black GIs held divergent opinions of the English, with 80 percent of Black soldiers viewing their hosts favorably but only 68 percent of whites holding that opinion.[16] White soldiers' lower opinion of English people was linked directly to the propensity of English women to socialize with African American soldiers. US Army censors charged with keeping tabs on white soldiers' comments regarding Black troops reported consistently that white soldiers commented "with amazement and indignation on the fact that the English do not recognize the color bar, and that English girls associate with the Negro Troops."[17] As one non-Southern white captain described the situation in England to those at home, "There are several gripes to the whole thing. One is the niggers—believe it or not—the English seem to actually prefer them to the white boys. Especially the girls—not that I give a hay for them anyhow, but it is disgusting, to say the least....That is enough to make me inclined to look down on the English in general to start with."[18]

Given the level of violence between Black and white troops in the segregated United States, army officials worried about their inability to forbid interracial dating in Great Britain. The directors of the European Theater of Operations (ETO) tried to contain it through strict leave policies and a system of pass rotation based on race. Yet the army recognized the reality that American soldiers' social freedom could not be curtailed abroad as easily as it was at home. "It will not be the policy to in any way force upon any individual the necessity of associating with or mingling with any other individual," instructed one official document from the fall of 1942. "Soldiers to be permitted freedom of action in selection of their associates." A letter from then Lieutenant General Dwight D. Eisenhower's office concurred. "Any attempt to curtail association of colored troops with British white population by official orders *or* restrictions is unjustified."[19]

A year later, the policy was amended, clearly in the wake of hard experience. "Races will not mingle while drinking, nor where women are intermingled," dictated an ETO memo from December 1943.[20] This directive proved unenforceable. "Everybody here adores the negro troops, all the girls go to their dances," enthused a Wiltshire woman in March 1943. "But," she added, "nobody likes the white Americans. They swagger about as if they were the only people fighting this war, they all get so drunk and look so untidy while the negroes are very polite, much smarter and everybody's pets."[21]

General Eisenhower (who had been promoted to full general in 1943), in Britain to oversee the preparations for D-Day, noted the popularity of African American troops as well as the irritation such popularity caused his white soldiers: "To most English people, including the village girls—even those of perfectly fine character—the negro soldier is just another man, rather fascinating because he is unique in their experience, a jolly good fellow and with money to spend."[22]

Eisenhower remarked on the propensity of white GIs to intervene, "even to the extent of using force," when they saw English girls accompanying Black men in public. This echoed Eleanor Roosevelt, who had noted in a letter tossed aside by Henry Stimson that "young Southerners were very indignant to find that the Negro soldiers were not looked upon with terror" by British girls. The letter home of a white sergeant in September 1942 confirmed his commander's observation: "One thing which would make you sick at your stomach tho is the niggers over here tell the English that they are North American Indians... so the English girls go with them. Every time so far that we have seen a nigger with a white girl we have run him away. I would like to shoot the whole bunch of them."[23]

Sexual competition between white and Black troops lowered morale on both sides, as white soldiers were angered and repulsed by the behavior of some Englishwomen and Black GIs, and Black soldiers were resentful of the strategies whites adopted to discourage interracial relations. In various towns in the Midlands and East Anglia, NAACP head Walter White learned, "white American soldiers had told the natives that Negroes wearing the American Army uniform were savages recruited in Africa who could not speak English and that they barked to communicate their wishes." Such vilification irritated Black soldiers from all regions and backgrounds. White soldiers and MPs "call you names in front of people," especially women, commented one Northern Black GI. "I don't like that at all." Recalled another, college-educated Northerner, "I have personally had the experience of being humiliated by having a young British child run and hide behind her mother, crying when she saw me approach."[24]

English civilians did not always remain on the sidelines during racial altercations. When a Black soldier dancing with an Englishwoman at a private party was attacked by a white Southern soldier, "a free-for-all followed in which the British took the side of the Negroes," Walter White reported. In London, a schoolmistress slapped a white airman who assaulted a Black GI in a pub. The worry was that serious violence would be next. An ETO survey from fall 1942 caught the mood of many white Southern GIs. "Negro troops have the girls coming down to camp and call for them," wrote one white soldier. "If anything will make [a] Southern's Blood run hot it is to see this happen....If it keeps on going as it is we will have a nice negro lynching down here and then things will be better."[25]

The British government was deeply afraid of exactly such a scenario—that the practice of lynching would follow American soldiers across the Atlantic. After a series of incidents in London in which colored British nationals, particularly West Indians, were "cursed, made to get off the sidewalk, leave eating places and separated from their white wives in public by American soldiers," the US Army made an effort to familiarize its troops with British social mores. An army training film, *Welcome to Britain*, featured a sequence about race relations that was set, in a studied challenge to Southern social conventions, in an integrated railway carriage. General Eisenhower issued emphatic instructions: "It must be realized by all ranks that it is absolutely essential that American officers and soldiers carefully avoid making any public or private statements of a derogatory nature concerning racial groups in the United States Army."[26]

The messages delivered by white officers in England varied considerably, however. Corporal Charles A. Leslie was informed by his chaplain that "there was no distinction made as to color in the U.K., and that we would see some negroes with beautiful white girls" and to "keep our tempers in check, and take no action, whatever." At the opposite end of the spectrum, English civilians were offered a short course in Black character by the chief of the Service of Supply, to which the majority of African American soldiers in Britain were assigned. Lieutenant General John C. H. Lee of Virginia explained that "colored soldiers are akin to well-meaning but irresponsible children...[who] cannot be trusted to tell the truth, to execute complicated orders, or to act on their own initiative except in certain individual cases." Furthermore, American Blacks, individually or collectively, could "change form with amazing rapidity from a timid or bashful individual to brazen boldness or madness or become hysterical."[27]

Back on base, Lee's chief of staff went on record as believing that "God created different races of mankind because he meant it to be so. He specifically forbade inter-marriage. Our Lord Jesus Christ preached the same tenet, the grounds for which were that such unions would make the blood of offspring impure." Rather than easing tensions between white and Black troops, the "actions & statements" of officers "definitely increased the friction," wrote one disgusted white GI. "What is taking place in our army today is nothing more disgraceful than what Hitler is doing to minorities in Germany. I joined the American Army to fight against the persecution of minorities," this young soldier concluded. "I resent that our Army actually practices the same type of persecution."[28]

Concerned about the potential for violence between Black and white troops in England, the army instituted "off-limits" and "every other night" rules for local pubs and theaters bordering the American camps. This "out of sight, out of mind" solution to the segregation problem "worked all right," one white GI recollected dryly, "until the white soldiers happened to ask their English girl friends who they went out with on the coloured nights."[29]

Unable to forbid interracial marriage in the United Kingdom outright, the army did all it could to discourage interracial unions. No soldier could marry outside the borders of the United States without the permission of his commanding officer, who could withhold his blessing for a variety of nebulous reasons, including that the marriage violated "public policy" or might "discredit" the military.[30] Pregnancy, which was known to speed up the nuptial process for white soldiers, was rarely seen as a mitigating factor for interracial couples. So unlikely were commanders to grant permission to a mixed-race couple to marry even under these circumstances that the NAACP accused the American government of acting as "a partner to bastardy." Black soldiers unhappy with their unit (and perhaps their looming paternal responsibilities) soon learned that the fastest way to be reassigned was to claim to be in love with a local white woman.[31]

The army's efforts to exert social control ran up against the sheer size of American forces. By the time of the invasion of Normandy in June 1944, more than 130,000 African Americans were stationed in Britain. Despite the concerted effort of both the British and the American military authorities, including a whisper campaign begun in 1942 to raise fears of an allegedly high rate of venereal disease among Black troops, social relationships between Black GIs and local white women flourished. As one incredulous white lieutenant wrote home, "I have not only seen the Negro boys dancing with white girls, but we have actually seen them standing in doorways *kissing the girls goodnight*."[32] Worried about what folks back home would think about all this after *Life* magazine published pictures of Black soldiers dancing with white girls in London, the War Department forbade the publication of photographs "showing negro soldiers in poses of intimacy with white women or conveying 'boy friend-girl friend' implications."[33]

The War Department's ban on intimate interracial photographs is comprehensible in light of what army censors were reading in the correspondence of white troops. These letters complained about African American social liberty in Europe and predicted that Black veterans would never willingly embrace white dominance after the war. A white captain who was no longer optimistic about the postwar racial situation in the United States complained that Black soldiers had been put in "the worst possible position to bring about any understanding or realization of their problem in a post-war U.S.A. Their acceptance by French women of the lower class and their jobs of supervising German P.O.W.s (also white) have built up a misguided sense of equality on one hand and superiority on the other that may take very severe measures" to remedy when they returned to the States.[34] General Eisenhower lifted the ban on photographs in March 1945, but white Southerners were already incensed enough.

By the end of the war, though white officers and GIs alike seemed to have realized that Black soldiers had earned certain rights through their service, whites nonetheless drew strict boundaries around those rights. "I don't think it is possible for anyone outside of the U.S. to understand just what the general attitude of the white people is toward the negro," wrote one white corporal in response to an interview with Walter White published in the *Sunday Dispatch*.

> In the first place it is not as bad as most outsiders seem to believe. The fact is that we are not opposed to the negro "getting ahead in the world" if he goes about it in the right way. We do object, however, to negro men sexing with white women. Even the most ardent race equality advocates in the States would be highly browned off if they suspected that any of their women folks were fraternizing, mating, marrying, or otherwise having truck with negro men. What the white soldiers see over here between negro soldiers and white girls has, very unfortunately, lowered the GI's respect for English girls, and for all the population, for that matter, about 99%—and it has most certainly not caused him to feel any more kindly toward the negro race.[35]

Complaining that white GIs in Britain felt "*forced* to accept race equality" by the absence of Jim Crow laws, this American soldier concluded, "The white GIs just can't stand to see [a] nice looking white girl necking with a big black negro. We're not fighting for that kind of 'democracy.' We could have it without fighting if we wanted it." Admitting that white GIs were "helpless at present," the white soldier ended ominously by adding that soon they would not be.[36]

WALTER WHITE, THE NAACP's executive secretary, was anxious to see how Black troops were faring in Europe and the Pacific and interested in gathering material for a book. White signed an agreement to send stories to the *New York Times* and then talked his way onto a plane to London. "On January 2, 1944," he would later write in his autobiography, "I left America for England as a war correspondent."[37]

Provided with a car and driver and unlimited access to military bases and personnel by the US Army, which decided in the end that it had little to lose by receiving White with open arms, he traveled extensively within England and visited the other theaters of operation as well. In addition to his book *A Rising Wind*, published in 1945, White provided specific recommendations to ease racial tensions within the armed forces in the latter days of the war. Among his most pressing concerns was what appeared to him—and to the Black troops with whom he spoke—to be systematic discrimination within the military-justice system, particularly when it came to the application of general courts-martial against African American soldiers. It seemed that "our second front" had accompanied Black troops to Europe.[38]

What Walter White suspected, army statistics later confirmed. Although African Americans constituted less than 10 percent of the troops that served in the European Theater of Operations, Black soldiers represented 20 percent of all courts-martial convictions there.[39] More disturbing than this African American overrepresentation at the level of general courts-martial statistics were two other facts. According to army statistics, 42.3 percent of servicemen convicted for sexual offenses were African American. Even more alarming, 74 percent of death sentences were pronounced against Black defendants in general courts-martial cases. Of the seventy US servicemen executed by hanging in the ETO between July 1942 and February 1946, 79 percent were Black and only 21 percent white.[40]

As in England, there was considerable socializing in Italy between African American soldiers and local troops and civilians. This friendliness on the part of Italians toward Blacks flourished in spite of the fact that the Italians were told by white troops that Blacks were cannibals—indeed, the warmth toward Blacks was sometimes matched by an antipathy toward whites. As Frank Penick, a light-skinned Black sergeant explained, "One awful problem I had was convincing the Italians I was not *blanco*. The American whites with their arrogance and contempt for these people, which they did not try to conceal, made themselves thoroughly disliked."[41]

The fruit of this dislike—and the need for prudent Black solidarity on the part of mixed-race troops—was apparent to all: white soldiers sometimes made "unwanted advances to Italian girls and women," Penick related. "Some of those guys would get out of line, even when invited as a guest into an Italian home." On some occasions, in response, "a white soldier would be knifed, castrated, and his body put in a big barrel and rolled down the hill into the white camp. They never caught the people who were carving up white GIs and delivering them downhill in a barrel. Funny thing," Penick mused, "whitey never seemed to learn. I am not trying to say every Negro soldier in Italy was a gentleman. I will say to my knowledge I never heard of one ending up in a barrel."[42]

Inquiries conducted by the military police frequently seemed to follow a "round up the usual suspects" system, particularly when the charge was rape. Frank Penick's unit was mustered out one time to be looked over by an Italian woman. According to Penick, "being mustered out only once for such a thing was something of a record. The practice was as soon as the word 'rape' was mentioned anywhere[,] the first guys hauled out to be looked over were Negroes, and you know during war rape is a hanging offense."[43]

Under US military law, and throughout much of America, particularly in the South, rape, like murder, was punishable by death or life imprisonment.[44] Whereas white soldiers convicted of raping civilian women almost always received a sentence of life imprisonment, Black soldiers were executed, not incarcerated. Twenty-five of the Black soldiers executed by the US military in England and France during the Second World War died for the crime of rape. During the same period, only four white men were executed for that offense. In England between 1942 and June 1944, 100 percent of the US soldiers executed for rape were Black or Hispanic; not a single white GI was executed for this crime alone.

Although Sir James Grigg of the British War Office pointed to "the natural propensities of the coloured man," the statistics pointed to the natural propensity of white officers to regard sex between Black men and white women as necessarily coerced, and to discount the testimony of Black men when it contradicted that of white women. Consistent with patterns of civilian executions for rape in the United States during the same era, the military execution numbers also signaled the vulnerability of minorities to institutionalized prejudice.[45]

The numbers are stark and bear repeating: Black soldiers represented less than 10 percent of the American armed forces in Europe, yet they constituted almost half of those convicted of sex crimes and were almost eight times as likely to be given the death penalty for rape.[46] In noting this statistical anomaly, Sam Weiss, a lawyer with the ETO branch office of the Judge Advocate General (JAG) who was sympathetic to the plight of Black military defendants, advised the NAACP that "there is alleged to be an unwritten policy that complaints of this nature against colored attackers will be brought to trial and that some colored man will pay for each such attack whereas where the attacker is white and identification difficult, charges are frequently not pressed." It was important to review the records of Black soldiers convicted of rape, Weiss suggested, because "the statistical paradox must be explained or else it must be admitted that such troops are incomparably more prone to such offenses than white troops." The job of disproving the enduring charge of sexual predation by Black soldiers assumed by W. E. B. Du Bois in France in 1919 was this time assigned to the legal department of the NAACP.[47]

Accused by Thurgood Marshall, chief counsel of the NAACP's Legal Defense and Educational Fund, of sentencing Black servicemen to death "on insufficient and fabricated evidence," the War Department responded vigorously, defending its review process and denying discrimination by either the officers of the courts-martial or the clemency review boards. Although the Secretary of War did what he could to hinder the NAACP investigation, the threat of independent review seems to have encouraged the department to scrutinize its courts-martial procedures.[48] Given the "overwhelmingly large number" of courts-martial cases involving African American soldiers, the NAACP limited itself to taking action "only in those instances where racial prejudice is flagrant," when the record showed that a sentence was "grossly disproportionate to the crime charged," or "when the case involved racial conflict, e.g., rape of a white woman."[49] Even with these limitations, the legal department was "swamped under" with courts-martial records by December 1945 and appealed to others, such as the Lawyers Veterans Committee, to help.[50]

Despite the impediments to reviewing these cases, there were notable successes in reducing sentences and even in overturning convictions. Death sentences for Frank Fisher and Edward Lowry, convicted of raping a French woman, were reduced to ten-year and eight-year prison sentences respectively after intervention by William Hastie, who had returned as a lawyer to the NAACP after resigning from the War Department, and by East Harlem congressman and president of the International Legal Defense Vito Marcantonio. In another case, the combined efforts of the NAACP and local English residents succeeded in saving the lives of two Black GIs sentenced to death on the basis of coerced confessions for the supposed rape of a woman known locally to traffic in sex.

One case that was not challenged by the NAACP concerned Private Louis Till, the young boxer who had previously violated a restraining order and opted for the army over a stint in jail. On the evening of June 27, 1944, Till and some friends from the 177th Port Company outside Civitavecchia, Italy, went looking for some wine in the nearby town of Cisterna. When air raids went off, Till got the bright idea, according to one of his friends, to run into a house where there were some women who "would be scared during the air raid and might give us some cunt." According to another companion, Till opened the conversation with the women in the house by saying "Fiky-fiky" (from the Italian *fica*, meaning cunt). The women subsequently filed rape charges but were unable to positively identify their supposed assailants because the men had worn face masks and there was a blackout owing to the air raid.

That same evening, American soldiers looking to buy wine shot through the door of a shack and hit an older woman, Anna Zanchi, in the stomach. Taken to the 93rd Evacuation hospital, she died the next morning. Although never identified by any of the inhabitants of Anna Zanchi's home, Till and his comrade Fred McMurry were convicted on the testimony of an accomplice who turned witness for the prosecution, and on the belief of Anna Zanchi's son, John Masi, that the men who had come to their door that night were Black, based on how they talked. It was circumstantial evidence, but the Army Review Board that evaluated the trial proceedings explained that "participation of an accused in a homicide may be established by circumstantial evidence." Furthermore, the board noted, "A conviction may be based on the uncorroborated testimony of an accomplice," although it did recognize that "such testimony is of doubtful integrity and is to be considered with great caution."[51]

The conviction was dubious, but the NAACP opted not to contest it. As a civilian, Louis Till had been a gambler and a boxer. As a soldier, he was accused by the US Army of double rape and a murder. As the NAACP reviewed courts-martial cases, JAG lawyer Sam Weiss reminded them that, as he put it to a colleague, "a lot of the boys convicted were pretty mean characters who maybe had it coming," and that war has a habit of making men into mean characters.

Till received a competent defense, but no mercy. His previous convictions—the AWOL in Chicago and a second for disobeying a standing order—were taken into consideration in the sentence, but they probably made no difference. He was sentenced to death and transferred to the Disciplinary Training Center near Pisa handcuffed to American poet Ezra Pound, whose radio broadcasts supporting Mussolini had resulted in a charge of treason. Then the twenty-four-year-old Till was caged alone in a wire and concrete pen that was open to the elements, awaiting his fate beneath the blazing summer sun. The man Pound referred to as "Saint Louis" was hanged at Averna on July 2, 1945, "for murder and rape with trimmings," as the poet wrote in canto 74 of his famous *Pisan Cantos*, composed during his incarceration in Italy.[52]

Although separated from his wife, Louis had sent a portion of his army pay, plus money he was making from boxing and gambling, to Mamie and the baby boy who had been born the summer before Louis was inducted into the army. That money stopped coming in 1945, and on July 13 of that year Mamie received a telegram informing her that Louis had died as a result of his own misconduct, via judicial asphyxiation.

The war in Europe was over, but all that came home of Louis Till was a ring he had bought in Casablanca and had engraved with his initials, "L.T.," and the date, May 25, 1943. Mamie put it away, to save for her son to wear when he became a man.[53]

Eight

WILL THE PEACE BRING
RACIAL PEACE?

W HEN HE CAME home from the war, Corporal John C. Jones rubbed the white folks in Minden, Louisiana, the wrong way. Described later as a "discharged veteran of European services," Jones refused to sell a Luger pistol he had brought back from Germany as a souvenir, and he suggested that he aimed to recover a piece of land that had once belonged to his grandfather. On August 8, 1946, Jones was arrested for loitering in the yard of a white woman. When the woman refused to press charges, Jones was joined in jail by his young cousin, seventeen-year-old Albert Harris, who had been beaten by the authorities until he "confessed" that Jones had planned to molest the woman.

Delivered that evening by white deputies into the hands of a waiting mob, Jones and Harris were driven to a nearby bayou. Harris was stripped naked, pistol-whipped, and held down and beaten with a strap. According to a later NAACP report, Jones was beaten with "some flat object—such as a wide leather belt or a thick plank." Both his hands were severed with a meat cleaver, and he was partially castrated. Then the mob burned his body and face with an acetylene torch so that his eyes "popped" out of his head and his normally light skin was scorched a deep black. After an investigation by local authorities and the FBI, five people, including two deputy sheriffs, were tried for the lynching of John Jones. All were acquitted.[1]

Jones was emblematic of the African American soldiers who returned from the Second World War with attitude. Whether it was because they had killed white men in the name of democracy, as one Black veteran of the European war put it, or violated foundational tenets of Jim Crow by socializing with white men and women, something had changed for them. "I carried myself in a different way after I came back, and people could tell I had been in the service," remembered Fred Hurns.[2] When questioned by the Army Research Branch in 1944 and 1945, nearly half of all Black GIs surveyed "believed that they would 'have more rights and privileges' after the war" than before.[3] A Black soldier writing from Okinawa was blunt about what that meant in practice: "Our people are not coming back with the idea of just taking up where they left off. We are going to have the things that are rightfully due us or else, which is a very large order, but we have proved beyond all things that we are people and not just the servants of the whiteman."[4]

White Southerners and federal officials had good reason to wonder if Black soldiers would return to the South peacefully. What were the boundaries of Black veterans' proposed rights? Was sexual access to white women among the American ideals expected now by Black men? It was common knowledge that African American soldiers had socialized with European women during the war—despite the Army's best efforts to discourage such relations, and to keep such stories, and especially photographs, out of the papers. Black servicemen who embarked on the war in the Pacific from Hawaii had socialized across the broad racial spectrum there. Black newspapers remarked routinely on wartime interracial romances, reported the NAACP's postwar efforts to lift the Army's and Navy's bans on mixed marriages overseas, and exhorted Congress to pass legislation to facilitate the entry into the United States of foreign wives of servicemen.[5] Now Black veterans were coming home to a region that limited their political participation, relegated them to the lowest ranks of the economy, circumscribed their educational possibilities and aspirations, and policed their social interactions.

The response of white Southerners to any challenge to Jim Crow was never in doubt. In August 1944, 83 percent of white Southerners and 66 percent of Black Southerners answered "no" to *Negro Digest*'s poll question "Will the peace bring racial peace?"[6] As they had during Reconstruction and after WWI, white Southerners responded to Black men in uniform and African American demands for full equality with pitiless violence. During the summer of 1946, Southern whites blinded, castrated, and killed fifty-six African Americans, many of whom were veterans. Local law enforcement agencies lent a hand, engaging in an orgy of official violence that was extreme even by Southern standards. When ex-marine Timothy Hood removed the Jim Crow divider from a segregated streetcar in Brichton, Alabama, he was shot five times by the conductor, and arrested, jailed, and executed by the chief of police with a single shot to the head. As many as five former Black GIs were killed at the hands of the Birmingham police in the first six weeks of 1946.[7]

Having monitored the behavior of white and Black GIs in Europe and the Pacific for the preceding four years, the War Department anticipated disorder during the deactivation process and advised that "precautionary measures must be taken against tension situations based on race." To this end, the military circulated a map of the United States that featured "a boundary zone of varying width" within which "conditions for Negro troops returning from overseas will probably be found tolerable." African American soldiers were, if possible, to be demobilized on bases within this zone, which, unsurprisingly, centered on the West, Midwest, and Northeast. Outside the zone, the army concluded, "conditions on military posts are frequently found to be undesirable, and conditions in the civilian environment intolerable, for Negro troops returning from overseas." Since eight out of nine of the largest army training camps—those capable of housing fifty thousand or more military personnel—were located in the South, the odds of releasing significant numbers of Black soldiers inside the comfort zone were slim.[8]

Given that the army's demobilization spectrum ran from "probably tolerable" to "undesirable" to "intolerable," the violence greeting returning Black servicemen was hardly unanticipated. New York congressman and International Labor Defense president Vito Marcantonio described the violence in a 1945 letter to Attorney General Tom Clark and denounced "a mounting campaign of terror…[designed] to re-subjugate the Negro GI returning to civilian life." Black veterans described what was happening to them more simply. As one told NAACP public relations director Oliver Harrington, "They're exterminating us."[9]

NOT EVERY BLACK soldier was transformed by the war, but many returned home determined to resist Jim Crow on a variety of fronts, especially by exercising the right to vote. During 1945 and 1946, an array of groups launched a full-blown campaign to expand Black political power. The roster included organizations ranging from the NAACP to the Congress of Industrial Organizations-Political Action Committee (CIO-PAC), the Southern Negro Youth Conference (SNYC), the Federal Council of Churches (FCC), the interracial American Veterans' Committee, and the state committees of the Southern Conference for Human Welfare (SCHW). To the alarm of white supremacists, the CIO launched "Operation Dixie," a combination voter-registration and union-organizing effort. South Carolina senator Burnet Maybank likened CIO operatives to Reconstruction-era carpetbaggers, a comparison that was not far off the mark. The meddling outsiders were, indeed, dedicated to amplifying African Americans' voice in public life through union organization and political assertion.[10]

The campaigns secured results immediately. An estimated six hundred thousand Black Southerners registered to vote in 1946, triple the number in 1940, including significant numbers of Black women. In Montgomery, Alabama, middle-class Black women, including seamstress and NAACP leader Rosa Parks and English professor Jo-anne Robinson, formed the Women's Political Council to help gain access to the political process. A seventeen-day registration drive in Savannah, Georgia, lifted the number of Black voters there from eight thousand to twenty thousand. Despite the obstructive tactics of registrars in Virginia, where only 11 percent of all eligible voters were registered, forty thousand new Black voters were added to the roster. In Montgomery, Alabama, NAACP branch president and Sleeping Car Porters union leader E. D. Nixon led 750 citizens to the courthouse to register to vote. Henry Lee Moon, an NAACP leader and field organizer for CIO-PAC from 1944 to 1946, reported that everywhere he went in the South, he found "a politically inspired people…who were registered and making the fight to get more registered."[11]

A small but significant number of white Southerners supported Black suffrage, acting on a variety of motives. Some could no longer stomach the discrepancy between America's professed values of freedom and equality, for which so many compatriots had given their lives, and the reality of white supremacy. Some were convinced by new arguments that racial discrimination undermined America's global mission to demonstrate the virtues of democracy to a broken and chaotic world. In 1945, a white Alabaman who had left his farm for a job in Mobile's shipyards set out the arguments for Black enfranchisement in a letter to his conservative congressman back home:

> After all we are taking a stand in world affairs as a nation against oppression and it looks to me as though it is high time we as southerners had better take the lead [against Jim Crow] and solve that much-kicked Republican football…it seems that the old tradition of damn nigger has gone and must be remedied by an enlightened and liberal stand by our own party.…I am as you know not what is called a "nigger lover." It is just something that has come out and I think we should do it before it explodes under us.[12]

Those who had commanded African American troops and experienced firsthand the conditions of life on the wrong side of the color line were often especially open to change. As Harold Fleming, under whose leadership the Southern Regional Council finally denounced racial segregation in 1951, recalled, "The nearest thing you could be in the army to being Black was to be a company officer with Black troops, because you lived and operated under the same circumstances they did, and they got crapped all over." Fleming's army experience did not transform him immediately into a civil rights activist, but it did awaken him to the structural bases of Jim Crow. As he explained years later, "It wasn't that I came to love Negroes; it was that I came to despise the system that did this."[13]

Efforts to change the system focused on jobs, housing, education, an end to mob violence, and voting. A potent public challenge to white supremacy, the 1946 Black voting results were modest in most Southern states—especially in Mississippi, where Senator Theodore Bilbo urged white Democrats to intimidate Black voters before the election and at the polls, and in Alabama, where voter restrictions were tightened in an effort to reject "those elements in our community which have not yet fitted themselves for self-government."[14] But in Georgia, which had the largest African American population of any state in the nation as well as the most progressive governor in the South, Ellis Arnall, Black registration swelled from about 30,000 to roughly 140,000, or approximately 20 percent of eligible Black voters.

When the Supreme Court refused in April 1946 to review a lower court decision allowing nonwhites to vote in Georgia's (previously all-white) Democratic primary election, Georgia became the first Deep South state to experience the mass enfranchisement of African Americans.[15] The July 17, 1946, Democratic gubernatorial primary between Arnall's successor, moderate James V. Carmichael, and Theodore Bilbo's Georgia counterpart, the race-baiting former governor Eugene Talmadge, marked the first time Black Georgians had a say in choosing their government since the early years of the twentieth century.[16]

FACED WITH A revival of the African American determination to join in democratic governance, white men in the South reasserted their political dominance through their traditional tactic of violence. In late June 1946, Willie Johnson, a fifty-five-year-old sharecropper and veteran of the First World War, registered to vote in the upcoming Georgia state primary through agents on the farm of his landlord, George Stokes. Johnson voted without incident on July 17, but later said that Stokes had hassled him about voting: "He said that, 'You niggers don't need to think that you are going to run this state.' I told him that the government had given us the right to vote and that I was sure that I had done right in voting. He seemed mad about this, but did not do anything about it then."[17]

A week later, Johnson and two friends saw a Dodge pickup truck driven by "a big white man" that contained two Black women and two Black men, one of whom "wore khaki like an Army uniform." According to Johnson, the truck was soon joined by two carloads of armed white men. Johnson continued: "The driver of the Dodge truck told the man in khaki to get out. He did. Then the driver said to him, 'You think that you are going to run the county.' He replied to him, 'I am not trying to run the county.' Then the driver slapped the man in khaki. One of the women screamed, 'Don't do that; I know you.'" Then, Johnson recalled, the men marched off with the four Black people into the woods, where they executed them. Johnson estimated they fired fifty or sixty shots before it was all over.[18]

Stories of horrific racial violence like this one were becoming a national embarrassment. On Friday, July 26, 1946, radio listeners tuned in to NBC news were informed that "140 million Americans were disgraced late yesterday, humiliated in their own eyes and in the eyes of the world by one of the most vicious lynchings to stain our national record....A gang of armed and degenerate poor whites waylaid a Negro man and another man and their wives on a country road 40 miles from Atlanta. The brief and sadistic orgy [in Monroe, Georgia] ended in the bodies being riddled by 60 bullets."[19] The *New York Times* was more temperate but equally somber in its front-page story on July 27: "Two young Negroes, one a war veteran who served in the Pacific, and their wives were lined up last night near a secluded road and shot dead by an unmasked band of twenty white men."[20]

At first it was assumed that the mob's primary target was twenty-four-year-old Roger Malcom, who was then out on bail for assaulting Loy Harrison, his former playmate and current landlord. The other man, George Dorsey, was a five-year veteran of the United States Army who was apparently, like the two women, an innocent bystander in the wrong place at the wrong time.[21] Local residents, however, eventually told the FBI what they had withheld from NBC and the *Times*—that Dorsey was also a target, perhaps the primary target, of the attack. Dorsey, they said, had been "associating with white girls," specifically Ruth and Effie May Adams, the daughters of his white next-door neighbors, who invited themselves to dance parties hosted by local Black youth. A white man told the FBI that he had heard "that George Dorsey was killed because he was talking about going with white women." Another white man, referring to the reform Democratic candidate for governor, James V. Carmichael, reported that Dorsey had declared that "as soon as Carmichael was elected governor, he was going to start going with the best-looking white woman in Oconee County and was going to start with Loy Harrison's wife."[22]

Harrison, a prosperous cotton planter and bootlegger, was responsible for putting George Dorsey in such close proximity to white girls. It was Harrison who settled the (Black) Dorsey and (white) Adams families next to each other on his land. Riden Farmer, a white neighbor, recalled that the families got along well until George returned from the war in September 1945—that's when relations between them got "too friendly." Farmer heard that Dorsey was having "sex relations" with the two oldest Adams daughters, and in January 1946 Farmer learned that Dorsey had spent three nights in the Adams house.[23]

Riden Farmer was not the only neighbor following George Dorsey's relations with the Adams sisters. Dorsey's friend Roy Jackson stopped going to the dance parties after George arrived home. "He'd get half-drunk and get to hugging on these gals and getting up against them," Jackson recalled. "All of us who had sense stopped going. We could see there was going to be trouble." Like Jackson, an African American woman who lived near the dance house had worried about the inter-racial contact. "Every evening they'd be out there on the road. I'd just stand there looking at them. Mrs. Adams"—the girls' mother—"come by my house one time and told me, 'George might have gone with white girls in the Army, but he can't do it here.'"[24]

White anxiety about the return of Black veterans was exacerbated by the demise of the white primary. Eugene Talmadge, who promised as governor to uphold the white primary despite the 1944 Supreme Court decision invalidating it, argued that the continued exclusion of African Americans from the franchise was justified by the horrific future Georgia would face if African Americans were allowed to vote. "If the Negro vote succeeds in defeating me…you will have to go around and politic with the Negroes," he warned crowd after crowd of white Georgians. If Black Georgians were enfranchised, Talmadge predicted, they would "become arrogant and drunk with their own power."[25] They would repeal the laws requiring segregation in schools, hotels, and trains—and the laws that prohibited interracial marriage.

Such rhetoric, especially the connection between voting rights and the preservation of sexual segregation, spoke to many white Georgians, including those recently discharged from the armed forces. Just as African Americans linked their campaign for political equality to the ideals for which they had fought overseas, so too did those who opposed any change in the Jim Crow regime. Emery Burke, cofounder of the neo-fascist Columbians, Inc., announced to the crowd at an election rally, "Our heroes didn't die in Europe to give Negroes the right to marry our wives [widows]." Veteran Maceo Snipes, the only Black man who dared vote in Taylor County, was shot and killed within hours of casting his ballot by a group of white men that included a former fellow GI.[26]

Adding to the growing tension in the South, Black GIs often demanded the respect they felt was owed them as veterans. A *New York Times* reporter wrote of white fears about "Negro war veterans 'getting out of their place' as a result of the aspirations for social equality which it is presumed they will have gained during their military service." In a moment of heightened Black influence in politics, Black attempts to redefine social relationships were, and were seen as, political acts. Black voting suggested that white supremacy was susceptible to reversal through politics, as the Talmadge campaign stressed, and had to be stamped out before it was too late.[27]

While Eugene Talmadge and his disciples expressed the challenges they saw in Georgia's volatile postwar political and social conditions in sexual terms, Willie Johnson, the witness to the Monroe lynching, grounded the violence in the 1946 Georgia primary election and in the notable local presence of Black veterans. There are reasons to doubt Johnson's allegedly eyewitness testimony to the Monroe lynching: his affidavit is undated, and many of the details he provided fail to correspond with others' versions of events that day. It is possible that Willie Johnson incorporated into his testimony details he had heard, just as others who were questioned about the lynching did. Yet by presenting both the violence he fled and the violence he encountered as explicitly political, Johnson created an alternative to the Talmadge narrative. Sex was the preferred language of white supremacists and the discourse through which the Monroe case was expressed most forcefully. But it was not the only language available to explain what had happened.

The assassination of Maceo Snipes for daring to assert his right to vote rattled Black Georgians. Responding to both the Monroe lynching and the murder of Snipes, a rising junior at Morehouse College in Atlanta wrote a letter to the *Atlanta Constitution* in August 1946:

> I often find when decent treatment for the Negro is urged, a certain
> class of people hurry to raise the scarecrow of social mingling and inter-
> marriage....Most people who kick up this kind of dust know that it is

simple dust to obscure the real question of rights and opportunities. It is fair to remember that almost the total of race mixture in America has come, not at Negro initiative, but by the acts of those very white men who talk loudest of race purity. We aren't eager to marry white girls, and we would like to have our own girls left alone by both white toughs and white aristocrats.

Despite this declared lack of interest, the author of the letter, seventeen-year-old M. L. King Jr., asserted African Americans' right to equal opportunities: "The right to earn a living at work for which we are fitted by training and ability; equal opportunities in education, health, recreation, and similar public services; the right to vote; equality before the law; some of the same courtesy and good manners that we ourselves bring to all human relations."[28]

Like the authors of *What the Negro Wants*, the young Martin Luther King insisted on separating the discursive dust of interracial sexual danger from questions of equal rights. This position was rejected outright by Eugene Talmadge and the white voters who returned him to office in 1946. Like their fathers before them, Talmadge and his ilk approached Black political power through a sexual lens that deflected their fear of the potential unraveling of white supremacy onto the sexual realm. In their eyes, the theoretical became concrete in 1946, when political power, demands for civility, and sexual potency merged in the figure of the enfranchised African American veteran. Black veterans, with their military discipline and pay, their presumed desire for (and experience with) white women, and their insistence on participation in the democratic polity, were powerful magnets for white fear and aggression. This left Black GIs terribly vulnerable to white violence. White men, however, were not to blame for this state of affairs, explained one of the suspected Monroe lynchers. "It was civil rights that got them killed."[29]

THE MAN WHO panicked half the East Coast with his radio presentation of H. G. Wells's *War of the Worlds* on October 30, 1938, which convinced many Americans that Martians had landed in Princeton, may seem an implausible crusader for Black equality. Yet Orson Welles had gotten his start in theater two years earlier, at age twenty, when he directed, as an employee of the Works Progress Administration's Federal Theater Project, an all-Black version of *Macbeth* for Harlem's American Negro Theater. The production was a triumph and led to a national tour, launching Welles's amazing career as a writer, director, filmmaker, radio commentator, editorialist, and political activist.[30]

An ardent supporter of FDR and the New Deal, Welles was also a disciple of Roosevelt's third vice president, Henry Wallace, who was an outspoken critic of racial discrimination. By the middle of the war, Welles was a featured speaker alongside Wallace and African American singer Paul Robeson. For an appearance in 1943, a year that had seen deadly race riots in Detroit and Harlem, Welles chose as his topic "Moral Indebtedness." He began, "To be born free is to be born in debt; to live in freedom without fighting slavery is to profiteer." He continued:

> By plane last night I flew over some parts of our republic where American citizenship is a luxury beyond the means of a majority. I rode comfortably in my plane above a sovereign state or two where fellow countrymen of ours can't vote without the privilege of cash. Today I bought my lunch where Negroes may not come, except to serve their white brothers, and there I overheard a member of some master race or other tell those who listened that something must be done to suppress the Jews. I have met Southerners who expect and fear a Negro insurrection. I see no purpose in withholding this from general discussion. There may be those within that outcast 10 per cent of the American people who someday will strike back at their oppressors. To put down the mob, a mob would rise. Who will put down that mob?[31]

Not another mob, Welles was quick to explain. Americans were going to have to take care of mob violence in a different way: through the

143

rule of law. The vote would have to be expanded and segregation ended. Extralegal violence—lynching—would have to be wiped out. The eyes of the world were upon America, and "what was excused in us before is no longer excusable. Our [r]epublican splendor in this new age will shine by its own virtues, not by virtue of contrasting tyranny," he intoned. It was not enough to be better than the Nazis. Adopting *Time* magazine publisher Henry Luce's description of the coming postwar era, Welles proclaimed that "there is no room in the American century for Jim Crow."

Heralded as "Plain Talk from the Man from Mars," Welles's speech was circulated widely and soon printed as a pamphlet by the Chicago United Nations Committee to Win the Peace. Never one to underestimate his talents, Welles considered a political career ("I thought I would be President," he said later) but returned to the theater and radio in 1944.[32]

On July 24, 1946, the day before the quadruple lynching in Georgia, NAACP executive secretary Walter White wrote to Welles, who was in New York presenting his production of another H. G. Wells story, *Around the World in Eighty Days*. White included with his letter some information concerning a brutal assault on an African American veteran and asked to meet with Welles to talk over the possibility of a publicity campaign on behalf of the soldier.[33]

Isaac Woodard Jr. was a twenty-seven-year-old decorated veteran of the US Army who had served in the South Pacific for fifteen months. Honorably discharged at Camp Gordon, Georgia, Woodard had a run-in with a Greyhound bus driver while on his way home to Winnsboro, South Carolina. At the next stop, in Aiken, Woodard reported, the driver summoned the police, who pinned Woodard's arms behind him and asked if he had been discharged. When Woodard's reply did not include the word "sir," an officer began beating the young veteran with his billy club. Woodard defended himself and wrung the billy out of the policeman's hand. A second policeman turned his gun on Woodard "and told me to drop the billy or he would drop me." Woodard dropped the club, and the first policeman began to punch Woodard in the eyes with the end of the billy. When it became clear the next day, after a night in jail, that Woodard was unable to see, he was transferred to the veteran's hospital in Columbia, South Carolina.[34]

The blinding of Isaac Woodard, which occurred in February 1946, was known to Black leaders, but not to the general public. The NAACP had first learned of the case in May, when Woodard spoke to members of the legal staff at the national office in New York.[35] However, it was not until the *Daily Worker*, the newspaper of the Communist Party USA, broke the Woodard story on July 13, 1946, that it became more broadly known. In a box to the side of the main story, the paper highlighted the aspect of the event that would eventually draw the Justice Department into the case. Beneath the headline "Get That Cop," the *Daily Worker* exhorted America to "get that policeman who stepped over to a Negro vet in uniform and gouged his eyes out with a billy. He is known. He spoke to the local judge down in South Carolina."[36]

The following Sunday, July 28, 1946, Welles opened his show by reading Isaac Woodard's affidavit. The broadcast had an electrifying effect. Letters and telegrams arrived from around the country, many from white people in the North and West who had previously felt removed from the racial violence occurring in the South. Another letter Welles received came from the mayor of Aiken, South Carolina, who insisted that Woodard had not been blinded in his town and demanded an on-air retraction. Welles was less than obliging the following Sunday afternoon: "If it turns out to be true that the City of Aiken is blameless of this hideous scandal, it is my duty to make that innocence as public as possible—and I hope to be able to. But I must warn you denials are never dramatic, and if I'm to say something exciting about Aiken, it will have to be something better than that a Negro [soldier] was never blinded in its streets." In response, Aiken police demanded that a local theater stop showing a movie in which Welles played a small role, and ordered all the advertising posters burned.[37]

The NAACP had hired a private investigator to smoke out the identity of "Officer X" before Walter White ever met with Welles about Woodard, and the Justice Department, prodded endlessly by the NAACP, had initiated an investigation as well. By the middle of August, however, the assailant still had not been identified, the city of Aiken was suing Orson Welles for $2 million, and the NAACP was, as Assistant Special Council Robert L. Carter explained in a letter to his chief South Carolina contact, "over a barrel about this whole Woodard incident." Still filtering through NAACP channels was a letter from a soldier who had traveled with Woodard all the way from the Philippines, a South Carolina local who confirmed Woodard's story and identified the location of the assault as Batesburg rather than Aiken. Confronted with this eyewitness testimony, the Batesburg chief of police, Lynwood L. Shull, confessed that he had beaten Woodard but nevertheless denied any wrongdoing.[38]

Welles exulted at having finally gotten the cop. Having solved the mystery of whodunit, he acquiesced to the requests of his sponsor and ABC and apologized to the people of Aiken on August 25. Welles then turned to his correspondence from the South and broached the question of motivation. The letter from "Former Fan" was, in its focus on sex, representative of the many critical letters Welles received regarding his coverage of the Woodard incident. "We want the Negro to have a fair chance," Welles read from the letter.

> We don't believe that the two races should mix, however, but it seems that the North is trying its damndest [*sic*] to make a mulatto nation of the whole South. Well, it isn't going to work! I believe that we would all die fighting, men and women side by side, before we would let a calamity like this happen to the glorious homeland of gallant men and their women, who have certain well-founded believes [*sic*] and never take anything from anybody.

Responding first to Former Fan's charge of Northern harassment, Welles reminded his audience that "Batesburg isn't another battlefield of the Civil War." Furthermore, Welles argued, "Isaac Woodard was not involved in a conspiracy to make a mulatto nation of the South. He was just taking a bus trip to Winnsboro to meet a young woman who belongs to his race and who bears his name....Even Chief Shull," Welles finished up, "doesn't claim he was defending the sanctity of white womanhood, or keeping Isaac Woodard from marrying his sister."[39]

Unlike the Monroe lynching, the Isaac Woodard blinding was never linked to sex; it revolved straightforwardly around white-supremacist police brutality. Also unlike the Monroe lynching, for which no arrests were ever made despite lengthy federal and state investigations, the Department of Justice prosecuted Lynwood Shull under Title 18, Section 52, of the US Code, which protected the right to be secure in one's person when in the presence of those exercising the authority to arrest.[40]

This unprecedented action was the result of adamant pressure by the NAACP via a national publicity campaign. After failing to fight for the Scottsboro Boys in 1931, the organization by 1946 had learned a thing or two about the power of a rapidly expanding mass media and the appeal of a squeaky-clean, blameless victim. As Walter White explained in a memo to NAACP branches, "Woodard was blinded for life for the sole reason that he is a Negro veteran."[41]

On Sunday, August 18, 1946, thirty-one thousand people—the largest crowd in its history—packed Lewisohn Stadium in New York to support Woodard and denounce mob violence. Welles, who broadcast on Sunday afternoons, could not attend, but he wired a message that called for passage of an antilynching law, exhorted Americans to "make prejudice illegal," and declared that "the only defense against the mob is the people."[42] On September 12, a packed Madison Square Garden heard political radical, singer, and actor Paul Robeson challenge the government to "Stop the lynchers!" Between the end of October and December 30, 1946, with memories of Monroe still fresh, approximately seventeen thousand people in twenty-three cities heard Woodard, billed by the NAACP as "the Living Lynching," tell his story on a nationwide tour sponsored by the NAACP—which estimated that more than five times that number became acquainted with the organization and current issues through the accompanying radio and newspaper coverage.

Batesville chief of police Lynwood Shull was tried in federal court the first week of November 1946 for having beaten Isaac Woodard and caused, in the words of expert medical testimony, "bruises and swelling about the eyes, rupture of both eyeballs, breaking of the right eye cornea and hemorrhage in both eyes."[43] The Justice Department sent a special assistant district attorney to bolster the local federal district attorney, who nevertheless apologized to the jury in his summation for having brought the suit and neglected to request a guilty verdict. This omission was probably of no consequence: the jury, persuaded that Chief Shull had acted in self-defense when confronted with a supposedly drunk and belligerent Black man, was in no mood to convict. Isaac Woodard, like George Dorsey, had returned from the war unwilling to be pushed around by the likes of a landlord, a Greyhound bus driver, or the local police. Such foolhardy behavior could only be explained by insanity or alcohol. As Shull's attorney explained in his summation, referring to Woodard's retorts to the bus driver and his admitted failure to address Chief Shull as "sir," "That's not the talk of a sober nigger in South Carolina."[44]

OPPONENTS OF EXTRAJUDICIAL violence had been trying for more than twenty years to make lynching a federal crime. Every year a progressive congressman affiliated with the NAACP introduced an antilynching bill; every year Southern conservatives prevented a floor vote. Franklin Roosevelt had refused to endorse an antilynching bill for fear of alienating the Southern states'-rights bloc, arguing that lynching's decline since 1930 demonstrated that a federal law was unwarranted.

That argument was not available to Roosevelt's successor in office. Eighty-two days after his inauguration as Franklin Roosevelt's fourth vice president in twelve years, former Missouri senator Harry S. Truman found himself president of the United States. A smallish man with a high, nasal voice, Truman inherited a world war, an explosive

domestic racial order, and a Congress dominated by Southern Democrats and their conservative GOP allies. This coalition of racial re-
actionaries and social conservatives was delighted with Truman's new
occupancy of the Oval Office. Lacking the charm and cunning of the
dead president and his outspokenly egalitarian First Lady, Truman
would be easy to control.

Conservatives often underestimated the progressivism of some
Southern whites, which was why their "race treason" came as such a
shock. The New Deal agencies most nondiscriminatory in their hiring practices and most committed to helping the poor—such as the
Farm Security Administration, the Public Works Administration,
and the FEPC—were all headed by progressive white Southerners.[45]
Truman was not a Southern liberal in this mold, but as a senator he
had at least refrained from allying himself with Southern filibusters or
states'-rights champions. The optimism of Southern conservatives on
the accession of Harry Truman was based more on relief that Franklin
Roosevelt was dead than on any clear-minded assessment of Truman's
stand on the race issue.

On September 19, 1946, President Harry Truman met with representatives of the NAACP and two new national organizations that
had formed in reaction to the postwar extralegal violence in the South,
the National Emergency Committee Against Mob Violence and the
American Crusade to End Lynching. His head in his hands, Truman
listened to the NAACP's Walter White describe recent events in the
South. Although he did not agree to press the entire agenda of the
National Emergency Committee Against Mob Violence, the president
did vow to create an executive committee to investigate the race question in the United States. This committee would not, he made clear,
include members of the more left-leaning American Crusade to End
Lynching, which was cochaired by Albert Einstein and Paul Robeson
and had already warned Truman at a private meeting that if the federal government would not protect African Americans, Black veterans
would do the job themselves.[46]

The racial violence of 1946 and the subsequent NAACP publicity campaign sounding the alarm convinced President Truman that he had to act. He appointed an interracial President's Commission on Civil Rights (PCCR) composed of public officials, clergymen, educators, businessmen, and labor leaders, and charged it to recommend ways to devise "more adequate means and procedures for protection of [the] civil rights of the people of the United States." At the same time, the president reassured white Americans that he was "not appealing for social equality for the Negro. The Negro himself knows better than that," he added, echoing Gunnar Myrdal, Mark Ethridge, and William Couch. Indeed, "the highest type of Negro leaders say quite frankly that they prefer the society of their own people." In flat contradiction of the demands of African American veterans and civil rights activists to choose their own companions, Truman concluded that "Negroes want justice not social equality."[47]

In June 1947, Harry Truman became the first American president to address the NAACP at its national convention. He also did what Franklin Roosevelt had resisted doing for more than a decade: he spoke openly on the race question. Broadcasting live, and carried by radio stations worldwide for the benefit of the people emerging from colonial rule, Truman introduced a term that was likely new to many white Americans. The president explained that novel "concepts of civil rights" meant that "there is no justifiable reason for discrimination because of ancestry, or religion, or race, or color." Echoing the expanded list of rights enunciated in FDR's 1944 "Second Bill of Rights" speech (the right to a home, an education, adequate medical care, and a job), Truman emphasized a theme Roosevelt had incorporated but submerged: "the right to an equal share in making the public decisions through the ballot."[48] Henceforward, African Americans would be acknowledged as part of "We the People."

In a special message to Congress in February 1948, President Truman laid out a ten-point legislative agenda based on the recommendations outlined in the PCCR's 1947 report, *To Secure These Rights*. The presidential commission called for desegregation of the armed forces and federal employment, a federal antilynching law, creation of a permanent FEPC, abolition of state poll taxes, and admission of Alaska and Hawaii as states. Although he did not adopt the committee's general condemnation of segregation and racial hierarchy, Truman did pledge to issue executive orders against racial discrimination in federal employment, to end segregation in the armed forces "as rapidly as possible," and to desegregate interstate transportation.[49] In endorsing the report, Truman outraged Southern whites who maintained that race relations were slowly improving. Syndicated columnist and perennially backsliding white liberal John Temple Graves II called the committee's report an attempt to "extinguish a smouldering and slowly dying fire by drenching it with gasoline." Finding Congress unwilling to pursue his legislative agenda, Truman used his executive powers to follow through on his pledges.[50]

In addition to the developing Cold War foreign-policy imperative and his own personal positions on the race issue, Truman's stance on civil rights was propelled by political calculations. The Northern Black vote had become pivotal in domestic politics. Appalled by the postwar violence and unhappy with the pace of progress on civil rights, Black voters who had supported the Democrats during the New Deal and the war returned to the Republican fold in the congressional elections of 1946. With an eye on the Black vote, presidential aide Clark Clifford urged President Truman to take action on civil rights despite Southern resistance. Looking forward to the 1948 presidential election, Clifford predicted that Truman could woo urban Black voters without losing the votes of white Southern Democrats.[51]

Clifford was half right. Despite considerable official backpedaling on civil rights at the Democratic National Convention in Philadelphia in July 1948, tempers flared. Led by Minneapolis mayor Hubert Humphrey, who was running for the US Senate, Northern liberals succeeded in passing a stronger civil rights plank than Southerners could tolerate and denounced the white South's commitment to states' rights as a violation of individual rights. When Humphrey challenged the delegates "to walk out of the shadow of states' rights and into the bright sunlight of human rights," thirty-five delegates from Alabama and Mississippi stalked out of the convention hall instead.[52]

The "Dixiecrats," as these breakaway delegates were dubbed by the press, formed the National States' Rights Party and nominated South Carolina governor J. Strom Thurmond for president. Although he advocated "complete segregation of the races" in order to protect the "racial integrity" of the race that mattered to him, Thurmond insisted that the real issue at stake in the 1948 election was one of sovereignty: "the right of the people to govern themselves." Like the Monroe lynchers and their apologists, Thurmond did not consider African Americans part of the people entitled to self-government. The president's plan to enforce civil rights through federal power was a violation of local sovereignty that would "convert America into a Hitler state," warned Thurmond. Or it might result in communism, since the expansion of federal power had its "origin in communist ideology." Either way, the future was totalitarian.[53]

In addition to Truman and Thurmond, there was a third presidential candidate in 1948: former vice president Henry A. Wallace, who challenged President Truman from the left. Until joining the Roosevelt government as one of three Republican members of the first New Deal cabinet, Wallace had edited the *Wallaces' Farmer*, a family journal dedicated to scientific agriculture and the modernization of farming. He served as Secretary of Agriculture from 1933 to 1940, before becoming FDR's vice presidential nominee. Too egalitarian on the race issue for most Democrats, Wallace was replaced by Harry Truman in the 1944 election. Wallace was appointed Secretary of Commerce by President Truman in 1945, but he was pushed out of his position the next year for criticizing the administration's increasingly bellicose anti-Soviet foreign policy. In 1948, Wallace decided to make an independent run for the presidency.

Despite his distinguished career as a public servant, Henry Wallace is probably most remembered for his response to *Time* magazine publisher Henry Luce's provocative 1942 editorial announcing the arrival of "The American Century." Where Luce exhorted the American people to "exert upon the world the full impact of our influence, for such purposes as we see fit," Wallace urged cooperation and collective action. "Some have spoken of the American Century," said Wallace. "I say that the century on which we are entering—the century which will come out of this war—can be and must be the century of the common man."[54] He was an early supporter of the Black press's wartime Double V campaign and identified Black suffrage as key to the domestic war against bigotry and discrimination. Campaigning for the Democrats in 1940, Wallace argued that the United States "cannot plead for equality of opportunity for people everywhere and overlook the denial of the right to vote for millions of our own people."[55]

The minute he left the government in 1946, a whisper campaign began about the reliability and extent of Wallace's "Americanism." A memo from White House aide Clark Clifford to the president recommended that the Truman campaign "identify and isolate [Wallace] in the public mind with the Communists."[56] This plan was furthered by the formation in 1946 of the Progressive Citizens of America (PCA) from the loose grouping of liberal and labor organizations that cohered around Wallace, and by the organization's agenda, which included full equality for African American citizens. In 1948, the PCA contributed to the formation of the United States Progressive Party, which coalesced to promote Wallace for president. In July of that year, the *Los Angeles Times* used the new Progressive Party's opposition to antimiscegenation laws to mark it and Henry Wallace as radically left-wing.[57] In the late 1940s, any challenge to antimiscegenation laws would inevitably be tagged by defenders of the status quo as evidence of communist inclinations.

Throughout 1948, Wallace, at the head of the new Progressive Party, traveled the nation, where he spoke exclusively to nonsegregated audiences. His open defiance of Jim Crow enraged white supremacists, who shouted down the candidate, manhandled his team, and disrupted rallies with violence. He and his running mate, Idaho senator Glen Taylor, made it out of the South alive but were catcalled, pelted with rotten eggs, and interrupted with cries of "Communist!" and "Nigger lover!" Both he and the Progressive Party, Wallace declared, "are fighting to end racial discrimination." A defiant Taylor scuffled with police and was arrested in Birmingham after entering a building through the "Negroes" entrance. By the summer of 1948, a Gallup poll reported that 51 percent of the public believed that the Progressive Party was controlled by communists.[58]

Wallace did not sound like a godless communist when he criticized segregation. To those who insisted that racial integration marked one as a communist, Wallace replied that toleration of segregation was incompatible with Christian faith. Everywhere he went, Wallace told crowds that "segregation is sin."[59] On live radio in Birmingham, Alabama, toward the end of his Southern tour in 1948, Wallace asked the listening audience to recite the Lord's Prayer with him. At the end, he added, "We believe in brotherhood. We believe in the brotherhood of man. The scriptures read: 'God hath made of one blood all the nations to dwell upon the face of the earth.'"[60]

The developing Cold War political context after 1946 shifted the terms of the civil rights conversation in unanticipated ways. A new emphasis on communists' rejection of religion empowered white-supremacist Christians, who explained that communists' support for racial equality was an offshoot of their atheism and lay at the heart of their plan to destroy America through racial amalgamation. To reject God was to endanger the United States, which was the only nation powerful enough to resist the communist onslaught. With one group of organized Christians connecting racial equality to communism and "moral foes of Christianity," and another stressing the codependence of democracy and race-blind Christian brotherhood, American race politics became unexpectedly an intramural Christian debate in which each side denounced the other in terms of true belief.

Nine

BROTHERHOOD

D<small>URING THE INTERWAR YEARS</small>, a series of high-level international conferences brought like-minded liberal Christians together. Protestant internationalists struggled to develop Christian solutions to the social and political problems that had led to the carnage of World War I and then doomed Woodrow Wilson's vision of a League of Nations.[1] When war broke out again in Europe in 1939, internationalists pushed the Federal Council of Churches (FCC), the largest interdenominational organization in the United States, to make the case for a new postwar international system akin to the League of Nations. In December 1940 the FCC formalized its support of this approach by forming the Commission to Study the Bases of a Just and Durable Peace (CJDP).

The CJDP was also known as the Dulles Commission after its chairman, John Foster Dulles. Remembered chiefly as Eisenhower's Secretary of State and an early Cold Warrior, John Foster Dulles had a foreign-policy career that, like those of so many of the cast of the Second World War, stretched back to the First. Serving under his uncle, Secretary of State Robert Lansing, as legal counsel to the American delegation at Versailles, twenty-three-year-old Dulles argued forcefully if unsuccessfully against a Carthaginian peace with Germany. After the war Dulles became a partner, along with his brother Allen, at the powerful New York City law firm Sullivan and Cromwell. There he specialized in international finance and assisted government efforts to renegotiate and manage German reparations payments in the 1920s. The son of a Presbyterian minister and the grandson of missionaries to India, Dulles was a deeply religious Presbyterian who believed that churches could play a decisive role in educating the public about the need for a new international political system after the war, one in which God's sovereignty overrode nations' claims to absolute dominion.[2]

In addition to his active engagement with the foreign-policy contingent in Washington, DC, Dulles was a leader in the ecumenical Protestant movement that came of age in the 1920s. As the word "ecumenical" implies, the various branches of this movement operated from an internationalist premise of the church universal. Groups like the YMCA and Britain's Student Christian Movement sought to transcend boundaries of nations and language to spread the Gospel and unite Christians in the pursuit of world peace and human advancement. In the shadow of the Great War, in which nationalist sentiments had overwhelmed international commitments, many people were eager to transcend sectarian differences in the interest of Christian unity.[3]

IN MARCH OF 1942, when an Allied victory was still far from certain, the Federal Council of Churches called a conference in Delaware, Ohio, on "the winning of the peace." There, delegates resolved that the "ultimate requirement" for a durable peace was "a duly constituted world government of delegated power" complete with legislature, courts, police, and "provision for world-wide economic sanctions." During their journey toward what was known popularly as "world government," the delegates hewed closely to the "Guiding Principles" drawn up by Dulles's CJDP, which sketched a Christian blueprint for the postwar world.[4]

The sheer number of distinguished Americans in attendance at the Delaware meeting, including several who, like Dulles, would go on to participate in the founding of the United Nations in 1945, made the conference easily the most important meeting of church leaders in a generation. In addition to eminent theologians, the group was stocked with Christian social progressives. Among these were Morehouse University president Benjamin Mays, young Martin Luther King's mentor, and pacifist A. J. Muste, an early and unbending white Christian advocate of racial equality whose expertise in nonviolent direct action left an indelible mark on the struggle for racial equality in America.[5]

The report produced by the Delaware Convention called for an end to the international colonial system and repudiated the notions of racial hierarchy that underpinned that system. Declaring that "no group of men is inherently superior or inferior to any other," the conference applied this reasoning to the United States as well as the rest of the world. If the United States wanted to "make its full contribution in securing a just and durable peace," announced the delegates, it would have to secure "justice now for racial groups." The United States could not be trusted to lead the world to peace "so long as our attitudes and policies deny peoples of other races in our own or other lands the essential position of brothers." Momentously, the conference acknowledged "with profound contrition the sin of racial discrimination" and called on the federal government to end racial discrimination in the United States.[6]

At the Delaware meeting, Benjamin Mays made the connection between sacred and civil explicit by linking theology and public policy. "To declare that 'we are all one in Christ Jesus' and deny, at the same time, the reality of that proclamation in the church and in everyday living is to deny God and repudiate the Lordship of Jesus Christ," he preached.[7] Mays had fought hard at the all-Black 1942 Southern Conference on Race Relations (also known as the Durham Conference) to demand the removal of all barriers to interracial intimacy. He lost that round but succeeded in including strong language in the so-called Durham Manifesto: "We regard it as unfortunate that the simple effort to correct obvious social and economic injustices continues, with such considerable popular support, to be interpreted as the predatory ambition of irresponsible Negroes to invade the privacy of family life."[8] Yet the Durham Conference was no more willing than any other interracial organization to affirm a notion of racial equality that addressed the interracial marriage taboo. Although the FCC urged churches to declare intermarriage "not a sin, but perhaps unwise," this was little better than downgrading interracial marriage from a religious felony to a misdemeanor.[9]

In 1943, the FCC created the Commission on the Church and Minority Peoples to gather information about social relations among various groups in America. A series of regional conferences in 1943, at the height of wartime social dislocation, revealed that the fear of intermarriage, especially between Black men and white women, was the biggest source of resistance to change in racial practices. This was the case for every region in the United States, and not simply the South—despite the committee's exasperated insistence that "it is not necessary to want a man for a brother-in-law before treating him as a brother."[10]

The FCC continued to wrestle with the race question throughout the war, especially after Benjamin Mays was elected vice president of the group in 1944. A follow-up conference held in Cleveland in January 1945 consolidated the liberal political orientation established at the 1942 Delaware meeting. Influenced by Mays and his co–vice president, former Commission on Interracial Cooperation director Will Alexander, the FCC declared war on Jim Crow laws: "The full influence of the Church should be exerted to remove all *legal* protection for or requirement of segregation, whether in the form of 'Jim Crow' laws, restrictive covenants in land titles, or in any other form. We hold it to be ethically wrong to protect or require segregation by legal enactment."[11] The Cleveland conference offered concrete proposals on how to combat domestic racism, including asking churches to support legislation for a permanent FEPC and to repeal "poll tax and other discriminatory laws" that limited participation in the political process, but was silent on the interracial marriage question.[12]

Neither Mays nor Will Alexander was willing to let it go. In an article published in *Harper's* magazine in January 1945, Alexander claimed every right for African Americans that any other American had. Just as white reformers reacting to *What the Negro Wants* had done in 1944, however, Alexander immediately undercut his own argument and reassured white readers that "American Negroes are not seeking an opportunity to mingle with whites. They desire freedom and opportunity to live as Americans."[13]

The FCC and civil rights organizations were well represented at the organizing conference for the United Nations held in San Francisco in the spring of 1945. Among those chosen by the State Department to serve as "consultants" to the official US delegation headed by Texas senator Tom Connally were Benjamin Mays; NAACP executive secretary Walter White; W. E. B. Du Bois; Mary McLeod Bethune, who had leveraged her relationship with Eleanor Roosevelt to organize the Federal Council of Negro Affairs (known popularly as the Black Cabinet); John Foster Dulles, who was part of the official US delegation; and Frederick Nolde, dean of the graduate school at the Lutheran Theological Seminary in Philadelphia and future Nobel Prize winner.[14] Together, they argued strenuously for an explicit commitment in the charter to uphold human rights.

At a May 2, 1945, meeting called by Secretary of State Edward Stettinius, the NAACP, the FCC, and the American Jewish Committee also pushed the State Department to insist on the inclusion in the UN charter of provisions defining and protecting human rights. Stettinius, who supported the human rights agenda, had intervened personally to bypass wartime travel restrictions for delegates to the FCC's Cleveland meeting. He was also content to attribute the campaign for human rights to unofficial lobbying even as he pledged to put the muscle of the United States behind the initiative.[15]

The Secretary of State was at the time buffeted from both the left and the right. On the one hand, the National Council of Negro Women insisted that "the blueprint of the post-war world must recognize that no lasting peace can be possible until the world is purged of its tradi-tional concepts and practices of racial superiority, imperial domination and economic oppression." This position was repudiated by unilater-alists like Ohio senator Robert A. Taft, who rejected the efforts by "do-gooders…to confer the benefits of the New Deal on every Hot-tentot," and by southern Democrats justifiably anxious about the future of Jim Crow in the dawning moment of "world government." Con-nally, who as chair of the Senate Foreign Relations Committee would shepherd the UN treaty through the Senate, kept an eagle eye on any potential dilution of local sovereignty over the internal government of member states, and was not appeased by Stettinius's insistence that "the negro question" was beyond his purview.[16]

Supported decisively by the powerful US delegation, the San Fran-cisco conference succeeded in adopting a charter for the United Nations that defined it as dedicated to the goals of achieving human rights and fundamental freedoms "for all without distinction as to race, sex, lan-guage, or religion" (Article 1 and Article 13), and of promoting respect "for the principle of equal rights and self-determination of peoples" (Articles 55, 62, and 68).[17] Rooted clearly in a rights-based tradition drawing on the Declaration of Independence and the French Decla-ration of the Rights of Man, the affinity between the values of liberal Christians and those expressed by the charter was not coincidental. Not only had the terms been shaped by government officials like John Foster Dulles; there was noteworthy overlap between delegates to the FCC's 1942 Delaware conference and the San Francisco meeting.[18]

Dulles, Mays, and others understood the importance of public rec-ognition of the correspondence between Christian principles and the founding values of the UN for American acceptance of the charter.[19] Dulles considered it vital to differentiate the UN from the failed League of Nations and to present the new organization as something American Christians had helped define and could therefore support. The FCC is-sued detailed charts and essays to guide discussion in church groups. The Methodists, led by Bishop G. Bromley Oxnam, called their campaign a

"Crusade for a New Order" and declared that isolationism denied "the Christian doctrine that all men are children of one Father and are members of one family."[20] Definitions of human rights were easily rendered into terms of Christian brotherhood, and vice versa: ideals of Christian brotherhood informed secular conversations about human rights, cosmopolitanism, and the worldwide community of mankind.

Urged ever forward by Mays and white allies like Will Alexander and A. J. Muste, in 1946 the FCC convened a special two-day meeting in Columbus, Ohio, to consider the Christian stance on segregation. President Harry Truman addressed the gathering on the theme of brotherhood, and the FCC delivered a formal statement on "The Church and Race Relations," in which it declared segregation a violation of the gospel of love and human brotherhood and entreated its affiliated churches to work for a nonsegregated society and a nonsegregated church. Mays fought once again for a strong denunciation of antimiscegenation laws in this latest FCC declaration on race. He proposed a statement that read, "In a democratic and Christian society such as we dream of in America, there can be no legal limitation, based on race, creed or national origin alone, upon free relationships among people," and a declaration stating that "the fear of inter-marriage cannot be allowed by the Christian Church to perpetuate the segregation pattern." Both made it into the final draft of the FCC's historic 1946 report on racial equality but were excised at the eleventh hour. The council's final report condemned segregation as "a violation of the gospel of love and human brotherhood" that was "always discriminatory," but said nothing about marriage, interracial or otherwise.[21]

When it formally declared racial discrimination a sin and a violation of the gospel, the FCC recast the language of the perennial public debate over American racial politics and moved the general conversation considerably to the left. Certainly, others before the FCC had considered racial hierarchy a sin against the divine origin of all mankind and the unity of believers in the body of Christ. Between Reconstruction and WWII, however, this language rarely crossed the line from personal confession to political advocacy. Individuals could, and did, denounce both segregation and racial hierarchy as un-Christian. But before the first FCC statement on the theological case for human brotherhood in 1942 and its later refinements in 1945 and 1946, no group with anything like the cultural currency of the FCC had turned its guns squarely on Jim Crow.[22]

By 1946, three groups of Americans had called openly for the end of all laws that distinguished by race: the NAACP, the Communist Party USA and its affiliated race organizations like the National Negro Congress (NNC), and the Federal Council of Churches. The FCC's "segregation is sin" argument was not a staple of the NAACP, which was led by lawyers, not ministers. Communists rejected racial hierarchy on ideological grounds but left God out of the equation. By the end of WWII, civil rights advocates, including the FCC, remained committed to the equalizing claims of liberalism prominent in their own publications and the founding documents of the United Nations, even as many recognized the insufficiency of equality arguments to make the civil rights case convincingly to whites.

The wholesale rejection of racial segregation and discrimination, including racially restrictive marriage laws, by exponents of the theology of brotherhood added a new register to civil rights discourse in the postwar United States and opened a new front in the struggle for equality by rejecting the proposition that racial purity was integral to, or even compatible with, the Christian belief system. A forceful intellectual and theological position in itself, the articulation of claims to racial equality in the language of Christian brotherhood smoothed popular acceptance of the United Nations, helped deflect charges of communism hurled at civil rights supporters, and even allowed them to portray themselves as part of the fight against global communism in the early Cold War.

THE DOMESTIC ANTICOMMUNISM that colored Henry Wallace's 1948 presidential bid had been foreshadowed in the 1946 congressional elections, which veered sharply to the right and brought to Washington rigidly anticommunist Republicans such as Joseph P. McCarthy and Richard M. Nixon (from Wisconsin and California, respectively). Nixon defeated one of the most liberal Democrats in Congress, Jerry Voorhies, by linking him to the "Moscow-CIO-PCA-Henry Wallace line." The Republicans' 1946 campaign slogan "Got enough communism?" touched nerves in many voters, especially formerly Democratic urban Catholics up in arms about communist suppression of the church in central and Eastern Europe. FBI director J. Edgar Hoover fanned the flames by charging that at least a hundred thousand communists roamed the nation's movie studios, universities, radio stations, and classrooms. The US Chamber of Commerce did its bit by publishing a widely distributed report, *Communist Infiltration in the United States*.[23]

In March 1947, President Truman established a loyalty program for all civilian government employees. Under its terms, no individual could work for the federal government if "reasonable grounds exist for belief" that he was "disloyal to the Government of the United States." Evidence of "disloyalty" included membership in "any foreign or domestic organization…designated by the Attorney General as totalitarian, fascist, Communist, or subversive." No definition of "subversive" was ever offered.[24]

Civil rights and labor activists in the South who had been red-baited in the 1930s interpreted anticommunism as an assault on Black rights because communists were both outspoken and unequivocal about racial equality. Deploying the same logic to the opposite end, white supremacists considered African American political action a barometer of communism. The louder the Black demand for civic equality, the greater the supposed communist foothold in the United States. "The fact that a person believes in racial equality doesn't *prove* that he's a Communist," admitted the chairman of a loyalty board. "But it certainly makes you look twice, doesn't it? You can't get away from the fact that racial equality is part of the Communist line."[25]

Much of the force of the equation of civil rights and communism derived from the fact that it was, in important ways, true. Communists *did* support racial equality and had fought for Black civil rights since the 1920s. The CPUSA party platform in 1928 *did* call for the complete abolition of all laws that discriminated on the basis of race, including antimiscegenation laws. Communists and others, especially members of the CIO, which aimed to organize Southern workers into unions, *did* strike at the racially stratified, low-wage labor system that underwrote the Southern economy. People who opposed racial discrimination *were* subversive, if by subversion one meant hostility to state-imposed racial segregation and white supremacy.

Unlike the Socialist Party, which drew hundreds of thousands of votes in the early twentieth century, the CPUSA as a *political* entity was never that important. More significant was the influence of communists in a variety of industries and institutions. Midcentury American communists played important roles in industrial unions, in the motion picture industry, in the world of art and literature, in progressive organizations such as the Southern Conference for Human Welfare, and in the Wallace campaign. Government agencies were crosscut with people who had rubbed shoulders, and sometimes more than that, with communists. Detroit police commissioner Harry S. Toy connected Jews with communism and political corruption and insisted that communists were entering the United States disguised as Canadian rabbis. Yet despite the common conviction that communists were foreign invaders, the vast majority of American communists were regular Joes who dreamed at night not of insurrection but of full employment and summer vacations.[26]

The successful red-baiting of Henry Wallace in 1948 was an early warning to advocates of equality. So was the impulse of white Southern politicians to push back against the "segregation is sin" argument. White supremacists correctly interpreted Wallace's denunciation of racial segregation as sinful as a direct threat to antimiscegenation statutes. An eight-point Statement of Principles issued by the States' Rights Party during the 1948 campaign linked defense of the Constitution, resistance to the

FEPC, the sanctity of segregation, and continued restriction of inter-racial marriage.[27] Acknowledging the potential power of "brotherhood" arguments, South Carolina Democrats went so far as to require voters to affirm by oath the "religious" reasons for segregation of the races.[28]

The South had viewed the Federal Council of Churches with suspicion since the organization's founding in 1908. Evangelical Christians considered ecumenism itself a dangerous development insofar as it threatened Protestant particularity and, it was feared, sacrificed doctrinal purity in the interest of Christian social and political cooperation. Before WWII, white Southern churchmen exhibited little concern about the FCC, which they considered a Northern entity.[29] But the FCC's close ties to national elites in politics, education, and business as well as its predilection to speak on behalf of all American Protestants raised concerns south of the Mason-Dixon Line that regional religious values were under attack.

The FCC's sequence of increasingly adamant critiques of racial segregation and discrimination and artful conceptualization of the essential brotherhood of man in Christ kindled rebellion among religious defenders of racial hierarchy and separation, who responded in kind. Following on the heels of the FCC's 1942 Delaware, Ohio, conference, evangelical Protestants convened in St. Louis in March 1943 to found the National Evangelical Association (NEA). Organized in explicit opposition to the ecumenicists, the NEA objected both to the FCC's dismissal of racial hierarchy and difference and to its support for "world government," positions that the NEA considered linked through an effacement of local sovereignty. Evangelicals also considered the ecumenicists' belief in the capacity of man to advance the goal of Christian perfection to be a dangerous theological fallacy. It was not man's place to bring peace to the earth; that could be accomplished only when the Messiah returned at the end of days. Alarmed that the UN conference did not begin with a prayer despite the presence of so many ecumenical leaders, evangelical pundits portrayed the United Nations as a godless organization dead set on destroying America's Christian foundations.[30]

During World War II, to the great dismay of pensive believers in racial hierarchy like William Couch and Mark Ethridge, advocates of racial equality had succeeded in equating racial oppression and discrimination in the United States with antidemocratic political movements, as the NAACP did when it asserted, "The man who discriminates against Negroes is a Fifth Columnist."[31] Building on the wartime connection of democracy with racial equality, in the immediate postwar period the NAACP and the State Department linked the domestic struggle for civil rights to the fight against international communism. The best way to rebut the postwar communist threat and export democracy abroad, they argued, was to practice it fully at home.[32]

This position was fiercely opposed by Southern white supremacists, who chipped away at the wartime link between racial discrimination and fascism, offering in its place an argument familiar to Southerners from the 1930s: that since communists believed in racial equality, anyone who believed in racial equality was a communist. Furthermore, since communists rejected organized religion, to embrace communism via opposition to segregation was to reject God as well, and to undermine the United States of America in its suddenly apocalyptic rivalry with the Soviet Union and international communism.

Rather than a marker of democracy, as African Americans and liberal whites had argued throughout the war, or of true Christianity, as the Federal Council of Churches insisted, or of basic human rights, as the United Nations announced, racial equality was represented by white supremacists as a communist aspiration. Its exponents were, if not card-carrying communists themselves, dangerous "fellow travelers," members of "subversive" organizations dedicated to undermining and potentially overturning "the American way of life."

Anticommunist Christians developed a convoluted critique of the United Nations, which they painted as a communist plot shored up with liberal Christian heresy. In addition to the harbinger of the one-world government spoken of in the Book of Revelation, the UN was easily seen as a Tower of Babel, where cultures and languages that God himself had separated were united in a sinful effort at international self-perfection.[33] White-supremacist Christians linked questions of national sovereignty and local control of Jim Crow, warning that supporters of Black-white interracial marriage and the UN's efforts to override American domestic sovereignty were part of a single communist-inspired plot to destroy American values in local self-government and the pure Anglo-Saxon blood that perpetuated that heritage.[34] In addition to working toward "one world" and "one race," the United Nations and its supporters aspired to "one religion."[35] By 1948, many white-supremacist Southern Christians were convinced that the Holy Trinity of the race mongrelizers consisted of communism, the UN, and liberal Christianity, each of which accepted, even supported, interracial sex and marriage.

From 1946 forward, the FCC and its successor organization, the National Council of Churches (NCC, founded in 1950), were race-baited by evangelical Christians, red-baited by Southern Democrats in Congress, and monitored by national security agencies. FBI director Hoover, whose thoughts frequently graced the pages of the NEA's journal, *Christianity Today*, was personally offended by the FCC's stance on racial equality, which was, he warned, a chief characteristic of "Christian Communists."[36]

Other critics of the FCC observed that its brand of Christianity was in accord with communist doctrine on racial equality, but thought liberal Christians had been converted to communism. Hoover, however, perceived that the FCC had accomplished something far more dangerous to white supremacy and to the American nation: Benjamin Mays and other FCC leaders had effectively Christianized what conservatives like Hoover considered a Soviet line.

In an influential 1946 pamphlet written to make churchgoers conversant in theological arguments against segregation, Mays asserted that racism was indicative of Americans' incomplete trust in God. Moving deftly back and forth between biological arguments about the unitary nature of the human family and familiar notions of Christian brotherhood, Mays argued that all human relations were a reflection of God's love. True Christianity, he insisted, required that people set aside fear and act on belief and "trust God for the results."[37] Rather than being a sign of communism, love and respect across the color line announced Christian faith.

When he argued that all human relations reflected God's love for man, including those forbidden by secular law, Mays did, as Hoover perceived, Christianize what many considered a communist precept. By transporting interracial relationships from the communist to the Christian sphere, Mays undercut the "free love" paradigm associated with communism, in which sexual exclusivity was discouraged as bourgeois, and placed interracial sex within the godly realm of marriage. Flipping segregationist terms, Mays made an implicit claim that advocates of interracial marriage adhered to the true Christian path, whereas white supporters of antimiscegenation laws protected conditions that fostered free love and adultery, positions that were effectively communist and inherently anti-Christian.[38]

Benjamin Mays did not believe that white supremacy could be defeated by law enforcement or appeals to the Constitution. He disagreed with those who, as Orson Welles had argued about the Monroe lynching in 1946, thought that white supremacy was a political doctrine that could be defeated through politics and legal challenges. Instead, Mays insisted that "this"—white supremacy in all its manifestations—"is a religious problem. It will never be settled on any other basis."[39]

The violent racial regime of Jim Crow, Mays reasoned, could not be overcome through liberal politics, constitutional debates and amendments, Supreme Court decisions, equal enforcement of voting laws, or federal intervention. Mays saw the civil rights struggle as a theological as well as a legal and political battle. African Americans had to be victorious on both fronts to succeed. Because "the Church is the only institution in America that lays claim to having a divine origin," it was uniquely positioned to bring down Jim Crow. Prescriptions for the future that relied on legal and political remedies alone were not enough. The fight for full emancipation of African Americans needed God on its side.

Racial equality may have been part of the communist line, but it was also a central tenet of the Federal Council of Churches' ecumenical Protestant line and the United Nations' emerging human rights stance. Henry Wallace, whom Benjamin Mays anointed in 1947 as "the greatest champion of human rights on the American platform today" and who was hated and feared by thousands of "professional Democrats and Christians," exemplified the fusion of liberal political rhetoric and Christian witness.[40] As Wallace put it in 1948 after his troubled Southern campaign tour, "I came back from the South with a deep conviction. It is this: So long as the brotherhood of Man is denied in any part of our land, all of our nation is in danger."[41] Whether that danger was external, in the form of communist critiques of American democracy as rotten at the core, or internal, in the form of white-supremacist violence, those who worshipped the idol god of segregation, as Benjamin Mays characterized it, endangered all Americans.[42]

Ten

WHITE SUPREMACY IN PERIL

L IKE MANY WARTIME COUPLES, Andrea Perez and Sylvester S. Davis Jr. met on the job. In their case it happened in 1941, on the factory floor of Lockheed Aviation's Burbank facility. A second-generation Californian, Sylvester Davis traced his family's roots, and its Catholic religion, to Louisiana. Raised in the multiethnic Central Avenue district of Los Angeles, Davis attended racially mixed Catholic schools and worshipped at the racially mixed St. Patrick's Church. Although Davis recalled that in his neighborhood "everything was mixed, everything," there were few interracial marriages, despite California's legal recognition of interracial marriages that had been contracted elsewhere and the proximity of Mexico, where anyone could marry interracially.[1] A graduate of Los Angeles City College, Davis was one of the first Black men employed at Lockheed after the Japanese attack on Pearl Harbor, long before President Roosevelt issued Executive Order 8802, which desegregated government employment in war industries.[2]

Andrea Perez was born in Texas, the second of nine children of Serafina and Fermín Pérez, who emigrated separately from central Mexico following the 1905 Mexican Revolution. During her high school years, Andrea worked as a babysitter for Dorothy Marshall, a newspaper reporter, and Dorothy's lawyer husband, Daniel. After graduation, Andrea found a defense job at Lockheed through an advertisement published in Los Angeles's leading Spanish-language newspaper, *La Opinión*.

The olive-complected daughter of Mexican immigrants, Andrea Perez was considered white in California thanks to the provisions of the Treaty of Guadalupe Hidalgo (1848), which ended the Mexican-American War. The treaty provided for the cession by Mexico of more than a half million square miles of territory, including all of California, and declared Mexican nationals eligible for US citizenship at a time when only "white persons" could naturalize—effectively making Mexicans white by default. Although those who later sought to limit Mexican immigration to the United States used antimiscegenation arguments to make their case ("Uncle Sam should look on each Mexican immigrant as a prospective son-in-law!" thundered prominent eugenicist Harry Laughlin in the mid-1920s), jurists generally followed the lead of an 1897 federal court decision in Texas that asserted the primacy of international treaties and held that national origin determined the citizenship status of Mexicans regardless of physiognomy.[3]

The draft took Sylvester Davis to war in 1944, but when he returned from Europe he was determined to marry Andrea Perez. Andrea agreed to this proposal, over the objections of her father, and the couple applied for a marriage license on August 1, 1947. They were denied the license by an employee in the marriage bureau of the county clerk, who cited California's antimiscegenation law, which forbade "all marriages of white persons with negroes, Mongolians, members of the Malay race, or mulattoes."[4]

This law was one of many written in the nineteenth century by representatives of "the great hegira of the land-hungry Anglo-Saxon" (as Jack London described California's early white leadership) that regulated land ownership, political participation, and social relationships. California's first code of criminal procedure prohibited legal testimony against whites by Blacks, mulattos, and Indians.[5] The legislature barred "Mongolians, Indians, and Negroes" from public schools in 1860 and prohibited the employment of Chinese laborers on public works projects in 1879.

Ever-evolving and frequently contradictory laws of racial identity constricted the lives of wave after wave of immigrants to the state. Were Armenians Asians, and therefore ineligible to become citizens? They were, briefly, in 1909, before a federal court admitted them into the Caucasian club for immigration purposes by virtue of their appearance, religion, and history ("the outlook of their civilization has been toward Europe").[6] Encouraged by federal legislation prohibiting Chinese from becoming naturalized citizens because of their supposed racial inferiority, and by a string of federal court rulings that extended this "logic" to Japanese immigrants, California's Alien Land Acts of 1913 and 1920 prohibited agricultural land ownership by Asians and their American-born children.[7]

California's anti-immigrant stance protected more than white men's jobs and political power; it protected their blood. Restrictive immigration policies were part of a broader governmental effort to preserve white racial fitness and hierarchy, as exhorted by prominent eugenicists like Charles B. Davenport, who insisted that states must "take positive measures to increase the density of socially desirable traits in the next generation—by education, segregation, sterilization, and by keeping out immigrants who belong to defective strains."[8]

Following venerable horticulturalist Luther Burbank's exhortations, California became the model eugenic state in the 1910s. In addition to limiting immigration, the state managed its population through sterilization of those deemed unfit to reproduce. Four-fifths of the people sterilized in the United States between 1910 and 1920 were sterilized in the state of California, which led the nation in the number of annual eugenic sterilizations until 1950. African Americans and foreign immigrants were sterilized at nearly twice the rate as the general population.[9] Given this energetic dedication to preserving the quality of the white race in California and the state's official hostility toward nonwhites, it is not surprising that as late as 1948 the Golden State boasted racially restrictive marriage laws that rivaled those of the Deep South.[10]

Rebuffed in their attempt to marry, Andrea Perez and Sylvester Davis turned for help to Dorothy and Daniel Marshall, Andrea's former employers. A graduate of Loyola Law School, Daniel Marshall, along with a small number of other liberal Catholics, had founded the Los Angeles Catholic Interracial Council (LACIC) in 1944 with the goal of promoting civic equality and interracial cooperation. Marshall offered his legal expertise to a number of race-discrimination cases in the 1940s, including several that resulted in landmark decisions by the California Supreme Court.

In 1946, for example, Marshall came to the aid of Henry Laws, a Black war worker who was jailed for the offense of building a house that he intended to live in on land he owned in violation of a restrictive residential covenant that forbade occupation by any person "not of the Caucasian race." Joined by the Anti-Defamation League and the NAACP's crack California lawyer Loren Miller, the case of "the house on 92nd Street" was a key challenge to restrictive covenants in filled-to-bursting Los Angeles County, which in 1945 saw more suits contesting residential housing restrictions than all the rest of the country combined.[11]

That same year, Marshall contributed an amicus brief in *People v. Oyama*, a groundbreaking challenge to California's Alien Land Law. When it came before the Supreme Court of the United States, this case elicited the strongest argument to date that the Fourteenth Amendment was designed, as Justice Hugo Black insisted, "to bar States from denying to some groups, on account of their race or color, any rights, privileges, and opportunities accorded to other groups." In this era, Daniel Marshall was a vital member of California's small cadre of civil rights lawyers.[12]

When Andrea and Sylvester presented their problem to Marshall in 1947, he consulted with his former Loyola roommate and current

LACIC member, Fr. George Dunne, SJ. Dunne advised that rather than mount an equal-protection challenge to the law (which would have asserted that it violated the Fourteenth Amendment's guarantee that no state "shall deny to any person the equal protection of the laws"), or contest the ascribed racial identity of either Andrea Perez or Sylvester Davis (who had identified themselves straightforwardly as "white" and "Negro" on their application for a marriage license), Marshall should attack California's antimiscegenation law on the grounds that it violated religious freedom.[13]

The US Supreme Court had recently ruled that fundamental liberties protected by the First Amendment, including the freedom of religion, "are susceptible of restriction only to prevent grave and immediate danger to interests which the State may lawfully protect."[14] In effect, Marshall's argument was that because marriage was a religious institution, the state could not constitutionally deny individuals the freedom to marry other individuals of their choice in the absence of a compelling justification.

A challenge to California's antimiscegenation law on First Amendment grounds was not implausible. At the time, a crucial swing vote on the California Supreme Court lay in the hands of Justice Douglas Edmonds, a Christian Scientist known for his interest in religious liberty.[15] Nevertheless, when Daniel Marshall stood before the California Supreme Court in October 1947 and challenged the constitutionality of the state's restrictive marriage laws, he stood alone. None of the civil rights advocates he had worked with in the past—not Thomas L. Griffith Jr., president of the Los Angeles branch of the NAACP; not David Coleman, director of the local Anti-Defamation League; not Charlotta Bass, publisher of Los Angeles's oldest Black newspaper, the *California Eagle*—would join the *Perez* lawsuit.

The American Civil Liberties Union kept an eye on the case, as did the Japanese American Citizens League, but neither would lend its voice to a cause "with so much dynamite in it."[16] This absence of support, explained California lawyer and journalist Carey McWilliams in *The Nation*, reflected the belief of local civil rights leaders that, as the foundation of Jim Crow, "miscegenation statutes could not be successfully challenged in the courts."[17]

A decision from outside the Deep South upholding the logic of *Plessy v. Ferguson* would damage the entire civil rights project. According to this view, it was essential to proceed in the courts cautiously and incrementally rather than to leap recklessly to challenge the most fundamental facet of Jim Crow—state antimiscegenation laws.

IN 1940, CALIFORNIA deputy attorney general Roger J. Traynor, a former University of California law professor then serving under California attorney general Earl Warren, was elevated unexpectedly to the California Supreme Court. He would sit there for the next thirty years, the last six as chief justice. Described later by *Time* magazine as a "law professor's judge," Traynor was always open to new ideas. He read widely in the social sciences and in the 1930s helped to revise California's tax structure along progressive New Deal lines. Traynor would eventually become legendary for his decisions reforming laws regarding divorce and products liability. He was, at all times, sympathetic to the need for the law to reflect changes in social circumstances and community values.[18]

As Traynor explained in a 1956 essay on law and social change in a democratic society, judicial precedents can become antiquated, they can lose touch with reality, and they should be "abandoned or reformulated to meet new conditions and new moral values." Objecting to the notion that "the overruling of ill-conceived, or moribund, or obsolete precedents somehow menaces the stability of the law," he asked his legal audience, "Who among us has not known a precedent that should never have been born?"[19]

In his October 1947 oral argument on behalf of Andrea Perez and Sylvester Davis, Daniel Marshall first noted that Sections 60 and 69 of the California Civil Code prohibited the intermarriage of whites with any other group except Indians. At the same time, the law allowed intermarriage of "any combination of yellow, black, red [Indian] and brown." This statutory permission for the intermarriage of all races, except where a white person was involved, revealed, Marshall concluded, that the antimiscegenation statute was "plainly not a declaration by the state that interracial marriage is, per se, an evil," but was rather "a prohibition used to implement the thesis of inherent racial superiority" through its ostensible protection of white "blood purity."[20]

Invoking his religion-based theory of the case, Marshall insisted that marriage was a Christian sacrament "instituted by the Founder of their faith" and that Section 69 therefore denied his clients the right to participate fully in the sacramental life of their religion. Charles C. Stanley, Los Angeles County's deputy council, challenged Marshall's argument that the right to marry was guaranteed by the First Amendment. Stanley stressed that the petitioners had no religious *obligation* to marry one another. It was not their religion, Stanley noted in oral argument, that compelled Andrea Perez and Sylvester Davis to marry, but rather "their own worldly choice," and he concluded that their case did not cross the threshold for First Amendment protection.[21]

Rather than engage the First Amendment issue, Justice Roger Traynor raised a question unaddressed by either Stanley or Marshall. "What about equal protection of the laws?" Traynor asked. Since the late nineteenth century, the equal protection clause of the Fourteenth Amendment had been interpreted as prohibiting laws that treat people differently without a legitimate justification, or that explicitly discriminate against historically oppressed racial minorities, unless the laws could be justified by a compelling state interest.[22] However, the Supreme Court had also held in *Plessy* that laws that treat the races separately but equally were constitutional as long as they served a legitimate state interest. As Stanley launched into a reply to Traynor's question about equal protection, Traynor asked him to explain what legitimate social purpose was served by California's restrictive marriage law. Stanley replied that there were biological and medical considerations upholding the law.

Stanley based this argument in part on an 1890 federal court of appeals decision, *State v. Tutty*, which quoted extensively from *Scott v. State*, an 1869 Georgia case that had upheld a ban on interracial marriage on biological grounds. The decision in *Scott* concluded, "The amalgamation of the races is not only unnatural, but it is always productive of deplorable results." Indeed, "the offspring of these unnatural connections are generally sickly and effeminate, and…they are inferior in physical development and strength to the full blood of either race." The court in *Scott* insisted that "such connections never elevate the inferior race to the position of the superior, but they bring down the superior to that of the inferior. They are productive of evil, and evil only, without any corresponding good."[23]

In response to Stanley's argument on this point, Marshall quoted extensively from *Mein Kampf* ("Every race-crossing leads necessarily sooner or later to the decline of the mixed product") and reminded the court that "the German Reich advocated and executed a policy and program for the defense of the so-called purity of the so-called Aryan race." Pitting the Nazis against the Founding Fathers, Marshall concluded, "The choice then must be between the dogma of the *Tutty* case, the decisions which have followed it[,] and the concepts of those leaders who adopted that dogma as their national aspiration, and the sublime expressions of our national aspiration forever imbedded in our constitutional documents," which, Marshall argued, sprang from the Declaration of Independence's affirmation of the equality of all men.[24]

Stanley dug in. First, he maintained, "there is evidence that any crossing of widely divergent races will have detrimental biological results. There is excellent evidence of loss of vitality and fertility in future generations." Furthermore, he added, "the thing which has been fairly well established is that certain disharmonic conflicts result." Because his task was not to establish the validity of a law preventing mixed marriages of races generally, but of a law prohibiting the mixing of Caucasians with a list of "specified colored races," Stanley expanded on the undesirability of interracial marriage involving whites. "I do not like to tie myself in with '*Mein Kampf*,'" he said, "but it has been shown that the white race is superior physically and mentally to the black race, and the intermarriage of these races results in a lessening of physical vitality and mentality in their offspring." Traynor's response to Stanley was immediate: "Are there medical men in this country today who say such a thing?"[25]

Roger Traynor would have been well aware that enough American medical men had said such things since the turn of the twentieth century to enable white supremacists to ground their beliefs in science and to agitate for laws to enforce the hierarchy of races they erected. The University of North Carolina Press's William Couch, who had defended scientific racism in his preface to *What the Negro Wants* in 1944, could have ticked off a list from memory. A generation before, any number of fully credentialed scientists could have been found to testify as to the division of mankind into races defined through the portentous Linnaean and Darwinian language of natural science.

By 1948, though, such language, with its straight-faced references to "certain disharmonic conflicts," carried a distinctly archaic sound. This shift, which in itself constituted one of the most dramatic signs of cognitive change in the shape of twentieth-century thought, reflected the rising influence of anthropologists such as German-born Columbia professor Franz Boas and his students Alfred Kroeber (Roger Traynor's colleague at Berkeley), Ruth Benedict, and Ashley Montagu, who questioned the biological category of "race" and redefined it in cultural terms.

Like his compatriot and coreligionist Albert Einstein, Franz Boas was outspokenly dedicated to human equality—social and political as well as biological—and frequently offended the interlocking WASP elite that governed the universities and the nation through the Second World War. Boas was from the first aware of the public policy repercussions of his anthropological conclusions, and much of the work of discrediting the nostrums of scientific racism was accomplished in courtrooms and on government committees. In 1911, after working on an immigration report for the United States government, Boas published *The Mind of Primitive Man*, in which he rejected "the belief of the hereditary superiority of certain types over others."

In several articles written for a popular audience after World War I, Boas questioned the methodology of the intelligence tests conducted by the US Army, which had seemingly demonstrated the mental inferiority of African Americans, and applied his conclusions to American race relations. Boas insisted that it should not be assumed that any individual Negro, simply because he was a Negro, was less intelligent than the average white, or that any individual white, simply because he was white, was more intelligent than the average Negro. Anticipating later Supreme Court rulings addressing individual rights, Boas argued in 1921 in the *Yale Quarterly Review* that African Americans had a right "to be treated as individuals, not as members of a class."[26]

As for the category of "race" itself, the anthropologists' most devastating argument was a basic one: that, all apparent differences aside, there was no such thing as "race," and any effort to define the supposed races was capricious. As Ashley Montagu explained in his influential book *Man's Most Dangerous Myth: The Fallacy of Race*, published in 1942, "In the biological sense there do, of course, exist distinctive populations of mankind. That is to say, mankind may be regarded as being comprised of a number of groups which as such are often physically sufficiently distinguishable from one another, in the sense defined above, to justify their being classified as distinctive populations but not as separate races."[27] Or as Boas had put it six years earlier, "We talk all the time glibly of races and nobody can give us a definite answer to the question what constitutes a race."[28]

Gunnar Myrdal summed up this thinking for a broad audience in 1944, when he wrote in *An American Dilemma* that "the concept of the American Negro is a social concept and not a biological one." He continued, "In modern biological and ethnological research 'race' as a scientific concept has lost sharpness of meaning, and the term is disappearing in sober writings."[29]

Although policy makers from both ends of the political spectrum would continue to speak in terms of racial groups,[30] by the time the California Supreme Court was asked to rule on racially restrictive marriage laws, the arguments of cultural anthropologists rebutting claims of racial *superiority* or inherent biological differences had gone from being a rearguard action to occupying the center of the discursive stage.

Americans of all ranks, including several members of the California Supreme Court, still believed in white racial superiority, which had its pseudoscientific defenders long past 1948. But scientific racism had lost the protection of academic credibility by then and was met with raised eyebrows by those who valued scientific expertise and read the work of popularizers such as Earnest Albert Hooton of Harvard.[31]

In his final question to Charles Stanley, Roger Traynor addressed the feasibility of the state's concept of racial classification:

MR. JUSTICE TRAYNOR: Before you go into that, it might help to explain the statute, what it means. What is a negro?

MR. STANLEY: We have not the benefit of any judicial interpretation. The statute states that a [white] cannot marry a negro, which can be construed to mean a full-blooded negro, since the statute also says mulatto, Mongolian or Malay.

MR. JUSTICE TRAYNOR: What is a mulatto? One-sixteenth blood?...If there is 1/8 blood, can they marry? If you can marry with 1/8, why not with 1/16, 1/32, 1/64?

MR. STANLEY: I agree that it would be better for the Legislature to lay down an exact amount of blood, but I do not think that the statute should be declared unconstitutional as indefinite on this ground.

MR. JUSTICE TRAYNOR: That is something anthropologists have not been able to furnish, although they say generally that there is no such thing as race.

MR. STANLEY: I would not say that anthropologists have said that generally, except such statements for sensational purposes.

MR. JUSTICE TRAYNOR: Would you say that Professor [H]ooton of Harvard was a sensationalist? *The crucial question is how can a county clerk determine who are negroes and who are whites?*
MR. STANLEY: He does it by taking a statement as to their race?[32]

This exchange revealed a fundamental flaw in California's antimiscegenation law: its failure to define any of the racial categories it invoked.

Although supporters of the law would point to almost a century of continuous operation as indicative of its strength, a quick detour to Mississippi reveals just how weak California's restrictive marriage law was, and how differences in each state's basic law of race contributed to strikingly different outcomes in contemporaneous, comparable cases.[33] California's expansive but vague antimiscegenation law was more vulnerable than Mississippi's, which relied explicitly on genealogy.

A FEW MONTHS after Andrea Perez and Sylvester Davis were turned away by a county clerk in Los Angeles in 1948, twenty-three-year-old Davis Knight was indicted in Mississippi for having knowingly contracted a miscegenous marriage with Junie Lee Spradley, a white woman. Davis Knight's navy induction and discharge papers identified him as white, but he was also the great-grandson of Newton Knight, who famously led a band of Confederate deserters turned Union supporters turned marauders, and Rachel Knight, a freed slave formerly owned by the Knight family. Between 1865 and 1870, Newton Knight established a small community in Jones County, Mississippi, consisting initially of two households: one headed by Knight and his white wife, Serena, the other by Rachel. Rachel's children, all apparently fathered by white men (including but not limited to Newton), grew up alongside the eight children of Newton and Serena Knight.

Sometime after 1878, Molly Knight and George Knight, two children of Newton and Serena, married Jeffrey Knight and Frances Knight, two of Rachel's children. These marriages began what local whites referred to as Jones County's "white negroes" or "Knight's negroes." By creating a community of mixed-race people, Newton Knight apparently convinced his neighbors that he had betrayed not only the Lost Cause but his race as well. They, in turn, drummed Knight out of the white race. In the 1900 census, Newton Knight, a Confederate veteran and former slaveholder, was designated as "Black."[34]

In Davis Knight's 1948 trial for marrying a white woman, the prosecution had the burden of establishing his race. Unlike Virginia's "one drop" regime, in which any documented African ancestry left a person outside the boundaries of whiteness, Mississippi law defined a Negro as any person with one-eighth or more African ancestry. In order for Davis Knight to be legally Black, his great-grandmother Rachel had to have been of full African ancestry.

The state's efforts to prove this foundered on the testimony of family and neighbors that Rachel had been at least part Indian, a "ginger-cake colored" woman with long, silky black hair. In addition to this sort of testimony, the extraordinarily tangled family relationships of the Knights further stymied the court's attempt to pin down Davis Knight's genealogy. To give but the most extreme example, Davis's grandparents Henry and Ella divorced, and Ella married Davis's other grandfather, Jeffrey, whose son Otho had previously married Ella's daughter Addie. After her remarriage, Ella became her own daughter's stepmother-in-law and was simultaneously Davis Knight's grandmother and step-grandmother.

Although convicted at trial, Davis Knight was freed on appeal when the Mississippi Supreme Court ruled that the prosecution had failed "to prove beyond all reasonable doubt that the defendant had one-eighth or more Negro blood." According to the state of Mississippi— not to mention the United States Navy—Davis Knight was a white man, and his marriage to Junie Lee Spradley stood.

However bizarre the trial proceedings may appear from a twenty-first-century perspective, the law worked as designed. Purists may have decried the fuzzy boundaries of whiteness and fretted over the individual outcome in this case, but Mississippi's racial conventions as a whole remained undisturbed.[35]

THIS WAS NOT the case in California. In a four-to-three ruling, the California Supreme Court in *Perez v. Sharp* became the first court since Reconstruction to find an antimiscegenation law unconstitutional.[36] As his prominent role in the oral argument presaged, Roger Traynor wrote the majority opinion, although two of his colleagues wrote concurring opinions that stressed different legal reasoning.

Conscious that he was writing for a national legal audience, Traynor crafted a tight decision on the narrowest possible grounds while still mounting a frontal assault on scientific racism, unconstitutional racial discrimination, and obsolete precedents that denied some Americans access to a fundamental right of citizenship.[37]

Affirming at the outset that "the regulation of marriage is considered a proper function of the state," Traynor rejected Daniel Marshall's argument that antimiscegenation laws violated religious liberty, noting that "although freedom of conscience and the freedom to believe are absolute, the freedom to act is not." Instead, Traynor concluded that restrictive marriage laws violated the due process clause of the Fourteenth Amendment. As he explained, "If the miscegenation law under attack in the present proceeding is directed at a social evil and employs a reasonable means to prevent that evil, it is valid regardless of its incidental effect upon the conduct of particular religious groups. If, on the other hand, the law is discriminatory and irrational," it more generally and unconstitutionally "restricts the liberty to marry."

Noting that the due process clause protects fundamental "personal liberty," Traynor listed the rights, including marriage, recognized by the Supreme Court as "essential to the orderly pursuit of happiness by free men." Marriage, Traynor concluded, is "something more than a civil contract subject to regulation by the state; it is a fundamental right of free men. There can be no prohibition of marriage except for an important social objective and by reasonable means."[38]

When he pronounced marriage a "fundamental right of free men" Traynor effectively added it to the list of recognized rights identified by the Supreme Court as not expressly mentioned in the Constitution, including the right of association, the right to educate a child in a school of the parents' choice, and the right to reproduce. These rights indicated that the "dignity of the person and worth of the human being are special objects of solicitude under the Constitution of the United States."[39] To support this conclusion, he invoked a string of Supreme Court rulings that protected the personal rights of individuals, two of which explicitly counted marriage as a civil right: *Meyer v. Nebraska* (1923), which recognized the right "to marry, establish a home and bring up children," and *Skinner v. Oklahoma* (1942), which defined marriage and procreation as among "the basic civil rights of man."[40]

Traynor also rejected the applicability of any notion of "separate but equal" to marriage. "Since the essence of the right to marry is freedom to join in marriage with the person of one's choice, a segregation statute necessarily impairs the right to marry," Traynor concluded. "Human beings," he added, "are bereft of worth and dignity by a doctrine that would make them as interchangeable as trains."[41]

According to the state of California, Sections 60 and 69 were constitutional because they protected the precious commodity of whiteness by prohibiting the contamination of the Caucasian race. Citing *An American Dilemma*, Traynor dismissed the claim that non-Caucasians were inherently physically inferior as "without scientific proof." On the question of mental inferiority, Traynor called on an impressive array of recent scientific literature to rebut any correlation between race and intelligence and noted that "in any event, the Legislature has not made an intelligence test a prerequisite to marriage." He also rebutted the claim that racially restrictive marriage laws played a vital role in maintaining the public peace. Citing the Supreme Court's decision in *Buchanan v. Warley* (1917), Traynor concluded that "it is no answer to say that race tension can be eradicated through the perpetuation of the prejudices that give rise to the tension."[42]

Finally, Traynor added that even if antimiscegenation laws were justifiable in principle, California's was impossible to implement because it failed to define any of its racial categories. Traynor raised the question of hybridity. "The fact is overwhelming," he remarked, "that there has been a steady increase in the number of people in this country who belong to more than one race....Some of these persons have migrated to this state; some are born here illegitimately; others are the progeny of miscegenous marriages valid where contracted and therefore valid in California."[43]

The apparent purpose of the antimiscegenation statute, Traynor continued, "is to discourage the birth of children of mixed ancestry within this state. Such a purpose, however, cannot be accomplished without taking into consideration marriages of persons of mixed ancestry. A statute regulating fundamental rights is clearly unconstitutional if it cannot be reasonably applied to accomplish its purpose."[44] By failing to define any of its racial categories, including the mixed-race group of mulattoes, Traynor held that California's restrictive marriage statutes were too vague and uncertain to be enforceable regulations of a fundamental right, and that they violated the Fourteenth Amendment's equal protection clause "by impairing the right of individuals to marry on the basis of race alone and by arbitrarily and unreasonably discriminating against certain racial groups."[45]

Roger Traynor's affirmation of a fundamental right to freedom of marriage spoke for a fragile majority of four. Two of the three justices who supported Traynor published their own separate, and divergent, concurring opinions. As anticipated by Marshall, the freedom of religion argument appealed to Justice Edmonds, whereas Justice Jesse Carter anchored his views, as we shall see, in a variety of texts. The three-judge dissent, on the other hand, was united in rejecting the arguments that antimiscegenation laws were unconstitutional. Written by Justice John W. Shenk, the dissent noted that racially restrictive marriage laws had been recognized as valid in California for nearly one hundred years, and that California had reaffirmed and broadened its law only a decade earlier to apply to Filipinos.[46] Moreover, when challenged at the state level, the constitutionality of such laws had been uniformly upheld across the nation.

Justice Shenk maintained that Traynor had not proved that the Constitution "confers upon a citizen the right to marry anyone who is willing to wed him." Shenk also held that antimiscegenation laws "have a valid legislative purpose even though they may not conform to the sociogenetic views of some people," that the states had sovereignty over the issue of marriage, and that substantial evidence existed to support the California legislature's conclusion that "intermarriage between Negroes and white persons is incompatible with the general welfare and therefore a proper subject for regulation under the police power."[47] In a stunt worthy of South Carolina, the California Senate signaled its opposition to *Perez* and Black assemblyman Augustus Hawkins's campaign to dissolve the state's antimiscegenation statute by voting twenty-five to eight to keep the law on the books.[48]

Eleven

ARCHITECTS OF A BETTER WORLD

R OGER TRAYNOR'S EMBRACE of marriage as a constitutionally protected interest, and his rejection of racialist thought, may seem
reasonable, even obvious, in the twenty-first century, but in 1948 those
views went far beyond settled doctrine. In 1948, thirty of forty-eight
states still had laws forbidding interracial marriage. *Perez*, limited to
California, did not immediately pose a threat to similar laws in the
other twenty-nine states that restricted interracial marriage.[1]

Nevertheless, two aspects of the decision troubled defenders of
white dominance. First, *Perez* threw into high relief the potentially revolutionary role of the judiciary in setting the boundaries of postwar racial politics. The California court held that marriage was a fundamental
right that could not constitutionally be restricted by race, consistent
with the Fourteenth Amendment's guarantee of equal protection of
the laws. Second, and potentially more troubling, one of the concurring opinions in *Perez* cited as authority for the decision the United
Nations Charter, which prohibited racial discrimination in all walks of
life, and which had been ratified by the United States in 1946.

The California ruling gained added meaning when considered alongside the emergence of a robust discourse of international human rights. Not two weeks before the opinion was issued in October 1948, the United Nations Commission on Human Rights, chaired by former first lady Eleanor Roosevelt, condemned restrictive marriage laws based on race. In the context of early Cold War criticism of American racial politics, the marriage question became a focal point for the tension between international law and national sovereignty, as well as a powerful, and potentially inflammatory, site of contestation between twenty-nine states and the national government.

ONE OF THE LESSONS of the Paris Peace Conference of 1919 had been the necessity to plan for peace well in advance of an armistice. In August 1941 Franklin Roosevelt and Winston Churchill had issued the Atlantic Charter, which called for a "wider and permanent system of general security" to replace the defunct League of Nations and offered suggestions to shape the postwar world. The peace envisioned by the charter was one "which will afford assurance that all the men in all the lands may live out their lives in freedom from fear and want." To speak in 1941 of individuals rather than states ("all the men in all the lands") was revolutionary. The idea that the dignity of the individual was an appropriate topic of international affairs was embraced immediately by groups already committed to fighting racism and colonialism as well as Nazism. It was, in short, the birth of the modern concept of human rights.

The "system of general security" that became the United Nations was sketched out by delegates of the four chief allies (Britain, the United States, the USSR, and China) at Dumbarton Oaks, a mansion outside Washington, DC, in late 1944. There, an exclusive group of diplomats and policy experts drafted the charter for an inclusive international organization. There were moments of rancor, especially when discussing veto power in the Security Council and the Soviets' idea to count all its recently acquired satellite states as independent nations for voting purposes. But in the end the delegates' work was rooted clearly in the Atlantic Charter, with two exceptions: there was no statement on the universal rights of the individual, nor a disavowal of racial discrimination.

On April 25, 1945, delegates from forty-six nations gathered in San Francisco to draft a charter for a new international agency dedicated to the maintenance of peace and security and the recognition of equal human rights. The proceedings were shadowed by the absence of Franklin Roosevelt, whose death two weeks earlier had removed the chief Western architect of the postwar order, and by the lack of representatives from Poland, whose invasion by Germany in September 1939 had set in motion the catastrophic war now coming to a close, and whose current domination by the Soviet Union suggested the need for an organization such as the United Nations.

Cheered by the last-minute attendance of Russian foreign minister Vyacheslav Molotov, whose presence had been thrown into doubt by a disagreeable first meeting with Harry Truman, and innocent yet of the knowledge that owing to food-rationing laws the only proteins they were likely to encounter in San Francisco restaurants were tripe and eggs, the delegates departed optimistically after the brief opening session. They were ferried to their hotels in US Army cars driven by California women chosen, according to the *New York Times*, "for their pulchritude as well as their driving ability."[2]

The delegates' optimism was laced with apprehension. Even as they celebrated the success of the Allied armies in Europe and their anticipated victory in the Pacific, the men and women gathered in San Francisco recognized that peace would be accompanied by disorder and uncertainty as the postwar world was recast. Acknowledging that moments of great possibility have multiple potential outcomes, President Truman cautioned these "architects of a better world" against retreat into parochialism and exhorted them to "build a new world—a far better world—one in which the eternal dignity of man is respected."[3]

Even the nations that supported the elevation of human rights in the UN Charter balked at the abridgement of national sovereignty required to protect them. Worried about getting the United Nations treaty past the Southern guard in the US Senate, John Foster Dulles negotiated an escape clause as the price of American support for the charter. Article 2, paragraph 7 protected national sovereignty over "domestic matters," such as education and marriage, by prohibiting the United Nations from intervening in things "essentially within the domestic jurisdiction of any state."

Wherever the charter's jurisdiction lay, the fundamental human rights enshrined in the United Nations' founding document remained undefined at the close of the San Francisco meeting. It was left to a nine-member subcommittee of the new Commission on Human Rights to draft an international bill of rights that would, it was hoped, ultimately produce a binding covenant to protect those rights.

During 1947 and 1948, the Human Rights Commission met in Lake Success, New York, where its members debated the fundamental rights of mankind and struggled to compose a Universal Declaration of Human Rights (UDHR) that would be acceptable to everyone. René Cassin, the French delegate to the commission and a Nobel Peace laureate, refined the preliminary draft. Aided by Monsignor Angelo Giuseppi Roncalli, papal nuncio in Paris and later the reformist Pope John XXIII, Cassin worked from two fundamental premises: first, "that every human being has a right to be treated like every other human being," and second, that the declaration should base its universal rights on the "great fundamental principle of the unity of all the races of mankind."[4]

Because of its implicit call for equality for women, the first of Cassin's principles challenged openly patriarchal societies such as Saudi Arabia's, which objected vehemently to women's rights. The second principle asserted the biological brotherhood of man and repudiated decades of "scientific racism" that upheld a hierarchy of races.

As relations between the United States and the Soviet Union descended into rancor and competition for world influence in 1947 and 1948, the deliberations of the Human Rights Commission became an irresistible location for communist condemnation of American racial inequality. American social practices left the nation vulnerable to criticism on many fronts—unequal educational opportunities, discriminatory housing laws, limited voting rights, segregated public accommodations with their photogenic "for Whites" and "for Colored" signs, and, most shocking of all, the acts of unspeakable violence perpetrated upon African Americans. The United States had signaled its commitment in theory to human equality when it signed the United Nations Charter in 1946. Now America's antagonists addressed the question of practice by raising the issue of freedom of marriage.

Ever since the modern campaign for female equality was inaugurated by Mary Wollstonecraft, who published *A Vindication of the Rights of Woman* in 1792, the institution of marriage has been critiqued as oppressive to women. In the context of the post-WWII/United Nations rights revolution, however, marriage was considered by many as emblematic of liberty. The deliberations of the Human Rights Commission linked freedom of marriage with citizenship and, more broadly, with a sense of state membership.

The UDHR went through six drafts. The first draft included "the right to contract marriage in accordance with the laws of the State."[5] This could be read, despite an accompanying declaration against discrimination "because of race, sex, language, religion, or political creed," as compatible with state antimiscegenation laws because, as whites had pointed out so many times, these laws treated whites and Blacks alike insofar as neither could marry the other.[6]

The commission's third effort, in June 1947, set the subject aside for further consideration. But at the next meeting, in Geneva, a nondiscrimination clause was added to the proposal on marriage that upheld the equal rights of men and women to marry "without distinction of race, religion, or origin." However, this was eventually reduced to "Men and women shall have the same freedom to contract marriage in accordance with the law."[7]

The records of the commission make clear that marriage rights were included in the UDHR in great measure to protect women. In addition to upholding the freedom to contract a marriage across lines of race and religion, the declaration upheld a woman's equal right to dissolve a marriage and to leave her own country in order to join her husband in another land.

But inclusion of freedom of marriage as a fundamental human right served political purposes as well. Both the mixed-marriage clause and the clause protecting couples' right to cross national boundaries in order to unite were clear swipes at state sovereignty that criticized specific policies of the two dominant powers in the UN: the United States and the USSR. Aimed squarely at the United States, the mixed-marriage clause of the declaration held up antimiscegenation laws to stand in for the broader Jim Crow regime and ultimately criticized America as a whole. Equally, condemnation of the forced separation of wives and husbands targeted the Soviet Union, which refused to allow Soviet women married to foreign nationals to leave the USSR, and stood in for the Soviet Union's broader curtailment of freedom of movement and its occupation of Eastern Europe.[8]

With no enforcement mechanisms, the UDHR had no real power over any of the nations that violated its principles.[9] Eleanor Roosevelt's characterization of the declaration as "a moral and spiritual milestone" emblematic of "the true spirit of Christianity" reflected the document's largely symbolic nature.[10] The United Nations Charter, which as a treaty *did* carry binding obligations for its signatories, posed a far more potent threat to American racial practices. To those worried about the erosion of national sovereignty, the omens were ill. In early 1947, the UN General Assembly denounced South Africa's apartheid regime and declared that the charter "imposed upon each member an obligation to refrain from policies based upon race discrimination."[11]

Any hope that the UN would not draw attention to violations of marriage rights evaporated in 1949, when the General Assembly censored the Soviet Union for its refusal to allow Soviet women married to non-Soviets to leave the country.[12] Supporters and opponents of African American civil and human rights raced to the same conclusion:

if the USSR could be censored and South Africa investigated and denounced, why not the United States?

The domestic jurisdiction clause inserted in the charter at the behest of the United States was designed to shield nations from "promiscuous international action" in matters of local concern.[13] But as the international effort brought to bear against South Africa and the Soviets suggested, the UN was alert to violations of individual rights whether or not they occurred within the realm of domestic sovereignty. Indeed, dissolving the boundary that fell between a nation's citizens and the citizens of the world, particularly where fundamental rights were concerned, was a founding purpose of the United Nations. After 1948, racially discriminatory laws that had been condemned by supporters of African American civil rights as violations of American ideals were now liable to be indicted as abuses of international human rights.[14]

Neither the UN's censorship of the Soviets nor its demand that South Africa turn from its apartheid ways resulted in any tangible policy changes in either country. Like the Declaration of Independence, whose bold assertion that "all men are created equal" carried no legal weight, the influence of the Universal Declaration of Human Rights lay entirely in the court of public opinion. This fact was soon recognized by African American civil rights groups, which petitioned the UN—what the National Negro Congress called "the highest court of mankind"—to "end the oppression of the American Negro."

When the UN Secretariat refused to receive a petition by the National Negro Congress and asked the organization to provide evidence of oppression, the NAACP assumed responsibility for the project. In October 1947, the same week that President Truman's Commission on Civil Rights released its report, the NAACP presented to the United Nations a 155-page petition titled *An Appeal to the World: A Statement on the Denial of Human Rights to Minorities in the Case of Citizens of Negro Descent in the United States of America and an Appeal to the United Nations for Redress.* Drafted by a committee of younger Black academics and lawyers under the supervision of W. E. B. Du Bois, the appeal claimed to speak on behalf of fourteen million Black citizens of the United States and demanded "elemental Justice against the treatment which the United States has visited upon us for three centuries."[15]

Uncertain about the UN's willingness to even receive the petition, Du Bois leaked the document to the press before presenting it to the General Assembly. Chicago's leading African American newspaper, the *Chicago Defender*, pronounced the appeal a "searing indictment" of America's "failure to practice what it preaches." The *New York Times* dutifully reported the NAACP's claim that Mississippi posed a greater threat to American democracy than the Soviet Union ("Not Stalin and Molotov but Bilbo and Rankin"), a sentiment applauded, naturally, by the Soviets, who took up the cause of the petition at the UN.[16]

Laws against interracial marriage were not the most visible racially discriminatory laws in America, nor were they a central target of the foreign press, which tended to highlight segregated public and private institutions, disenfranchisement, and racial violence. But because of the commission's inclusion of freedom of marriage on its list of fundamental human rights, America's antimiscegenation laws provided a sturdy platform from which to launch accusations of hypocrisy and to discredit American democracy.

The Soviet Union, predictably, launched the most frontal attack on American antimiscegenation laws. This strategy reflected a desire to embarrass the United States, but it was also based on the Soviets' own ideological priorities. Whatever its other human rights failures, the Communist Bloc was from the first dedicated to the incorporation of clear antidiscrimination language in the UN's declaration.[17] In a direct provocation of the United States and other nations reluctant to abandon racial hierarchies, the Soviet delegate, Alexi Pavlov, proposed an amendment to the UDHR that condemned "the racial practice... of prohibiting mixed marriages between persons who are subjects of the same State but differ from each other by the colour of their skin or their racial, national or religious membership." It was not impossible, he maintained, "that racial practices in the United States might be found to be even more objectionable than those formerly obtaining in Germany."[18] Pavlov's use of the past tense with respect to German anti-Jewish codes acknowledged the fact that an Allied commission was at that very moment purging German law of such restrictions. Indeed, both East and West Germany barred discrimination by race in their 1949 constitutions.[19]

Conversations about human rights transcended Long Island. Also in 1948, at a conference organized in Bogotá, Colombia, the (Pan) American Declaration of the Rights and Duties of Man was drafted. It announced, "Every person has the right to establish a family, the basic element of society." The final text of Article 16, Section 1 of the UDHR was more specific than the American Declaration, and read, "Men and women of full age, without any limitation due to race, nationality or religion, have the right to marry and to found a family." Both the American and the British representatives argued unsuccessfully against Article 16, insisting that its contents were covered elsewhere in the declaration.[20]

Article 16 made headlines even at the drafting stage ("Mixed Marriages Win a U.N. Vote," announced the *New York Times*) and was prominent in other reporting. When considered in combination with the UDHR's Article 2, which announced that "everyone is entitled to all the rights and freedoms set forth in this Declaration, without distinction of any kind, such as race, colour, sex, language, religion, political or other opinion, national or social origin, property, birth or other status," it did not take a great leap of imagination to consider Article 16 in particular and the United Nations in general a serious threat to racial segregation and discrimination in America.[21]

ROGER TRAYNOR'S OPINION in *Perez* in 1948 had been rooted entirely in state and American constitutional law and made no reference to international norms, beyond suggesting that there were universal rights and that marriage was one of them.[22] Traynor's colleague on the bench

Jesse Carter was less restrained in his concurrence. Known in California legal circles as "the great dissenter," Carter refused to sign a loyalty oath when he was appointed to the California Supreme Court in 1930 and declared such oaths unconstitutional in a series of cases through the McCarthy era. Carter ranged widely in his *Perez* concurrence, citing in support of the decision the Declaration of Independence, Thomas Jefferson, the Charter of the United Nations, and, for good measure, the Apostle Paul.

In coming years, the Acts of the Apostles would assume unanticipated political significance with regard to questions of race mixing, but in 1948 the UN Charter was the more oft-cited text. Noting that "the rest of the world never has understood and never will understand why and how a nation, built on the premise that all men are created equal, can three times send the flower of its manhood to war for the truth of this premise and still fail to carry it out within its own borders," Carter pled to bring the United States into accord with world opinion as well as with its own basic law. "Pray let us so resolve Cases here," Carter quoted Lord Nottingham from 1682, "that they may stand with the Reason of Mankind when they are debated abroad. Shall that be Reason here that is not Reason in any part of the World besides?"[23]

Whereas many American foreign-policy analysts considered American race politics dangerous for the nation's role in global politics, the guardians of Jim Crow considered American participation in international organizations such as the United Nations a threat to the nation's established social order.[24] Petitions aside, the danger to the sovereign status quo lay in the interpretive possibilities of the UN Charter and its relationship to American law. Howard Law School dean William H. Hastie, who had resigned from the Roosevelt administration in 1943 over the issue of segregated troops and training, lost no time in explaining how the charter affected American public policy. In a 1946 challenge to segregated interstate transportation, Hastie argued that when the United States ratified the UN Charter, it "embedded in its national policy a prohibition against racism and pledged itself to respect fundamental freedoms for all without distinction as to race, sex, language or religion."[25]

This position was reinforced in 1948. As the Human Rights Commission prepared to release the UDHR, the California Supreme Court annulled its state's racially restrictive marriage laws, and four justices of the US Supreme Court included references to the UN Charter in their opinion in *Oyama v. California*, which invalidated provisions of that state's alien land laws. Noting that the United States had recently pledged to "promote…universal respect for, and observance of, human rights and fundamental freedoms for all without distinction as to race, sex, language, or religion," Justice Hugo Black asked, "How can this nation be faithful to this international pledge if state laws which bar land ownership and occupancy by aliens on account of race are permitted to be enforced?"[26]

The objections to Black's argument were vehement. In a speech before the State Bar of California that same year, Frank Holman, a prominent Utah lawyer and the president of the American Bar Association (ABA), warned that the Human Rights Commission headed by Mrs. Roosevelt was formulating "a so-called bill of rights program" that if ratified as a treaty by the US Senate would, under Article VI of the Constitution, "supersede any conflicting state constitutions and state legislative enactments."

After posing a number of legal questions (such as how far could a treaty affect or nullify a state statute? The provisions of state constitutions? Judicial decisions of state supreme courts?), Holman noted that the executive treaty power raised "important legal-political questions" as well. "How far can a treaty increase the powers of the Federal Government at the expense of the States?" Holman asked. "In the field of so-called civil rights, it has been definitely suggested that this can be done." Although acknowledging that the "treaty-making power is an admitted attribute of sovereignty," Holman warned that international treaties on human rights had the potential to seriously disrupt American social conventions. For example, if the Treaty of Guadalupe

Hidalgo could make Andrea Perez white, why could another not allow her to marry any man she wished?[27]

Although Holman was dismissed at the time as an alarmist, his fears took on greater weight two years later, after a California court found the state's remaining restrictions on alien ownership of land unconstitutional on the grounds that they conflicted with the Universal Declaration of Human Rights and the UN Charter, which, as a federal treaty, prevailed over state law. In his 1950 opinion in *Sei Fujii v. California*, Judge Emmet H. Wilson explained that when the United States ratified the UN Charter, it pledged to uphold its guarantees, including racial equality. To ensure the "rights and benefits" of UN membership, the member nations were obliged to "fulfill in good faith" the standards set by the organization.[28]

In this decision, the California court echoed both the conclusion of President Truman's Commission on Civil Rights, which had noted in 1947 that the doctrine of the supremacy of treaties had "an obvious importance as a possible basis for civil rights legislation," and the US Justice Department's 1948 Amicus curiae brief in the NAACP challenge to restrictive housing covenants, which reminded the Supreme Court that international treaties, including specifically the UN Charter, constituted components of public policy.[29]

The decision in *Sei Fujii* caused an immediate uproar. The headlines from the *Chicago Daily Tribune* in the days following the court's ruling give a flavor of the negative reaction: "Rules Charter of U.N. Cancels California Law" (April 25); "Way to Cast Off U.N. Yoke Sought by California" (April 26); "U.N. Makes No Laws for America" (April 26); "Can U.N. Lay Down the Law of the Land?" (April 27).[30]

The California decision also received an extraordinary amount of attention in the nation's leading law journals, where scholars debated the finer points of treaty law and the relevance of the UN Charter to racially discriminatory state legislation.[31] The *Sei Fujii* decision was denounced in Congress. Southern senators complained that it paved the way for Congress to legislate issues that the Constitution had reserved to the states. Noted *New York Times* editorial writer Arthur Krock predicted a national crisis should the California court's reasoning be sustained. The court's "subservience to the Charter" decision was quickly undone by the California Supreme Court, which ruled that the United Nations Charter "was not intended to, and does not, supersede existing domestic legislation."[32]

Roger Traynor did not mention the UN Charter in his decision in the *Perez* case. This did not prevent opponents of American adherence to international standards of human rights from associating the United Nations Charter and the UDHR with the *Perez* decision, or discourage them from suggesting that judges, by invoking national treaties as the supreme law of the land, could effect domestic social reform against the wishes of the elected representatives of the people.

In an editorial about the *Sei Fujii* case in the ABA's monthly journal, Frank Holman referred to Jesse Carter's concurring opinion in *Perez* to remind his readers that the "precedent shattering 4 to 3 decision" of the California Supreme Court rested "in part on the United Nations charter," and warned that "many laws relating to women, to miscegenation (intermarriage of races), to citizenship or property qualifications for numerous purposes, veterans' preference laws, possibly even state laws undertaking to outlaw the Communist party" were imperiled by the UN treaty.[33] The editors of the *Chicago Daily Tribune* duly informed their readers that the laws that governed Americans would soon be drafted by foreigners.[34]

However far-fetched some interpretations of the possible impact of the *Sei Fujii* decision—Russians would buy up all of California; Africans would write the laws that governed white men's family life—the question of the relationship of the UN Charter and the Universal Declaration of Human Rights to American law was deeply divisive. When it presented its work to the world, the Human Rights Commission exhorted UN member states to "endeavor as soon as possible to bring their legislation in line with the principles" enunciated in the UDHR.[35] In January 1951, a leading scholar of international affairs defended the California court's interpretation of the charter. "It is difficult, if not impossible," wrote University of Chicago political scientist Quincy Wright, "to say that a Member is acting in cooperation with the United Nations 'for the achievement' of 'universal respect for, and observance of, human rights and fundamental freedoms'" if its courts enforced their own jurisdiction's laws that conflicted with the United Nations charter.[36]

Although not a treaty, Wright continued, the Universal Declaration of Human Rights was "of great interpretative value," constituting "an authoritative interpretation of the words 'human rights and fundamental freedoms' in Articles 55 and 56 of the Charter." It was the duty of judges to respect international human rights by refusing to apply laws that violated them, as the Ontario High Court did in 1945 when, citing the charter, it refused to enforce a restrictive residential covenant against Jews. As for state sovereignty, Wright concluded that enforcing human rights and fundamental freedoms under the UN Charter was a mere variation of the way "American courts, in applying the 14th Amendment, have done much to achieve respect for, and observance of, Constitutional guaranties within the States of the Union."[37]

By empowering judges, federal treaties threatened majoritarian rule (in this case, the rule of white supremacists). In 1952 the omnipresent Frank Holman teamed up with Ohio senator John W. Bricker to try to constrain the executive treaty-making powers of the president. The timing was not insignificant, nor was it unrelated to recent interpretations of the Fourteenth Amendment by judges like Roger Traynor.

Indeed, in the five years surrounding *Perez*, judges outside California had begun overturning racially discriminatory laws. California quietly desegregated its public schools in response to a suit brought by the League of United Latin American Citizens (LULAC).[38] Federal district court judge J. Waties Waring ruled against South Carolina's effort to preserve the white primary despite the Supreme Court's 1944 ruling outlawing it. In 1948, Waring all but dared the NAACP to mount a frontal assault on segregated education in his dissenting opinion in *Briggs v. Elliott*, a South Carolina school equity case that would eventually be bundled together with *Brown v. Board of Education*. The South Carolina General Assembly responded to this ruling by demanding that Judge Waring, a prominent native son, leave the state.[39]

Human rights principles and rhetoric were also becoming more prominent in domestic politics. In 1945, fifty bills proposing either the creation of state Fair Employment Practices Committees or the granting of antidiscrimination authority to existing agencies were introduced in twenty-one state legislatures. In 1949, the Arizona Council for Civic Unity issued a pamphlet urging repeal of that state's ban on interracial marriage and an end to school segregation.[40]

Furthermore, 1950 was not only the year of the *Sei Fujii* decision; it was also the year of the NAACP's Supreme Court trifecta. In three unanimous decisions, the court insisted that "separate but equal" be truly equal in higher education (*Sweatt v. Painter* and *McLaurin v. Oklahoma State Regents*) and in railroad dining cars (*Henderson v. United States*).[41] In language reminiscent of Roger Traynor's analysis in *Perez*, the Justice Department's amicus brief in *Henderson* called "separate but equal" a "constitutional anachronism." While segregationists were reeling from all this, the UN Educational, Scientific, and Cultural Organization (UNESCO) pushed defenders of racial hierarchy closer to the wall when it endorsed a report of eight scientists that announced that "race discrimination has no scientific foundation in biological fact," that all human races are essentially alike, and that no biological harm comes from mixed marriages.[42]

SENATOR BRICKER'S 1952 proposal was for a Constitutional amendment to severely limit the treaty-making power of the president and the Senate, which ratifies treaties.[43] The pushback was fierce. Under the terms of the Bricker Amendment, treaties would have to be passed by the House of Representatives as well as by the Senate, and ratified by two-thirds of state legislatures. This populist move was designed to insulate cherished local social institutions, such as restrictive marriage laws and segregated schools. Students of the Bricker Amendment have noted that there is good evidence that opposition to civil rights was a driving motivation in the effort to limit federal treaty-making power. Georgia senator Walter George, for example, worried that the Genocide Convention might enable passage of congressional antilynching legislation. As Frank Holman explained in Senate testimony, a treaty "can increase the power of the Federal Government at the expense of the States. For example, in the so-called field of civil rights, a treaty can do what the Congress has theretofore failed to do." In a monumental understatement, Holman added, "The Congress has to date refused to enact the civil rights program."[44] Indeed, it was increasingly clear that, given the use of executive power to desegregate the armed forces and of judicial power to limit segregation under the authority of the Fourteenth Amendment, Congress was the last, best line of defense for preserving states' rights.[45]

Once it became clear that the Bricker Amendment had some traction in Congress, the newly elected administration of President Dwight D. Eisenhower acted forcefully against it, but not before making an enormous concession. In testimony before the Senate in 1953, Secretary of State John Foster Dulles, who had helped merge Christian faith with human rights discourse during the deliberations over the UN Charter in 1945, subordinated his own beliefs in the interest of protecting the Eisenhower administration. Charged with undermining states' rights in the South, Dulles announced that the United States would not ratify any UN human rights treaties, such as the pending Genocide Convention.[46] "We do not ourselves look upon a treaty as a means which we would now select as the proper and most effective way to spread throughout the world the goals of human liberty," explained America's ambassador to the world. In an oblique reference to the NAACP's strategy of exposing America's racial regime through petitions to the UN, and in an effort to distance Eisenhower from human rights–driven agendas at home, Dulles announced that the administration would welcome "a reversal of the trend toward trying to use the treaty-making power to effect internal social changes."[47]

This accommodation by Dulles reflected the interpretational power of those who considered both the *Perez* ruling and the UN commitment to freedom of marriage direct threats to Jim Crow. In this early Cold War moment, supporters of racial hierarchy cast the debate over evolving national and international standards of constitutional and human rights as one of imperiled state sovereignty in the South.

Neither the *Perez* decision nor the Universal Declaration of Human Rights nor the UN Charter had a demonstrable effect on race-based prohibitions on marriage or other forms of segregation and discrimination in the United States outside California. Yet by 1950, as we have seen, there was a growing constitutional argument in the United States as well as an articulated international vision of human rights that treated the complete dismantling of racially discriminatory regimes, including antimiscegenation laws, as normative. The increased visibility of these arguments, and the willingness of certain courts to entertain them, was cause for optimism. Even Thurgood Marshall declared in 1950, "The complete destruction of all enforced segregation is in sight."[48]

By 1953, however, neither the constitutional notion that marriage is a fundamental right nor the argument that international human rights norms should trump discriminatory local practices had inspired the domestic political will necessary to support those rights in American law. Instead, they ignited strenuous resistance that was aimed at African American civil rights exponents and at the judiciary, the branch of government least susceptible (ideally) to political pressure.

In the years to come, as the battle for civil rights became just that, the billboards erected alongside Southern highways reflected the extent to which the constitutional and international arguments for human rights merged in the minds of Dixie's defenders. This was especially apparent in 1954, after the Supreme Court overturned segregated public education in *Brown v. Board of Education*. Directed at the chief justice who wrote the opinion, former California governor Earl Warren, the slogans "Impeach Earl Warren" and "Get the U.S. Out of the U.N." were tied together both logically and pragmatically. America's rejection of international human rights norms and treaties was rooted directly in the civil rights struggle at home.

Twelve

GRAPPLING WITH *BROWN*

T HERE IS A REASON the Supreme Court does not reconvene after its summer holiday until the first Monday in October: September in Washington, DC. The morning of September 11, 1953, was unusually cool, however, and Solicitor General Philip Elman hardly sweated as he made his way to Union Station to pick up his old boss, Supreme Court Justice Felix Frankfurter. Three days earlier the chief justice of the Supreme Court, Frederick M. Vinson, who opposed ruling segregated education unconstitutional in the school cases then pending before the court, had died unexpectedly of a heart attack at the age of sixty-three. Frankfurter was coming from his summer home in Massachusetts to attend the funeral mass at Washington Cathedral. As he stepped off the train from Boston, Frankfurter's thoughts focused, appropriately, on death and the divine. As he explained to Elman on the way to the chief justice's funeral, "This is the first solid piece of evidence I've ever had that there really is a God."[1]

Frankfurter's irreverent quip reflected the strained relations among the justices of the Supreme Court, nine men whose arguments over basic questions of jurisprudence had become so toxic that they could barely shake hands. Fractured along personal and political lines, the court had not ruled on a racial discrimination case since 1950. It was divided between those who considered segregation "Hitler's creed," in the words of Justice Robert Jackson, who had prosecuted leading Nazis at the Nuremberg trials after World War II, and those, like Vinson, who were unprepared to impose a social revolution on the South. All the justices were aware of the pitfalls of tackling *Plessy v. Ferguson*; none cared to be blamed for what one white Southerner referred to as "race suicide by judicial interpretation."[2] When five separate NAACP-sponsored school-desegregation cases from four states and the District of Columbia came before the court in December 1952, the justices stalled and ordered the cases to be reargued in October 1953.[3]

Divinely ordained or not, Vinson's sudden death created an opportunity for President Dwight D. Eisenhower to change the tenor of the court. California governor Earl Warren appeared to be just the man for the job. Then serving an unprecedented third term as the Republican governor of the nation's second-largest and most racially heterogeneous state, Warren was a master politician who could be expected to create consensus among the peacocks on the court. In addition, Warren had been Thomas Dewey's vice presidential running mate in 1948 and might have threatened Eisenhower's second-term presidential ambitions. Although the president was personally conflicted about the wisdom of school desegregation and came down decisively on the side of enforcing the law only in 1957, when he was backed into a corner by events in Little Rock, Arkansas, he was surely aware that in 1953 California had, in response to a lawsuit brought by the League of United Latin American Citizens (LULAC), desegregated its public schools.[4]

Patient, genial, and aware of the depth of white Southerners' commitment to racial segregation in public life, the new chief justice worked assiduously to find the judicial common ground in which to root an opinion on segregated schools. This was no simple task. Recognizing the overlapping aims of Jim Crow's underlying arguments—white superiority and white supremacy—Warren believed that the Jim Crow "separate but equal" standard was based "on the premise that the Negro race is inferior" and designed to relegate African Americans to a permanent status of second-class citizenship.[5]

This understanding of segregation was denied explicitly in *Plessy v. Ferguson* (1896), however. As Justice Henry Billings Brown put it in the majority opinion in that case, "We consider the underlying fallacy of the plaintiff's argument to consist in the assumption that the enforced separation of the two races stamps the colored race with a badge of inferiority. If this be so, it is not by reason of anything found in the act, but solely because the colored race chooses to put that construction upon it." Although he rejected *Plessy's* "it's all in their heads" interpretation of Black critiques of racial segregation, Warren was respectful of the doubts of several of his fellow justices about overturning this long-standing precedent.[6]

To ease worries that the court's decision in *Brown v. Board of Education* could be interpreted as applying to segregation across the board, Warren limited the *Brown* decision scrupulously to segregated public education alone. The opinion, written by Warren and delivered by him on behalf of a unanimous court on May 17, 1954, was short and to the point. The heart of the opinion was the court's declaration that "in the field of public education the doctrine of 'separate but equal' has no place. Separate educational facilities are inherently unequal. Therefore, we hold that the plaintiffs…are, by reason of the segregation complained of, deprived of the equal protection of the laws guaranteed by the Fourteenth Amendment."[7]

Because the Fourteenth Amendment applies to the states but not to the District of Columbia, public school segregation there was invalidated in a companion case, *Bolling v. Sharpe*, via the Fifth Amendment's due process clause. In both cases, Warren deferred the crucial question of implementation, leaving others to decide later what states with dual school systems and the District of Columbia would have to do to comply with the Constitution. A vague implementation decision a year later, known as *Brown II*, directed local authorities to move with "all deliberate speed" toward the goal of desegregated public schools.[8]

The *Brown* decision has become so iconic that it can be difficult to recognize the jurisprudential strength of segregation's defenders in 1954. By any reckoning, precedent was on the side of the South. Of the forty-four challenges to school segregation mounted between 1865 and 1935, none succeeded. In the early 1950s, twenty-one states and the District of Columbia had mandatory or optional segregated school systems.[9] An "original intent" argument about the framers of the Fourteenth Amendment was unlikely to come out on the side of integration, as the Supreme Court discovered after commissioning such a study in 1953.[10]

It could not be said that the authors of the Fourteenth Amendment had considered racial segregation incompatible with equality. The same members of Congress who wrote and ratified the Fourteenth Amendment in 1868 mandated segregated schools for the District of Columbia, and many of the states that ratified the amendment, including those whose ratification was a requirement for readmission to the Union, operated dual school systems. Even the late nineteenth-century leaders of Southern interracial political movements, white and Black men who championed public education as well as African American suffrage and office-holding, fought to keep public schools segregated in order to protect the quest for state-supported education from charges of miscegenation.[11]

On the other hand, as the court noted in its decision in *Brown*, "'separate but equal' did not make its appearance in this court until 1896"—twenty-eight years after passage of the Fourteenth Amendment. Furthermore, the court had begun chipping away at the notion of separate but equal within two decades of *Plessy*, beginning in 1914 with *McCabe v. Atchison, Topeka and Santa Fe Railway*, which upheld the argument that railroad companies that provided first-class cars for whites had to do the same for Blacks. In 1917, in *Buchanan v. Warley*, the court rejected the residential checkerboard law, which segregated neighborhoods block by block, as an unconstitutional limit on individual property rights.[12]

Responding to the NAACP's transition from trains to schools, in 1938 the court, drawing on *McCabe*, ruled that a law that forced Black, but not white, residents of Missouri to leave the state to obtain a legal education was a denial of equal protection of the law.[13] Between 1938 and 1948, the court did not decide any Fourteenth Amendment "separate but equal" cases, but it did hold the white primary unconstitutional, invalidate racial discrimination in jury selection, rule that Congress could constitutionally forbid racial segregation in interstate transportation facilities, declare racially restrictive residential covenants unconstitutional, and decide that Oklahoma had violated the equal protection clause when it excluded a Black student from the University of Oklahoma law school.[14]

Building on these precedents, in 1950 the court ruled in *Sweatt v. Painter* that a "separate but equal" law school established for Black Texans was inherently inferior to the University of Texas Law School. *McLaurin v. Oklahoma State Regents*, decided on the same day as *Sweatt*, concluded that forcing a Black student to sit apart at his own table in the cafeteria did not meet the *Plessy* "separate but equal" standard. After *Sweatt*, constitutional scholar David A. Strauss has remarked, "a state could not satisfy separate but equal by establishing a new all-black graduate school, because any such school, however equal tangibly, could not possibly match the intangible assets that the white school had. After *McLaurin*, a state could not segregate African-Americans within the established white school. What was left?" By 1950, it seemed, *Plessy* was pinned down if not yet sent away: in the view of the *New Republic*, segregation was "in handcuffs."[15]

Several of the justices who voted in favor of *Sweatt* and *McLaurin* did not see things this way in 1954. Justice Robert Jackson, who favored desegregation as a matter of moral principle, fretted that he could not argue "that the Constitution this morning forbids what for three-quarters of a century it has tolerated or approved." Precedent, meaning state, federal, and Supreme Court decisions "rendered by judges, many of whom risked their lives for the cause that produced" the Reconstruction amendments, "is almost unanimous in the view that the [Fourteenth] Amendment tolerated segregation by [government] action."[16]

People who supported other rights for African Americans still balked at integrated schools. Philip Perlman, who as solicitor general had signed off on government briefs opposing the constitutionality of restrictive housing covenants and of laws requiring segregation in railroad dining cars and higher education, hesitated to support school desegregation in the years leading up to *Brown*. According to Philip Elman, then one of Perlman's lawyers in the solicitor general's office, Perlman shrank from supporting school desegregation because "you can't have little black boys sitting next to little white girls....The country isn't ready for that. This would lead to 'miscegenation and mongrelization of the races.'"[17]

Justice Felix Frankfurter, who had been associated with the NAACP for his entire legal career, also believed that judicial precedent was firmly on the side of school segregation. Justice Stanley Reed, a Kentuckian who insisted that he did not consider African Americans an inferior race, nonetheless argued that segregation served a vital purpose: it "protects people against [the] mixing of races." Despite this belief, Reed joined the other eight justices in June 1953, when they upheld a Washington, DC, law that prohibited racially segregated restaurants in the District. Like so many other white Southerners, though, Reed approached this attack on segregation in terms of its probable effects on white women. "This means," fretted Reed, who lived with his wife at the Mayflower Hotel, "that a nigra can walk into the restaurant at the Mayflower and sit down to eat at the table right next to Mrs. Reed."[18]

White anxiety about racial mixing and the erosion of white supremacy was also basic to the ideological structure of Southern society. The argument that segregation protected "racial integrity" remained a common rationale for Jim Crow, and courts across the country upheld segregation laws based on the idea that the state had a public interest in protecting "racial purity."[19]

The court in *Plessy* had held that a state law requiring "separate but equal" railway cars for Blacks and whites did not violate the equal protection clause because separate was not unequal, and because the policy was therefore constitutional because it rationally furthered a state interest. Under the *Plessy* standard, the preservation of "racial purity" was a legitimate state interest. There were at least two ways to attack this reasoning. One was to argue that the preservation of "racial purity" was not a legitimate state interest—which was the tack Roger Traynor took in *Perez v. Sharp* in 1948. Another was the NAACP's position, which was that separate *was* unequal, and that decisions like *Strauder* and *Sweatt* therefore governed.

A central question in 1954 was thus whether *Plessy* was right in denying that separate was unequal. The NAACP challenged this argument, and it was an important strategic move. Rather than disputing the assertion that preserving "racial purity" was a legitimate state interest, the NAACP lawyers maintained that separate was inherently unequal and therefore unconstitutional under the equal protection clause.

Were separate public schools unequal? Was the education that African American children received in segregated Black schools equal to the education whites received in white schools? Did the fact of segregation itself render segregated schools unequal?

The court in *Plessy* had maintained that "the underlying fallacy" of the plaintiffs' challenge to racially segregated railway cars rested "in the assumption that to enforce separation of the two races stamps the colored race with a badge of inferiority." In *Brown*, noting the importance of education in American life and its vital role in molding citizens, the court insisted that "to separate" Black children "from others...solely because of their race generates a feeling of inferiority as to their status in the community that may affect their hearts and minds in a way unlikely ever to be undone.... Whatever may have been the extent of psychological knowledge at the time of *Plessy*, this finding is amply supported by modern authority. Any language in *Plessy* contrary to this finding is rejected."

This was the core of the difference between *Plessy* and *Brown*: the understanding that racial segregation, at least in the realm of education, was not innocuous but harmful, and that the reason for imposing it was not neutral but discriminatory. As the court announced in *Brown*, "in the field of public education, the doctrine of 'separate but equal' has no place. Separate educational facilities are inherently unequal." Side-stepping the implementation question, the chief justice explained that the court would consult with Southern state attorneys general about compliance. These consultations informed the court's vague implementation decision a year later in *Brown II*, which directed local authorities to move with "all deliberate speed" toward the goal of desegregated public schools. The tokenism and foot-dragging achieved via "minimum compliance" with the court's implementation decree in *Brown II* succeeded in delaying school desegregation for years.[20]

WHAT WAS SO combustive about public school desegregation? In many ways an extension of the family, public schools are an agency of the state and as such occupy an intermediate space between public and private. Try as they might, parents can influence but not control the education, or the experiences, of their children in the public schools. Public schools are the place where social values are both reinforced and transformed. In this space, it is hoped—or dreaded—that old social hierarchies based on race or class or gender or language or religion or national origins will be erased, and new generations of children will take what they learn at school home with them and create a new social reality.

The very arguments that the NAACP and the Supreme Court found so persuasive—that the public school, "even more than the family, the church, business institutions, political and social groups and other institutions, has become an effective agency for giving to all people that broad background of attitudes and skills required to enable them to function effectively as participants in a democracy"— suggested that school desegregation would, as white Southerners feared and predicted, change everything.[21] White supremacists rightly saw desegregated schools as a direct challenge to belief in racial hierarchy and white superiority and to the culture of white supremacy. Many connected these strands and predicted that school desegregation was a prelude to finding antimiscegenation laws unconstitutional.

The Supreme Court may have moved the question of civil rights to the center of American politics with the desegregation cases, but it did not define the ideological boundaries within which the fight over civil rights would occur. Just as the NAACP had done in the long run-up to *Brown*, everyone connected with the "Segregation Cases," as they were known in the court, went to great trouble to avoid the impression that school desegregation was connected in any way with sex and marriage. Although the court quickly extended *Brown* to apply not only to segregated schools but also to segregated golf courses, public buses, and beaches, when presented with the opportunity in 1954 and 1955 to rule on the constitutionality of racially restrictive marriage, adultery, and fornication laws from Virginia and Alabama, the justices who backed *Brown* refused to do so.

In November 1954, the court failed to grant certiorari (petition for review) to a case testing Alabama's antimiscegenation law.[22] The next year, the Department of Justice declined to support a challenge to Virginia's law upholding "racial integrity," and the Supreme Court embarrassed itself by ducking the case.[23] ("That's what you get when you turn your ass to the grandstand," remarked a rueful Earl Warren, who supported taking on the miscegenation issue.) With *Brown II* pending and compliance in doubt, a majority of the court feared provoking the white South further. As Justice Harlan put it to his law clerk, "One bombshell at a time is enough."[24]

Challenged by Federal Judge Learned Hand, one of the most respected legal authorities in America, Felix Frankfurter explained to his old friend that "the miscegenation issue is not immediately here, but vividly in the offing. We [have] twice shunted it away and I pray we may be able to do it again, without being too brazenly evasive."[25]

Hand was unconvinced. "I cannot see how we can possibly say that it does not deny 'equal protection' to Negroes to forbid their marriage with Whites....If I could see any honest way of escaping the conclusion that the taboo on race discrimination [in the Fourteenth Amendment] was an 'absolute,' I should seize upon it. I do not see any and the 'Segregation' case has closed it, if there was one I do not see."[26]

To Frankfurter's increasingly contrived explanations of the inapplicability of *Brown* to miscegenation, and his pronouncement that "I will work, within the limits of judicial decency, to put off [a] decision on miscegenation as long as I can," Hand replied laconically, "As to miscegenation, I don't see how you lads can duck it."[27]

Brown disappointed those who hoped the justices would tackle *Plessy* directly and identify the maintenance of white supremacy as the core rationale for school segregation and thus find it constitutionally illegitimate on that ground. Enthusiasm and anxiety about the extent of *Brown*'s reach were voiced in different registers of society simultaneously: in terms of "dignity," which Benjamin Mays reached for in his response; in legal logic (did *Brown* declare all segregation in public places unconstitutional? If not, why the unembroidered per curiam decisions?); in religious arguments of the sort seen in *Berea* and *Buchanan* (did God change His mind about the evils of racial amalgamation on May 17, 1954? Had the Divine Writ that helped justify Jim Crow society been overturned along with school segregation?); and in personal encounters that revealed the inability of white Southerners to gauge the resistance of African Americans to Jim Crow. The interpretational system of white supremacy was breaking down, and what anthropologists refer to as the "hidden transcript" of African American resistance was becoming visible to whites, a great many of whom received that knowledge with disbelief, as William Couch had when he published

What the Negro Wants.[28] After the *Brown* decision, white Southerners angry about the "betrayal" of the Supreme Court reacted more decisively to Black behavior that challenged racial norms, as fourteen-year-old Emmett Till discovered tragically.

MAMIE TILL KNEW him by his ring—the signet ring that his father, Louis Till, her ex-husband, had bought in Casablanca in 1943, and which the US Army had sent home in lieu of Louis's body in July 1945. She had given her son the ring the day before he boarded the City of New Orleans train in Chicago on August 20, 1955, on his way to visit family in the Mississippi Delta.

In giving Emmett his father's ring, Mamie had hoped to forge a bond of memory between the living and the dead. Now, the ring had become a talisman gone wrong, a symbol of what happens to Black men accused of interacting too closely with white women. The defense attorneys for the men who murdered her boy would claim that the body was too decomposed to be identified, but she could tell by the ring that it was Emmett. As if Mamie could not recognize her baby, even though half his face had been shot away and his body submerged for three days in the pink silt of the Tallahatchie River.[29]

When Emmett Till, who had been born and raised in Chicago, entered the Mississippi Delta that summer, he crossed more than state lines. The Delta, as described by native son Willie Morris, dominated a singular state, a place "eternally wild,…savagely unpredictable,…fraught with contradictory deceits and nobilities"; a place cloven by "the gulf between its manners and morals" and marked by "the extraordinary apposition of its violence and kindliness."[30] Mississippi in the best of times was a place of extremes: extreme heat, extreme poverty, extreme beauty; a downtrodden state familiar to the world through Nobel laureate William Faulkner's fictionalized depictions of it. Relaxed, Mississippi was the gracious hostess, seeing to every need. Mississippi under pressure was like Bill Faulkner drunk: incoherent, suspicious, volatile.

In June 1954, a month after the Supreme Court declared segregated public education unconstitutional in *Brown*, a group of Delta businessmen came together to form a new organization, the White Citizens' Council (WCC). Founded by Robert Patterson, a thirty-two-year-old plantation manager, and composed of the local white elite, by October the WCC claimed twenty-five thousand members in Mississippi and outposts in neighboring states.[31]

Between June 1954 and May 1955, when the Supreme Court issued *Brown II*, the WCC concerned itself chiefly with building its organizational base and harassing local African Americans. These pillars of the white community did nothing violent or ugly—nothing that would strain their consciences on Sunday. They simply used the weapons at hand, which, since many of them were bankers and businessmen, included economic intimidation. When he came to the attention of the WCC, for example, NAACP leader Amzie Moore, a WWII veteran and one of the most influential Black men in Mississippi, suddenly found the mortgages on his house and service station called by the bank that held them.[32]

While the WCC coalesced, the Mississippi legislature took a variety of official actions in response to *Brown*. In a deliberate effort to tie up the NAACP in court, Mississippi and other states abolished mandatory school-attendance laws.[33] The Mississippi State Sovereignty Commission, a secret police force designed to "prevent encroachment upon the rights of this and other states by the Federal Government," augmented individual acts of intimidation. Reviving tactics used against Black voter-registration drives in the late 1940s, many of Dixie's defenders turned to violence to protect their privileged way of life. The summer of 1955 was a veritable white reign of terror in Mississippi. Between May and August, three Black political leaders were gunned down in the Delta. Two, the Reverend George Lee, an NAACP activist, and Lamar Smith, a farmer and WWII veteran active in voter-registration efforts, were killed. A third, Gus Courts, a grocer and NAACP member, recovered from his wounds and fled the state.

Emmett Till was neither an NAACP activist nor a local political leader. He was a teenage boy from Chicago who was used to the everyday brutalities of segregation and white racism but unfamiliar with the elaborate social rules of Jim Crow Mississippi.[34] His mother tried to instruct him before he left for the Delta—always say "yes, Sir" and "no, Ma'am" to whites; hold the door for white men and women alike; step aside for whites on the sidewalk; don't talk back, don't get fresh; and never look a white woman in the eye—but no crash course in white-supremacist manners was adequate for the extraordinarily tense atmosphere in the post-*Brown* Deep South. It is also true that Emmett was not the most retiring of adolescent boys. A beloved only child used to having his way and talking himself out of tight spots, Emmett was temperamentally unsuited for the Deep South in the best of times. August 1955 was not, by anyone's measure, the best of times in Mississippi. There were men in the state that summer who were prepared to kill children to uphold Jim Crow.

In a remarkable postacquittal interview with white Southern journalist William Bradford Huie published in *Look* magazine, Emmett Till's murderers offered two reasons for his death: first, Emmett offended twenty-two-year-old Carolyn Bryant, who was minding the counter of a family grocery store in Money, Mississippi, when Till entered and supposedly propositioned her, or whistled, or was otherwise overly familiar (accounts varied); and second, Emmett was allegedly boastful and unrepentant even after Carolyn's young husband, Roy Bryant, and his older half brother J. W. Milam had pistol-whipped him half to death.[35]

Despite the testimony of Till's uncle Moses Wright, who verified the body and courageously identified Milam and Bryant as the men who came to his home in the middle of the night, demanded his nephew, and took him away, the all-white, all-male jury assembled in tiny Sumner, Mississippi, accepted the claim of the local sheriff that the killing was an NAACP plot and responded enthusiastically to the defense lawyer's challenge to "summon their Anglo-Saxon courage" and acquit the defendants.[36] In addition to the broader denial of justice, the jury's action was a public relations nightmare for Mississippi, whose political establishment had tried to protect their state's reputation by providing a fair trial. In addition to Mamie Till and Michigan representative Charles Diggs, who acted as a sort of African American congressman-at-large, nearly a hundred newspaper reporters, thirty photographers, and television and radio crew members crowded into the courtroom to report the Till trial worldwide. Radio journalists raced to telephones with stories to broadcast live.[37]

NAACP executive secretary Roy Wilkins depicted Mississippi in the summer of 1955 as "at war with the United States."[38] White Mississippians saw things in reverse. As far as they were concerned, the school desegregation decisions were an assault on their society by a national government clearly at war with them. At another time, it is unlikely that Emmett Till would have been killed for any perceived breach of racial etiquette. There had been no lynchings in Mississippi since 1951.[39] But in the turbulent months following *Brown I* and *II*, the impetuous actions of a fourteen-year-old-boy could be interpreted as challenging the entire Jim Crow system. Emmett Till was caught between two worlds that summer: between Southside Chicago, a racially divided realm that nonetheless offered its youth some independence, and rural Mississippi, where self-assertion could result in a death sentence. He also straddled the line between the old world of legal segregation and the emerging, and violently resisted, world of desegregation and potential racial equality.

It is not coincidental that Till's "crime" was being fresh to a white woman.[40] In the context of the *Brown* decision and the rise of the White Citizens' Council, even the rumor of a single whistle or "ugly remark" aimed at a white woman by a Black male of any age was liable to be seen by Delta whites as an assault on the broader "Southern way of life." Even before *Brown*, with African American veterans asserting the right to vote, and potentially other rights, white blood ran hot. In 1951, Mack Ingram, a Black North Carolina sharecropper, was sentenced to two years hard labor for the "eye rape" of his landlord's daughter, whom Ingram had seen at a distance on a path leading to his landlord's home.[41]

Nor is it coincidental that Till's killers portrayed themselves as compelled to act in the defense of white womanhood and white supremacy. As defendant J. W. Milam explained to *Look* magazine's Huie, Emmett sealed his fate by asserting his own equality via sexual access to white women and to whiteness itself through a purported white grandmother (who, presumably, had engaged in miscegenation). Recalling for Huie his "interrogation" of Till in a toolhouse, the sentence Milam attributed to Till contains within it everything white Southerners had dreaded since WWII: "You bastards, I'm not afraid of you. I'm as good as you are. I've 'had' white women. My grandmother was a white woman."[42]

In Milam's view, these words justified Emmett's death: "Well, what else could we do? He was hopeless," Milam explained. "I'm no bully; I never hurt a nigger in my life.… But I just decided it was time a few people got put on notice. As long as I live and can do anything about it, niggers are gonna stay in their place." Making the traditional link between the vote, education, and sexual rights, Milam continued, "Niggers ain't gonna vote where I live.… They ain't gonna go to school with my kids. And when a nigger gets close to mentioning sex with a white woman, he's tired o' livin'.… Me and my folks fought for this country," the WWII veteran concluded, "and we got some rights." Among those rights was counted a proprietary right to white women, a right Milam performed dramatically when, upon his acquittal, he kissed his wife Juanita in a prolonged fashion more suitable for the bedroom than for a courtroom.[43]

The regulation of Black sexuality—both the denial of Black men's access to white women and the unrestricted access of white men to Black women—had been counted among the traditional rights of white men and their "folks" since slave times. It is emblematic of the shift in American race relations that occurred between 1945 and 1955 that this "right," while asserted, did not go unchallenged that summer in Mississippi. Mamie Till was determined to impart meaning to Emmett's death. Insisting that her son's body be sent by train to Chicago rather than buried in Mississippi, Mamie staged an open-casket funeral attended by fifty thousand grim-faced Black Chicagoans.[44]

In September 1955, *Jet*, a leading African American magazine published in Chicago, brought Southern violence before the eyes of the world when it published sickening photographs of Till's mutilated corpse. William Faulkner, then in Rome, was shocked and apocalyptic: "If we in America have reached that point in our desperate culture when we must murder children, no matter for what reason or what color, we don't deserve to survive, and probably won't."[45]

Emmett Till's murder, which was grounded in miscegenation anxiety and clashes over white power and dominance, was politically galvanizing for white supremacists like Bryant and Milam and their supporters, and also for civil rights activists such as Amzie Moore, who identified the death of the boy from Chicago as a turning point. "Personally," Moore recalled years later, "I think this was the beginning of the Civil Rights Movement in Mississippi in the twentieth century.... From that point on, Mississippi began to move."[46]

White Citizens' Council founder Robert Patterson agreed and extrapolated the argument across the region. "I think it all started probably with a case of a young Negro boy named Emmett Till getting killed in Mississippi for offending some white woman.... That made every newspaper on the face of the earth." Referring to the civil rights movement, Patterson concluded, "Following that there were other incidents that happened in the South," and "whenever something happened to a Negro in the South, it was made a national issue against the South."[47]

Whatever their disagreements, and they were legion, Moore and Patterson agreed that a lynching that was justified as preserving the taboo against interracial sex and intimacy, and as protecting white men's purported "right" to exclusive sexual access to white women, triggered the modern civil rights movement in the Deep South. In other words, it is impossible to understand neither the timing of the movement there nor its impetus without recognizing the power of white anxiety about interracial sex, the political work accomplished by arguments articulated in terms of sexual threats to white supremacy, and the reaction of Blacks North and South to the murder and its rationale.

Thirteen

BREACHING THE INNER SHRINE

DESEGREGATION INITIALLY proceeded largely without incident in the North and the West, although the number of nonwhite children to enter previously all-white schools remained minuscule until the mid-1960s. The Upper South (Delaware, Maryland, West Virginia, Tennessee, and Arkansas) followed a similar trajectory, particularly in cities. Most of west Texas desegregated peacefully after 1955, as did North Carolina and southern Missouri. In October 1955, NAACP executive secretary Roy Wilkins reported that "approximately 100 communities in Oklahoma, including all major cities, have desegregated their school systems." There had been no violence and no friction, and "apparently no one is worried to death about his bloodstream."[1]

This was not the case in the Deep South. The prediction of NAACP lawyer Thurgood Marshall, who argued the school desegregation cases before the Supreme Court, that the South now had "to yield to the Constitution" was belied by events there. Southern politicians and journalists denounced what they called the "activism" of the Supreme Court. Mississippi senator James Eastland, who chaired the Senate Judiciary Committee's subcommittee on civil rights, warned in 1954 that the South would not "abide by or obey this legislative decision by a political court." Many raised the miscegenation worry—such as Alabama state senator Walter Givhan, who thundered that the true goal of the NAACP in bringing the desegregation cases was "to open the bedroom doors of our white women to Negro men."[2]

Despite the precautions of the NAACP and the court, *Brown* was interpreted by a large and vocal segment of white Southerners in explicitly sexual terms. "The first reaction to the Supreme Court's decision was almost psychotic," former FEPC director Mark Ethridge and current editor of the *Louisville Courier Journal*, recalled. To give but one example, the *Jackson Daily News* (Mississippi) denounced the school decision as "the first step, or an opening wedge, toward mixed marriages, miscegenation, and the mongrelization of the human race."[3] Those inclined to suspect African American men of coveting white women had not forgotten the 1949 marriage of NAACP leader Walter White to Poppy Cannon, a white journalist from South Africa. White had been harshly criticized at the time for reinforcing white-supremacist beliefs that the NAACP and other groups were determined to erase all racial barriers. As one columnist complained, "It will take us another 50 years to convince the white man that this is not true when our leader has so betrayed us."[4]

Interpretations of *Brown* that linked the decision to sex were not limited to the Deep South. The NAACP's Roy Wilkins complained that Virginia "is pronouncing in rounded phrases what Mississippi says in whoops and hollers." In the Old Dominion, "we have the Defenders of State Sovereignty and Individual Liberties knocking down once more that battered old straw man, intermarriage." Southern resistance to school integration, FBI director J. Edgar Hoover explained matter-of-factly to President Eisenhower, was rooted in fears of "mongrelization," which was, everyone knew, a key element of the communist plot to destroy America.[5]

Bags of letters sent to Southern governors struck the same theme. In a letter to Georgia governor Herman E. Talmadge, who had declared that "God himself segregated the races" and continued to assert that "segregation is not inconsistent with Christianity,"William A. Robinson Jr. worried about the future. Making precisely the connection between integrated schools and interracial marriage that Felix Frankfurter had energetically denied, Robinson mused, "Of course, we may abolish the public schools, but when the NAACP procures from an obliging Court, as seems quite likely in the near future, a ruling adverse to our marriage restrictions, we cannot meet that issue by abolishing marriage."[6]

While white Southern opponents of *Brown* were making dire predictions of communist triumph and syphilis in the schools, Southern moderates and reformers leapt to take the moral high ground. With Southern newspapers and politicians almost unanimously opposed to the Supreme Court decision, *Brown*'s supporters turned to the white churches. The relative silence of white ministers on the race issue through 1954 may have encouraged moderates to try to co-opt the church. Mississippi's Hodding Carter, who won the Pulitzer Prize in Editorial Writing in 1946 for a series of antilynching columns, made a claim for religious authority and a link between Christianity and democracy when he wrote in the *Delta Democrat-Times* that "the Court could not have made a different decision in the light of democratic and Christian principles and against the background of today." A group of thirty-seven college students and counselors attending the Southeastern Regional Methodist Student Conference in Virginia made the same rhetorical move in a letter to Governor Thomas Stanley. The *Brown* decision, the students explained, was "in keeping with the spirit of democracy and Christianity and should not be side-stepped in any way."[7]

Black Southerners also tried to tie *Brown* to Christian ideals. The National Baptist Convention, the leading forum of Black Baptists, announced that on May 17, 1954, "the Social Gospel of Jesus received its endorsement by the Highest Court of the nation." Other African Americans reacted less reverently. Boxer Joe Louis, who had wandered into the office of *Ebony* magazine as editors there received news of

Brown, smiled broadly and said, thinking of the race-baiting governor of Georgia, "Tell me, did Herman Talmadge drop dead?"[8]

Civil rights supporters understood immediately the importance of having God—and his spokesmen—on their side. "If the ministers speak out bravely, quietly, persuasively they can give direction to the feelings of millions of white southerners who don't know what to do or where to turn," wrote liberal author Lillian Smith from her home in Georgia.[9] Although Smith was hardly representative of either Southern Protestantism or white Southern thought more generally, her hopes were not entirely unfounded. There is evidence that white Christian consciences were strained by many aspects of segregation.

CERTAINLY, MANY SOUTHERN religious leaders, especially those connected with seminaries or foreign mission work, had questioned segregation long before 1954. Just two weeks after the Supreme Court decided *Brown*, the ten thousand messengers of the Southern Baptist Convention (SBC) endorsed the decision, proclaiming it "in harmony with the constitutional guarantee of equal freedom to all citizens, and with the Christian principles of equal justice and love for all men." The Catholics, Methodists, and Presbyterians agreed with the SBC. The Southern Presbyterian General Assembly accompanied its support for school integration with the assurance that interracial marriage would not follow.[10]

The proclamations of the national church organizations were useful to supporters of Black civil rights. As one Virginia minister lectured his governor, in trying to circumvent *Brown* Virginia was ignoring "the expressed wishes of the four, largest religious bodies in our State." But these organizations, especially the SBC's progressive Christian Life Commission, which authored the denomination's official response to *Brown*, were not necessarily representative of the masses of white Christian Protestants or of the clergy. For every Protestant minister who declared that *Brown* "showed the hand of God in it," there were others who saw the diabolical machinations of the Kremlin instead, and who denounced "pinkos in the pulpit" for their support of integration.[11]

To be sure, some Baptist ministers defied the SBC's guidance that local churches should accept *Brown*. Douglas Hudgins, pastor of Jackson, Mississippi's, powerful First Baptist Church, led a congregation studded with state leaders and almost never preached on contemporary events. But now he took the opportunity to remind his flock of the congregational autonomy at the heart of Baptist associational life. Decisions taken by the Southern Baptist Convention had no binding authority on local churches, he insisted. Furthermore, Hudgins explained, the Supreme Court decision was "a purely civic matter" and thus an inappropriate topic for the Christian Life Commission in the first place. In this, Hudgins echoed SBC president J. W. Storer, who endorsed the *Brown* decision on civic rather than theological grounds. Repudiating the religious arguments of his organization's Christian Life Commission, Storer argued that Baptists should obey the Supreme Court decision because "we 'Render to Caesar the things that are Caesar's, and to God the things that are God's.'"[12]

Public schools belonged to Caesar. Racial purity belonged to God. In *Brown*'s wake, many white Southern Christian leaders tried to find a way to obey both the law of man and that of God, and at the same time to chart a middle course between massive resistance and capitulation to the theology of the emerging civil rights movement. Worried about the sexual and theological implications of *Brown* and anxious about schism, in 1956 the Episcopal church's National Council backtracked on its belief, expressed just a year earlier, that desegregation was "the will of God."

Replacing this explicitly theological justification for desegregation with a secular/civic concern for justice, the Episcopalians substituted "free access to institutions" for the goal of "integration"—a loaded term that suggested intermarriage, from which "the majority of church leaders still shrank." In 1957 an interdenominational group of Atlanta clergymen published a statement that disavowed support for racial amalgamation but declared that "as Americans and Christians we have an obligation to obey the law." The *Alabama Baptist's* Leon Macon went further, arguing, "When we violate a law we hurt man and grieve God." Liberal clergymen in Little Rock during the school integration crisis there in September 1957 took the same tack, insisting that good Christians could disagree about segregation but not about upholding the law.[13]

But what were good Christians to do when the law of the land contradicted God's holy word? *Brown* raised practical moral and theological issues for many Southern white Christians. While liberal Presbyterians worried that "the courts have shown more sympathy toward the Negro than has the church" and admonished the church to "strive to keep apace of its Master or become bereft of his spirit," segregationist Christians suspected that the state was following not the Master but his principal challenger. Like the Reverend James F. Burks of Bayview Baptist Church in Norfolk, Virginia, who argued that "modern-day Christianity has substituted a social Gospel for the Blood-purchased Gospel of Christ," many white Southerners considered the *Brown* decision at direct odds with God's moral codes.[14]

White Southerners had a rich arsenal of arguments against desegregation, and they deployed them against different targets. Even when white supremacists accused civil rights organizations of fostering dreams of miscegenation, they did not necessarily turn to religious arguments to back up their claims. Segregationists did not make religious arguments against Black suffrage, for example, or against integration of the armed forces. For all they loathed the FEPC, Southern white conservatives did not hurl scripture against it. White supremacists made religious arguments in very specific instances, under specific circumstances, at specific moments. One of those moments was immediately following the announcement of the *Brown* decision, which sharpened dramatically the theological debate among Southern Christians.

In the midcentury South, religion became the vessel for one particular language crucial to upholding racial segregation: the language of miscegenation. It was through sex that racial segregation in the South moved from being a local social practice to a part of the divine plan for the world. It was thus through sex that segregation assumed, for Christian defenders of racial hierarchy and separation, cosmological significance.

IN THEIR RESPONSE to the challenges of progressive believers in 1954, Christian segregationists entered an argument as old as the church itself: in what ways could and should the world of the flesh be made like the world of the spirit? Taking the tack that normative Christians have taken since the second century, anti-integrationists pitted the pastoral Apostle Paul, who provided guidelines for the day-to-day administration of Christian communities, against the eschatological Apostle Paul, who proclaimed the impending end of time and the irrelevance of life in the flesh. There are distinctions on earth (different languages, races, sexes), segregationists argued; these distinctions are created by God. And although humans can all become one in spirit through conversion to Jesus, and although once the Messiah returns all earthly distinctions will pass away, in this world and in this flesh the distinctions are real—and Christians should not rebel against them.

Turning to their Bibles, anti-integrationists found many narratives that supported a segregated world. White ministers and laymen across the South offered a biblically based history of the world that accounted for all the significant tragedies of human history, from the Fall and the Flood through the Holocaust, in terms of race relations. Binding the narrative together and linking the catastrophes of the past with the integrated apocalypse to come was the chief sin in the service of the Antichrist: miscegenation.

The notion that the sin committed in the garden of Eden was sexual in nature stretches back centuries. By the middle ages, rabbinical readings of the Fall commonly considered the serpent a male, since it lusted after Eve. Proslavery apologists in the nineteenth century favored a variant of this theory, in which Eve was tempted not by a snake but by a pre-Adamite Black man (even, in one version, a "negro gardener").[15]

Most Southern Christians rejected as heretical the notion that Negroes were created before Adam and were therefore soulless beasts incapable of salvation, but several influential postemancipation writers persisted in arguing precisely this point.

Buckner H. Payne, a Nashville publisher and clergyman who wrote under the pseudonym Ariel, insisted that the tempter in the garden was a talking beast—a Black man—and his interactions with Eve the first cause of the Fall. Writing at the height of Radical Reconstruction in 1867, Ariel concluded his argument by reminding his readers that "a man can not commit so great an offense against his race, against his country, against his God, in any other way, as to give his daughter in marriage to a negro—a *beast*—or to take one of their females for his wife." Should America fail to heed his warning, Ariel predicted disaster: "The states or people that favor this equality and amalgamation of the white and black races, *God will exterminate.*"[16]

Although rebutted at the time and later, Ariel's argument remained in use through the middle of the twentieth century, buttressed along the way by such widely read books as Charles Carroll's *The Negro a Beast* and *The Tempter of Eve*, both of which considered miscegenation the greatest of sins. Denounced by mainstream Christians for its acceptance of separate creations, *The Negro a Beast* was nonetheless enormously influential. Recalling the door-to-door sales campaign that brought the book to the notice of whites across the South, an early historian of religion lamented, "During the opening years of the twentieth century it has become the Scripture of tens of thousands of poor whites, and its doctrine is maintained with an appalling stubbornness and persistence." In this tradition, miscegenation—or, more colloquially, amalgamation or mongrelization—was the original sin, the root of all corruption in humankind.[17]

The expulsion from Paradise did not solve the problem of miscegenation. By the time of Noah, race mixing was so prevalent that, in the words of one civil rights–era pamphleteer, "God destroyed '*all flesh*' in that part of the world for that one sin. Only Noah was '*perfect in his generation'*...so God saved him and his family to rebuild the Adamic Race." That perfection did not last long, however; according to some traditions, the cursed son of Ham, already doomed to a life of servitude, mixed his blood with "pre-Adamite negroes" in the Land of Nod. Again and again God's wrath was aroused by the sin of miscegenation, and the people felt the awful weight of His punishment. Sodom and Gomorrah were destroyed for this sin, as was the Tower of Babel, where, in a failed effort to protect racial purity, God dispersed the peoples across the globe. King Solomon, "reputed to be the wisest of men, with a kingdom of matchless splendor and wealth was ruined as a direct result of his marrying women of many different races."[18]

The "physical mixing of races" that occurred between the Israelites and the Egyptians who accompanied Moses into the wilderness "resulted in social and spiritual weakness," leading God to sentence the Exodus generation to die before reaching the Promised Land. For evidence that the God of Noah remained as adamantly opposed to racial mixing as ever, white Southern believers could look back a mere fifteen years to the Holocaust. The liquidation of six million people was caused, author D. B. Red explained in his pamphlet *Race Mixing a Religious Fraud*, by the sexual "mingling" of the Jews, who suffered what Red represented as God's final solution to the miscegenation problem: "Totally destroy the people involved." Here surely was proof that segregation was "divine law, enacted for the defense of society and civilization."[19]

Narratives like these had two key pedagogical aims: to make the case for segregation as divine law, and to warn that transgression of this law would inevitably be followed by divine punishment. In the 1950s and 1960s, this punishment was imagined to be directed at the nation in the form of the communist partisans of the Antichrist and at local communities and congregations. Referring to the fate of Sodom and Gomorrah, Carey Daniel, pastor of the First Baptist Church of West Dallas, Texas, and active in local segregationist politics, explained, "Anyone familiar with the Biblical history of those cities during that period can readily understand why we here in the South are deter-mined to maintain segregation."[20]

A Virginia minister was more explicit. As he lectured shortly after the *Brown* decision: "Spurning and rejecting the plain Truth of the Word of God has always resulted in the Judgment of God. Man, in overstepping the boundary lines God has drawn, has taken another step in the direction of inviting the Judgment of Almighty God. This step of racial integration is but another stepping stone toward the gross immorality and lawlessness that will be characteristic of the last days, just preceding the Return of the Lord Jesus Christ." If this happened, it would be the fault of no one but white Southern Christians them-selves, for did not the Bible make clear, as Mississippi senator Theodore G. Bilbo warned in 1946, that "miscegenation and amalgamation are sins of man in direct defiance with the will of God?"[21]

Racial extremists like Bilbo were not the only people who believed this. Evidence of the political and social influence of these ideas is everywhere—in legal decisions, in personal correspondence, in sermons and pamphlets and speeches and newspapers. The argument that God was against sexual integration was articulated across a broad spectrum of Southern society—by senators and Klansmen, by housewives, soror-ity sisters, and Rotarians, and not least of all by mainstream Protestant clergy, many of whom turned on their liberal ecumenicist brethren.

The Reverend Burks of Norfolk, in his May 30, 1954, sermon, "In-tegration or Segregation?," which followed on the heels of *Brown* and was reprinted widely in newspapers and circulated in pamphlet form, rebutted the efforts of integrationists to cloak themselves in Chris-tian righteousness. "The spiritual 'oneness' of believers in the Lord Je-sus Christ actually and ethically has nothing to do" with the issue of segregation, Burks explained. Spiritual kinship differed from physical kinship, just as the spiritual and secular worlds differed. "If integration of races is based upon the contention that men are all 'one in Christ,' then the foundation is not secure. The idea of 'Universal Fatherhood of God and Brotherhood of Man' is MAN'S concoction and contradicts the Word of God," Burks charged. Citing Paul's pastoral letters, Burks warned, "The Anti-Christ will consummate this [rebellious] attitude by opposing and exalting Himself above God."[22]

The argument for divine segregation had great power in its day and fueled opposition to school desegregation as well as intermarriage. Segregationist ministers who believed that the Bible "gave clear guidance on the integration-segregation issue" were prominent in the crowds preventing the integration of Little Rock's Central High School in 1957. Editorialists and congregations elsewhere spoke out as well. "In integrating the races in schools, we foster miscegenation, thereby changing God's plan and destroying His handiwork," resolved the Cameron Baptist Church in Cameron, South Carolina. David M. Gardner, writing in the *Baptist Standard*, agreed: "God created and established the color line in the races, and evidently meant for it to remain. Therefore, we have no right to try and eradicate it."[23]

This argument, it is important to note, was not about school integration per se but about its consequences, which segregationists considered to be interracial sex and marriage, leading to race corruption. A common line of argument among the more than six hundred letters that Virginia governor Thomas B. Stanley received in the two weeks following the *Brown* decision insisted that school integration led inevitably to intermarriage, which violated God's plans for the universe.

Mrs. Jesse L. West supported equal education for Black Virginians ("they should have good, clean schools, buses to ride there, etc."), but she drew the line at integration, which she believed was a sin. "Having attended my beloved little county church from infancy I believe I know the fundamentals of the teachings of God's Holy Word....Nowhere can I find anything to convince me that God intended us living together as one big family in schools, churches and other public places."[24]

In April 1956 the *Citizens' Council* complained that "many ministers of the Gospel and laymen are telling us that integration is the word of God....Many others, equally devout and, one is to assume, equally prayerful in their search for Divine guidance, have received no word from the Throne of Grace that public school integration is God's wish." Admitting that there was ample biblical justification to support notions of the brotherhood of man and the equality of all men in God's sight, the official publication of the White Citizens' Council maintained, nonetheless, that "it does not follow that God intended the different races of men to inter-marry."[25]

The 1955 opinion of Henry Louttit, Episcopal bishop of South Florida, that only a few "sincere but deluded folk" would use scripture to back up their belief in segregation turned out to be optimistic. Organizations acted on this assumption. In 1958 the Daughters of the American Revolution denounced interracial marriage and resolved that "racial integrity" was a "fundamental Christian principle." Judges even incorporated these positions into legal decisions, illustrating the compatibility of legal and theological discourses. Upholding segregation in a 1955 ruling, for example, the Florida Supreme Court preferred its own reading of the Bible to that of Bishop Louttit. "When God created man," the Florida justices explained, "He allotted each race to his own continent according to color, Europe to the white man, Asia to the yellow man, Africa to the Blackman, and America to the red man."[26]

Not every white Southern response to *Brown* or to miscegenation anxiety touched on religion. Roy Bryant and J. W. Milam never claimed to have killed Emmett Till in defense of the faith. But other white Southerners *did* see resistance to the *Brown* decision as a Christian imperative. Because of the ways school desegregation raised worries about miscegenation, *Brown* allowed for the amplification of a religious discourse that had always been associated with antimiscegenation arguments but which had, until the mid-1950s, been relatively muted.

To recognize pervasive white anxieties about race mixing in the 1950s and the power of antimiscegenation arguments is not to suggest that white Southerners lacked other reasons to resist the push for Black equality. The concentrated efforts of the Supreme Court, the NAACP, and individual civil rights activists to remove race mixing as an issue from the public debate about desegregation after the *Brown* decision reveals, however, the seriousness with which supporters of civil rights took this argument. Defusing it was not easy. In 1959, Little Rock journalist Harry Ashmore published an article in *Saturday Review* in which he despaired of eluding the grip of the antimiscegenationists.

Throughout the twentieth century, Ashmore wrote, white Southerners had delayed economic and political reform out of fear that there would be social consequences. Preventing race mixing was "the inner shrine, where the mildest dissent is treason, the one place where that vaunted individuality that is so much a part of the Southern style is denied." Referring to the reality of interracial sex between white men and Black women and the construal of white women as the last and only barricade to white racial identity, Ashmore predicted that this effort to "counter the reality of the present with the unreality of the past" was suicidal and destined to failure.[27] Be that as it may, exactly *how* the inner shrine would be breached remained a mystery in 1959.

Fourteen

DEATH GROANS FROM A
DYING SYSTEM

WHEN THE SUPREME COURT ruled on public school segregation in 1954, the limitations of the *Brown v. Board of Education* decision, particularly its lack of an enforcement mechanism, were visible. Justice Robert Jackson, well aware of the court's reluctance to act definitively on racial discrimination, incorporated that knowledge into his *Brown* memo. Misquoting the nineteenth-century English poet Matthew Arnold, Jackson wrote that the court and the nation were "hesitating between two worlds—one dead, the other powerless to be born."[1] With these words ("hesitating between two worlds"), Jackson highlighted his sense of being suspended in time and in history.

Three years later, Martin Luther King Jr. appropriated the same text but endowed it with more forward momentum. In a speech to an NAACP Emancipation Day rally on January 1, 1957, King declared that all Americans were living in "an age in which a new world order is being born. We stand today between two worlds: the dying old and the emerging new."[2]

Where Justice Jackson had seen a ship of state becalmed, King saw motion. Celebrating the decision that had created such stress among the justices, King exulted that "as a result of [the *Brown*] decision, we can gradually see the old order of segregation and discrimination passing away and the new order of justice and freedom coming into being." The "loud noises" of protest heard in the South, said King, were nothing but the "death groans from a dying system. The old order is passing away, and the new order is coming into being."[3]

Unlike Jackson, who lacked confidence in his ability to midwife this new world, King exhorted his audience to "speed up the coming of the inevitable. We must speed up the coming of this new order." Deftly appropriating Christianity and melding it with notions of freedom and justice, King proposed a "Prayer Pilgrimage for Freedom" to Washington, DC, on May 17, 1957—the third anniversary of the *Brown* decision.[4] At the rally, King urged Congress to pass civil rights legislation then pending. The House passed the bill in June, but Senate debates ground on through the summer. An amended—some said emasculated—version of the bill finally cleared Congress at the end of August, and in September President Eisenhower signed into law the first federal civil rights legislation since Reconstruction.

Passage of the 1957 Civil Rights Act was not the big civil rights story that fall. That honor went to Central High School in Little Rock, Arkansas, where nine African American students were welcomed to the otherwise all-white school by a threatening mob dedicated to the preservation of white racial purity through resistance to enforcement of the *Brown* decision. The mob, in turn, was greeted by the 101st Airborne Division, which was dispatched, reluctantly, by the commander in chief when it became clear that Arkansas governor Orval E. Faubus did not intend to uphold the law. Local anti-integrationists turned to familiar arguments against racial integration, presenting school desegregation as leading inevitably to miscegenation.[5] Cartoons and buttons depicted little white girls forced at federal bayonet point into the arms of African American schoolmates. Such depictions also made clear, as

Governor Faubus intended, which branch of government was responsible for this state of affairs.[6]

The standoff in Little Rock was a public relations nightmare. In the context of competition between Cold War superpowers, people around the world paid close attention to the civil rights battles in America. From Germany to Latin America, American leaders were greeted with banners reading "What's Up with Little Rock?" in multiple languages.[7] African Americans argued that white supremacy handicapped the United States in its struggles against both international and domestic communism. In 1950, Benjamin Mays blamed the appeal of communism in the United States on white supremacy, writing, "Make no mistake, racialism breeds communism."[8]

The oft-cited notion that the African American community was uninterested in interracial marriage was rebutted by a cursory look at Black newspapers and magazines. Even as Yale law professor Alexander Bickel was pronouncing a deafening lack of interest in marriage across the color line, Martin Luther King was recommending it—with suitable caution—in his monthly Advice for Living column published in *Ebony*. In 1958, King engaged the Christian arguments against interracial marriage. Antimiscegenation laws existed "because of certain misguided religious views as well as long entrenched social customs. Many people sincerely feel that the Bible prohibits interracial marriage." But: "Of course, there is no justification for laws against interracial marriages either on religious or rational grounds. The Bible neither condemns nor condones intermarriage. It simply does not deal with the question....There should be no laws against intermarriage." King frequently fielded questions about intermarriage, writing soothingly, "Individuals marry, not races."[9]

There was one part of America where race mixing was celebrated: the island territory of Hawaii, where a mix of native Hawaiians, Japanese, Filipinos, and Chinese labored in the pineapple and sugarcane fields and manned the docks. A backwater until Pearl Harbor, by the end of WWII Hawaii had been transformed into an indispensable military outpost, a way station for thousands of US troops on their way east. Many of these troops appreciated the lack of racial segregation in Hawaii and the refusal of General Delos G. Emmons, the islands' military governor, to establish Jim Crow there.[10]

The island colonial world created by white elites in the mid-nineteenth century had become, by the middle of the twentieth, the "melting pot of the Pacific." By 1950, more than a third of Hawaii's marriages were interracial. The *Chicago Tribune* reported in 1952 that mixed marriages had increased over 35 percent since 1941. How better to communicate America's commitment to racial equality than to admit Hawaii as a state? As the *New York Times* editorialized in 1950, Hawaiian statehood would be "a most convincing demonstration to our friends in Asia, at a time when we badly need friends in Asia, that this nation as a democratic state has no place for any theory of racial supremacy or superiority."[11]

Hawaii was useful to the State Department because it embodied interracial democracy and social life. This was precisely what made statehood unpalatable to Southern senators, who blocked Hawaii's admission as a state for a decade, a fact trumpeted by the Soviets as evidence of American unwillingness to tolerate nonwhite political power. Secretary of the Interior Oscar L. Chapman, a long-serving Roosevelt appointee, argued that Hawaiian statehood would deny the communists a powerful issue in their "problem of persuasion" to potential Asian allies. He testified in 1950 at a congressional hearing, "Hawaii should not be required to apologize for or minimize the significance of its heterogeneous racial complexion."[12]

Hawaiian statehood hearings dragged on in the US Senate until 1959, blocked at every turn by white Southerners charging that the islands were hotbeds of communist infiltration.[13]

The chairman of the Hawaiian statehood committee, Joseph C. O'Mahoney, addressed the communist question straightforwardly, using a secular version of the Christian brotherhood argument advanced by the Federal Council of Churches. Noting that much of the testimony against Hawaiian statehood concerned communist infiltration, O'Mahoney announced, "We shall be confronted here with the same question that we will have to face on the world stage: Whether or not communism can best be fought by thoroughgoing application of American principles of human brotherhood or by reliance on force and...isolation."[14]

Intended to signal America's commitment to racial egalitarianism to the rest of the world, the question of Hawaiian statehood became a proxy for civil rights arguments at home. The African American press consistently framed statehood as part of the civil rights struggle. In 1954, *Chicago Defender* reporter Enoch Waters relayed the news that Hawaii had stopped noting racial identity on birth certificates. "Interracial marriages," Waters wrote, "have so confused the situation that no one can determine how to classify anyone."[15]

This state of affairs was what restrictive marriage laws were supposed to prevent: they were designed to guard against racial "amalgamation" and to protect white "racial purity" through regulation of marriage. Antimiscegenation laws sanctioned the broader system, including the legal racial classification codes that guarded white "race purity."[16] Hawaii offered a glimpse of the future, a model of what a world without racial restrictions on marriage looked like. Other states could regulate marriage in ways Hawaii declined to—or they could follow its example.

IN MAY 1961 an integrated group from the Congress of Racial Equality (CORE, established in Chicago in 1942) embarked on a "Freedom Ride" through the South. Their aim was to draw a reluctant federal government into the civil rights struggle by testing a recent Supreme Court decision that barred segregation in facilities involved in interstate transit and, it was expected, by exposing Southern noncompliance with federal law. The Freedom Riders were mauled by segregationists in Anniston, Alabama, and in Birmingham, where Commissioner of Public Safety Eugene "Bull" Connor allowed an armed mob to attack the riders without police interference for exactly fifteen minutes. They were further assaulted in Montgomery, where a Justice Department official sent to monitor the proceedings was knocked unconscious by a mob armed with clubs, chains, and iron bars.

The argument against the Freedom Riders was familiar: massive integration will mean future intermarriage. As the *Meridian Star* fumed, "Intermarriage in the South, where we are so evenly divided white and colored, means the end of both races as such, and the emergence of a tribe of mongrels."[17]

Alabama's one-two assault on the rule of law and its federal representatives drew a reluctant Robert Kennedy into the fray, as CORE had intended. The attorney general instructed the Interstate Commerce Commission to ban segregation and discrimination in interstate travel. At the same time, Kennedy implored civil rights leaders to back away from these direct-action tactics, which were stoking a worsening public relations debacle for President John F. Kennedy and American diplomats, and to focus on something less confrontational: voter registration. The Student Nonviolent Coordinating Committee (SNCC), organized in April 1960 at Shaw University in Raleigh, North Carolina, by young Black men and women veterans of the direct-action campaigns, was glad to comply.

In the summer of 1964, SNCC leader Robert Parris Moses, a former high school mathematics teacher from New York, journeyed to Mississippi, where only 5 percent of eligible African American voters were registered. Local civil rights leaders convinced Moses of three things: first, that white supremacy rested on disenfranchisement and that only voters could break the back of Jim Crow; second, that a voter-registration drive in the Deep South was as direct a challenge to white power as any sit-in; and third, that such a campaign would provoke an even more dramatic response from local whites than the Freedom Rides had in Alabama. As one worker put it, "If you went into Mississippi and talked about voter registration, they [were] going to hit you on the side of the head and that's about as direct as you can get."[18]

This final assessment proved tragically accurate. Violence followed the SNCC workers as they fanned out across southwest Georgia and the delta counties of Mississippi and Alabama. After only a few weeks of activity, four Black churches in Georgia that were being used as voter-registration centers were firebombed. SNCC workers in Mississippi were arrested and beaten. Robert Zellner, a white Alabaman, nearly lost an eye when an assailant gouged it from its socket; Fannie Lou Hamer, a Black Mississippian, suffered for the rest of her life from a brutal beating she received while in police custody. In a calculated warning to local Blacks with civic ambition, E. H. Hurst, a member of the Mississippi state legislature, shot and killed local civil rights activist Herbert Lee, a farmer and WWII veteran.

IN SEPTEMBER 1962, the House of Representatives began to draft new federal civil rights legislation. Building on this momentum, Martin Luther King led a group to Birmingham, Alabama, to force a showdown against segregation in one of the most violently racist cities in America. The images of Police Chief "Bull" Connor's officers attacking young Black men and women with batons, snarling police dogs, and high-pressure fire hoses shocked the world and embarrassed the United States. Criticized for pushing his agenda beyond the social breaking point, King penned his famous "Letter from Birmingham Jail" in April 1963 while serving a sentence for violating a state ban on protest marches. In it, he blasted the complacency of "whites of good-will" and capitalized on the violence in the Deep South by declaring that the only alternative to civil disobedience was revolution.

The assassination of John F. Kennedy in Texas on November 22, 1963, spurred passage of the slain president's proposed civil rights act. Lyndon B. Johnson propelled the 1964 Civil Rights Act through Congress, and then, understanding that Black economic inequality was as severe as Black political inequality, he launched the social welfare programs he called the "Great Society." Voting rights still remained at the top of civil rights organizations' agenda, however, and for good reason:

as of 1964 only two million of the South's five million Blacks of voting age were registered to vote.

SNCC's interracial Freedom Summer group was also greeted by the surveillance state. The Mississippi State Sovereignty Commission was charged to "watch the movements of subversive persons and institutions within the South."[19] Citizens were encouraged to report anything that looked like "suspicious behavior." Thousands of reports made their way to commission headquarters.

The heart of the Sovereignty Commission was its undercover agents, who infiltrated Freedom Houses, monitored conversations in public, and befriended hangers-on. The agents were concerned with two things: communism and interracial sex. Like the White Citizens' Councils, which equated the drive for Black equality with a Soviet plot to destroy America "by sapping its Caucasian energies through miscegenation," the Sovereignty Commission considered the civil rights activists traitors to their race and country.[20] Agent Tom Scarborough reported on July 29, 1964, "All kinds of rumors can be heard everywhere one goes concerning indecent conduct by Negro males and white females, who are traveling about over this state." Scarborough concluded that the people he referred to as the "summer project invaders" were doing it "to drive white Mississippians crazy."[21] In one report, Agent 79 focused on a conversation he had had with the mayor of Jackson. Local white residents were anxious over the interracial housing arrangements of the student workers, he related. Worse, "White women had been seen kissing Negroes and walking arm in arm with Negroes down the street." This could easily ignite violence, he warned.[22]

The Sovereignty Commission's call for Mississippi whites to report *anything* that looked like "suspicious behavior" reflected a secondary role: to surveil the Klan and the Citizens' Councils and short-circuit, if possible, their planned violence and disruption against the summer activists. On this front, the Sovereignty Commission failed. The Summer Project workers faced an unprecedented campaign of violence and intimidation. A thousand people were arrested in Mississippi; many of them were brutalized by the police. To the consternation of Mississippi authorities trying to keep the feds out of their state, the Ku Klux Klan launched what it considered a counteroffensive to the students, thereby issuing an open invitation to the FBI. Thirty-five churches—the most common site for civil rights meetings—were burned to the ground that summer, and six people were murdered. Three of them—Black Mississippian James Chaney and white New Yorkers Andrew Goodman and Michael Schwerner—were killed together and buried in an earthen dam. News of their deaths, broadcast by a riveted media, clarified for white Americans outside the region the degree of violent resistance to Black equality in the South.

The extent of that resistance was demonstrated once again in Selma, Alabama, where King and the Southern Christian Leadership Council (SCLC) chose to mount their own voter-registration campaign in 1965. Rising from the northern banks of the Alabama River in the heart of the fertile plain linking central Alabama and northeastern Mississippi (known as the Black Belt), the small town of Selma seemed an unlikely site for the climax of the civil rights movement. Home to a rigidly controlled political machine, Selma has also been described by its most thorough historian as Alabama's "most inflexibly and fervently segregationist" city.[23] Faced with the *Brown* decision, the different elements among the white citizenry had reacted in a variety of ways. The more respectable segregationists in town joined the White Citizens' Council, which announced that it intended "to maintain complete segregation of the races ...[and] make it difficult, if not impossible, for any Negro who advocates de-segregation to find and hold a job, get credit or renew a mortgage." Less savory whites turned to their own form of direct action: in September 1964, arsonists burned two Dallas County Black schools to the ground.[24]

Most ominous of all for Selma's Black residents was the merging of these two strands of white response within the county government. In the spring of 1960, the Dallas County sheriff, cattle rancher James G. Clark Jr., organized a four-hundred-man posse to serve as the county's first line of defense against integration. Drawn from the ranks of the Citizens' Council and the Klan, the posse was divided into a small mounted cavalry and a much larger group of foot soldiers.[25] Led by the combative Sheriff Clark, the posse represented a challenge both to local Black supporters of civil rights and to Selma's emerging white moderates.

Although described by Martin Luther King in early 1965 as the "symbol of bitter-end resistance to the civil rights movement in the Deep South," Selma was by that point already deep in political transition. Since 1962, the city had been the site of voting-rights demonstrations organized by the local Dallas County Voters League (founded in the mid-1920s) with the aid of SNCC. The 1964 mayoral race—Selma's first truly competitive municipal election since 1932—ended with the defeat of the local machine. The new mayor, an enterprising small-business owner named Joe Smitherman, was elected with the support of the Black community, which also posted the first Black candidates for municipal office since Reconstruction.[26]

Drawn by this vital local movement, in late 1964 SCLC focused its own voter-registration efforts on Dallas County and its abusive sheriff—who could be relied on, SCLC thought, to respond to the voter drive with an explosion that would catch the nation's attention in the way Bull Connor's water hoses and police dogs had in Birmingham the previous year.[27] This reading of Clark was all too accurate: on February 18, 1965, four hundred activists in Marion, an outlying town, were attacked during a night march by a gang made up of Jim Clark's posse, state troopers, local police, and assorted hooligans. A twenty-six-year-old Black man, Jimmie Lee Jackson—the youngest deacon in his small Baptist church—was shot while protecting his mother and eighty-two-year-old grandfather from state troopers. He died eight days later.[28]

Conceived in response to Jackson's death as a protest against the violence of the state, the March 7 Selma-to-Montgomery march became an unforgettable example of that violence when Sheriff Clark's mounted posse and Alabama state troopers met the marchers on the Edmund

Pettus Bridge and gassed, clubbed, and trampled them. The attack was caught on film, and the grainy images of gas-masked, blue-helmeted state troopers and whip-wielding mounted police bludgeoning Black men and women who moments before had been kneeling in prayer transfixed the nation. What was immediately dubbed "Bloody Sunday" ignited sympathy demonstrations across the country. The participation of religious leaders in these demonstrations was striking. Two hundred nuns marched alongside fifteen thousand other people in Harlem; 150 clergymen joined SCLC's Walter Fauntroy and Episcopal bishop Paul Moore in a denunciation of President Lyndon Johnson's passivity.[29]

SCLC was determined to march again. But this time it would be more than a march; it would be a procession, and, like all proper processions, it would be led by holy men. Shrewdly building on the reaction of religious leaders outside the South, Martin Luther King issued a national call to clergymen to join him in Alabama. The call represented a significant rhetorical shift. Prior to Bloody Sunday, SCLC presented the Selma voting-rights campaign in terms of citizenship and equal justice. A nine-by-sixteen-inch advertisement published in the *New York Times* on February 5 and titled "A Letter from MARTIN LUTHER KING from a Selma, Alabama Jail" called for help from "all decent Americans" to support equal rights and "to advance dignity in the United States." What had been a secular campaign for civil rights was now transformed into a holy crusade to redeem the blood spilled in Selma.

Shortly after the first march, on the evening of Sunday, March 7, King sent telegrams to clergy around the country. Insisting that "no American is without responsibility" for what happened at Selma, King continued, "The people of Selma will struggle on for the soul of the nation, but it is fitting that all Americans help to bear the burden. I call therefore, on clergy of all faiths…to join me in Selma for a ministers march to Montgomery on Tuesday morning, March ninth."[30]

The response was overwhelming: by March 9 more than 450 white clergymen and religious women (including a contingent of nuns) had gathered in Selma, with more on the way. Contemporaries remarked on the sense of pilgrimage shared by those who traveled to Selma. Arriving from New York, NAACP lawyer Stanley Levison was "struck by the unfamiliarity of the participants. They were not long-committed white liberals and Negroes. They were new forces from all faiths and classes."[31] Believers who did not themselves journey to Selma could still participate vicariously in the march; denominational leaders in New York and Washington urged that the coming weekend's sermons be on Selma. And the next Sunday (March 14), upwards of fifteen thousand people gathered across the street from the White House in Lafayette Park to take part in an ecumenical protest sponsored by the National Council of Churches.[32]

In the end, the "march" became three marches: the original March 7 march, known as "Bloody Sunday" for the police violence on the Edmund Pettus Bridge; a truncated protest on March 9, in which protesters led by King approached the Edmund Pettus Bridge and then turned around; and the final march from Selma to Montgomery. The violence escalated after the March 9 march, when a group of white supremacists murdered the Reverend James Reed, a Unitarian Universalist minister from Boston.

After negotiations with Alabama governor George Wallace, who refused to protect the marchers, and President Lyndon Johnson, who nationalized the Alabama National Guard, the third march began on March 21. That march, which achieved the goal of reaching the state capitol of Montgomery, can be read in many ways, but there is much to support an interpretation of the event as a contest over Christian orthodoxy—a collision of religious communities presenting themselves as defenders of two conflicting theological views. As its very name implies, the Southern Christian Leadership Conference was always aware that men of the cloth lent the movement moral and social power.[33] As we have seen, King and other SCLC preacher-politicians encouraged the conflation of Black protest and Christian righteousness throughout the civil rights era. King used it to particularly good effect, as when he chose to be arrested in Birmingham, Alabama, on Good Friday.[34] But religious leaders were equally important for their theological imprimatur. Calling the March 21 march a "pilgrimage," as the Black press and leading rights workers did (including King, in his end-of-the-march speech at the Alabama capitol in Montgomery), invested it with religious, and not just political, significance.[35] So did SCLC's decision to call those who would be allowed to walk the entire fifty-mile distance "the chosen few." The ranks of marching priests, ministers, and rabbis represented a concrete witness to the rightness of integration, a walking testimony to an ecumenical belief in racial equality rooted in a common Judeo-Christian heritage. This, at least, is how *Ebony* saw it. The Reverend King, the magazine declared, had "accomplished the virtually impossible: he had converted leaders of the so-called white church" to civil rights.[36] The participation of "pure-faced nuns" and "clerics with high collars" in the march merged with SCLC's long-standing campaign to portray desegregation and Black equality as right Christian doctrine in a strategy to assault at its root the most powerful language supporting segregation, a language that was thoroughly Christian.

Understanding the march in religious terms helps explain not only SCLC's tactics but also segregationists' response to those tactics: an emphasis on the sexual sins of the clergy and on the desecration of holy spaces. Surely good Christians—Christians whose behavior found favor in the sight of the Lord—could not behave the way these supposedly religious supporters of civil rights did in Alabama. In a speech before the US Congress, Alabama representative William Dickinson denounced the morals of SCLC's supporters and declared that "Negro and white freedom marchers invaded a Negro church in Montgomery and engaged in an all-night session of debauchery within the church itself." "I saw numerous instances of boys and girls of both races hugging, kissing and fondling one another openly in the church," another source reported. "On one occasion I saw a Negro boy and a white girl engaged in sexual intercourse on the floor of the church." As the marchers reached Montgomery, Alabama governor George Wallace sent all female state employees home.[37]

Worse yet was what the clergy were up to. Publications ranging from the *Fiery Cross* to the *Memphis Press-Scimitar* described the march as a week-long interracial orgy, with men of the cloth leading the way. These stories were picked up by the mainstream press; during the first week in May, *Newsweek, Time,* and *U.S. News & World Report* all carried features with titles like "Kiss and Tell" and "Orgies on the Rights March." Riffing on Martin Luther King's appeal for clergy to come to Selma, white supremacists charged that marchers were offered "$15 a day, 3 meals a day, and all the sex [they] could handle."[38] In a letter to the Episcopal bishop of Alabama that made its way into the *New York Times,* Frances H. Hamilton complained about the behavior of civil rights activist Reverend Jonathan Daniels and other priests during the march, and claimed that a white girl had died of exhaustion after providing "sexual comfort to the visiting clergy." As Representative Dickinson summed things up a month later, in another speech before Congress, "Mr. Speaker, our modern Canterbury Tales make Chaucer's pilgrims look like veritable paragons of virtue and piety."[39]

This testimony should not be read as descriptive of actual clerical behavior on the march. Indeed, Congressman Dickinson's allegations regarding sexual activity during the march were refuted at the time. Hearing the rumors, Bob Craig, a South Carolina editor, worked hard to substantiate the stories but came up empty. "I spent the entire night trying to find an orgy in a church and checked a lot of churches and found no such thing," he reported.[40] Nuns, seminarians, and clergymen who had participated in the march insisted in telegrams and affidavits that they had observed no sexual misconduct. (Or sexual conduct of any sort: as one SNCC official noted wryly, "Baby, everyone was too tired from all that marching.")[41] When McBee Martin of Bristol, Virginia, complained that the *Presbyterian Survey* had failed to cover the sexual angle of the story, the *Survey's* editor replied soberly, "We seldom report rumors of sex orgies in connection with religious events."[42]

The ease with which the *Presbyterian Survey* referred to the Selma-to-Montgomery march as a religious event reveals the victory of Martin

Luther King's vision of Christianity as firmly allied with the civil rights movement. Yet this victory should not obscure the conflict behind it. However inaccurate, representations of clerical sex orgies should be taken seriously as efforts to demonize civil rights activists in religious terms that would resonate with Southern Christians—just as SCLC's use of "pilgrims" was an attempt to sanctify them in the same language.[43] In casting the clergy in Selma and Montgomery as miscegenators—as sexual sinners—white opponents of integration were able to represent them as apostles of the Antichrist. This was Congressman Dickinson's position: "I feel very deeply that when the genuine devout men and women devoted to God's work participate in activities as I have described and lend their dignity and prestige they are doing themselves and those whom they represent"—including, presumably, Jesus—"a very grave disservice."[44]

THE FALL, WITHOUT A WHIMPER, OF AN EMPIRE

Mildred Jeter Loving and her husband, Richard, grew up down the road from each other in Caroline County, Virginia, during and after World War II. Although he was from a nominally white family, Richard Loving did not live in a Black-white world, either physically or imaginatively. Caroline County was known locally as "the passing capital of America" because it was full of people who traced their heritage to one or more of three groups: Europeans, Africans, and Native Americans. Indeed, Mildred Jeter's family faced the world from their home on Passing Road. Mildred identified as Indian on her application for a marriage license, which still disqualified her from marrying a white man under the laws of Virginia.[1] Many mixed-race people left the county and passed as white elsewhere; Richard later insisted that "everybody looked alike to me."[2]

Richard Loving's family stood out for their disaffection for white supremacy. Richard's father worked as a truck driver for twenty-three years for Boyd Bird, a wealthy Black farmer. Addicted to NASCAR, Richard formed a highly successful integrated drag-racing team with two African American friends, who shared communal ownership of a car. In this context, nobody paid much attention when Richard, then age seventeen, began to date young Mildred Jeter, who traced her family along a bumpy genealogical road that included ancestors from three continents. As one of Mildred's uncles put the matter later, after the young couple had married, "Richard isn't the first white man in our family, and he won't be the last."[3]

In June 1958, when Richard was twenty-four and Mildred just eighteen, they decided to get married. Because he knew that interracial marriage was illegal in Virginia, Richard drove his bride an hour north, to Washington, DC. After the ceremony the newlyweds returned to Virginia, where they moved in with Mildred's parents. Before they had time to feel cramped by this arrangement, Sheriff Garrett Brooks and two deputies barged in on the Lovings in bed, shined a flashlight in their faces, and arrested them. Richard pointed to their marriage license, which was framed and hanging on the wall, but Brooks said it was no good in Virginia. It was two o'clock in the morning. "Somebody had to tell, but I have no idea who it could have been," Mildred, who was six months pregnant, mused later. "I guess we had one enemy."[4]

Richard posted bond and was released the day after the arrest, but Sheriff Brooks inexplicably kept Mildred jailed for another five days. Released from detention, Richard and Mildred found themselves before Circuit Court Judge Leon M. Bazile, where they pled guilty to violating Virginia's antimiscegenation law. Despite his clear aversion to such a marriage, Judge Bazile imposed the lightest sentence possible— one year in jail each—and then suspended the sentences for a period of twenty-five years provided that the Lovings leave Caroline County and the state of Virginia at once. Exiled from their home, Richard and Mildred moved in with some of Mildred's cousins in Washington, DC.

The Lovings had some options. They could have stayed in Washington, where they were legally married, or moved to any of the states north or west of Virginia that had repealed their antimiscegenation laws by 1958.[5] But Richard never took to city life. He was a mason and preferred to work back home in Virginia and commute to DC. "I burned up $35 worth of gasoline a month," he recalled later, "but it was worth it." The family returned clandestinely to Virginia, traveling in two cars as a precaution. Nevertheless they were caught twice and rearrested.[6]

The commute took a toll on the Lovings' marriage, and by 1963 Mildred, left alone all day in Washington with three children, had had enough. Inspired by the March on Washington that August, Mildred, who had never participated in any aspect of the organized civil rights movement, contacted the Justice Department. She wanted to know if they could do anything about Virginia's antimiscegenation law. Justice passed Mrs. Loving's request to the National Capital Area Civil Liberties Union (a branch of the ACLU), where Bernard S. Cohen agreed to challenge the Lovings' conviction. He was soon joined by another young ACLU lawyer, Philip J. Hirschkop.

In January 1965, Cohen and Hirschkop went before Judge Bazile and asked him to set aside his 1958 decision. Predictably, he did not oblige. Instead, he referred to the 1955 Virginia case *Naim v. Naim*, in which the Virginia Supreme Court of Appeals held that the state's antimiscegenation law was justified in order to "preserve the racial integrity of its citizens" and to prevent the "corruption of blood." (This was the case the Supreme Court had gone to such trouble to avoid ruling on, to sidestep the miscegenation issue.) Bazile refuted the ACLU's contention that antimiscegenation laws were unconstitutional by insisting that marriage was "a subject which belongs to the exclusive control of the States." ("We are not marrying the state," remarked Mildred.) After citing a series of other cases that supported antimiscegenation laws, Bazile left the realm of jurisprudence altogether and concluded, "Almighty God created the races white, black, yellow, malay and red, and he placed them on separate continents. And but for the interference with his arrangement there would be no cause for such marriages. The fact that he separated the races shows that he did not intend for the races to mix." The Virginia Supreme Court of Appeals affirmed Bazile's opinion. The Lovings, violators of both man's and God's laws, were not welcome in Virginia as husband and wife.

There was nothing left to do but appeal to the United States Supreme Court and hope it would agree to hear the case. It did, in December 1966. Bolstered by friend-of-the-court briefs from the Catholic Church, the Japanese American Citizens League, and the Anti-Defamation League, Cohen and Hirschkop presented Virginia's antimiscegenation statute as both a relic of slavery and an expression of modern-day racism that clearly violated the equal protection and due process clauses of the Fourteenth Amendment. In oral argument in April, Cohen passed on Richard Loving's plea to the justices: "Mr. Cohen, tell the Court I love my wife, and it is just unfair that I can't live with her in Virginia."

The justices agreed. In a ringing unanimous decision written by Chief Justice Earl Warren (who had authored the *Brown* decision thirteen years before), the Supreme Court declared that Virginia's justifications for the state's antimiscegenation law were "obviously an endorsement of White Supremacy."[7]

Those two words—"white supremacy"—had not made it into the *Brown* decision. But in *Loving v. Virginia*, legal historians have noted, the court struck a much more confrontational tone than it did in *Brown*.[8] *Brown* focused narrowly on public education. *Loving* denounced "invidious racial discrimination" generally. Warren declared that marriage was a "vital personal right," a "fundamental freedom." Echoing Roger Traynor's twenty-year-old decision in *Perez v. Sharp* (1948), Warren explained that the due process clause of the Fourteenth Amendment guaranteed the fundamental right to marry, and that in this case the fundamental right was paired with the constitutional guarantee of equal protection of the laws. "There can be no doubt that restricting the freedom to marry solely because of racial classifications violates the central meaning of the Equal Protection Clause."[9] The court dismissed Virginia's argument that its antimiscegenation law did not discriminate on the basis of race because whites could no more marry nonwhites than nonwhites could marry whites, ruling that the antimiscegenation law had no purpose other than to further "invidious racial discrimination." The right to marry, as the Universal Declaration of Human Rights had announced in 1948, was a human right—even in Virginia. The decision in the *Loving* case represented the collapse of the most fundamental, and longest-standing, color barrier in America. At the time of *Loving*, sixteen states, mostly in the South, still had laws forbidding interracial marriages.

DOWN IN MISSISSIPPI, Governor Ross Barnett exploded. The man who in 1962 had defied a court order to desegregate the University of Mississippi with the declaration "We will not drink from the cup of genocide" denounced the *Loving* decision as "without question the most flagrant, irresponsible, and frightening decision ever decreed by the Warren Court" and predicted that it would "lead to chaos, strife, and dissension never before equaled on this earth."[10]

Yet the popular reaction to *Loving* was relatively calm. Which leads one to ask: why did *Loving* fail to inspire white Southern rage? How could the same people who had ardently resisted *Brown* because it allegedly led to miscegenation accept *Loving*, which actually did the things wrongly attributed to *Brown* thirteen years earlier?

Given the pedigree and longevity of antimiscegenation laws, the prominence of miscegenation concerns throughout the civil rights era, and the difficulty of the freedom struggle, repeal of racial barriers to marriage in 1967 should have been seen as catastrophic for the white South. Such an event might have been expected to produce a crisis of identity in a society confronted for the first time by the possibility that the differences by which it defined itself would actually disappear, and that white Southerners would be swallowed up, as they had worried for years, in a sea of brown-skinned mulattoes.

It took a while for white Americans to warm to the new legal possibilities for interracial marriage. In 1968, 72 percent of Americans disapproved of white-nonwhite marriages. A decade later, 54 percent still disapproved of such marriages. Public approval for interracial marriage did not cross the majority threshold until 1997, three decades after the decision in *Loving*. By 2013, 84 percent of whites and 96 percent of Blacks approved of interracial marriage.[11] At the time of *Loving*, only 3 percent of all marriages in the United States were interracial. Heading into the third decade of the twenty-first century, 17 percent of marriages are interracial (this includes Hispanics and Asian Americans).

There is a stark partisan difference on intermarriage. In 2015, nearly half of all Democrats or Democrat-leaning Independents thought intermarriage was good for society, whereas only 28 percent of Republicans or Republican-leaning Independents shared this view.

The most significant outlier on the spectrum of acceptance of interracial marriage is evangelical Christians, who are "the most opposed to interracial marriage." Only 9 percent of Americans overall opposed interracial marriage in 2011, but 16 percent of white evangelicals embraced that position, nearly double the percentage of other Americans. On the flip side, of Americans overall, 27 percent said that more interracial marriage was good for society, but only 17 percent of evangelicals did. Of Black Protestants, 97 percent considered intermarriage a positive good.[12]

As so often since *Brown*, Baptists have been at the center of these discussions. At the congregational level, the debate has raged over the issue of integrated churches. After a string of "kneel-ins" in the 1960s, the problem gained national attention in 1976, when the deacons of Plains Baptist Church, the home church of Democratic presidential candidate Jimmy Carter of Georgia, enforced its closed-door policy against the Reverend Clennon King and three other African Americans. The specter that haunted Baptists wrangling over integrated churches was a familiar one: miscegenation. In 1971, the Baptist Sunday School Board revised 140,000 copies of *Becoming*, a quarterly magazine for teenagers, because it contained an article supporting open churches illustrated with a photograph of an African American boy talking to two white girls. Although by the mid-1980s most Baptists agreed that whites had no right to exclude Black Americans from their neighborhoods, 53 percent of Southern Baptists still favored laws that prohibited interracial marriage.[13]

More important than the way antimiscegenation concerns fueled internal debates over open churches has been the effort to use the constitutional protection of religion to expand the social sphere in which segregation could remain. The main battleground here has been private religious schools.[14] In 1979, the Southern Baptist Convention (SBC) adopted by an overwhelming margin a resolution that opposed a federal proposal to deny tax-exempt status to private schools that discriminated on the basis of race. While the SBC resolved, the federal government sued. Their target was well chosen: Bob Jones University in South Carolina, which until the spring of 2000 prohibited interracial dating among its students. Founded in 1927, Bob Jones excluded Black students until 1971. Revealing a deep concern about interracial marriage, from 1971 to 1975 the university accepted a small number of Black students who were already married to other African Americans. In 1975 the university began to accept unmarried Black students but prohibited interracial dating and marriage.

Because of this policy, in 1976 the Internal Revenue Service stripped the university of its tax-exempt status, arguing that federally supported institutions could not enforce policies "contrary to established public policy" even if those policies were grounded in religious belief. In 1983, the Supreme Court upheld the IRS's decision in *Bob Jones University v. United States*.[15] In this important ruling, the court held that the religion clauses of the First Amendment did not give a religion-based university an exemption from complying with the government's compelling interest in eradicating racial discrimination.

Although the federal government was not constitutionally required to subsidize the racially discriminatory behavior of Bob Jones University, the Supreme Court nonetheless recognized in its 1983 decision that some Americans might "engage in racial discrimination on the basis of sincerely-held religious beliefs." White supremacists haven't been shy about embracing such beliefs, especially if the move gains them the protection of the First Amendment's Religion Clause.

Perhaps the most extreme example of the use of the First Amendment to shelter racially discriminatory beliefs is the World Church of the Creator. Led by the Reverend Matt Hale—who set off down the path of radical racist politics when he, as a child in the 1970s, witnessed white girls at a dance "betraying their race" by kissing Black boys—the World Church is identified by the Anti-Defamation League as one of America's most dangerous white-supremacist movements. The World Church of the Creator is not a religion, and Hale is not a minister in any recognized church. He is, instead, a lawyer who has drained the concept of "religion" of all content except its constitutional privilege to justify resistance to state laws. The World Church's logo is revealing: it features a masked white man and woman aiming automatic weapons beneath the slogan "Freedom of Religion."[16]

The language of sexual anxiety about racial purity and religious arguments against intermarriage persists more broadly on the far right. Speaking of white nationalists in the 1980s, historian Kathleen Belew has remarked that "the rhetorical defense of white women from miscegenation, racial pollution, and other dangers continued to structure the worldview…of white power movement activists." Some white-power leaders have justified their stance through religion, as when Robert Miles, a leader in the Mountain Church, announced, "Miscegenation…is the ultimate abomination and violation of the law of God."[17]

The overall disappearance of antimiscegenation anxiety as an acceptable public language is momentous; it represents the collapse of the most enduring color barrier in the United States. Today, interracial couples are elevated as poster children for interracial progress. For many contemporary commentators in the era of integration, interracial romance and marriage rates are considered the most reliable barometer of American race relations. As a columnist for the *Chicago Tribune* put it at the turn of this century, "The change in sentiments about what used to be referred to as 'miscegenation' is one of the most dramatic and hopeful developments of the last generation."[18]

WHY WERE ANTIMISCEGENATION laws, the very foundation of segregation, the last piece of Jim Crow to fall? Why did the NAACP, the premier African American civil rights organization, fail to mount an organized challenge to restrictive marriage laws in the 1950s? Why, instead, did it focus on schools?

Political philosopher Hannah Arendt asked exactly this question in 1959, five years after the *Brown* decision and two after the Little Rock High School integration crisis. The response she provoked suggests the difficulties the NAACP would have encountered by raising the marriage issue. In an essay called "Reflections on Little Rock," published in the December 1959 issue of the leftist magazine *Dissent*, Arendt suggested that the leaders of the civil rights movement had their priorities confused. Instead of fighting Jim Crow in the schoolyard, Arendt thought they should focus on voting rights and on "what the whole world knows to be the most outrageous legislation in the whole western hemisphere": the restrictive marriage laws that, in 1959, made marriages between white and nonwhite citizens a criminal offense in twenty-four states. Echoing California Supreme Court justice Roger Traynor's 1948 decision in *Perez v. Sharp*, Arendt argued that restrictive marriage laws were at odds with American constitutionalism and with the new articulations of human rights associated with the United Nations and the emerging civil rights movement.[19]

White public intellectuals who were committed to civil rights had no sympathy for this high-minded argument. Responding to Arendt's article before it was even published, Sidney Hook accused her of giving priority to "agitation for equality in the bedroom rather than equality in education."[20] In a response printed in another issue of *Dissent*, Hook echoed William Couch and other midcentury white liberals and insisted that African Americans were "profoundly uninterested" in antimiscegenation laws.[21] Arendt's argument was so controversial that the editors of *Dissent* included two rebuttals in the same issue in which "Reflections on Little Rock" appeared. In his response, political philosopher David Spitz advised Arendt to limit her philosophical interventions to the realm of the possible: "Surely what is today possible, and what is today sought *first* by those who are oppressed, is not the right to be accepted as a brother-in-law but as a brother."[22]

Whether in 1930 or 1960, this kind of false dichotomy (between brothers and brothers-in-law) typified the response of white liberal supporters of civil rights when they were forced to address marriage. Like Hook and Spitz in 1959, those few whites willing to advocate complete equality and the abolition of all segregation laws after WWII could only articulate their position on the grounds that sex and marriage between Blacks and whites were off the table. Even in the late 1950s, whites were unaware of or resistant to the basic message of *What the Negro Wants*, which made perfectly clear African Americans' desire for full equality in all realms of society and their capacity to speak for themselves. (That book retained its subversive implications for white supremacy and was pulled off the shelves of overseas US Information Service libraries by Joseph McCarthy's henchmen.)[23] Like African Americans during World War II, Arendt recognized racially restrictive marriage laws for the hallmark of tyranny that they were. The German refugee had met them before.

IT TOOK ROUGHLY forty years for Americans to apply—even weaponize—the reasoning of *Loving* to same-sex marriage. Over the past twenty years, the right to marry has moved to the center of discussions about civil rights in contemporary America. The argument over gay marriage rights, for example, is founded in part on the assumption that marriage is both a human and a constitutional right. As historian George Chauncey explains in his book *Why Marriage? The History Shaping Today's Debate over Gay Equality*, "the freedom to marry, and above all the freedom to choose one's partner in marriage, has come to be seen by the courts and the American people as a fundamental civil right."[24]

Although the Jim Crow South was exceptional in many ways, in its regulation of marriage it was not: it was normative. Any discussion of marriage rights in the Jim Crow era necessarily ventures beyond the boundaries of the South and reminds one that state-supported racial segregation and discrimination were national, and not simply regional, phenomena.

At the end of the twentieth century, arguments for freedom of marriage and against racial discrimination took the United States in unprecedented directions. Justifications by African Americans about marriage as a basic right laid the foundation for same-sex marriage. Advocates of marriage equality embraced the premise, set forth in the *Brown v. Board* and *Loving v. Virginia* decisions, that marriage is indeed a fundamental right. This noteworthy expansion of rights is also under assault by members of the Christian right who, as they did with interracial sex and marriage, deploy the religion clauses against them. The Supreme Court, in *Masterpiece Cakeshop v. Colorado Civil Rights Commission*, ruled that long-established religious scruples do not necessarily overcome civil rights laws. Justice Anthony Kennedy, who wrote the majority decision, cited *Newman v. Piggie Park Enterprises*, a 1968 case that rejected a claim of religious exemption for a barbecue joint whose owner asserted that serving Black people offended his religion. In this instance, Kennedy wrote, the Colorado Civil Rights Commission, in its hearing, did not afford the owner of the cakeshop "neutral and respectful consideration of his claims" for religious exemption.[25]

Since emancipation, African Americans have openly and consistently claimed the right to marry whomever they wished. Questions about sex and marriage have been at the core of civil rights conversations since 1866, but equality of marriage never drove the civil rights agenda and only burst on the political scene beginning in the 1990s, with cases in Massachusetts and Hawaii, when same-sex-marriage advocates linked freedom of marriage in theory and practice to the Black freedom struggle. The success of this strategy represents the dramatic evolution and expansion of family and sexual rights in America, as well as the gradual acceptance by all subgroups of Americans of interracial marriage over the course of forty years. After World War II, it was extremely difficult for "whites of goodwill" to deny the importance of sex and marriage rights to African Americans.

Toward the end of WWII, a lieutenant from the Deep South wrote to Margaret Halsey of the Stage Door Canteen in New York—recall, one of a handful of integrated USO facilities. Describing himself as one of those "who seek democracy in a nation where it is sometimes hard to find," the lieutenant continued, "even I am not sure how far I would go to [e]nsure that democracy."

> I want my colored friend to vote; I want him to be free from prejudice in the courts; I want him to go to college; I want him to have the best of living conditions; I want him to be paid what he is worth; I want him to be an active and respected member of any union he desires; I want him to know and enjoy the Four Freedoms. I will work and work hard to see that he—or his sons—gets these things, but—I do not want him to live next door to me; I do not want him to be my house guest; and I do not want him to dance with my daughter. How can I reconcile these conflicting desires?

Halsey responded that she did not think the lieutenant, or most white Southerners of that generation, could reconcile those conflicting desires. She thought they would just have to live with the tension the conflicting desires produced. Join an organization dedicated to racial justice, Halsey advised the white man, and "stock up on bicarbonate of soda and try not to think of posterity."[26]

Acknowledgments

This book has taken slightly longer to complete than anticipated. Indeed, in the span of the few years that I have spent on this project, my first graduate research assistant, Scott Marler, became a tenured professor. My son Alex, who was seven years old when I began, recently refinanced his mortgage. The Blackhawks won the Stanley Cup *three times*. The Cubs even won the World Series.

Nobody researches a book entirely alone. I have benefited from some talented and resourceful research assistants: Emma Broder, Ann Fefferman, Rachel Feinberg, Kayla Ginsburg, Alex Hofmann, Katherine Jones, Scott Marler, Rachel Rosenberg, Alyssa Smith, and Daniel Vivian have all enriched this project through their work and conversation. Angelina Keating of the Library of Congress Publishing Office explored the National Archives for me while I was abroad for a year. Amazingly, Anji managed to sweet-talk Louis Till's court-martial trial transcript out of a reluctant government, and she slipped into the reputedly restricted NAACP Legal Defense Fund papers while no one was looking.

My colleagues at the University of Chicago, especially the participants in the American History Workshop, have improved this book

Acknowledgments

through their careful reading and smart questioning of several papers I've presented. I am especially indebted to Thomas Holt, Adam Green, Jon Levy, Matthew Briones, Amy Lippert, Matthew Kruer, Amy Dru Stanley, Linda Zerilli, and Curtis Evans (who generously shared his work in progress on the Federal Council of Churches). Mary Anne Case invited me to present at her workshop and inadvertently introduced me to my now husband. I am grateful on both counts. I am thankful for Mark Phillip Bradley's friendship (and that of our gustatory partner in crime Jim Ketelaar), and for Mark's sharp thinking about the book and support as faculty director of the Pozen Family Center for Human Rights.

Graduate students at Rice University, Johns Hopkins University, and the University of Chicago have kept my interest in this project from flagging and contributed to its completion through conversations, research assistance, and pub dates. Thanks to Richard Brust, Rachel Feinmark, Alex Hofmann, Nick Kryczka, Sarah Levine-Gronningsater, Naama Maor, Scott Marler, Emily Masghati, John McCallum, Sarah Miller-Davenport, Shaul Mitelpunkt, Guy Mount, Carlos Rangel, Emily Remus, Allison Robinson, Rachel Rosenberg, Kathryn Schumaker, Savi Sedulak, Robert Suits, Emily Swafford, Katherine Turk, Sarah Weicksel, and Lael Weinberger.

I WOULD LIKE to thank the many colleagues who have read pieces of this book, commented on presentations at conferences, and/or participated in learned conversations at bars across the South. Please forgive the long list: so many people have been so generous over the years that I think it only right to thank them publicly. Ray Arsenault, Tony Badger, Manfred Berg, Elizabeth Borgwardt, William Chafe, Katherine Charron, Andrew Cohen (who also got me a gig on a comedy blog, which was the best antidote to writing), David Chappell, Stephanie Cole, Joe Crespino, Mary Dudziak, Laura Edwards, Adam Fairclough, Sarah Flynn, Eric Foner, Ute Frevert, Sarah Gardner, Sarah Barringer Gordon, Grace Hale, Jacqueline Dowd Hall, Peter Jelavich, Martha Jones, Laura Kalman, Stephen Kantrowitz, Ira Katznelson, Michael Klarman, John

Acknowledgments

Kneebone, Robert Korstad, Kevin Kruse, Pnina Lahav, Karen Leathem, Adrienne Lenz-Smith, Ken Mack, Tim Mennel of the University of Chicago Press, Simon Newman, Ted Ownby, Nell Irvin Painter, Jennifer Rittenhouse, Richard Rosengarten, Christopher Schmidt, Daniel Sharfstein, Manisha Sinha, J. Douglas Smith, Marjorie Spruill, Christine Stansell, Steven Stowe, David Tanenbaum, Brent Tarter, Heather Ann Thompson, Christopher Tomlins, Sandra Treadway, Steven Tuck, Allen Tullos, Timothy Tyson, Anders Walker, Peter Wallenstein, Brian Ward, Jason Morgan Ward, Clive Webb, and my dear friend Michael Willrich, whom I have known since our bright college days.

The late Michael O'Brien was an inspiration and, more directly, a brilliant interlocutor. The world of American history is poorer for his absence.

I might have been able to write this book without presenting parts of it at other universities and institutes, but it would not have been nearly as much fun, and the book would have suffered from a lack of engagement. An astonishing number of colleagues at institutions in the United States and abroad welcomed me to their universities, and frequently their homes. I thank my hosts at: the University of Leipzig; the Max Planck Institute for Human Development; the Historisches Seminar der Universität Heidelberg; Oxford University; University of Cambridge; University of Glasgow; University of Leiden; the American Academy in Berlin; Hebrew University; the German Historical Institute in Washington, DC; Lycoming College; Princeton University; Boston University Law School; University of Pennsylvania Law School; University of Delaware; University of Texas-Arlington; University of North Carolina Asheville; University of North Carolina Chapel Hill Law School; University of North Carolina Charlotte; University of Virginia; University of Michigan Law School; Houston Holocaust Museum; Brandeis University; University of Mississippi; University of Alabama; Virginia Military Institute; University of Notre Dame; University of Georgia; University of California Los Angeles; University of Sussex; and University of Newcastle upon Tyne.

Acknowledgments

There are a few people who have truly gone beyond all expectations in helping me write and, especially, finish this book.

Thank you, Larry Lessig, for your unexpected random acts of encouragement over the past few years. Your enthusiasm was contagious.

I met Brenda and Charles Eagles on my first trip to Oxford, Mississippi. After enduring an impromptu oral exam in Southern history from Charles, I was allowed to stay for dinner. Over the years, Charles has mailed me documents from whatever archive he was working in, with notes saying, "Thought you might find this interesting." Some of them were very interesting indeed!

Historians would be lost without archivists. I am grateful for the able and helpful archivists and librarians at the William David McCain Library and Archives at the University of Mississippi, the Wilson Library at the University of North Carolina at Chapel Hill, the Rare Book and Manuscript Library at Duke University, the University of Southern Mississippi, the Jean and Alexander Heard Libraries at Vanderbilt University, and the Library of Congress.

I have benefited enormously from a variety of organizations that coordinate conferences where conversations take place around a bar. I am deeply indebted to the Southern Historical Association for offering an annual conference in which to learn, grow, and make lifelong friends; to the members of the Southern Association for Women Historians for their concentrated scholarship, professional support, and friendship; to the Southern Intellectual History Circle (and to Orville Vernon Burton for opening the gates to the riffraff); to the American Association for Legal History, and the American Studies Association for having a conference in Puerto Rico at a hotel with a swim-up bar. I am so glad to have been welcomed into the British American Studies Association, and to have benefited from many conferences and refreshing conversations with colleagues in England and Scotland.

I spent the fall of 2004 in Berlin as a Berlin Prize Fellow, courtesy of the American Academy in Berlin. The Hans Arnhold Center in

Acknowledgments

Wannsee was a sublime setting to dig into a book. Through the American Academy I met American historians in Heidelberg and Leipzig, who inevitably altered my perspective on American history.

Three other funding organizations supported my work through fellowships: the American Council of Learned Societies, the John Simon Guggenheim Memorial Foundation, and the Alphonse Fletcher Sr. Foundation, Johns Hopkins University and the University of Chicago, including the Center for the Study of Race, Politics and Culture and the Pozen Family Center for Human Rights. Each provided crucial institutional support in the form of leave time and research funds. I could not have asked for more generous support.

My family has been relentlessly encouraging even when no solid evidence of a book appeared. Thanks to: Judy Dailey, Scott Dailey, Sue Mara, Laura Hanley, Mark Phillips, Julie Stone, Scott Mendeloff, Madeline Mendeloff, Jackson Mendeloff, Bethany Bailey, Mollie Stone, Patty Culyer, and precious Amaya Bee and Leni. My son Alexander Nirenberg is, in addition to being a mensch, a very clear thinker who helped me formulate several key arguments in this book. Glenda Gilmore and Bryant Simon have been family for more than thirty years. What would I do without them? My father, Bill Dailey, did not live to see this book—but there's a chance he might have read it if given the opportunity.

This book is vastly improved thanks to the labor of my very talented and thoughtful editor at Basic Books, Connor Guy. I am grateful to him for adopting this book. Brandon Proia was a knowledgeable and uncompromising line editor. Many thanks to Ann Kirchner, the designer of the book jacket, and Chin-Yee Lai, the art director, for imagining such a beautiful cover. I am grateful for Melissa Veronesi's organization and her patience, and for Kelley Blewster's meticulous copyediting.

"Agent" doesn't begin to describe the relationship I have with Geri Thoma, of Writers' House. She has believed in me and this project for years, and I thank her for her bottomless support and good humor.

Acknowledgments

Thanks to the Space Penguins and the Revival theater for keeping me sane as I finished this book, and to Randy Picker for introducing me to improv.

My husband, Geoffrey R. Stone, came along about halfway through the process of writing *White Fright*. This poor man has participated in endless conversations about it. He has read every single word of this book and erased quite a few of them. In addition to being a razor-sharp reader, Geof is a magnificent editor, and this book benefited substantially from his purple pen. He corrected numerous imprecise formulations of the law. Without his support for this project and his unwavering faith in its author, there would be no book. I thank him from the bottom of my heart—which overflows with love for him.

Notes

Introduction: Origins of White Fright

1. "Emily W. Reed, 89, Librarian in '59 Alabama Racial Dispute," *New York Times*, May 29, 2000. Cf. "Emily Reed; Librarian Resisted Racists," *Los Angeles Times*, June 5, 2000; Werner Sollors, "Can Rabbits Have Interracial Sex?" in *Mixing Race, Mixing Culture: Inter-American Literary Dialogues*, ed. M. Kaup and D. Rosenthal (Austin: University of Texas Press, 2002).

2. On interracial sex in Virginia during this period, see Martha Hodes, *White Women, Black Men: Illicit Sex in the 19th-Century South* (New Haven, CT: Yale University Press, 1997); Thomas E. Buckley "Unfixing Race: Class, Power, and Identity in an Interracial Family," *Virginia Magazine of History and Biography* 102 (1994), 349–380; Joshua D. Rothman, *Notorious in the Neighborhood: Sex and Families Across the Color Line in Virginia, 1789–1861* (Chapel Hill: University of North Carolina Press, 2003); and Philip D. Morgan, "Interracial Sex in the Chesapeake and the British Atlantic World, c. 1700–1820," in *Sally Hemings and Thomas Jefferson: History, Memory and Civic Culture*, ed. Jan Ellen Lewis and Peter S. Onuf (Charlottesville: University of Virginia Press, 1999), 52–84. More broadly, see Diane Miller Sommerville, *Rape and Race in the Nineteenth-Century South* (Chapel Hill: University of North Carolina Press, 2004).

3. Joel Williamson makes this point in his book *New People: Miscegenation and Mulattos in the United States* (Baton Rouge: Louisiana State University Press, 1995), 93–94.

4. There is a rich and growing literature on racial definition and passing. See, among others, Paul R. Spickard, *Mixed Blood: Intermarriage and Ethnic Identity in Twentieth-Century America* (Madison: University of Wisconsin Press, 1989); David Roediger, *The Wages of Whiteness: Race and the Making of the American Working Class* (New York: Verso, 1991), Grace Elizabeth Hale, *Making Whiteness: The Culture of Segregation in the South, 1890–1940* (New York: Pantheon, 1998); Matthew Frye Jacobson, *Whiteness of a Different Color: European Immigrants and the Alchemy of Race* (Cambridge, MA: Harvard University Press, 1998); Ariela Julie Gross, *What Blood Won't Tell: A History of Race on Trial in America* (Cambridge, MA: Harvard University Press, 2008); Peggy Pascoe, *What Comes Naturally: Miscegenation Law and the Making of Race in America* (New York: Oxford University Press, 2009); Daniel Sharfstein, *The Invisible Line: A Secret History of Race in America* (New York: Penguin, 2012); Allyson Hobbs, *A Chosen Exile: A History of Racial Passing in American Life* (Cambridge, MA: Harvard University Press, 2014); Kali Nicole Gross, *Hannah Mary Tabbs and the Disembodied Torso: A Tale of Race, Sex, and Violence in America* (New York: Oxford University Press, 2016). This literature builds on an outpouring of work published in the mid- and late 1990s that revolved around issues of miscegenation and racial classification: for example, Shirlee Taylor Haizlip's autobiography of her mixed-race family, *The Sweeter the Juice* (New York: Simon and Schuster, 1994); Gregory Howard Williams's recollections of his discovery of his own mixed heritage, *Life on the Color Line: The True Story of a White Boy Who Discovered He Was Black* (New York: Dutton, 1995); Edward Ball's excursions into the history of the other side of his privileged white family, *Slaves in the Family* (New York: Farrar, Straus and Giroux, 1998); Henry Wiencek's amazing reconstruction of an enormous interracial clan, *The Hairstons: An American Family in Black and White* (New York: St. Martin's, 1999); and Jeffrey Lent's fictional saga of an interracial family from the Civil War through the Depression, *In the Fall* (New York: Atlantic Monthly Press, 2000). The foundational novel for all of this, of course, is Nella Larson's *Passing* (New York: Alfred A. Knopf, 1929).

5. Hodes, *White Women, Black Men*, 70.

6. Eugene D. Genovese, *Roll, Jordan, Roll: The World the Slaves Made* (New York: Vintage, 1974), 461–462. Cf. Calvin Hernton, *Sex and Racism in America* (New York: Grove, 1966). On white women and slave men, see Hodes, *White Women, Black Men*, and Diane Miller Sommerville, *Rape and Race in the Nineteenth-Century South*.

7. Steven Hahn, *A Nation Under Our Feet: Black Political Struggles in the Rural South from Slavery to the Great Migration* (Cambridge, MA: Harvard University Press, 2003), 57, 219, 163.

8. Hahn, *A Nation Under Our Feet*, 308. General Phillip Sheridan concluded that between the end of the war and 1875, some 2,141 African Americans had been killed by whites in Louisiana alone. The perpetrators escaped punishment in every case. See James Gray Pope, "Snubbed Landmark: Why *United States v. Cruikshank* (1876) Belongs at the Heart of the American Constitutional Canon," *Harvard Civil Rights–Civil Liberties Law Review* 49 (2014): 385–447, 398. Pope cites Nicholas Lemann, *Redemption: The Last Battle of the Civil War* (New York: Farrar, Straus and Giroux, 2006), 11. For Louisiana, see Pope, "Snubbed Landmark," 48; for Mississippi, see Pope, "Snubbed Landmark," 414. See also Michael Perman, *The Road to Redemption: Southern Politics, 1869–1879* (Chapel Hill: University of North Carolina Press, 1984), 169–170.

9. On marriage and the Thirteenth Amendment, see Amy Dru Stanley, "Instead of Waiting for the Thirteenth Amendment: The War Power, Slave Marriage, and Inviolate Human Rights," *American Historical Review* 115, no. 3 (June 2010): 732–765.

10. Mutilation might include cutting off an ear as punishment for running away, or "hobbling": cutting the leg tendons to prevent running.

11. Quoted in Stephen Kantrowitz, *More Than Freedom: Fighting for Black Citizenship in a White Republic, 1829–1889* (New York: Penguin Press, 2012), 313.

12. Congressional debates on the Civil Rights Act, February 2–3, 1866, in Jane Dailey, *The Age of Jim Crow: A Norton Documentary History* (New York: Norton, 2008), 8.

13. Aside from upholding the 1866 Civil Rights Act's definition of national citizenship and threatening diminished representation in Congress for states that prohibited Black men from voting, the Fourteenth Amendment referenced no positive rights at all.

14. President Andrew Johnson's veto message to Congress, March 27, 1866. Quoted in Peter Wallenstein, *Tell the Court I Love My Wife: Race, Marriage and Law—An American History* (New York: Macmillan, 2003), 59. Alabama, which had no antimiscegenation statute before the Civil War, declared interracial marriage "null and void *ab initio*" in its first postwar state constitution (1865). The Alabama Code of 1867 criminalized interracial cohabitation, adultery, and fornication (Sections 3598 and 3602). A state Supreme Court composed entirely

of Republicans declared Section 3602 unconstitutional in 1872 (*Burns v. State*). In *Burns*, Justice Benjamin F. Saffold made exactly the argument Andrew Johnson dreaded: "The civil rights bill...confers...the right to make and enforce contracts, amongst which is that of marriage with any citizen capable of entering into that relation." The revised Alabama Code of 1876 reinstated the antimiscegenation law, and an all-Democratic court reversed the *Burns* decision in *Green v. State* (1878). The laws were reinstated, along with the Democrats, in the 1870s. See Wallenstein, *Tell the Court*, 70–72, 75–77.

15. Pascoe, *What Comes Naturally*, 29–30. A majority of states had antimiscegenation statutes at some point in their history. At the end of WWII, for example, thirty of forty-eight states still had these laws on the books. For a detailed look at this history, see Wallenstein, *Tell the Court*.

16. Wallenstein, *Tell the Court*, 69–93, especially 80. Legislatures acted in Florida, Arkansas, Mississippi, South Carolina, and Louisiana. State courts acted in Texas, Alabama, Mississippi, and Louisiana. During Reconstruction six Republican state legislatures in the South either repealed their states' restrictive marriage laws or found them unconstitutional under the Fourteenth Amendment. Five states either repealed their antimiscegenation laws (South Carolina, Louisiana, and Mississippi) or simply omitted them when drafting new codes of law (Arkansas and Florida).

17. *Congressional Globe*, 39th Cong., 1st Sess., Pt 1 at 322 (1899). Cf. Alfred Avins, "Anti-Miscegenation Laws and the Fourteenth Amendment: The Original Intent," *Virginia Law Review* 52 (1966): 1224–1255.

18. For an illuminating discussion of the "social equality" question and its relationship to the Civil Rights Act and the Fourteenth and Fifteenth Amendments, see Kate Masur, *An Example for All the Land: Emancipation and the Struggle Over Equality in Washington, D.C.* (Chapel Hill: University of North Carolina Press, 2010), 119–138, quote from 136–137. On the sexualization of Reconstruction politics, see Hodes, *White Women, Black Men*, 147–175.

19. *Congressional Globe*, 39th Cong., 1st Sess., Pt 1, January 10 (1866), 180. Cf. Hodes, *White Women, Black Men*, 145.

20. *State v. Gibson*, 36 Ind. 389 (1871), at 400–403.

21. "Marriage," lectured the Texas Court of Appeals, "is not a contract protected by the Constitution of the United States, or within the meaning of the Civil Rights Bill. Marriage is more than a contract within the meaning of the act. It is a civil *status*, left solely by the Federal Constitution and the laws to the discretion of the states, under their general power to regulate their domestic affairs." *Frasher v. State*, 3 Tex. Ct. App. 263 (1877).

22. *Pace and Cox v. State*, 69 Ala. 231 (1881); *Pace v. Alabama*, 106 U.S. 583 (1883). See Wallenstein, *Tell the Court*, 110–114, 120–121; Julie Novkov, *Racial Union: Law, Intimacy, and the White State in Alabama, 1865–1954* (Ann Arbor: University of Michigan Press, 2007), 58–65.

23. *McLaughlin v. Florida*, 379 U.S. 184 (1964).

24. For a Northern example see *West Chester and Philadelphia Railroad Co. v. Miles*, 55 Pa. 209 (1867).

25. For a detailed exploration of this argument see Jane Dailey, *Before Jim Crow: The Politics of Race in Postemancipation Virginia* (Chapel Hill: University of North Carolina Press, 2000). This is not to deny that certain spaces were segregated already in the antebellum era (such as most churches and cemeteries), or that in many ways segregation was preferable for African Americans to their outright exclusion of access (for instance, to schools) before emancipation. See Howard N. Rabinowitz, "From Exclusion to Segregation: Southern Race Relations from 1865–1890," *Journal of American History* 63, no. 2 (September 1976): 325–350.

26. Glenda Elizabeth Gilmore, *Gender and Jim Crow: Women and the Politics of White Supremacy in North Carolina, 1896–1920* (Chapel Hill: University of North Carolina Press, 1996), 83–88.

27. Manly quoted in Adam Fairclough, *Better Day Coming: Blacks and Equality, 1890–2000* (New York: Viking, 2001), 9.

28. On the Wilmington Riot see Timothy B. Tyson and David S. Cecelski, *Democracy Betrayed: The Wilmington Race Riot and Its Legacy* (Chapel Hill: University of North Carolina Press, 1998).

29. Mississippi quote from Edward L. Ayers, *The Promise of the New South: Life After Reconstruction* (New York: Penguin Books, 1992), 147.

30. Mississippi's 1890 constitution limited Black political participation through a combination of complicated registration procedures, a poll tax, a literacy requirement, and what was dubbed an "understanding clause" designed to guard the interests of illiterate white Democrats.

31. Statistic from Fairclough, *Better Day Coming*, 16.

Chapter One: Fighting for Justice

1. *Plessy v. Ferguson*, 163 U.S. 537, 559 (1896).

2. *Plessy*, 163 U.S. at 560, 544, 561, 563. For a concise history of the *Plessy* case see Charles A. Lofgren, *The Plessy Case: A Legal-Historical Interpretation* (New York: Oxford University Press, 1987).

3. *Plessy*, 163 U.S. at 544, 545, 550–551. *Plessy v. Ferguson* said nothing at all about equality and, indeed, rejected equality as a condition for segregation. The Louisiana statute, and not the court, imposed the standard of equality. Indeed, only three years later, the court accepted unequal conditions for segregation in the first segregated public school case that came before them after ruling in *Plessy*. Benno C. Schmidt Jr., "Principle and Prejudice: The Supreme Court and Race in the Progressive Era. Part 1: The Heyday of Jim Crow," *Columbia Law Review* 82, no. 3 (April 1982): 444–524, esp. 468; Michael J. Klarman, *From Jim Crow to Civil Rights: The Supreme Court and the Struggle for Racial Equality* (New York: Oxford University Press, 2004), 46. On *Cumming v. Richmond County Board of Education*, 29 S.E. 488 (Ga. 1898), affirmed, 175 U.S. 528 (1899), see J. Morgan Kousser, "Separate but *Not* Equal: The Supreme Court's First Decision on Racial Discrimination in Schools," *Journal of Southern History* 46 (1980), 17–44. The court also upheld its earlier finding in *Pace v. Alabama* (106 U.S. 583 [1883]), where it had upheld a law that imposed on members of both races a heavier penalty for fornication across the color line than for fornication within race boundaries.

4. *Plessy*, 163 U.S. at 561, 562; *West Chester and Philadelphia R.R. v. Miles*, 55 Pa. 211-12 (1867). On the gendered aspects of rail segregation, see Barbara Y. Welke, "When All the Women Were White, and All the Blacks Were Men: Gender, Class, Race, and the Road to *Plessy*, 1855–1914," *Law and History Review* 12, no. 2 (1995), 261–316, esp. 307. Welke notes that educated, propertied, urban Black women brought a majority of the lawsuits challenging segregation on common carriers. For a broader consideration of women and the railroads, including the race issue, see Amy G. Richter, *Home on the Rails: Women, the Railroad, and the Rise of Public Domesticity* (Chapel Hill: University of North Carolina Press, 2005), esp. 99–104.

5. Quoted in Schmidt, "Principle and Prejudice," 447. *Berea College v. Commonwealth*, 123 Ky. 209, 94 S.W. 623 (1906). See also "Experiment in Interracial Education at Berea College," *The Nation* 87 (1908), 480–481, which pointed out that the same logic that made it a crime to educate Blacks and whites under the same roof could be used to prohibit the coeducation of Jews and Gentiles. The *Richmond Times Dispatch* justified the separate-car law thusly: "It is necessary that this principle be applied in every relation of Southern life. God Almighty drew the color line and it cannot be obliterated. The negro must stay on his side of the line and the white man must stay on his side, and the sooner both races recognize this fact and accept it, the better it will be for both." Quoted

in C. VannWoodward, "The Case of the Louisiana Traveler," in *Quarrels That Have Shaped the Constitution*, ed. John A. Garraty (New York: Harper and Row, 1964), 145–158.

6. "Constitutionality of a Statute Compelling the Color Line in Private Schools," *Harvard Law Review* 22 (1909): 217, 218.

7. Richard Kluger, *Simple Justice: The History of* Brown v. Board of Education *and Black America's Struggle for Equality* (New York: Knopf, 1975), 108. Baltimore enacted the first residential segregation law in 1910. By 1913, Atlanta, Richmond, Norfolk, and Roanoke had followed suit, as had Winston-Salem, North Carolina. In the next three years the laws spread westward, to Louisville, St. Louis, Oklahoma City, and New Orleans. See Roger L. Rice, "Residential Segregation by Law, 1910–1917," *Journal of Southern History* 34, no. 2 (May 1968): 179–199.

8. Kluger, *Simple Justice*, 109.

9. *Buchanan v. Warley*, 245 U.S. 60 (1917), at 7, quoted in Schmidt, "Principle and Prejudice," 505.

10. See J. R. Pole, *The Pursuit of Equality in American History* (Berkeley: University of California Press, 1978), 258. On residential segregation in the South, see Rice, "Residential Segregation by Law, 1910–1917," 34.

11. *Guinn v. United States*, 238 U.S. 347 (1915), is the Oklahoma grandfather case.

12. Schmidt, "Principle and Prejudice," 506.

13. Regarding the view that antimiscegenation laws constituted a legitimate state power: "Laws forbidding the intermarriage of the two races may be said in a technical sense to interfere with the freedom of contract, and yet have been universally recognized as within the police power of the State." *Plessy v. Ferguson*, 163 U.S. 537, 545 (1896). The "universal," of course, was an exaggeration, as several Southern states repealed their antimiscegenation laws during Reconstruction. Day quote is from *Buchanan*, 245 U.S. at 76–82; quoted in Schmidt, "Principle and Prejudice," 507–508.

14. Schmidt, "Principle and Prejudice," 508.

15. Schmidt, "Principle and Prejudice," 509.

16. *Dred Scott v. Sandford*, 60 U.S. 393 (1857).

17. Glenda Elizabeth Gilmore, *Defying Dixie: The Radical Roots of Civil Rights, 1919–1950* (New York: Norton, 2008). On the experiences of African American soldiers in WWI, see Adriane Lentz-Smith, *Freedom Struggles: African Americans and WWI* (Cambridge, MA: Harvard University Press, 2009).

18. I have leaned on Daniel T. Rodgers's formulation of the state of postwar European society here. See Rodgers, *Atlantic Crossing: Social Politics in a Progressive Age* (Cambridge, MA: Harvard University Press, 1998), esp. 290–318.

19. Address of the President of the United States to the Senate, January 22, 1917, outlining the American position on the war.

20. Adam Fairclough, *Better Day Coming: Blacks and Equality, 1890–2000* (New York: Viking, 2001), 91, 93.

21. Richard Dalfiume, *Desegregation of the U.S. Armed Forces: Fighting on Two Fronts, 1939–1953* (Columbia: University of Missouri Press, 1969), 15, quoting the 92nd's former chief of staff and General Robert Lee Bullard, commander of the Second Army, to which the 92nd was assigned.

22. Dalfiume, *Desegregation of the U.S. Armed Forces*, 19. For a history of Black soldiers in WWI, see Arthur E. Barbeau and Florette Henri, *The Unknown Soldiers: Black American Troops in World War I* (Philadelphia: Temple University Press, 1974) and Emmett J. Scott, *Scott's Official History of the American Negro in the World War* (Chicago: Homewood Press, 1919).

23. Dalfiume, *Desegregation of the U.S. Armed Forces*, 21; W. E. B. Du Bois, "An Essay Toward a History of the Black Man in the Great War," *The Crisis*, June 1919, in *W. E. B. Du Bois: A Reader*, ed. David Levering Lewis (New York: Holt Paperbacks, 1995).

24. Du Bois, "An Essay Toward a History of the Black Man in the Great War," 706–709. Du Bois refers to the death of a Black corporal shot by a lieutenant from North Carolina on 716.

25. Du Bois, "An Essay Toward a History of the Black Man in the Great War," 707, 708; Dalfiume, *Desegregation of the U.S. Armed Forces*, 18.

26. Quoted in Graham Smith, *When Jim Crow Met John Bull: Black American Soldiers in World War II Britain* (London: St. Martin's, 1987), 10–11. Cf. Dalfiume, *Desegregation of the U.S. Armed Forces*, 16, and Du Bois, "An Essay Toward a History of the Black Man in the Great War," 710, 731. Smith quotes Stephen Graham, "a young British author," who wrote in 1920, "The rape legend was imported, and every effort was made to infect the French male with race prejudice." According to Stephen Graham, the attempt failed because "Puritanism does not easily take root in a French heart" (Smith, *When Jim Crow Met John Bull*, 13).

27. Stephen Graham, quoted in Graham Smith, *When Jim Crow Met John Bull*, 13.

28. Du Bois, "An Essay Toward a History of the Black Man in the Great War," 710, 731.

29. Du Bois, "An Essay Toward a History of the Black Man in the Great War," 731–732; Jenna Rae McNeil, *Groundwork: Charles Hamilton Houston and the Struggle for Civil Rights* (Philadelphia: University of Pennsylvania Press, 1984), 44.

30. Smith reports that there were "about 1,000–2,000" marriages between Black Americans and French women during WWI (*When Jim Crow Met John Bull*, 12); Gilmore, *Defying Dixie*, 19. Vardaman quoted in M. Ellis, *Race, War, and Surveillance: African Americans and the United States Government During WWI* (Bloomington: University of Indiana Press, 2001), 222.

31. *Moore v. Dempsey*, 261 U.S. 86 (1923). The NAACP put the number of dead in Phillips County at 250; Fairclough says, "The true number was probably smaller" (*Better Day Coming*, 105).

32. Glenda Gilmore counts twenty-six race riots in 1919 (*Defying Dixie*, 18). Cf. Wilma Dykeman and James Stokley, *Seeds of Southern Change: The Life of Will Alexander* (Chicago: University of Chicago Press, 1962), 56–57.

33. Jacquelyn Dowd Hall, *Revolt Against Chivalry: Jessie Daniel Ames and the Women's Campaign Against Lynching*, rev. ed. (New York: Columbia University Press, 1993), 61.

Chapter Two: Protecting "Racial Purity"

1. Sharon Davies, *Rising Road: A True Tale of Love, Race, and Religion in America* (New York: Oxford University Press, 2009), 197. Indeed, the marriage license confirmed, if it did not actually produce, Gussman's race—as it had already in his first marriage. Gussman had previously married a white woman, who had died. Had he been reclassified by law as nonwhite, Gussman had more to lose than his wife. Pedro and Ruth did not live as husband and wife after the trial, and divorced in 1923. Davies, *Rising Road*, 285. On anti-Catholicism see John Higham, *Strangers in the Land: Patterns of American Nativism, 1860–1925* (New Brunswick, NJ: Rutgers University Press, 1955).

2. Peggy Pascoe, *What Comes Naturally: Miscegenation Law and the Making of Race in America* (New York: Oxford University Press, 2009), says, 9, that "marriage licensing was the most common, and surely the most effective, means of preventing interracial marriage and enforcing miscegenation laws."

3. "Racial reassignment" from J. Douglas Smith, *Managing White Supremacy: Race, Politics, and Citizenship in Jim Crow Virginia* (Chapel Hill: University of North Carolina Press, 2003), 122.

4. Elizabeth M. Smith-Pryor, *Property Rites: The Rhinelander Trial, Passing, and the Protection of Whiteness* (Chapel Hill: University of North Carolina Press, 2009), 98, 99.

5. Smith-Pryor, *Property Rites*, 177.

6. Smith-Pryor, *Property Rites*, 98–99.

7. Allyson Hobbs, *A Chosen Exile: A History of Racial Passing in American Life* (Cambridge, MA: Harvard University Press, 2014), 142. *Opportunity* article is from 1926.

8. *Leonard Rhinelander v. Alice Rhinelander*, 219 A.D. 189; 219 N.Y. Supreme Court of New York, Appellate Division, Second Department (1927); "Rhinelander Sues to Annul Marriage; Alleges Race Deceit," *New York Times*, November 27, 1924.

9. New York State never had an antimiscegenation law. However, the Dutch colony of New Amsterdam did. See Peter Wallenstein, *Tell the Court I Love My Wife: Race, Marriage and Law—An American History* (New York: Macmillan, 2003), Appendix 1.

10. Mrs. Caroline Astor's list of four hundred society families in New York included no "new" money gained during the Industrial Revolution. The Rhinelander family came to the New World in the 1680s. They were colonial shipbuilders and developed a large carrying (shipping) business. They also had extensive landholdings in Manhattan.

11. Smith-Pryor, *Property Rites*, 174, cites Joel Williamson, *New People: Miscegenation and Mulattoes in the United States*, rev. ed. (Baton Rouge: Louisiana State University Press, 1995), on white Southern anxiety over "invisible blackness" in the early twentieth century. W. E. B. Du Bois wrote about Leonard (Kip) Rhinelander's racial knowledge, asking "Did He Know?" *The Crisis*, January 1926, 112–113.

12. The Las Vegas divorce was not valid in New York State as long as Alice had a separation suit filed. In any case, New York allowed for divorce only in cases of adultery. Eventually Alice and Leonard came to a separation agreement. Leonard died in 1936 at the age of thirty-two. Alice never remarried and died in 1989 at age eighty-nine or ninety (there is disagreement about her birth date).

13. *Opportunity*, January 1926, 4.

14. Quoted in Smith, *Managing White Supremacy*, 94.

15. T. Lothrop Stoddard quoted in David Levering Lewis, *W. E. B. Du Bois: The Fight for Equality and the American Century* (New York: Holt Paperbacks, 2001), 235–237.

16. Davenport, *State Laws* 36 (1924), quoted in Edward J. Larson, *Sex, Race, and Science: Eugenics in the Deep South* (Baltimore, MD: Johns Hopkins University Press, 1995), 22.

17. The act was also known as the Johnson-Reed Act, in part after Congressman Albert Johnson, who served as president of the Eugenics Research Association from 1923 to 1924. See Smith-Pryor, *Property Rites*, 47. See also Mai Ngai, *Impossible Subjects: Illegal Aliens and the Making of Modern America* (Princeton, NJ: Princeton University Press, 2004), 21–55.

18. The congressman most aligned with congressional legislation and/or a constitutional amendment outlawing interracial marriage was Georgia congressman Seaborn Rodenberry. Reacting to African American boxer (and world champion) Jack Johnson's marriage to a white woman in 1910 (his second, in fact), Rodenberry introduced a bill calling for a constitutional amendment to ban interracial marriage from states where it was legal. Smith-Pryor, *Property Rites*, 318. In 1910 and 1913, New York legislators who were dismayed about Jack Johnson's marriages to white women introduced bills in the state legislature to prohibit interracial marriage. The NAACP worked hard throughout the 1920s to defeat "anti-intermarriage laws." David H. Fowler, *Northern Attitudes Towards Interracial Marriage: Legislation and Public Opinion in the Middle Atlantic and the States of the Old Northwest, 1780–1930* (New York: Garland Publishing, 1987), 299, 307–308; Nancy F. Cott, *Public Vows: A History of Marriage and the Nation* (Cambridge, MA: Harvard University Press, 2000), 163–164.

19. Quote and statistic from Pauline Maier et al., *Inventing America: A History of the United States* (New York: Norton, 2000), 690.

20. Daniel J. Kevles, *In the Name of Eugenics: Genetics and the Uses of Human Heredity* (New York: Knopf, 1985), 118.

21. Lewis, *W. E. B. Du Bois*, 237. On Stoddard, see Thomas F. Gossett, *Race: The History of an Idea in America* (New York: Oxford University Press, 1997), 390–398. On the Du Bois–Stoddard debate, see *Report of a Debate by the Chicago Forum: Shall the Negro Be Encouraged to Seek Cultural Equality?* March 17, 1929 (Chicago: Chicago Forum Council, 1929); see also Herbert Aptheker, ed., *Pamphlets and Leaflets by W. E. B. Du Bois* (White Plains, NY: Kraus-Thompson Organization, 1986), 226–229; "Du Bois Shatters Stoddard's Cultural Theories," *Defender*, March 23, 1929, 1–3; and Du Bois, "Postscript," *The Crisis*, May 1929, 167–168.

22. Lewis, *W. E. B. Du Bois*, 235–236.

Chapter Three: The United States of Lyncherdom

1. Quoted in Glenda Elizabeth Gilmore, *Gender and Jim Crow: Women and the Politics of White Supremacy in North Carolina, 1896–1920* (Chapel Hill: University of North Carolina Press, 1996), 200. The title of this chapter has been borrowed from an essay of the same name written in 1901 by Mark Twain after a lynching in his home state of Missouri; the piece remained unpublished until after his death.

2. Statistic from Equal Justice Initiative, *Lynching in America: Confronting the Legacy of Racial Terror*, 3rd ed. (Montgomery, AL: Equal Justice Initiative, 2017), 4. The *Chicago Tribune* first began to collect lynching data in 1881. This work was continued by the Tuskegee Institute and the NAACP. The phenomenon of lynching has generated an extensive historiography. For an introduction to the literature, see: Ida B. Wells, *Southern Horrors: Lynch Law in All Its Phases* (New York: New York Age Print, 1892) and *A Red Record: A History of Lynching Documented by Ida B. Wells Barnett* (Chicago: Donohue and Henneberry, 1895); Walter White, *Rope and Faggot: A Biography of Judge Lynch* (Notre Dame, IN: University of Notre Dame Press, 1929); W. J. Cash, *The Mind of the South* (New York: Vintage Books, 1991 [1941]); Jacquelyn Dowd Hall, *Revolt Against Chivalry: Jessie Daniel Ames and the Women's Campaign Against Lynching* (New York: Columbia University Press, 1974); James R. McGovern, *Anatomy of a Lynching: The Killing of Claude Neal* (Baton Rouge: Louisiana State University Press, 1982); Edward L. Ayers, *Vengeance and Justice: Crime and Punishment in the 19th-Century South* (New York: Oxford University Press, 1984); Nancy MacLean, "The Leo Frank Case Reconsidered: Gender and Sexual Politics in the Making of Reactionary Populism," *Journal of American History* 78, no. 3 (1991), 917–948; W. Fitzhugh Brundage, *Lynching in the New South: Georgia and Virginia, 1880–1930* (Chicago: University of Illinois Press, 1993); E. M. Beck and Stewart T. Tolnay, *A Festival of Violence: An Analysis of Southern Lynchings, 1882–1930* (Chicago: University of Illinois Press, 1995); W. Fitzhugh Brundage, *Under Sentence of Death: Lynching in the South* (Chapel Hill: University of North Carolina Press, 1997); Crystal N. Feimster, *Southern Horrors: Women and the Politics of Rape and Lynching* (Cambridge, MA: Harvard University Press, 2009); Michael Ayers Trotti, "What Counts: Trends in Racial Violence in the Postbellum South," *Journal of American History* 100, no. 2 (September 2013): 375–400; Equal Justice Initiative, *Lynching in America*.

3. White, *Rope and Faggot*, 20. Grace Elizabeth Hale links spectacle lynchings with a burgeoning consumer culture in the early twentieth century. Hale,

Making Whiteness: The Culture of Segregation in the South, 1890–1940 (New York: Random House, 1998).

4. Quoted in James C. Cobb, *Away Down South: A History of Southern Identity* (New York: Oxford University Press, 2005), 96–97.

5. Definition from Robert L. Zagrando, *The NAACP Crusade Against Lynching, 1909–1950* (Philadelphia: Temple University Press, 1980), 243; "two to three lynchings per week, nationally" from Hall, *Revolt Against Chivalry*, 133; "An uncomfortably large percentage" from White, *Rope and Faggot*, vii–viii.

6. Tillman quoted in Francis Butler Simkins, *Pitchfork Ben Tillman, South Carolinian* (Baton Rouge: Louisiana State University Press, 1944), 397; White, *Rope and Faggot*, 55.

7. Philip Dray, *At the Hands of Persons Unknown: The Lynching of Black America* (New York: Random House, 2002), 259–260.

8. Dray, *At the Hands of Persons Unknown*, 264.

9. Hall, *Revolt Against Chivalry*, 99.

10. Hall, *Revolt Against Chivalry*, 99.

11. Hall, *Revolt Against Chivalry*, 99.

12. Hall, *Revolt Against Chivalry*, 100.

13. Lillian Smith, *Killers of the Dream* (New York: Norton, 1994 [1949]), 121.

14. Cash, *The Mind of the South*, 115.

15. Cash, *The Mind of the South*, 115; Wells, *Southern Horrors*, 54 (electronic text).

16. Cash, *Mind of the South*, 116.

17. This synopsis is based on that provided by James Goodman in *Stories of Scottsboro* (New York: Pantheon, 1994), xi–xii.

18. Goodman, *Stories of Scottsboro*, 18.

19. Goodman, *Stories of Scottsboro*, 26.

20. Goodman, *Stories of Scottsboro*, 27, 29. Cf. Dan T. Carter, *Scottsboro: A Tragedy of the American South* (Baton Rouge: Louisiana State University Press, 1969).

21. Glenda Elizabeth Gilmore, *Defying Dixie: The Radical Roots of Civil Rights, 1919–1950* (New York: Norton, 2008), 40–42.

22. Goodman, *Stories of Scottsboro*, 65.

23. Gilmore, *Defying Dixie*, 32, 65, 98–100. See also Harry Haywood, *Black Bolshevik: Autobiography of an Afro-American Communist* (Chicago: Liberator Press, 1978), 170–171. Gilmore argues that "southern-born people" (i.e., those

who migrated north to Chicago and Harlem) "helped make the South and African Americans central to Soviet policy." African American Communists "had an influence on domestic and international Communist policy disproportionate to their meager numbers."

24. "The Social Equality of Whites and Blacks," *The Crisis*, November 1920, 16–18, in *W. E. B. Du Bois: The Crisis Writings*, ed. Daniel Walden (Greenwich, CT: Fawcett Publications, 1972), 104–107.

25. Monthly circulation of *The Crisis* in 1919 was one hundred thousand (the high-water mark), which exceeded circulation for *New Republic*, *The Nation*, and *Liberator* (Max Eastman's successor to the banned *Masses*). David Levering Lewis, *W. E. B. Du Bois: The Fight for Equality and the American Century, 1919–1963* (New York: Henry Holt, 2000), 2.

26. Gilmore, *Defying Dixie*, 124–125 ("disrupted the long-standing"); Goodman, *Stories of Scottsboro*, 57 ("amazed beyond expression").

27. *Powell v. Alabama*, 287 U.S. 45 (1932); *Norris v. Alabama*, 294 U.S. 587 (1935).

28. *Herndon v. Lowry*, 301 U.S. 242 (1937).

29. Gilmore, *Defying Dixie*, 165.

30. Zechariah Chafee Jr., *Free Speech in the United States* (Cambridge, MA: Harvard University Press, 1941), 392.

Chapter Four: "Nobody Is Asking for Social Equality"

1. Speech, "America's Obligation to Its Negro Citizens," August 4, 1938, p. 11, f. 108, Mark F. Ethridge Papers, Coll. No. 3842, Southern Historical Collection, University of North Carolina, Chapel Hill.

2. Significantly, white Southern liberals did not join the NAACP, which they considered a Northern critique of the South. A handful of more radical Southern whites did join up.

3. Quoted in John T. Kneebone, *Southern Liberal Journalists and the Issue of Race, 1920–1944* (Chapel Hill: University of North Carolina Press, 1985), 150.

4. Quoted in Kneebone, *Southern Liberal Journalists*, 91.

5. Quoted in J. Saunders Redding, "Southern Defensive," *Common Ground* (Spring 1944), 37. Cf. Charles S. Johnson, "The Present Status of Race Relations in the South," *Social Forces* 23, no. 1 (1944), 29–30. The Southern Conference on Race Relations met in Durham, North Carolina, in October 1942. The so-called Durham Manifesto (or sometimes Durham Statement) called for African American participation in the polity and an end to racial segregation.

6. The Southern states thwarted New Deal spending after President Roosevelt rocked the states'-rights boat by threatening to increase the size of the Supreme Court to preserve the New Deal; "$10 billion" statistic from John Egerton, *Speak Now Against the Day: The Generation Before the Civil Rights Movement in the South* (New York: Knopf, 1994), 207.

7. Egerton, *Speak Now Against the Day*, 206–208.

8. Karen Tucker Anderson, "Last Hired, First Fired: Black Women Workers During World War II," *Journal of American History* 69, no. 1 (June 1982): 82.

9. On the defense industry exclusion, see *Baltimore Afro-American*, November 28, 1942, 8, quoting US Bureau of Employment Security survey. Cf. Richard M. Dalfiume, *Desegregation of the U.S. Armed Forces: Fighting on Two Fronts, 1939–1950* (Columbia: University of Missouri Press, 1969), 51, and Patricia Sullivan, *Days of Hope: Race and Democracy in the New Deal Era* (Chapel Hill: University of North Carolina Press, 1996), 157. By late 1942, the Detroit area had a female work force of 96,000; a mere 100 of these were Black women. Jacquelyn Jones, *Labor of Love, Labor of Sorrow* (New York: Vintage Books, 1986), 239. The army operated from a "balanced force principle," according to which Black men would serve in proportion to their representation in the overall population. The army's goal for the war was to have 10.6 percent of its strength be Black soldiers, a goal it never reached. On the selective service quota system see Dalfiume, *Desegregation of the U.S. Armed Forces*, 50–53, 91.

10. On the March on Washington, see "Call to Negro America, 'To March on Washington for Jobs and Equal Participation in National Defense,'" *Black Worker*, May 1941, reprinted in *Reporting Civil Rights*, eds. Clayborne Carson, David J. Garrow, Bill Kovach, and Carol Polsgrove (New York: Library of America, 2003), 1:3.

11. Ottley quoted in Adam Fairclough, *Better Day Coming: Blacks and Equality, 1890–2000* (New York: Vintage, 2001), 155–157. Cf. Ottley, "Negro Morale: November 1941," *New Republic*, November 10, 1941, reprinted in *Reporting Civil Rights*, 1:5–10.

12. Jason Morgan Ward, *Defending White Democracy: The Making of a Segregationist Movement and the Remaking of Racial Politics, 1936–1965* (Chapel Hill: University of North Carolina Press, 2011), 39.

13. Ward, *Defending White Democracy*, 30 ("Of equal importance"), 79 ("Under cover of this clause,"); Fairclough, *Better Day Coming*, 186 ("kangaroo court"). On the FEPC see Merl E. Reed, *Seedtime for the Modern Civil Rights Movement: The President's Committee on Fair Employment Practice, 1941–1946*

(Baton Rouge: Louisiana State University Press, 1991). This was not the South's first experience with wartime efforts by the federal government to ameliorate conditions for Black workers. During WWI, the National War Labor Board (NWLB) intervened on the side of Black workers in disputes with white employers. Memories of the NWLB may help explain the hysterical white Southern reaction to the FEPC. On the NWLB see Robert Zieger, *America's Great War: World War I and the American Experience* (Lanham, MD: Rowman and Littlefield, 2000), 131–134.

14. Louis Ruchames, *Race, Jobs, and Politics: The Story of the FEPC* (New York: Columbia University Press, 1953), 94 (Rankin quote); Mss. tract, I.X.L., 1944, "The Insidious American Cancer," 1950 (dated in pencil), supposedly written in 1944 and "Found in the effects of a soldier killed on Leyte in November, 1944," Administrative Files, 1924–1953, Propaganda, Letters, 1944–50, Earl Warren Papers, California State Archives, Sacramento (white correspondent's quote)—hereafter Warren Papers.

15. Quoted in Ward, *Defending White Democracy*, 78 (Russell), 85 (Cox).

16. Quoted in Ward, *Defending White Democracy*, 85.

17. Carl Sandburg, "Dignity: White and Black," *Negro Digest*, November 1942.

18. Ethridge speech at Birmingham printed in its entirety in *Baltimore Afro-American*, July 11, 1942, 14.

19. *Pittsburgh Courier*, June 19, 1943, in CIC Clip Sheet, Series II, No. 12, June 30, 1943, D-15 Smmss 76–78, folder 6, CIC, Alfred H. Stone Collection, J. D. Williams Library, University of Mississippi (hereafter CIC Papers).

20. "FEPC Denies Full OK to Ethridge," *Baltimore Afro-American*, July 18, 1942, 4.

21. "FEPC Denies Full OK to Ethridge." Ethridge did, in fact, resign shortly thereafter, although more out of frustration that the FEPC had no power to achieve even the limited goals he had outlined in Birmingham than out of a sense of obligation to the *Afro-American*'s readers.

22. Wartime manufacturing and government spending more than doubled the gross national product between 1940 and 1945, from $100 billion to $214 billion.

23. *Gourmet Magazine*, 1943, quoted in Madeline Grimes, "'Summum Bonnum of Living': Food in the 1940s," website of Four Freedoms Park Conservancy, January 6, 2016, www.fdrfourfreedomspark.org/blog/2016/1/6/food-in-the-1940s.

24. Mobile water pressure story from Pete Daniel, "Going Among Strangers: Southern Reactions to World War II," *Journal of American History* 77, no. 3 (December 1990): 904–905; population statistics for Detroit from Harvard Sitkoff, *Toward Freedom Land: The Long Struggle for Racial Equality in America* (Lexington: University of Kentucky Press, 2010), 66. In 1943 President Roosevelt established the Committee for Congested Production Areas (CCPA), which tried to establish some order in dangerously congested key defense areas. Daniel, "Going Among Strangers," 899.

25. James N. Gregory, *The Southern Diaspora: How the Great Migration of Black and White Southerners Transformed America* (Chapel Hill: University of North Carolina Press, 2005), 34–35.

26. Sullivan, *Days of Hope*, 162.

27. Harvard Sitkoff, "The Detroit Race Riot of 1943," *Michigan History* 53 (Fall 1969): 188.

28. James Baldwin, *Notes of a Native Son* (Boston: Beacon Press, 1955), 99. Charles S. Johnson noted in 1944 that "the point of most frequent physical contact between whites and Negroes is in transportation, and more minor clashes have occurred in these relationships than in any other." Johnson, "The Present Status of Race Relations in the South," 28.

29. Ralph Ellison, "An Extravagance of Laughter," in *The Collected Essays of Ralph Ellison*, ed. John F. Callahan (New York: Modern Library, 1995), 621.

30. Dixon quoted in J. Mills Thornton III, "Segregation and the City: White Supremacy in Alabama in the Mid-Twentieth Century," in *Fog of War: The Second World War and the Civil Rights Movement*, ed. Kevin M. Kruse and Stephen Tuck (New York: Oxford University Press, 2012), 57.

31. Johnson, "The Present Status of Race Relations in the South," 28. Virginia E&P official quote from Bruce Nelson, "Organized Labor and the Struggle for Black Equality in Mobile During World War II," *Journal of American History* 80, no. 3 (December 1993): 967. On public transportation as a special site of resistance to Jim Crow during the war, see Robin D. G. Kelley, "The Black Poor and the Politics of Oppression in a New South City, 1929–1970," in *The "Underclass" Debate: Views from History*, ed. Michael B. Katz (Princeton, NJ: Princeton University Press, 1993), 293–333, esp. 305–309. Fairclough, in *Better Day Coming*, reports that in 1941–1942, the police in Birmingham recorded "fifty-five incidents in which Black passengers defied white drivers by refusing to give up their seats or by sitting in the white section" (191–192), and that bus drivers in Mobile, Alabama, and Alexandria, Louisiana, shot and killed Black servicemen in quarrels over segregation (193).

32. Examples are legion, but see Dr. F. D. Patterson (President of Tuskegee Institute) to Virginius Dabney, November 26, 1943, file "Segregation Correspondence 1943," box 4, Papers of Virginius Dabney, #7690, Alderman Library, University of Virginia (hereafter Dabney Papers).

33. Sterling Brown, "Out of Their Mouths: November 1942," reprinted in Carson et al., *Reporting Civil Rights*, 1:35.

34. Anderson connected shoving with interracial marriage: "I do not believe in intermarriage, of course; I don't believe in residential mixing, believing that the colored folks should live in their respective sections and fraternize among themselves, not feel they have a right to 'mix' with the whites." J. F. Anderson to Earl Warren, n.d. (received Dec. 9, 1944), F3640:3676, 1924–1953, Administrative Files, Public Works, Race Relations, Negro, 1943–1944 file, Warren Papers.

35. Nelson, "Organized Labor and the Struggle for Black Equality," 967.

36. Dabney to Louis Jaffe, November 16, 1943, file "Segregation Correspondence 1943," box 4, Dabney Papers.

37. "To Lessen Race Friction," *Richmond Times-Dispatch*, November 13, 1943; clipping, "Virginians Speak on Jim Crow," *The Crisis*, February 1944, 47, in file "Segregation Correspondence 1943," box 4, Dabney Papers.

38. Dabney to Warren M. Goddard, November 19, 1943; Warren M. Goddard to Dabney, November 23, 1943; clipping, editorial, Norfolk *Journal and Guide*, November 27, 1943; all in file "Segregation Correspondence 1943," box 4, Dabney Papers.

39. Clipping, *Baltimore Afro-American*, August 28, 1943, "Negroes, Clippings, 1942–43," box 4, Dabney Papers; Dabney to Dr. Robert H. Tucker (Dean of Washington and Lee), January 13, 1944; both in file "Segregation Correspondence 1943," box 4, Dabney Papers.

40. Howard Odum, *Race and Rumors of Race* (Chapel Hill: University of North Carolina Press, 1943), 7.

41. Steven Hahn, "'Extravagant Expectations' of Freedom: Rumour, Political Struggle, and the Christmas Insurrection Scare of 1865 in the American South," *Past and Present* 157 (November 1997): 122–158.

42. Odum, *Race and Rumors of Race*, 54–55; Sullivan, *Days of Hope*, 158–159. Numerous editorials in the CIC clip sheets from summer 1943 asserted Eleanor Roosevelt's responsibility for, among other things, the 1943 Detroit and Harlem race riots. CIC Clip Sheet, Department of Field Work, Series III, No. 10, November 30, 1943, CIC Papers.

43. Odum, *Race and Rumors of Race*, 96–104.

44. Edith M. Stern, "Riddle of the Race Riots," *Negro Digest*, October 1943, 37. Odum cites similar stories. *Race and Rumors of Race*, 58–62.

45. Odum, *Race and Rumors of Race*, 57–58.

46. Virginius Dabney to Howard Odum, August 17, 1943, folder "The Southern Regional Council, 1943–44," box 8, Dabney Papers.

47. Odum, *Race and Rumors of Race*, 56–57.

48. Quoted in Ward, *Defending White Democracy*, 53.

Chapter Five: What the Negro Wants

1. Background on Couch from John Egerton, *Speak Now Against the Day: The Generation Before the Civil Rights Movement in the South* (New York: Knopf, 1993); "parlor Bolshevik" quote from 133–134.

2. Couch to H. C. Brearley, September 22, 1932, quoted in Daniel Joseph Singal, *The War Within: From Victorian to Modernist Thought in the South, 1919–1945* (Chapel Hill: University of North Carolina Press, 1982), 283.

3. Gunnar Myrdal, *An American Dilemma: The Negro Problem and Modern Democracy* (New York: Harper and Brothers, 1944), 466. On the making of *An American Dilemma*, especially the contributions of the African American scholars, see Emily Masghati, "The Rosenwald Explorers: Race and Social Science in the Age of Jim Crow" (PhD diss., University of Chicago, 2019), Chapter 3.

4. *What the Negro Wants*, ed. Kenneth Robert Janken, African American Intellectual Heritage Series (Notre Dame, IN: University of Notre Dame Press, 2001 [1944]), xii. This edition includes Rayford Logan's introduction to a 1969 reprint as well as a new introduction by Janken. (Hereafter *WTNW*.)

5. "Who's Who," in *WTNW*, 345–352.

6. *WTNW*, xxxiii.

7. *WTNW*, 65.

8. *WTNW*, 117, 133, 161, 254. Randolph's formulation was drawn from the demand of the March on Washington Movement, as quoted by W. E. B. Du Bois in "A Chronicle of Race Relations," *Phylon* 4, no. 1 (1943): 82.

9. *WTNW*, 297, 305, 328, 326.

10. *WTNW*, xvi.

11. *WTNW*, xvi–xix.

12. *WTNW*, xxii, and Singal, *The War Within*, 299.

13. Quote from the *Times* (London) in Deborah Lipstadt, *Beyond Belief: The American Press and the Coming of the Holocaust, 1933–1945* (New York: Free Press, 1986), 189–190.

14. *WTNW*, xi. All quotes from Couch in the passage that follows come from his Publisher's Preface.

15. Quoted in *WTNW*, xxiii (Ethridge), xii (Hughes). Couch's formulation of Black inferiority in *WTNW* does not differ substantially from the view he espoused in his essay "The Negro in the South" for *Culture in the South*, in which he echoes *Dred Scott* on racial hierarchy: "The reality is the notion that the Negro is so far inferior that he has no rights which the white man is bound to respect. The racial customs, habits, and laws of the southern states are merely the external aspects of this one deep-lying reality. It is a thousand headed hydra, but unlike the mythical beast it seems to have no heart—or perhaps it has many hearts—to be pierced before it will finally die." Couch, "The Negro in the South," in *Culture in the South*, ed. W. T. Couch (Chapel Hill: University of North Carolina Press, 1934), 471.

16. Couch was referring to work by anthropologists Ruth Benedict, Melville J. Herskovits, and John Dollard, among others.

17. Ruth Benedict and Gene Weltfish, *The Races of Mankind* (New York: Public Affairs Committee, 1943), 4; Glenda Elizabeth Gilmore, *Defying Dixie: The Radical Roots of Civil Rights, 1919–1950* (New York: Norton, 2008), 396, quoting "What South Doesn't Want Soldiers to Read About Negroes," *Chicago Defender*, March 18, 1944, 1. In 1947, Walter White queried Robert Patterson, secretary of war, about the location of the recalled pamphlets, asking if the NAACP could obtain the pamphlets "by purchase or otherwise so that they may be distributed?" White to Patterson, April 16, 1947, in box 719, Record Group 407, National Archive Records Administration, Washington, DC.

18. *WTNW* coauthors who contributed to the research of *An American Dilemma* were Doxey Wilkerson and Sterling Brown. Prominent Chapel Hill scholars who were consulted for the project included Charles S. Johnson, Guion G. Johnson, and Howard Odum. Gunnar Myrdal et al., *An American Dilemma: The Negro Problem and Modern Democracy* (New York: Harper and Brothers, 1944).

19. W. E. B. Du Bois, "My Evolving Program for Negro Freedom," in *WTNW*, 31–70 (quote on 65). The Du Bois quotes in the following paragraphs are all from this source unless otherwise attributed.

20. The "great gift to mankind" reference is to Alexandre Dumas and his siblings.

21. W. E. B. Du Bois, "A Social Program for Black and White Americans," commencement address at Florida A&M College, Tallahassee, delivered May 31, 1943, in Du Bois, *Against Racism: Unpublished Essays, Papers, Addresses,*

1887–1961, ed. Herbert Aptheker (Amherst: University of Massachusetts Press, 1985); 206–219 (quote on 209). "If every law restricting marriage between races in the United States were repealed tomorrow there would be no appreciable increase in intermarriage." Du Bois, "A Social Program for Black and White Americans," 215.

22. J. Saunders Redding, "Fourteen Negro Voices," *New Republic*, November 20, 1944.

23. William Shands Meacham, "The Negro's Future in America," *New York Times Book Review*, November 5, 1944.

24. J. Saunders Redding, "Southern Defensive," *Common Ground*, Spring 1944.

25. Myrdal, *American Dilemma*, 61; Eleanor Roosevelt, "The Four Equalities," *Negro Digest*, September 1943, 81.

26. David Levering Lewis, *W. E. B. Du Bois: The Fight for Equality and the American Century, 1919–1963* (New York: Henry Holt, 2000), 453; Sparks quoted in J. Mills Thornton III, "Segregation and the City: White Supremacy in Alabama in the Mid-Twentieth Century," in *Fog of War: The Second World War and the Civil Rights Movement*, ed. Kevin M. Kruse and Stephen Tuck (New York: Oxford University Press, 2012), 59.

27. "Is Social Equality a Red Herring?," CIC Clip Sheet, Series III, No. 8, October 30, 1943, D-15 SmmSS 76-78, folder 6, CIC, Alfred H. Stone Collection, J. D. Williams Library, University of Mississippi (hereafter CIC Papers).

28. "How the South Feels About the Race Problem," *Reader's Digest*, June 1944, folder 36, box 9, David L. Cohn Papers, Special Collections, J. D. Williams Library, University of Mississippi. For more on Cohn, see James C. Cobb, ed., *The Mississippi Delta and the World: The Memoirs of David L. Cohn* (Baton Rouge: Louisiana State University Press, 1995), especially the "Editor's Afterword," 183–213. Cohn's position that sex is at the core of life is neither radical nor original, although it did shock a number of his readers. Schopenhauer said more or less the same thing (sexual instinct is the "Sovereign of the World") in his critique of Hegel in the nineteenth century. "Über die Metaphysick der Geschlechtsliebe," *Die Welt als Wille und Vorstellung*, Ergänzungen zum vierten Buch, Kap. 44. Cohn probably got his Schopenhauer via Freud.

29. "A Texan," n.d. (1944); Wm. J. Frazier Jr., June 1, 1944; Vivan Thomas and Phyllis Freeman, May 2, 1944. All in folder 36, box 9, David L. Cohn Papers, Special Collections, J. D. Williams Library, University of Mississippi. Thanks to Neil McMillen for drawing my attention to this collection.

30. Editorial, *Southern Frontier*, March 1944.

31. Margaret Anderson to Virginius Dabney, January 21, 1943, "Southern Regional Council, 1943–44" folder, box 8, Dabney Papers #7690, Alderman Library, University of Virginia (hereafter Dabney Papers).

32. Lillian Smith to Dr. Guy B. Johnson, Executive Director of SRC, June 12, 1944, "Southern Regional Council, 1943–44" folder, box 8, Dabney Papers.

33. *Pittsburgh Courier*, quoted in CIC Clip Sheet, Series II, No. 9, May 15, 1943, in report on "The Public's Reaction to the Atlanta Conference, April 8, 1943," CIC Papers.

34. McKensie quoted in CIC Clip Sheet, Series III, No. 7, October 15, 1943, CIC Papers; Will W. Alexander, "Our Conflicting Racial Policies," *Harper's*, January 1, 1945.

Chapter Six: Fighting Hitler and Jim Crow

1. Background and quotes from Mamie Till-Mobley and Christopher Benson, *Death of Innocence: The Story of the Hate Crime That Changed America* (New York: Random House, 2003), 13–17.

2. Chester Himes's 1945 novel about a Black war worker, *If He Hollers, Let Him Go* (New York: Doubleday, 1945), includes a judicial conscription. Adam Fairclough, *Better Day Coming: Blacks and Equality, 1890–1920* (New York: Vintage, 2001), 185, writes, "By the time of Pearl Harbor, blacks in the South were organizing more openly, speaking more confidently, and acting more militantly than they had been for a generation." Fairclough also notes, 192, that "black servicemen joined the NAACP in droves."

3. *Christian Science Monitor*, April 18, 1933, quoted in Deborah E. Lipstadt, *Beyond Belief: The American Press and the Coming of the Holocaust, 1933–1945* (New York: Free Press, 1986), 35. Lipstadt writes, "The persecution of the Jews…was never the central theme of the reports about the new [Nazi] regime" (15). Had Lipstadt read African American newspapers, she would have noted the difference in their reporting from that of the mainstream white press. Not that Lipstadt should be singled out for reproach; her principal source, the daily *Press Information Bulletin*, prepared by the Division of Press Intelligence for FDR, did not include a single African American paper (p. 5). James Q. Whitman makes a similar error in *Hitler's American Model: The United States and the Making of Nazi Race Law* (Princeton, NJ: Princeton University Press, 2017), 17, when he says that US newspapers soft-pedaled the race laws.

4. *Philadelphia Tribune*, May 10, 1934, 4. Lipstadt, in *Beyond Belief*, writes, "Rarely was news of the persecution of the Jews handled by journalists…as an inherent expression of Nazism. This failure to see Nazi antisemitism [*sic*] as a reflection of the fundamental principles of Nazism was to have important consequences for the interpretation and comprehension of the news of the persecution of European Jewry" (p. 15). Rather, other strands of the story took precedence: the Reichstag fire, the crackdown on communists and socialists, etc. Those reporters who did focus on Nazi atrocities toward Jews, such as the *New York Evening Post*'s H. R. Knickerbocker, Edmond Taylor of the *Chicago Tribune*, and the *Chicago Defender*'s George Padmore, were forced to leave Germany. Padmore was arrested in 1933 and deported from Germany for criticizing Hitler's treatment of Negroes from the former German African colonies living in Germany. "Hitler Will Treat Jews like Blacks: Adopts South African Methods to Deal with Problem," *Chicago Defender*, November 13, 1937, 24. Cf. Lipstadt, *Beyond Belief*, 14. Johnpeter Horst Grill and Robert L. Jenkins, "The Nazis and the American South in the 1930s: A Mirror Image?" *Journal of Southern History* 58 (November 1992): 668, note that "white southern newspaper editorials condemned Nazi racism but refused to acknowledge the obvious similarities between the German racial system and that of the South in the 1930s." Cf. John T. Kneebone, *Southern Liberal Journalists and the Issue of Race, 1920–1944* (Chapel Hill: University of North Carolina Press, 1985), 181, who says that liberal Southern journalists made racial prejudice (but not segregation per se) "unrespectable" by identifying it with the Klan and the Nazis.

5. *Baltimore Afro-American*, September 21, 1935, 12; September 9, 1939, 4. Du Bois quoted Stalin on the absence of racial prejudice in the Red Army in "A Chronicle of Race Relations," *Phylon* 3, no. 2 (1942): 208.

6. Du Bois, "The Present Plight of the German Jew," *Pittsburgh Courier*, December 19, 1936, in *W. E. B. Du Bois: A Reader*, ed. David Levering Lewis (New York: Henry Holt, 1995), 81; "American Nazis Quite as Bestial as Their German Brothers," *Baltimore Afro-American*, August 24, 1935, 6. For further examples of the African American press drawing equivalences between Germany and the American South, see *Baltimore Afro-American*, October 18, 1941 ("Nazism in Wilmington"); September 20, 1941 ("Nazis Ape American Jim Crow"); October 25, 1941 ("Germs of Hitlerism in U.S."). See also *Philadelphia Tribune*, October 12, 1933.

7. Although there were significant differences between German and Italian thinking on race when it came to Jews during those countries' respective fascist

regimes, regarding Africans and their descendants the distance was not great. Mussolini declared theories of racial equality "absolutely inadmissible" in the Manifesto of Race (1938) shortly after attacking Ethiopia, which he considered an act in the defense of "western civilization against the colored races." Harvard Sitkoff, "African Americans, American Jews, and the Holocaust," in *The Achievement of American Liberalism*, ed. William Chafe (New York: Columbia University Press, 2002), 181–203, esp. 182, and Dennis Mack Smith, *Mussolini* (New York: Random House, 1982), 182.

8. J. A. Rogers, *Pittsburgh Courier*, October 17, 1936, 2. *Opportunity* magazine editorialized in 1939, "Germany is modeling its program of Jewish persecution after American persecution of Negroes." *Opportunity*, January 1939, 2. Cf. Grill and Jenkins, "The Nazis and the American South in the 1930s," 667–694, esp. 675. See also the compilation from Black newspapers by Lunabelle Wedlock, "Comparisons by Negro Publications of the Plight of the Jews in Germany with That of the Negro in America," in *Strangers and Neighbors: Relations Between Blacks and Jews in the United States*, ed. Maurianne Adams and John Bracy (Amherst: University of Massachusetts Press, 1999), 427–433.

9. Whitman, *Hitler's American Model*, 12; Pierre L. van den Berghe, "Miscegenation in South Africa," *Cahiers d'etudes africaines* 1, no. 4 (1960): 68–84, esp. 71.

10. Whitman, *Hitler's American Model*, 113; see also pages 33, 46–47, 78, and 79 for more on the Nazi interest in American immigration policies. See also Stefan Kuehl, *The Nazi Connection: Eugenics, American Racism, and German National Socialism* (New York: Oxford University Press, 1994), 39, and Philipp Gassert, *Amerika im Dritten Reich: Ideologie, Propaganda und Volksmeinung, 1933–1945* (Stuttgart: Steiner, 1997), 95–97.

11. Kelly Miller, "Race Prejudice in Germany and America," *Opportunity*, April 1936.

12. "Foster Says We Are Worse Off Than Jews," *Baltimore Afro-American*, October 21, 1939.

13. *The Crisis* quoted in Harvard Sitkoff, *Toward Freedom Land: The Long Struggle for Racial Equality in America* (Lexington: University Press of Kentucky, 2010), 156; "A Negro Pursuit Squadron," *Opportunity*, April 1941.

14. Quoted in Kneebone, *Southern Liberal Journalists*, 175. Probably from John Temple Graves, *The Fighting South* (New York: G. P. Putnam's Sons, 1943). Odum called the Klan "un-American, un-democratic, and un-Christian." Quoted in Daniel Joseph Singal, *The War Within: From Victorian to Modernist Thought in the South, 1919–1945* (Chapel Hill: University of North Carolina

Press, 1982), 123. Odum wasn't the only member of the Chapel Hill intelligentsia to see both parallels and significant differences between the segregated South and Nazi Germany. William Couch, who read German newspapers regularly, worried that the antagonistic relationship between majority and minority populations created the conditions for fascism, and he worried that a fascist demagogue could find a following in the South of the 1930s. Singal, *The War Within*, 294. Other white conservatives use language derived from a critique of the Nazis in the 1950s to talk about more extremist whites. In 1956 John Temple Graves referred to Asa Carter's White Citizens' Council group as "an outlaw and fascist element of the Citizens Councils" in Birmingham, and Virginius Dabney called Carter the "loathsome fuehrer." In David L. Chappell, *A Stone of Hope: Prophetic Religion and the Death of Jim Crow* (Chapel Hill: University of North Carolina Press, 2004), 163.

15. W. E. B. Du Bois, "Hitler Far Ahead of Simon Legree," *New York Post*, January 27, 1937, 16; Du Bois, "Germany and Hitler," *Pittsburgh Courier*, December 5, 1936, in Lewis, *Du Bois: A Reader*, 735.

16. For schools, see "Nazi Prejudice Against Jews Is Like Dixie's," *Baltimore Afro-American*, September 21, 1935, 12. For Jim Crow streetcars, see *Philadelphia Tribune*, December 29, 1938, 1. For marriage, see *Philadelphia Tribune*, July 5, 1934, 4; *Afro-American*, June 18, 1938, 1–2.

17. "A Negro Pursuit Squadron."

18. Miller, "Race Prejudice in Germany and America."

19. Glenda Elizabeth Gilmore also makes this point about democracy in *Defying Dixie: The Radical Roots of Civil Rights, 1919–1950* (New York: Norton, 2008). The general critique of Nazi Germany by African Americans seems to have caught the attention of Julius Streicher, publisher of the virulently anti-Semitic propaganda magazine *Der Stürmer*. Comparing marriage laws, segregation statutes, Black education, Black business opportunities, and rates of extra-legal violence, Streicher complained, "The treatment of Negroes in America [is] far worse than that accorded Jews by the Nazis and America's criticism should be turned in that direction rather than toward Germany." Quoted in Gilmore, *Defying Dixie*, 171. On domestic Nazis, see Sander A. Diamond, *The Nazi Movement in the United States, 1924–1941* (Ithaca, NY: Cornell University Press, 1974).

20. Quoted in Kuehl, *The Nazi Connection*, 98.

21. Henry L. Stimson, diary entry, June 24, 1943. Quoted in Richard M. Dalfiume, *Desegregation of the U.S. Armed Forces: Fighting on Two Fronts, 1939–1950* (Columbia: University of Missouri Press, 1969), 31.

22. See W. E. B. Du Bois, "Close Ranks," *The Crisis*, July 1918, 111; "Resolutions of the Washington Conference," *The Crisis*, June 1917, 59–60.

23. Charles Hamilton Houston, "Saving the World for Democracy," *Pittsburgh Courier*, October 5, 1940. Houston wrote a series of articles recalling his wartime experience; see the *Courier*, July 20 and 27, August 10, September 7, 14, and 28, 1940. The *Baltimore Afro-American* ran a similar series of WWI reminiscences; see December 9 and 30, 1930. See also Walter Wilson, "Old Jim Crow in Uniform," *The Crisis*, February 1939.

24. *Baltimore Afro-American* survey of Black leaders, "For Manhood in National Defense," September 16, 1939, 1–2.

25. Wilkins quoted in Dalfiume, *Desegregation of the U.S. Armed Forces*, 26–27; Charles C. Diggs, *Baltimore Afro-American*, June 29, 1940, 5; George Rouzeau, *Pittsburgh Courier*, January 1, 1944; W. E. B. Du Bois, "For Manhood in National Defense," *The Crisis*, December 1940.

26. White quoted in *Baltimore Afro-American*, June 29, 1940, 12. "Benevolent neutrality" was one description of FDR's concern for the race question. Frank Freidel, *F.D.R. and the South* (Baton Rouge: Louisiana State University Press, 1965), 97.

27. Dalfiume, *Desegregation of the U.S. Armed Forces*, 35–36. See *Baltimore Afro-American*, October 19, 1940.

28. Roosevelt and Knox quoted in Dalfiume, *Desegregation of the U.S. Armed Forces*, 54–55.

29. Walter White quoted in *Baltimore Afro-American*, June 29, 1941, 12.

30. On the meeting with FDR, see Walter White, *A Man Called White: The Autobiography of Walter White* (New York: Viking Press, 1948), 186–187.

31. On the Harvard-Navy game, see Dalfiume, *Desegregation of the U.S. Armed Forces*, 30.

32. Ralph Matthews, *Baltimore Afro-American*, December 20, 1941, 4.

33. Carpenter quoted in *Time*, March 2, 1942; Macdonald quote from *The War's Greatest Scandal: The Story of Jim Crow in Uniform* (pamphlet), March on Washington Movement, 1942, p. 15, folder, "Negroes, Clippings, 1942–43," box 4, Coll. 7690, Alderman Library, University of Virginia; New Jersey man quoted in *Baltimore Afro-American*, June 29, 1940, 5.

34. John Hope Franklin, "Their War and Mine," *Journal of American History* 77, no. 2 (September 1990): 578.

35. Quoted in *Baltimore Afro-American*, December 20, 1941, 1–2.

36. *The Crisis*, quoted in Adam Fairclough, *Race and Democracy: The Civil Rights Struggle in Louisiana* (Athens: University of Georgia Press, 1995), 75–76.

37. Ralph Bunche, "The Negro in the Political Life of the United States," *Journal of Negro Education* (July 1941), 583, quoted in Gunnar Myrdal et al., *An American Dilemma: The Negro Problem and Modern Democracy* (New York: Harper and Brothers, 1944), 1007.

38. *Baltimore Afro-American*, May 23, 1942, 4; Samuel A. Stouffer et al., *The American Soldier* (Princeton, NJ: Princeton University Press, 1949), 1:516–517; Roi Ottley, *New World A'Coming* (New York: Arno Press, 1968 [1943]), 287.

39. Bethune quoted in *Baltimore Afro-American*, June 27, 1942, 2. See also Office of Facts and Figures, *The Negro Looks at the War: Attitudes of New York Negroes Toward Discrimination Against Negroes and a Comparison of Negro and Poor White Attitudes Toward War-Related Issues*, 1942. Cited in Leo Wynn, *The Afro-American and the Second World War* (London: Elek, 1976), 100. Lee Finkle, "The Conservative Aims of Black Rhetoric: Black Protest During World War II," *Journal of American History* 60, no. 3 (December 1973): 692–713, argues that Black newspapermen actually lagged behind the masses in militancy toward domestic war aims.

40. This skepticism was reciprocated: Franklin Roosevelt considered the *Chicago Defender* and the *Baltimore Afro-American* seditious, and tried to get Attorney General Francis Biddle to prosecute editors for sedition. Fairclough, *Better Day Coming*, 193–194; Geoffrey R. Stone, *Perilous Times: Free Speech in Wartime* (New York: Liveright, 2004), 255–256. Circulation of Black newspapers increased 40 percent during the war. See Ralph N. Davis, "The Negro Newspapers and the War," *Sociology and Social Research* 27 (May–June 1943): 373–380, and Thomas Sancton, "The Negro Press," *New Republic*, April 26, 1943, 557–560.

41. *Baltimore Afro-American*, May 23, 1942, 1.

42. The Supreme Court upheld the notion that political parties were private, voluntary organizations with the right to control their membership, and the court considered poll taxes constitutional because they applied equally to all voters.

43. Gilmore, *Defying Dixie*, 337; Patricia Sullivan, *Days of Hope: Race and Democracy in the New Deal Era* (Chapel Hill: University of North Carolina Press, 1996), 204.

44. Virginia Durr, *Outside the Magic Circle: The Autobiography of Virginia Foster Durr* (Tuscaloosa: University of Alabama Press, 1990), 102. There were, naturally, no Black women on the committee.

45. Durr, *Outside the Magic Circle*, 175, 172.

46. Gilmore, *Defying Dixie*, 338.

47. Quoted in Jason Morgan Ward, *Defending White Democracy: The Making of a Segregationist Movement and the Remaking of Racial Politics* (Chapel Hill: University of North Carolina Press, 2011), 57. On Southern domination of Congress and its effects, see Ira Katznelson, *Fear Itself: The New Deal and the Origins of Our Time* (New York: Liveright, 2013), Part II ("Southern Cage").

48. Darlene Clark Hine, *Black Victory: The Rise and Fall of the Black Primary in Texas* (Milwood, NY: KTO Press, 1979), 234–235.

49. Hine, *Black Victory*, 222. The 1941 case (which originated in Louisiana) is *United States v. Classic*, 313 U.S. 299 (1941). On the white primaries see Michael Klarman, "The White Primary Rulings: A Case Study in the Consequences of Supreme Court Decisionmaking," *Florida State University Law Review* 29, no. 1 (Fall 2001): 55–109. The lone dissenter in *Smith v. Allwright* was Justice Owen Roberts, the only justice who had been sitting the previous time the Supreme Court decided a primary election question, in *Grovey v. Townsend*, 295 U.S. 45 (1935), and one of the few non-Roosevelt appointees.

50. "Primaries Are Not Private," *New York Times*, April 5, 1944, 18, quoted in Klarman, "The White Primary Rulings," 64.

51. Jackson quoted in Sullivan, *Days of Hope*, 149; Juan Williams, *Thurgood Marshall: American Revolutionary* (New York: Times Books, 1998), 112.

52. John Dittmer, *Local People: The Struggle for Civil Rights in Mississippi* (Urbana: University of Illinois Press), 1–9; Fairclough, *Race and Democracy*, 111; Lawson, *Black Ballots: Voting Rights in the South, 1944–1969* (New York: Columbia University Press, 1976), 102; Michael J. Klarman, *From Jim Crow to Civil Rights: The Supreme Court and the Struggle for Racial Equality* (New York: Oxford University Press, 2004), 238–239.

53. Southern white civilians were more prepared to accept Black suffrage than their elected representatives were. Klarman, *From Jim Crow to Civil Rights*, 83. Klarman also determines that many white Southerners (including judges) were much less resistant to Black voting than they were to school desegregation (p. 89).

54. Klarman, "The White Primary Rulings," 73.

55. Hughes quoted in Barbara Dianne Savage, *Broadcasting Freedom: Radio, War, and the Politics of Race, 1938–1948* (Chapel Hill: University of North

Carolina Press, 1999), 211. The Hughes broadcast was on February 17, 1944; the *Smith* decision was announced on April 3, 1944.

56. Quoted in Katznelson, *Fear Itself*, 206.

57. "Soldier Voting Deal," *Pittsburgh Courier*, January 29, 1944. Quoted in Katznelson, *Fear Itself*, 216.

58. *Baltimore Afro-American*, February 7, 1942, 1, 4.

59. Pete Daniel, "Going Among Strangers: Southern Reactions to World War II," *Journal of American History* 77, no. 3 (December 1990): 892; Victor H. Bernstein, "No Belief in Democracy," *Baltimore Afro-American*, September 19, 1942, 17.

60. Bernstein, "No Belief in Democracy."

61. *Baltimore Afro-American*, September 27, 1941, 4; Wilkins's keynote address to the NAACP's convention in Los Angeles in July 1942 quoted in Virginius Dabney, "Nearer and Nearer the Precipice," *Atlantic Monthly*, January 1941, 94. "Social revolution" from "Address of Roy Wilkins to the Thirty-Third Annual Convention of the NAACP," July 14, 1942, Part I, Reel II, NAACP Records, Library of Congress.

62. Smith quoted in Nancy MacLean, "The Leo Frank Case Reconsidered: Gender and Sexual Politics in the Making of Reactionary Populism," *Journal of American History* 78 (December 1991), 948.

63. In addition to the men roaming the country in uniform, 3.2 million people left Southern rural areas during the war, most of them heading for the centers of the wartime defense industry in the North and West. A quarter of the 250,000 new people living in the Detroit-Willow Run area hailed from just four Southern states. During the war it is estimated that 300,000 Black Southerners migrated to the border and Northern states, a further 100,000 Blacks from the border states moved further north or west, and an additional 250,000 African Americans moved to the West Coast. Statistics from Carey McWilliams, *Brothers Under the Skin* (Boston: Little, Brown, 1964 [1942]), 7. On the USO, see "Historical Overview of the USO," Skylighters.org, accessed May 2020, http://www.skylighters.org/canteen. Not all the segregated canteens were in the South; one Black girl tried to volunteer at the White Plains, New York, canteen but was rejected as unnecessary because the canteen did not admit Black soldiers. See *Negro Digest*, March 1944, 3.

64. Margaret Halsey, *Color Blind: A White Woman Looks at the Negro* (New York: Simon and Schuster, 1946), 36–37, 69; Halsey, "Memo to Junior Hostesses," *Negro Digest*, October 1943, 51–53.

65. Halsey, *Color Blind*, 20; on Jane White's employment at the canteen, see *Negro Digest*, March 1944, 3.

66. Halsey, *Color Blind*, 55.

67. Halsey, *Color Blind*, 20, 70–71. On white soldiers' disinclination to dance with Black hostesses, see Michael Carter, "Trouble in the Canteen," *Negro Digest*, April 1944, 7–9, esp. 8.

Chapter Seven: The "Second Front"

1. Description from John Dos Passos, *State of the Nation* (Boston: Houghton Mifflin, 1944), 67.

2. *Baltimore Afro-American*, March 21, 1942, 4; *Baltimore Afro-American*, February 13, 1943, 12 (Phoenix); December 12, 1942, 1 (Fort Dix); November 21, 1942, 1 (Luke Field); January 24, 1942, 3 (Alexandria, LA).

3. On Woods, see Bruce Nelson, "Organized Labor and the Struggle for Black Equality in Mobile During World War II," *Journal of American History* 80, no. 3 (December 1993): 952–988, esp. 967. Mary Penick Motley, ed., *The Invisible Soldier: The Experience of the Black Soldier, World War II* (Detroit: Wayne State University Press, 1987), 40.

4. Cumulative statistics from Pete Daniel, "Going Among Strangers: Southern Reactions to World War II," *Journal of American History* 77, no. 3 (December 1990): 886–911, esp. 893–894. Social Science Institute numbers cited in Harvard Sitkoff, "Racial Militancy and Interracial Violence in the Second World War," *Journal of American History* 58, no. 3 (December 1971): 661–681, esp. 671; Sitkoff also notes that at least fifty Black soldiers were killed in race riots (668). The most complete treatment of wartime interracial violence remains James A. Burran III, "Racial Violence in the South During World War II" (PhD diss., University of Tennessee, 1977). Col. Howard Donovan Queen, Foreword, in *The Invisible Soldier: The Experience of the Black Soldier, World War II*, ed. Mary Penick Motley (Detroit: Wayne State University Press, 1987), 40.

5. Quoted in Motley, *The Invisible Soldier*, 57.

6. "Army Voids Death Penalty Order for Mixing of Races," "Stupid Army Orders," both from *Baltimore Afro-American*, January 10, 1942, 1, 4.

7. James Baldwin, *Notes of a Native Son* (Boston: Beacon Press, 1955), 109–110. Walter White, *A Man Called White: The Autobiography of Walter White* (New York: Viking Press, 1948), 233–241, confirmed that the altercation in the lobby began when a Black soldier intervened on behalf of a Black woman arguing with the white policeman (p. 234).

8. Clipping, "The Harlem Riot," *The Crisis*, September 1943, 263, in folder, "Negroes, Clippings, 1942–43," Papers of Virginius Dabney, Coll. #7690, Special Collections, Alderman Library, Charlottesville, University of Virginia. Poet Langston Hughes caught this spirit: "*They didn't kill the soldier,* / A race leader cried. / Somebody hollered, / *Naw! But they tried!*" Quoted in Leo Wynn, *The Afro-American and the Second World War* (London: Elek, 1976), 70.

9. Report from Hastie to Stimson, September 1941, quoted in Richard M. Dalfiume, *Desegregation of the U.S. Armed Forces: Fighting on Two Fronts, 1939–1950* (Columbia: University of Missouri Press, 1969), 46. The report was printed in the *Pittsburgh Courier*, February 6, 1943, after Hastie resigned his position in protest at the army's continued treatment of Black men in arms. The official army report on the riot blamed it on white MPs. On Hastie, see Dalfiume, *Desegregation of the U.S. Armed Forces*, 84–86. On riots on military bases, see *Baltimore Afro-American*, January 24, 1942, 4.

10. Ralph Matthews, *Baltimore Afro-American*, January 24, 1942, 4.

11. Untitled report, NAACP Legal Department 1943–1945, pp. 17–18, Legal Reports, Group II: B96, NAACP Records, Library of Congress (hereafter NAACP Records).

12. Statistic on increase in circulation of Black newspapers from Dalfiume, *Desegregation in the U.S. Armed Forces*, 78.

13. Baldwin, *Notes of a Native Son*, 101.

14. Graham Smith, *When Jim Crow Met John Bull: Black American Soldiers in World War II Britain* (New York: St. Martin's Press, 1987), 48.

15. Harvey quoted in Smith, *When Jim Crow Met John Bull*, 48. Law quoted in David Reynolds, *Rich Relations: The American Occupation of Britain, 1942–1945* (New York: Random House, 1995), 226–227. England was not the only country that hoped to avoid the stationing of Black troops. Iceland, Greenland, Trinidad, Panama, Chile, and Venezuela all tried to exclude African Americans. See Morris J. MacGregor Jr., *Integration of the Armed Forces, 1940–1965* (Washington, DC: Center of Military History, United States Army, 1981), 38.

16. *A Preliminary Report on Attitudes of Negro Soldiers in ETO*, February 7, 1944, ETO-B2, Box 1018, Survey B2, Entry 94, Record Group 330, National Archives, College Park, MD.

17. "Extracts on Negro Morale," from Base Censor Office No. 1, for the period March 1–15, 1944, in Negro Troops, Entry 578, RG 498, National Archives, College Park, MD.

18. Morale Report, August 15–31, 1943, Base Censor Office No. 4, Box 23, File 353.8, McCloy, Entry 180, RG 107, National Archives, College Park, MD. A March 1944 Morale Report concurred, noting that "white soldiers are prejudiced against the English because some white girls go about with Negro soldiers." See "Extracts on Negro Morale."

19. Brig. Gen. B. O. Dans to Commanding General, ETOUSA, October 25, 1942; Lt. Gen. Dwight D. Eisenhower to Col. Pleas B. Rogers, September 5, 1942 (corrected by hand to read 1943). Both in file 218 (Negro Troops), Entry 578, RG 498, National Archives, College Park, MD.

20. Memo, "Uniform Policy Governing Racial Inter-Relations of Soldiers, and of Soldiers and Civilians, ETO," n.d. (stamped December 8, 1943). For more military conversation on this topic see memo, "Colored Troops," March 14, 1944, quoting memo of February 14, 1942. Both in file 218 (Negro Troops), Entry 578, RG 498, National Archives, College Park, MD.

21. Quoted in Reynolds, *Rich Relations*, 303.

22. Quoted in Reynolds, *Rich Relations*, 218.

23. Quoted in Reynolds, *Rich Relations*, 218 (Eisenhower), 219 (Roosevelt), 133 (white sergeant).

24. All three quotes from Walter White, *A Rising Wind* (Garden City, NY: Doubleday, Doran and Company, 1945), 56. Army records documented the abuse directed at African American troops and the roles played by white soldiers. See *A Preliminary Report on Attitudes of Negro Soldiers in ETO*. ETO officials tried to stop this behavior; General Eisenhower directed in September 1942, "Spreading of derogatory statements concerning the character of any [member] of US groups, either white or colored, must be considered as prejudicial to good order and military discipline." Dwight David Eisenhower to Gen. Lee, March 1, 1944, file 218 (Negro Troops), Entry 578, RG 498, National Archives, College Park, MD. A similar campaign was conducted by white Southern officers in Hawaii. There, however, the whites encountered New York's all-Black 369th Coast Artillery—known by their nickname, "the Harlem Hellfighters"—who soon put such rumors to rest, and resisted, with the aid of Hawaii's fair-minded military governor General Delos G. Emmons, other attempts to establish Jim Crow in Hawaii. On Hawaii, see White, *A Man Called White*, 274, and Beth Bailey and David Farber, *The First Strange Place: The Alchemy of Race and Sex in World War II Hawaii* (New York: Free Press, 1992), 133–166, esp. 150.

25. White, *Rising Wind*, 11 (dance); Reynolds, *Rich Relations*, 302 (schoolmistress), 313 (white GI). White notes in *A Rising Wind*, 30, "Most of the clashes

between white and Negro troops had occurred when white soldiers physically resented the association in public of British people—particularly women—and American Negroes." Ralph Ellison, who was stationed in Swansea, published a short story, "In a Strange Country," in *Flying Home and Other Stories* (New York: Random House, 1996 [1944]), in which a Black merchant seaman anxious to see South Wales is beaten up by white GIs and rescued by Brits.

26. Smith, *When Jim Crow Met John Bull*, 85, 88; Eisenhower quoted in White, *A Rising Wind*, 17.

27. Smith, *When Jim Crow Met John Bull*, 113, credits this text to Col. E. W. Plank, commanding officer of Eastern Base Section. Complaints about Lt. Gen. Lee seem to have prompted Eisenhower to reiterate his views on this topic in a detailed letter from March 1944, in which the commanding general reminded his subordinate, "Any person subject to military law who makes statements derogatory to any troops of the United Nations will be severely punished for conduct prejudicial to good order and military discipline." Gen. Eisenhower to Gen. Lee, March 1, 1944, file 218 (Negro Troops), Entry 578, RG 498, National Archives, College Park, MD.

28. Reynolds, *Rich Relations*, 231, 313.

29. Quoted in Smith, *When Jim Crow Met John Bull*, 114. Black soldiers' venereal disease rates were measured as six times those of white GIs. Reynolds, *Rich Relations*, 225.

30. James D. Givens, ASC, US Strategic Air Forces in Europe, AAP. Sta. 379, APO 633, US Army January 8, 1945, responding to inquiry about US policy regarding interracial marriages, Part 9, Series B, Reel 15, Group II, Box B-153, NAACP Records. On wartime marriages involving GIs in England, see Jenel Virden, *Goodbye, Piccadilly: British War Brides in America* (Chicago: University of Chicago Press, 1996), 30–48. The Air Force seemed particularly jealous of its reputation in this regard. In 1944 the judge advocate of the 8th Air Force Service Command, Col. J. L. Harbough, warned that the 8th's ban on mixed marriages in England was "not strictly in accord with the directives of higher authority," and noted that the army in the United States would have approved such marriages if they did not break the law in a soldier's home state. Eighth AFSC story in Reynolds, *Rich Relations*, 231, who notes that pregnant British girls and their families protested the army's ban on interracial marriages (232).

31. White, *Rising Wind*, 50; Reynolds, *Rich Relations*, 232. "Partner to bastardy" comment in Walter White to Secretary of War Robert Patterson, December 20, 1945, *Papers of the NAACP*, Part 9: Discrimination in the U.S.

Armed Forces, 1918–1955, Series B, NAACP 1940–1955: Legal File—Soldier Marriages, 1944–1949 (Frederick, MD: University Publications of America, 1982), microfilm, reel 15. The NAACP formally requested that the War and Navy departments lift the ban on marriages between African Americans in the armed services and women of the countries where the men had served. *Chicago Defender*, December 29, 1945, 3. A 1943 British poll found that one in seven Brits disapproved of interracial marriages. Smith, *When Jim Crow Met John Bull*, 200. Smith reports, "It is not possible to estimate how many mixed marriages took place during the years of the war" because British authorities refused to furnish such statistics to the Department of State (206). Statistics about mixed-race babies born in Britain during the war are equally dodgy; the most careful investigation, carried out by Sylvia McNeill for the League of Coloured Peoples in 1945, tabulated 553 "brown" babies born to 545 mothers. Smith, *When Jim Crow Met John Bull*, 208. The policy of the United States government after the war was to assign servicemen in interracial marriages according to the miscegenation laws of the states. Walter B. Richardson, Office of the Adjutant General, draft report, "Miscegenation Laws of Various States of the Union," June 4, 1954, folder 12 (Race 291.2), box 129, RG407, National Archives, College Park, MD.

32. Reynolds, *Rich Relations*, 305 (white lieutenant).

33. Smith, *When Jim Crow Met John Bull*, 197. According to Smith, Eisenhower lifted the ban in March 1945 in response to "vigorous protest" in Europe. The Army censored the photograph of the interracial winners of a dance contest at an Italian Red Cross Club. See Renee Christine Romano, *Race-Mixing: Black-White Marriage in Postwar America* (Cambridge, MA: Harvard University Press, 2003), 21 (with photo). See also George H. Roeder Jr., *The Censored War: American Visual Experience During World War II* (New Haven: Yale University Press, 1993), 57.

34. *Censorship Report on Inter-Racial Relations for Period 16 to 30 June 1945*, file 212 (Morale), Entry 578, RG 498, National Archives, College Park, MD; *A Preliminary Report on Attitudes of Negro Soldiers in ETO*.

35. "Extracts on Negro Morale."

36. "Extracts on Negro Morale."

37. White, *A Man Called White*, 242; Kenneth Robert Janken, *The Biography of Walter White, Mr. NAACP* (New York: Free Press, 2003), 281–286.

38. For specific examples of White's concern with courts-martial, see Walter White to Secretary of War Stimson, July 6, 1945, and Sherman Minton (chair of Clemency Boards), September 25, 1945, both in Group II: B193, U.S. Army Regulations and Disposals (of Courts-Martial), 1945–1949, NAACP Records.

39. "Statistical Survey: General Courts Martial in the European Theater of Operations," *History of the Branch Office of the Judge Advocate General with the United States Forces European Theater (USFET)*, 1:3–17, esp. 4, 8. According to the NAACP, African Americans constituted only 8.24 percent of ETO personnel as of V-J Day (August 8, 1945). See memorandum to Mr. White from Franklin H. Williams, May 14, 1946, Group II: B193, U.S. Army Regulations and Disposals (of Courts-Martial), 1945–49, NAACP Records.

40. "Statistical Survey," 9; memo to Mr. White. These numbers appear not to include executions carried out in the Mediterranean Theater of Operations, which covered North Africa and Italy. The European Theater of Operations included Europe north of Italy and the Mediterranean coast, to the north.

41. Motley, *The Invisible Soldier*, 312.

42. Motley, *The Invisible Soldier*, 52–53. Lieutenant Wade McCree Jr., a Fisk University graduate and Harvard Law student who fought with the 92nd Infantry Regiment, also recalled that there was a rapport between the Italians around Naples and the Black troops "which apparently did not exist in the same intensity between the Italians and our white troops." Motley, *The Invisible Soldier*, 299.

43. Quoted in Motley, *The Invisible Soldier*, 53.

44. "The penalty for rape is death or life imprisonment as the court-martial may direct." Article of War 92, Appendix 39, "Forms and Methods of Citation for Use in Board of Review Holdings and Opinions," *History Branch Office of the Judge Advocate General with the United States Forces European Theater, 18 July, 1942 to 1 November, 1945* (St. Cloud, France, 1946), 425–436, esp. 428.

45. Grigg quoted in Reynolds, *Rich Relations*, 232; "Statistical Survey," 11. On England alone see J. Robert Lilly, "Dirty Details: Executing U.S. Soldiers During World War II," *Crime and Delinquency* 42, no. 4 (1996): 493–494, 496–497. Between 1930 and 1967, when antimiscegenation laws were overturned by the Supreme Court's decision in the *Loving* case, 405 out of 455 men executed for rape were African American. J. Robert Lilly and J. Michael Thomson, "Executing US Soldiers in England, World War II," *British Journal of Criminology* 37, no. 2 (Spring 1997): 263. On courts-martial, see also Elizabeth Hillman, *Defending America: Military Culture and the Cold War Court-Martial* (Princeton, NJ: Princeton University Press, 2005).

46. "Statistical Survey," 13–14. This number is matched by statistics from the Pacific Theater of Operations, in which Black soldiers were roughly nine times as likely to be executed as white soldiers. See Walter A. Luszki, *A Rape*

of Justice: MacArthur and the New Guinea Hangings (Lanham, MD: Madison Books, 1991), 108–109. The military's racial imbalance on death row continued long after WWII: of the twelve executions carried out by the military between 1954 and 1961 (the last military execution to date), eleven were African American. As Dwight Sullivan, a managing attorney with the ACLU in Maryland, noted in 1998, "No state comes close to the military's astounding 87.5 percent minority death row population." Dwight Sullivan, "A Matter of Life and Death: Examining the Military Death Penalty's Fairness," *Federal Lawyer* (June 1998): 44. See also Richard A. Serrano, "Prvt. John Bennett Is the Only U.S. Soldier Executed for Rape in Peacetime," *Los Angeles Times Magazine*, September 10, 2000, 10–13, 35.

47. Sam Weiss to "Dear Marian," January 29, 1946, Group III: B16, Court Martial/General/1944–46, NAACP Records.

48. Thurgood Marshall to Secretary of War Stimson, July 6, 1945; Under Secretary of War Robert P. Patterson to Thurgood Marshall, July 17, 1945; Under Secretary of War Kenneth C. Royall to Franklin H. Williams, February 4, 1946; memorandum from Franklin H. Williams to Thurgood Marshall, November 30, 1948. All in Group II: B193, U.S. Army Regulations and Disposals (of Courts-Martial), 1945–49, NAACP Records.

49. Untitled Report, Group II: B96, Legal Reports, NAACP Legal Department, 1943–45; memorandum to Thurgood Marshall from Franklin H. Williams, November 30, 1948. Both in Group II: B193, U.S. Army Regulations and Disposals (of Courts-Martial), 1945–49, NAACP Records.

50. Franklin H. Williams to Hon. Arthur P. McNulty, Chairman, Lawyers Veterans Committee, New York, December 29, 1945, Group II: B193, U.S. Army Regulations and Disposals (of Courts-Martial), 1945–49, NAACP Records.

51. Branch Office of the JAG, Mediterranean Theater of Operations, June 13, 1945, pp. 13–14 (Till Trial Transcript, 41–42), National Archives and Records Administration, Suitland, MD.

52. Headquarters, Mediterranean Theater of Operations, US Army, June 13, 1945, General Court-Martial Orders Number 89 (Till Trial Transcript, p. 14); Incoming Classified Message, from Commanding General, U.S. Army Forces, Mediterranean Theater of Operations, Caserta, Italy, to War Department, July 11, 1945. Fred McMurray was hanged the same day at Aversa; see Headquarters, Mediterranean Theater of Operations, US Army, June 13, 1945, General Court-Martial Orders Number 88 (Till Trial Transcript, p. 10), National Archives and

Records Administration, Suitland, MD. John Tytell, *Ezra Pound: The Solitary Volcano* (New York: Anchor Press, 1987), 277; Ezra Pound, *The Pisan Cantos*, ed. Richard Sieburth (New York: New Directions, 2003 [1948]), canto 74.172–173.

53. Mamie Till-Mobley and Christopher Benson, *Death of Innocence: The Story of the Hate Crime That Changed America* (New York: Random House, 2003), 17.

Chapter Eight: Will the Peace Bring Racial Peace?

1. Description of the Jones lynching from Walter Francis White, *A Man Called White: The Autobiography of Walter White* (New York: Viking, 1948), 323–335, and Philip Dray, *At the Hands of Persons Unknown: The Lynching of Black America* (New York: Random House, 2002), 374–376. The FBI became involved because the participation of law officers made the lynching a federal crime.

2. Maggi M. Morehouse, *Fighting in the Jim Crow Army: Black Men and Women Remember World War II* (Lanham, MD: Rowman and Littlefield, 2000), Henry Peoples, quote about killing in the name of democracy, 197; Fred Hurns quote, 196.

3. Jennifer E. Brooks, *Defining the Peace: WWII Veterans, Race, and the Remaking of Southern Political Tradition* (Chapel Hill: University of North Carolina Press, 2004), 17.

4. Black soldier on Okinawa quote from Leo Wynn, *The Afro-American and the Second World War* (London: Elek, 1976), 106; Neil R. McMillen, "How Mississippi's Black Veterans Remember World War II," in *Remaking Dixie: The Impact of World War Two on the American South*, ed. Neil R. McMillen (Jackson: University Press of Mississippi, 1997), 95; and Timothy B. Tyson, *Radio Free Dixie: Robert F. Williams and the Roots of Black Power* (Chapel Hill: University of North Carolina Press, 1999), 48.

5. "Lift Ban on Mixed Marriages Overseas: NAACP," *Chicago Defender*, December 29, 1945, 3; "House Says GI's May Send for Their White Brides," *Chicago Defender*, October 27, 1945, 5.

6. *Negro Digest*, August 1944, 48. Cited in Gayle Brenda Plummer, *Rising Wind: Black Americans and Foreign Affairs, 1935–1960* (Chapel Hill: University of North Carolina Press, 1995), 88.

7. Flyer, *Stop This Slaughter!*, Hollywood Independent Citizens' Committee of the Arts, Sciences and Professions, n.d. (late 1946), August 20–26, folder 1946, box 3, LMC 2009, Orson Welles Papers, Lilly Library, Indiana University, Bloomington (hereafter Welles Papers); on Birmingham, see John Egerton, *Speak Now Against the Day: The Generation Before the Civil Rights Movement in*

the South (New York: Knopf, 1993), 362. The number killed in Birmingham is inexact thanks to Bull Connor's control of information as city police commissioner.

8. Map, "Zones of Influence: Negro Troops," with explanatory memorandum, quoted in Maggi M. Morehouse, *Fighting in the Jim Crow Army: Black Men and Women Remember World War II* (Lanham, MD: Rowman and Littlefield, 2000), 192; Morton Sosna, "Introduction," in *Remaking Dixie*, xvi.

9. *Chicago Defender*, October 13, 1945, 1; "Ex-Marine Slain for Moving Jim Crow Sign," *Chicago Defender*, February 23, 1946, 1; excerpt from Vito Marcantonio letter to Tom Clark, "Asks Federal Action to Halt KKK Terror in Dixie," *Chicago Defender*, December 1, 1945, 18; "they're exterminating us" quoted in Brooks, *Defining the Peace*, 24.

10. Ira Katznelson, *Fear Itself: The New Deal and the Origins of Our Time* (New York: Liveright, 2013), 190.

11. Patricia Sullivan, *Lift Every Voice: The NAACP and the Making of the Civil Rights Movement* (New York: New Press, 2009), 306, 218 (Moon quote); Danielle L. McGuire, *At the Dark End of the Street: Black Women, Rape and Resistance—A New History of the Civil Rights Movement from Rosa Parks to the Rise of Black Power* (New York: Knopf, 2010), 63; on Parks and Montgomery race politics, see J. Mills Thornton III, *Dividing Lines: The Struggle for Civil Rights in Montgomery, Birmingham and Selma* (Tuscaloosa, AL: University of Alabama Press, 2002), 60.

12. C. C. Hodge to George Andrews, March 4, 1945, Papers of George Andrews, Auburn University, Auburn, AL, quoted in Tony Badger, "Whatever Happened to Roosevelt's New Generation of Southerners?," in *New Deal, New South: An Anthony J. Badger Reader* (Little Rock: University of Arkansas Press, 2007), 66.

13. Fleming quoted in Jason Sokol, *There Goes My Everything: White Southerners in the Age of Civil Rights, 1945–1975* (New York: Knopf, 2006), 21. David Brion Davis had a similar moment while aboard a ship bound for postwar Europe, when he witnessed the poor treatment of African American US soldiers. See Drew Faust, "The Scholar Who Shaped History," *New York Review of Books*, March 20, 2014.

14. Jason Ward, *Defending White Democracy: The Making of a Segregationist Movement and the Remaking of Racial Politics, 1936–1965* (Chapel Hill: University of North Carolina Press, 2011), 93.

15. Brooks, *Defining the Peace*, 30. Brooks says "somewhere between 135,000 and 150,000" Black Georgians registered to vote in 1946; Sullivan, *Lift Every Voice*, 211–212, says 135,000.

16. Brooks, *Defining the Peace*, 33–35. About eighty-five thousand Blacks succeeded in voting in the Georgia primary. Sullivan, *Lift Every Voice*, 212.

Carmichael carried the popular election by fifteen thousand votes, but Talmadge still won the election by taking the county-unit vote by a margin of two to one.

17. Willie Johnson deposition, n.d., Part 8, Series B (Reel 128), Group II, Box B-219, Correspondence, June–August 1946, NAACP Records, Library of Congress (hereafter NAACP Records). This deposition was filed incorrectly with material regarding the blinding of Isaac Woodard. Cf. *New York Times*, July 27, 1946, 1, 32.

18. Johnson deposition.

19. Quoted in Laura Wexler, *Fire in a Canebreak: The Last Mass Lynching in America* (New York: Scribner, 2003), 81–82.

20. "Georgia Mob of 20 Men Massacre 2 Negroes, Wives," *New York Times*, July 27, 1946, 1, 32.

21. This is the preferred argument of historians, e.g., Mary Dudziak, *Cold War Civil Rights: Race and the Image of American Democracy* (Princeton, NJ: Princeton University Press, 2000), 18. On Loy Harrison's account of the lynching, see "Farmer Describes Slaughter of Four," *New York Times*, July 27, 1946, 21. On George Dorsey, see Egerton, *Speak Now Against the Day*, 329.

22. Wexler, *Fire in a Canebreak*, 155. None of the four Monroe victims was registered to vote, and because of their illiteracy, none would have been able to qualify. Wexler, *Fire in a Canebreak*, 54.

23. Wexler, *Fire in a Canebreak*, 157.

24. Quoted in Wexler, *Fire in a Canebreak*, 167, 157.

25. Quoted in Wexler, *Fire in a Canebreak*, 37–38.

26. Burke quoted in Brooks, *Defining the Peace*, 64; Snipes killing in Brooks, *Defining the Peace*, 33–35.

27. Harold B. Hinton, "Klan in South Keeps Under Cover," *New York Times*, September 1, 1946, 65.

28. M. L. King Jr., letter to the editor, *Atlanta Constitution*, August 6, 1946.

29. "It was civil rights that got them killed" from Hyde Post, Andy Miller, and Peter Scott, "Murder at Moore's Ford," *Atlanta Journal-Constitution*, May 31, 1992, A/01. Statewide NAACP membership in Georgia plummeted after the 1946 election from eleven thousand to three thousand. In Ward, *Making White Democracy*, 111.

30. Simon Callow, *Orson Welles* (New York: Viking, 1996), vol. 1.

31. "Moral Indebtedness," Orson Welles broadcast, August 11, 1946, Welles mss., Radio, folder 14, box 13, Welles Papers.

32. Orson Welles to Kathleen Tynan, quoted in Callow, *Orson Welles*, 2:179.

33. Walter White to Orson Welles, July 24, 1946, Correspondence, June–August 1946, Group II, Box B-219 (Reel 28), Series B, Part 8, NAACP Records.

34. Transcript of "Orson Welles' Commentary," July 28, 1946, folder 13, box 13, Fourteen August, 1945, Miscellaneous Recordings, 1938–1945, Welles mss., Welles Papers.

35. Donald Jones, Assistant Field Secretary, to Franklin Wallin, Chairman Inter-Racial Committee, November 7, 1946, Correspondence, September–November 1946, Box B-219, Group II (Reel 28), Series B, Part 8, NAACP Records.

36. "Get That Cop," *Daily Worker*, July 13, 1946, Clippings 1946–1947, Box B-29, Group II (Reel 28), Series B, Part 8, NAACP Records. Had a private citizen blinded Isaac Woodard, the case would have been left to local law enforcement authorities. The allegation that Woodard was assaulted by an officer of the law made the attack a federal crime, because federal law guarded a prisoner's right "not to be beaten and tortured by persons exercising the authority to arrest." *PM*, September 27, 1946, Clippings, 1946–1947, Box B-29, Group II (Reel 28), Series B, Part 8, NAACP Records. (*PM* was a left-leaning newspaper in New York.)

37. "Aiken Police Ban Showing of Orson Welles Movie," *Augusta Chronicle*, August 12, 1946, 1.

38. Memorandum to Mr. White from Robert L. Carter, July 19, 1946; memorandum to Ollie Harrington from Robert L. Carter, July 17, 1946, instructs Harrington to urge organizations concerned about Woodard to write to the Department of Justice and demand an investigation; Thomas Clark, AG, to Walter White, July 25, 1946, confirming investigation; Robert L. Carter to Harold R. Boulware, August 13, 1946; Lincoln Miller to Walter White, July 27, 1956 [*sic*]; Lincoln Miller deposition, August 8, 1946. All in Correspondence, June–August 1946, Group II, Box B-29 (Reel 28), Series B, Part 8, NAACP Records.

39. "Orson Welles' Commentary," August 25, 1946 (tape indicates August 18, 1946), f. 14, Welles Papers; Former Fan to Orson Welles, n.d. (July 1946), in 1946, July 21–31 Correspondence folder, Welles Papers. Welles's correspondence files contain at least five other letters accusing Welles of supporting interracial sex and marriage. All in box 3, Letters to Welles, Welles Papers.

40. United States Code of Federal Regulations, Title 18, Section 52, 1940 ed.

41. Memorandum, Walter White to NAACP Branches, July 25, 1946, "Press Releases, 1946–1947," Group II, Box B-219, Reel 29, Legal File: Isaac Woodard, Series B, Part 8, NAACP Records.

42. Text of wire, dated August 16, 1946, from Orson Welles read at Joe Louis Benefit at Lewisohn Stadium, Correspondence 1946, August 12–19 file, Welles Papers; *New York Herald Tribune*, August 17, 1946.

43. Quoted in *Columbia Record*, November 6, 1946, in Clippings, 1946–1947, Group II, Box B-219, Reel 28, Series B, Part 8, NAACP Records.

44. The NAACP objected strenuously to the conduct of the Shull trial. Thurgood Marshall to Tom Clark, November 14, 1946; handwritten notes from trial (Franklin Williams), typed report on trial, November 8, 1946. All in Correspondence, September–November 1946, Group II, Box B-219, Reel 28, Series B, Part 8, NAACP Records.

45. Egerton, *Speak Now Against the Day*, 341.

46. Martin Duberman, *Paul Robeson: A Biography* (New York: Knopf, 1988), 306–307; White, *A Man Called White*, 330–331; Fred Jerome, *The Einstein File: J. Edgar Hoover's Secret War Against the World's Most Famous Scientist* (New York: St. Martin's Press, 2002), 82.

47. A 1947 report to the PCCR from the Civil Rights Section of the Department of Justice listed the top public civil rights concerns. Lynching topped the list, followed by the Klan and the Columbians, white primaries, segregation in transportation and public places, and police brutality. Turner L. Smith, Chief, Civil Rights Section, to President's Committee on Civil Rights, February 21, 1947, box 5, Records of the President's Committee on Civil Rights, Papers of Harry S. Truman, Roosevelt Institute for American Studies, Abbey of Middelburg, Netherlands. Truman quotes from *To Secure These Rights: The Report of the President's Committee on Civil Rights* (Washington, DC: Government Printing Office, 1947), 34, President's charge to the committee. Truman declared his opposition to "social equality" in an interview with the *Pittsburgh Courier*. William C. Berman, *The Politics of Civil Rights in the Truman Administration* (Columbus: Ohio State University Press, 1970), 15–20.

48. Harry S. Truman, "Address Before the National Association for the Advancement of Colored People," June 29, 1947, in *Public Papers of the Presidents: Harry S. Truman* (Washington, DC: Office of the Federal Register, National Archives and Record Service, 1947), 311–313. Truman also emphasized "the right to a fair trial in a fair court." The *Pittsburgh Courier* noted, "The NAACP was never able to get Mr. Roosevelt on its conference platform at any time during his occupancy of the White House....Although Mr. Roosevelt meddled with the affairs of the outer world, he never insisted that his Department of Justice show any of the activity it has displayed under Mr. Truman in investigating

mob violence and efforts to deprive Negroes of the vote; nor in all the torrent of words coming from the former President during his fourteen-year administration was there one sentence urging passage of an anti-lynch bill." Editorial, "Mr. Roosevelt and Mr. Truman," July 12, 1947.

49. "Message from the President of the United States Transmitting His Recommendations for Civil Rights Program," February 2, 1948, box 20, Elsey Papers, Harry S. Truman Library, Independence, Missouri (hereafter Truman Library).

50. *Birmingham Post*, October 31, 1947. Graves apparently lifted the quote from the *New Orleans Times-Picayune*, n.d. Quoted in Monroe Billington, "Civil Rights, President Truman, and the South," *Journal of Negro History* 58 (April 1973): 127–139; 131. Other critics hit closer to home. An irate woman from Corinth, Mississippi, demanded, "You wouldn't want your [daughter] Margaret to make a cross country trip on a bus seated by a dirty, evil smelling, loud mouthed negro man, now would you?" Surely conscious of the sexual double-entendre, she added, "You wouldn't want your Margaret to sleep in a Pullman section with a negro man above or below her, now would you?" Virginia Hart Lide to Truman, March 10, 1948, box 200, President's Personal Files, Truman Library.

51. On the politics of race in the 1948 election, see Harvard Sitkoff, "Harry Truman and the Election of 1948: The Coming of Age of Civil Rights in American Politics," *Journal of Southern History* 37 (1971): 597–616.

52. Speech of Hubert Humphrey, 1948 Democratic National Convention, July 14, 1948.

53. Address of J. Strom Thurmond at Augusta, Georgia, September 23, 1948. On the Dixiecrats and the Democratic schism, see Kari Frederickson, *The Dixiecrat Revolt and the End of the Solid South, 1932–1968* (Chapel Hill: University of North Carolina Press, 2001). Not all the white-supremacist Southern Democrats bolted the party that year. Georgia senator Richard Russell, one of the most powerful men in Congress, stayed to fight from within Truman's civil rights program, which Russell condemned as "a crime against our civilization and a sin against nature's God." Nominated by a fellow Georgian for president, Russell received over a quarter of all delegate votes in the first balloting round, including the united support of the remaining delegates of the former Confederacy. Russell quoted in Numan V. Bartley, *The New South, 1945–1980* (Baton Rouge: Louisiana State University Press, 1995), 95; on Charles Bloch (who nominated Russell), see Clive Webb, "Charles Bloch, Jewish White

Supremacist," *Georgia Historical Quarterly* 83, no. 2 (Summer 1989): 267–292, esp. 268–269.

54. Wallace's "The Century of the Common Man" speech was delivered on May 8, 1942, to the Free World Association in New York City. On the speech see John Culver, *American Dreamer: The Life and Times of Henry A. Wallace* (New York: Norton, 2000), 275–278.

55. Quoted in Patricia Sullivan, *Days of Hope: Race and Democracy in the New Deal Era* (Chapel Hill: University of North Carolina Press, 1996), 182. A Gallup poll on the eve of the convention reported that Northern Democrats supported Wallace by a three-to-one margin, and 43 percent of Southern Democrats supported him as well. Sullivan, *Days of Hope*, 182.

56. According to Wallace biographer John Culver, a widely distributed report by the Americans for Democratic Action "sought to bond Wallace with communism." Culver, *American Dreamer*, 465.

57. "Third Party Platform Offers Free Rein to Reds," *Los Angeles Times*, July 25, 1948, 12. Dara Orenstein, "Void for Vagueness: Mexicans and the Collapse of Miscegenation Law in California" *Pacific Historical Review* 74, no. 3 (Summer 2005): 367–408, reports that the Progressive Party "named miscegenation laws as one of the evils of Jim Crow that it intended to vanquish" at its state convention in Sacramento, and suggests that it did so at the request of civil rights lawyer Daniel Marshall (391). In the 1950s, Marshall was red-baited after representing schoolteachers who were blacklisted for supposed communist connections, and for contributing to Ethel and Julius Rosenberg's appeal in 1953.

58. Culver, *American Dreamer*, 457, 481. We know now from documents tied to the Venona Project, the secret counterintelligence initiated during World War II, that the PCA was, in fact, run by communists, but it is not at all clear that Wallace knew this (it seems unlikely, in fact).

59. Palmer Weber to Thurgood Marshall, quoted in Sullivan, *Lift Every Voice*, 366.

60. Quoted in Culver, *American Dreamer*, 494.

Chapter Nine: Brotherhood

1. George C. Herring, *From Colony to Superpower: U.S. Foreign Relations Since 1776* (New York: Oxford University Press, 2008), 412.

2. Heather A. Warren, *Theologians of a New World Order: Reinhold Niebuhr and the Christian Realists, 1920–1948* (New York: Oxford University Press, 1997), 99.

3. Warren, *Theologians of a New World Order*, 14–17.

4. Warren, *Theologians of a New World Order*, 99. Dulles was simultaneously a member of another influential American think group, the Commission to Study the Organization of the Peace (CSOP), which was chaired by University of Chicago international lawyer Quincy Wright. On the CSOP see Mark Mazower, *No Enchanted Palace: The End of Empire and the Ideological Origins of the United Nations* (Princeton, NJ: Princeton University Press, 2009), 15, and Robert P. Hillman, "Quincy Wright and the Commission to Study the Organization of the Peace," *Global Governance* 4 (1998): 485–499.

5. David A. Hollinger, *After Cloven Tongues of Fire: Protestant Liberalism in Modern American History* (Princeton, NJ: Princeton University Press, 2013), 65, 66.

6. Hollinger, *After Cloven Tongues of Fire*, 62.

7. Quoted in Randal Maurice Jelks, *Benjamin Elijah Mays, Schoolmaster of the Movement: A Biography* (Chapel Hill: University of North Carolina Press, 2012), 133.

8. W. E. B. Du Bois quoted that text in a 1943 commencement address at Florida A&M College and concluded that the demand for repeal of restrictive marriage laws was an attempt to force "the admission…by whites that Negroes are human beings." W. E. B. Du Bois, "A Social Program for Black and White Americans," commencement address at Florida A&M College, Tallahassee, May 31, 1943, in Du Bois, *Against Racism: Unpublished Essays, Papers, Addresses, 1887–1961*, Herbert Aptheker, ed. (Amherst: University of Massachusetts Press, 1985), 206–219, esp. 209, 212, 215.

9. Barbara Dianne Savage, *Broadcasting Freedom: Radio, War, and the Politics of Race 1938–1948* (Chapel Hill: University of North Carolina Press, 1999), 791.

10. This finding accorded with Gunnar Myrdal's conclusion in *An American Dilemma: The Negro Problem and Modern Democracy* (New York: Harper and Brothers, 1944). See vol. 1, 587.

11. Curtis J. Evans, "A Theology of Brotherhood: The Federal Council of Churches and the Theology of Race," (unpublished manuscript, in author's possession), 144.

12. Hollinger, *Cloven Tongues*, 68–69; 30.

13. Will W. Alexander, "Our Conflicting Racial Policies," *Harper's*, January 1, 1945, 177.

14. Dulles attended the conference as an assistant to Michigan senator Arthur Vandenberg. Nolde later authored the freedom of religion segment of

the Universal Declaration of Human Rights. Other organizations included as consultants ranged across the political spectrum, from the National Lawyers' Guild and Council of African Affairs on the left to the National Association of Manufacturers on the right.

15. Elizabeth Borgwardt, "Race, Rights and Nongovernmental Organizations at the UN San Francisco Conference," in *Fog of War: The Second World War and the Civil Rights Movement*, ed. Kevin M. Kruse and Stephen Tuck (New York: Oxford University Press, 2012), 189–190, 196. On Stettinius's intervention, see John S. Nurser, *For All Peoples and All Nations: The Ecumenical Church and Human Rights* (Washington, DC: Georgetown University Press, 2005), 101.

16. Borgwardt, "Race, Rights and Nongovernmental Organizations," 199–200.

17. Borgwardt, "Race, Rights and Nongovernmental Organizations," 188.

18. Hollinger, *With Cloven Tongues of Fire*, 70–71; Nurser, *For All Peoples and All Nations*. So associated was Dulles with liberal Protestant notions of human equality and oneness that his appointment as an official advisor to the US delegation in San Francisco was denounced as an "insult" to American Catholics and Jews. *The Pittsburgh Press*, April 7, 1945. The FCC called for special services in American churches on April 22, 1945 (the Sunday before the San Francisco convention began) to pray for success. The FCC also pressed the Senate to ratify the treaty. Lukas Haynes and Michael Ignatieff, "Mobilizing Support for the United Nations" (working paper, Center for Public Leadership, n.d.), 68, 70, accessed May 2020, http://dspace.mit.edu/bitstream/handle/1721.1/55800 /cpl_wp_03_2_haynesignatieff.pdf?sequence=1.

19. Churches ultimately played an important educational/lobbying role for US ratification of the charter.

20. Warren, *Theologians of a New World Order*, 103. The phrase "The World Is Our Parish" is Methodist. Nurser, *For All Peoples and All Nations*, 108, n. 25.

21. Evans, "A Theology of Brotherhood," 154–157 (quote from 157); "The Churches v. Jim Crow," *Time*, December 13, 1948.

22. Hollinger, *With Cloven Tongues of Fire*, 72–73, emphasizes the importance of the political reorientation of ecumenical Protestantism at the Delaware conference and in the following meetings as a landmark moment. On the early engagement of the FCC with racial issues, see James F. Findlay Jr., *Church People in the Struggle: The National Council of Churches and the Black Freedom Movement, 1950–1970* (New York: Oxford University Press, 1993), esp. 11–47.

23. John C. Culver, *American Dreamer: The Life and Times of Henry A. Wallace* (New York: Norton, 2000), 430.

24. Quoted in Geoffrey R. Stone, *Perilous Times: Free Speech in Wartime; From the Sedition Act of 1798 to the War on Terrorism* (New York: Liveright, 2005), 326–327.

25. Quoted in Andrea Friedman, "The Strange Career of Annie Lee Moss: Rethinking Race, Gender, and McCarthyism," in *Liberty and Justice for All? Rethinking Politics in Cold War America*, ed. Kathleen G. Donahue (Amherst: University of Massachusetts Press, 2012), 91–123 (quote on 96). John Egerton, *Speak Now Against the Day: The Generation Before the Civil Rights Movement in the South* (New York: Norton, 1994), 448–460, notes that white supremacy was a "salient feature" of the anticommunist crusade.

26. Culver, *American Dreamer*, 468 (Canadian rabbis).

27. States' Righters affirmed belief in the Constitution and opposition to "the elimination of segregation, the repeal of miscegenation statutes [no one had proposed this], the control of private employment by federal bureaucrats called for by the misnamed civil rights program." "Statement of Principles," *States' Rights Information and Speakers' Handbook*, 4–5, quoted in Kari Fredrickson, *The Dixiecrat Revolt and the End of the Solid South, 1932–1968* (Chapel Hill: University of North Carolina Press, 2001), 139.

28. Fredrickson, *Dixiecrat Revolt*, 112, recounts that Black and white South Carolina Democrats protested a party pledge required to vote. The oath was retained but replaced with one that did not require the voter to actively work against the FEPC or profess belief in the "religious" foundation of the segregation of the races. This suggests that the previous oath *did* require people to profess belief in the religious segregation of the races. See *The State*, May 30, 1948.

29. Darren Dochuk, *From Bible Belt to Sunbelt: Plain-Folk Religion, Grassroots Politics, and the Rise of Evangelical Conservatism* (New York: Norton, 2011), 41–42.

30. Dochuk, *From Bible Belt to Sunbelt*, 105.

31. Fifth Column quote from Jason Ward, *Defending White Democracy: The Making of a Segregationist Movement and the Remaking of Racial Politics, 1936–1965* (Chapel Hill: University of North Carolina Press, 2011), 38.

32. Mary Dudziak, *Cold War Civil Rights: Race and the Image of American Democracy* (Princeton, NJ: Princeton University Press, 2000), 29.

33. Paul Harvey, *Freedom's Coming: Religious Culture and the Shaping of the South from the Civil War Through the Civil Rights Era* (Chapel Hill: University of North Carolina Press, 2005), 238, writes that Christian critics of the United

Nations worried that it promoted the "permanent integration of the peoples of the earth" in defiance of God's destruction of the Tower of Babel.

34. Dochuk, *From Bible Belt to Sunbelt*, 164.

35. Quoted in Stephen A. Berrey, "Racial Discourses" (unpublished manuscript, in author's possession), 14.

36. Curtis J. Evans, "White Evangelical Protestant Responses to the Civil Rights Movement," *Harvard Theological Review* 102, no. 2 (April 2009): 245–273, 272.

37. Benjamin E. Mays, *Seeking to Be a Christian in Race Relations* (New York: Friendship Press, 1957); Randal Maurice Jelks, *Benjamin Elijah Mays: Schoolmaster of the Movement* (Chapel Hill: University of North Carolina Press, 2012), 168–173.

38. This formulation of the argument is the product of my clear-headed son Alexander Nirenberg.

39. Benjamin E. Mays, "A Religious Problem: Inability of Authorities to Apprehend Monroe Lynchers Unconvincing to Dr. Mays," *Pittsburgh Courier*, January 25, 1947, 7, quoted in Jelks, *Benjamin Elijah Mays*, 183. See also Benjamin E. Mays, *Born to Rebel: An Autobiography*, Orville Vernon Burton, ed. (Athens: University of Georgia Press, 2003).

40. Benjamin E. Mays, *Pittsburgh Courier*, December 20, 1947.

41. Quoted in Culver, *American Dreamer*, 494.

42. Benjamin Mays, "The Idol God of Segregation," *Pittsburgh Courier*, May 7, 1949.

Chapter Ten: White Supremacy in Peril

1. Dara Orenstein, "V for Vagueness: Mexicans and the Collapse of Miscegenation Law in California," *Pacific Historical Review* 74, no. 3 (August 2005): 386. Sylvester Davis's uncle was among those who did take the train down to Mexicali and Tijuana to get married, which perhaps influenced Davis's later recollections. The other proximate safe haven for interracial marriages in California was the Pacific Ocean: in 1914 the *Los Angeles Times* reported that white women and Japanese men were subverting California law by marrying at sea. "Would Unite East and West," *Los Angeles Times*, October 13, 1914, 115; "White Brides of Japs Prepare to Flee Law," *Los Angeles Times*, October 14, 1914, 111. Cited by Orenstein, "V for Vagueness," 386, n. 39.

2. Biographical details from Orenstein, "V for Vagueness," 367–408. On the Central Avenue neighborhood in the 1930s and 1940s, see Douglas Flamming, *Bound for Freedom: Black Los Angeles in Jim Crow America* (Berkeley: University of California Press, 2005), 92–125, esp. 103. Flamming describes "a kind of racial

separateness" within the district, "its stunning heterogeneity notwithstanding." On Black Los Angeles, see Josh Sides, *L.A. City Limits: African American Los Angeles from the Great Depression to the Present* (Berkeley: University of California Press, 2003).

3. *In re Rodriguez*, 81 F. 337 (W.D. Tex., 1897); Orenstein, "V for Vagueness," 382. See also Ian Haney López, *White by Law: The Legal Construction of Race*, rev. ed. (New York: New York University Press, 2006); Matthew Frye Jacobson, *Whiteness of a Different Color: European Immigration and the Alchemy of Race* (Cambridge, MA: Harvard University Press, 1998), 223–245. In a 1934 ruling on California's Alien Land Law, Justice Benjamin Cardozo, citing *Rodriguez*, noted nonetheless that Mexicans' eligibility for citizenship was "still an unsettled question." *Morrison v. California*, 291 U.S. 82 (1934), at 96. In 1935 a federal court in Buffalo, New York, denied the petition of three Mexicans for citizenship because they had "a strain of Indian blood." See "Indian Blood Bars Mexicans as Citizens," *New York Times*, December 12, 1935, 4.

4. Cal. Civ. Code §69 (1906) (amended 1937, 1959); Cal. Civ. Code §60 (West 1906) (amended 1937, repealed 1959).

5. *People v. Hall*, 4 Cal. 399 (1854) upheld the code.

6. *In re Halladjian*, 174 F. 834 (1909).

7. The Chinese Exclusion Act of 1882 (22 Stat. 58, 1882) declared Chinese immigrants ineligible for citizenship. The federal court cases were *In re Saito*, 62. F. 126 (C.C.D. Mass. 1894); *In re Yamashita*, 30 Wash. 234, 70 F. 482 (1902); *In re Buntaro Kumagai*, 163 F. 922 (W.D. Wash. 1908); *Bessho v. United States*, 178 F. 245 (4th Cir. 1910). Two US Supreme Court decisions, *Takao Ozawa v. U.S.*, 260 U.S. 178 (1922) and *U.S. v. Bhagat Singh Thind*, 261 U.S. 204 (1923), established that immigrants from Japan and India were likewise barred from citizenship. On Asians and unassimilability, see Mae M. Ngai, *Impossible Subjects: Illegal Aliens and the Making of Modern America* (Princeton, NJ: Princeton University Press, 2004), 37–50.

8. Davenport quoted in Edward J. Larson, *Sex, Race, and Science: Eugenics in the Deep South* (Baltimore, MD: Johns Hopkins University Press, 1995), 22.

9. According to Larson, "this apparently reflected the higher commitment rates of these groups rather than a practice of targeting them for sterilization within institutions." *Eugenics in the Deep South*, 37–38.

10. *In re Halladjian*, 174 Fed. 834 (1909). On racially restrictive legislation in California see Tomás Almaguer, *Racial Fault Lines: The Historical Origins of White Supremacy in California* (Berkeley: University of California Press, 1994); Ronald

Tagaki, *Strangers from a Different Shore: A History of Asian Americans* (Boston: Little Brown, 1989); Ngai, *Impossible Subjects*, 30–55; Rachel F. Moran, *Interracial Intimacy: The Regulation of Race and Romance* (Chicago: University of Chicago Press, 2001), 30–36. On the legal construction of race, see López, *White by Law*.

11. Carey McWilliams, "The House on 92d Street," *The Nation*, June 8, 1946. In 1948, Miller joined Thurgood Marshall to argue the bundle of residential covenant cases from Michigan and Missouri that came before the Supreme Court in *Shelley v. Kramer*. On overcrowding and unhygienic conditions in Los Angeles's segregated Black neighborhoods in the 1940s, see Leo Wynn, *The Afro-American and the Second World War* (London: Elek, 1976), 66. On Kelly Miller see Flamming, *Bound for Freedom*, 368–369.

12. Orenstein, "V for Vagueness," 404, n. 82.

13. Orenstein, "V for Vagueness," 389–390.

14. *West Virginia State Board of Education v. Barnette* 319 U.S. (1943), at 639.

15. In 1939, a pair of NAACP lawyers challenged Maryland's antimiscegenation law and also made a freedom-of-religion argument (in addition to challenging the law on Fourteenth Amendment grounds). See *Baltimore Afro-American*, November 18, 1939; October 21, 1939; October 28, 1939.

16. Orenstein, "V for Vagueness," 391–392. The NAACP, the ACLU, and the JACL joined forces in 1947 to challenge California's segregated school law.

17. Carey McWilliams, *The Nation*, October 16, 1948, 415.

18. "Pioneering California," *Time*, January 21, 1966. Court of Appeals judge Henry J. Friendly considered Traynor the "ablest judge of his generation"; he was frequently compared to Judge Learned Hand. Henry J. Friendly, "Ablest Judge of His Generation," *California Law Review* 71, no. 4 (1983): 1039–1044. On Traynor's receptivity to new ideas, see Gerald N. Rosenberg, *The Hollow Hope: Can Courts Bring About Social Change?* (Chicago: University of Chicago Press, 1991), 11, and Lawrence M. Friedman, *A History of American Law*, 3rd ed. (New York: Oxford University Press, 2017), 551. On Traynor's biography, see Ben Field, *Activism in Pursuit of the Public Interest: The Jurisprudence of Chief Justice Roger J. Traynor* (Berkeley, CA: Institute of Governmental Studies, 2003), xiii, 7. Traynor was elevated to chief justice in 1964, and during his tenure the California Supreme Court became the most frequently cited court by other courts outside California. A study of state supreme courts by Lawrence Friedman, Robert Kagan, and colleagues revealed that 92 percent of the California cases cited in the study sample were cited at least three times by out-of-state courts. Lawrence M. Friedman, Robert A. Kagan, Bliss Cartwright, and Stanton

Wheeler, "State Supreme Courts: A Century of Style and Citation," *Stanford Law Review* 33 (1981): 773–818.

19. Roger J. Traynor, "Law and Social Change in a Democratic Society" (1956), in *The Traynor Reader: Nous Verrons; A Collection of Essays* (San Francisco: Hastings Law Journal, 1987), 37; Traynor, "The Courts: Interweavers in the Reformation of Law" (1967), in *The Traynor Reader*, 126.

20. *Perez, et al. v. Maroney, etc.*, Oral Argument in Support of Petition Before the Supreme Court of the State of California, October 6, 1947, pp. 1, 2, 9, California Supreme Court Papers; *Perez v. Lippold*, LA20305, October 1, 1948, California State Archives, Sacramento. *Perez v. Lippold*, 198 P.2d 17, 32 Cal. 2d 711 (1948). Case names change according to the trial level and recording system. "Lippold" refers to Earl O. Lippold, County Clerk of Los Angeles.

21. Orenstein, "V for Vagueness," 389; "Catholics Start Test of California Race Law," *Christian Century* 64 (1947), 1067–1068.

22. *Strauder v. West Virginia*, 100 U.S. (10 Otto) 303 (1880); *United States v. Caroline Products Co.*, 304 U.S. 144 (1938); *Korematsu v. United States*, 323 U.S. 214 (1944).

23. *Scott v. State*, 39 Ga. 321 (1869).

24. *Perez, et al. vs. Maroney, etc.*, Oral Argument in Support, 11–12, esp. 6. Because the case involved a public official who refused to carry out his office, Marshall was able to file a writ of mandamus (from the Latin "we command") with the California Supreme Court, bypassing the lower courts entirely.

25. *Perez* case file, oral argument, 5–6, quoted in Orenstein, "V for Vagueness," 396.

26. George W. Stocking, *Race, Culture and Evolution: Essays in the History of Anthropology* (New York: Free Press, 1968), 192, 194; Franz Boas, "The Problem of the American Negro," *Yale Quarterly Review* 10 (1921), reprinted in Boas, *Race and Democratic Society* (New York: Augustin, 1945), 79. In *Missouri ex rel. Gaines v. Canada*, 305 U.S. 337 (1938), Chief Justice Charles Evans Hughes reached back to his ruling in the *McCabe v. Atchison, Topeka and Santa Fe Railway*, 235 U.S. 151 (1914), and highlighted the individual rights of the citizen that lay at the heart of the Fourteenth Amendment. The plaintiff Lloyd Gaines's right to a legal education was, said the court, "a personal one. It was as an individual that he was entitled to the equal protection of the laws."

27. Ashley Montagu, *Man's Most Dangerous Myth: The Fallacy of Race* (New York: Columbia University Press, 1942), 6.

28. Franz Boas, "History and Science in Anthropology: A Reply," *American Anthropologist* 38 (1936), 140.

29. Gunnar Myrdal, *An American Dilemma: The Negro Problem and Modern Democracy* (New York: Harper and Brothers, 1944), 136, 115.

30. The 1948 United Nations Convention on the Prevention and Punishment of the Crime of Genocide, for example, defined "genocide" as the "intent to destroy, in whole or in part, a national, ethnical, racial or religious group, as such."

31. On the declining academic credibility of scientific racism, see Elazar Barkan, *Retreat of Scientific Racism: Changing Concepts of Race in Britain and the United States Between the World Wars* (Cambridge, UK: Cambridge University Press, 1992). Regarding the continued popularity of many of these arguments, Justice John Shenk embraced them in his dissent in *Perez*, in which he insisted there was reason to believe that "the crossing of the primary races leads generally to retrogression and to eventual extinction of the resultant type unless it is fortified by reunion with the parent stock." Cf. "Mixed Marriages Upheld by Court," *New York Times*, October 2, 1948, 13. A contemporary of Franz Boas, Earnest Albert Hooton was one of the founders of physical anthropology in the United States and was known especially for his work on evolution and on nonhuman primates. A well-known public speaker, Hooton also wrote widely for the public, authoring a number of popular successes, including *Up from the Ape* (1931, reprinted in 1946) and *Man's Poor Relations* (1942), the first comprehensive treatise on primates. *Life* magazine devoted a six-page spread to Hooton ("Hooton of Harvard," August 7, 1939, 60–66). See also Stanley M. Garn and Eugene Giles, *Earnest Albert Hooton, 1887–1954: A Biographical Memoir* (Washington, DC: National Academies Press, 1995), www.nasonline .org/publications/biographical-memoirs/memoir-pdfs/hooton-earnest.pdf; and H. L. Shapiro, "Earnest Albert Hooton, 1887–1954," *American Anthropologist* 56 (1954): 1081–1084. In his essay "The Antropometry of Some Small Samples of Negroes and Negroids," in *A Study of Some Negro White Families in the United States*, ed. Caroline Bond Day (Cambridge, MA: Peabody Museum of Harvard University, 1932), 107, Hooton says that a white person and a person who passed for white could not produce Black offspring, refuting the old "blood will out/retrogressive black trait" argument.

32. *Perez* case file, oral argument, 3–4. Italics mine.

33. Justice Shenk made this argument in his dissent.

34. "Vet Sentenced to 5 Years for Mixed Marriage," *Chicago Tribune*, December 19, 1948, 37. Knight's designation as "white" in his navy discharge papers did not figure in the evidence in his favor.

35. Victoria E. Bynum, *The Free State of Jones: Mississippi's Longest Civil War* (Chapel Hill: University of North Carolina Press, 2001); "Court Reverses Conviction in Mixed Marriage," *Chicago Tribune*, November 15, 1949, 2.

36. The fact that antimiscegenation laws had been repeatedly upheld by state supreme courts (although never by the United States Supreme Court) was noted prominently by the dissenting justices.

37. Roger J. Traynor, "Badlands in an Appellate Judge's Realm of Reason," *Utah Law Review* 7 (1960): 157, 166, cited in Ben Field, *Activism in Pursuit of the Public Interest: The Jurisprudence of Chief Justice Roger J. Traynor* (Berkeley, CA: Institute of Governmental Studies, 2003), 10.

38. *Perez v. Sharp*, 32 Cal.2d 711; 198 P.2d 17, 18–19 (1948).

39. Quote from Noel T. Downing, "Protection of Human Rights Under the United States Constitution," *Annals of the American Academy of Political and Social Science* 243, Essential Human Rights (January 1946): 100. Downing was Nash Professor of Law at Columbia University and a former special assistant legislative counsel to the United States Senate.

40. *Meyer v. Nebraska*, 262 U.S. 390 (1923); *Skinner v. Oklahoma*, 316 U.S. 535 (1942), at 541. In his argument, Traynor also relied on *Pierce v. Society of Sisters*, 268 U.S. 510 (1925), as well as three cases that originated in California: *Yick Wo v. Hopkins*, 118 U.S. 351 (1886), in which the court wrote that "distinctions between citizens solely because of their ancestry are by their very nature odious to a free people whose institutions are founded upon the doctrine of equality"; *Hirabayashi v. United States*, 230 U.S. 81 (1943), which held that racial discriminations might be allowable in a national emergency such as a war; and *Oyama v. California*, 332 U.S. 633 (1948), which established that only the most exceptional circumstances could excuse racial discrimination in the face of the equal protection clause.

41. *Perez*, 198 P.2d at 21 ("to marry") and 25 ("as trains").

42. *Perez*, 198 P.2d at 24 and 25; *Buchanan v. Warley*, 245 U.S. 60 (1917): "As important as is the preservation of the public peace, this aim cannot be accomplished by laws or ordinances which deny rights created or protected by the Federal Constitution."

43. *Perez*, 198 P.2d at 28. Unlike many states with antimiscegenation laws, California recognized mixed-race marriages contracted elsewhere according to law.

44. *Perez*, 198 P.2d at 28.

45. *Perez*, 198 P.2d at 29. The California Constitution, Article 1, Section 7(a) guarantees equal protection of the laws.

46. *Roldan v. Los Angeles County*, 129 Cal. App. 267, 18 P.2d 706 (1933) defined Filipinos as "Malays" under the antimiscegenation law. On Filipinos and California's antimiscegenation regime, see Leti Volpp, "American Mestizo: Filipinos and Antimiscegenation Laws in California," *UC Davis Law Review* 33, no. 4 (Summer 2000): 795.

47. *Perez*, 198 P.2d at 40 (Shenk, J., dissenting), 35 ("some people"), and 45 ("police power").

48. "Racial Bill Retained," *New York Times*, May 17, 1951. The legislature finally revised the statute in 1959, after repeated demands by Augustus Hawkins, a Black assemblyman from Los Angeles. Orenstein, "V for Vagueness," 401. See *Statutes of California*, 1959, Chapter 146, 2043–2044.

Chapter Eleven: Architects of a Better World

1. *Perez v. Sharp*, 32 Cal.2nd 711 (1948). During Reconstruction, six Republican state legislatures in the South either repealed their states' restrictive marriage laws or found them unconstitutional under the Fourteenth Amendment. See *Burns v. State*, 48 Ala. 195 (1872); *Ex parte Francois*, 9 F. Cas. 699 (C.C.W.D. Tex. 1879) (No. 5047); *Hart v. Hoss and Elder*, 26 La. Ann. 90 (1874). Three states repealed their antimiscegenation laws (South Carolina, Louisiana, and Mississippi), and two others omitted them when drafting new codes of law (Arkansas and Florida). Peter Wallenstein, *Tell the Court I Love My Wife: Race, Marriage and Law—An American History* (New York: Macmillan, 2003), 80.

2. "Blaze of Lights Limns the Scene," *New York Times*, April 26, 1945, 4; "Eggs and Tripe, Three Times a Day, Fail to Make Delegates Gay; Hotels and Restaurants Lack Red Meat," *New York Times*, April 25, 1945, 16. On Molotov's irritation with Truman and Stettinius's anxiety that the Russians would not be represented at San Francisco, see Alger Hiss, *Recollections of a Life* (New York, Seaver Books, 1988), 136–137.

3. Address to the Delegates of the United Nations Conference on International Organization, April 25, 1946, Truman Official File, Harry S. Truman Papers, scanned online at www.trumanlibrary.gov/library/public-papers/10/address-united-nations-conference-san-francisco.

4. Quotes from Mary Ann Glendon, *A World Made New: Eleanor Roosevelt and the Universal Declaration of Human Rights* (New York: Random House,

2001), 67. Of the various drafts of a declaration of rights offered to the commission, the most influential was that of the American Law Institute (ALI), a distinguished association of jurists and law professors that included Roger Traynor among its members. (Traynor was at the opening session of the United Nations in San Francisco.) The ALI's Statement of Essential Human Rights was published in pamphlet form in 1945 by Americans United for World Organization. On the ALI and the UDHR, see Sarah Sao, "A Shattered Dream: The American Law Institute and the Drafting of the International Bill of Rights," *Thomas Jefferson Law Review* 30 (2007): 179–195.

5. "Humphrey Draft," in Glendon, *A World Made New*, Appendix I, 272.

6. Article 17 of the UDHR: "Every person has the right to contract marriage in accordance with the laws." Glendon, *A World Made New*, Appendix II, 277, 93.

7. Glendon, *A World Made New*, 3.

8. Glendon, *A World Made New*, 194. Freedom of movement is included in Article 13 of the UN Charter. The Soviets argued strenuously and repeatedly against this. Johannes Morsink, *The Universal Declaration of Human Rights: Origins, Drafting, and Intent* (Philadelphia: University of Pennsylvania Press, 1999), 74–75.

9. The General Assembly vote in 1948 affirmed the principles contained in the declaration and committed the members to work toward the creation of a covenant of binding obligations in the future. The United States refused to sign the covenant.

10. Quoted in William H. Brackney, series ed., *Human Rights and the World's Major Religions*, vol. 2, *The Christian Tradition* (Westport, CT: Praeger, 2005), 119.

11. Quoted in Carol Anderson, *Eyes off the Prize: African Americans, the United Nations, and the Struggle for Human Rights, 1944–1955* (New York: Cambridge University Press, 2003), 88; Paul Lauren, *Power and Prejudice: The Politics and Diplomacy of Racial Discrimination* (Boulder, CO: Westview Press, 1996), 168–172.

12. Glendon, *A World Made New*, 194.

13. John Foster Dulles's description of the clause he had designed. Quoted in Anderson, *Eyes off the Prize*, 87.

14. The National Negro Congress's Max Yergan, who was in San Francisco for the UN conference, recognized this as early as 1946, when India challenged South Africa's proposal to absorb South-West Africa. The Indian action, Yergan wrote, broke "the barrier of national sovereignty—the international equivalent of the 'states' rights' obstacle." In Glenda Elizabeth Gilmore, *Defying Dixie: The Radical Roots of Civil Rights, 1919–1950* (New York: Norton, 2008), 407.

15. "Statement of Dr. W. E. B. Du Bois to the Representatives of the Human Rights Commission and its Parent Bodies, the Economic and Social Council and General Assembly," October 23, 1947, Reel 60, Correspondence, frame 1079, Du Bois Papers, Library of Congress. Quoted in Lauren, *Power and Prejudice*, 173. See also David Levering Lewis, *W. E. B. Du Bois* (New York: Henry Holt, 1993–2000), 2:521–522, 528–530. On the National Negro Congress, see Herbert Aptheker, "The Oppression of the American Negro: The Facts," and National Negro Congress, "The Jurisdiction of the Economic and Social Council of the United Nations," both quoted in Anderson, *Eyes off the Prize*, 80–81.

16. Anderson, *Eyes off the Prize*, 103 (Du Bois leak). Quotes from Anderson, *Eyes off the Prize*, 103 and 108; Lauren, *Power and Prejudice*, 173.

17. Morsink, *Universal Declaration*, 93.

18. Document E/1003, USSR: amendment to the Chilean amendment (E/981 and Corr.1) to draft resolution D in the report of the Human Rights Committee (E/950), United Nations Economic and Social Council, Official Records, 3rd year, 7th session, August 23, 1948, Annex, 178.

19. United Nations Economic and Social Council, Official Records, 3rd year, 7th session, July 19–August 28, 1948, 580–582. On Germany, see Glendon, *A World Made New*, 154, and Heide Fehrenbach, *Race After Hitler: Black Occupation Children in Postwar Germany and America* (Princeton, NJ: Princeton University Press, 2005), 7.

20. Adopted at the Ninth International Conference of American States in the spring of 1948, the (Pan)American Declaration upheld the equality of all human beings before the law without distinction of race, sex, language, creed "or any other factor." See Morsink, *Universal Declaration*, 255.

21. Headline from *New York Times*, August 24, 1948. The addition of "colour" to the list reflected an increasing uncertainty about establishing a scientific definition of "race." Roger Traynor was not the only one abandoning the quest. Morsink, *Universal Declaration*, 102–103.

22. *Plessy v. Ferguson* is notable for its absence in the *Perez* decision.

23. *Perez*, 198 P.2d at 34 (Carter, J., concurring).

24. For a discussion of American race politics in the context of the nation's role in global politics, see Mary Dudziak, *Cold War Civil Rights: Race and the Image of American Democracy* (Princeton, NJ: Princeton University Press, 2000), passim.

25. "Hastie Seeing Court Reversal," *Washington Tribune*, April 2, 1946, quoted in Gilmore, *Defying Dixie*, 407.

26. *Oyama v. California*, 332 U.S. 633 (1948).

27. Frank E. Holman, "Treaty Law-Making: A Blank Check for Writing a New Constitution," *American Bar Association Journal* 36 (September 1950): 708, 710. This article is from 1950, in which Holman reminisces about what he supposedly said in his speech of 1948. In 1948, the ABA, under Holman's leadership, passed a resolution condemning the Universal Declaration of Human Rights. See Margaret E. Galey, "The Universal Declaration of Human Rights: The Role of Congress," *PS: Political Science and Politics* 31, no. 3 (September 1998): 524.

28. *Sei Fujii v. State of California*, 97 A.C.A. 154, 217 Pac. (2d) 481 (1950); rehearing denied on May 22, 1957. 97 A.C.A. 718, 218 Pac. (2d) 595.

29. *To Secure These Rights: The Report of the President's Committee on Civil Rights* (1947), quoted in "Can U.N. Lay Down the Law of the Land?," *Chicago Daily Tribune*, April 27, 1950; Brief for the United States as Amicus Curiae, *Shelley v. Kraemer*, 334 U.S. 1 (1948), 97–102.

30. "Can U.N. Lay Down the Law of the Land?"

31. Bert B. Lockwood Jr., "The United Nations Charter and United States Civil Rights Litigation: 1946–1955," *Iowa Law Review* 69 (1983–1984): 901–956, esp. 927–928. The crucial question was whether or not the charter, as a treaty, was self-executing, which would require the United States to fulfill its pledge to promote respect for and observance of human rights and freedom, or whether it required enabling legislation by Congress to take effect.

32. Arthur Krock, *New York Times*, May 16, 1950, 27; *Sei Fujii v. State of California*, 38 Cal.2d 718, 242 P.2d 617 (1952).

33. Holman excerpted in "Fears Nation's Laws Imperiled by U.N. Charter," *Chicago Daily Tribune*, September 11, 1950, B12.

34. "Can U.N. Lay Down the Law of the Land?"

35. United Nations Economic and Social Council, Official Records, 7th session, July–August 1948, 581–582; United Nations, Commission on Human Rights, 7th session, item 10 of Provisional Agenda, August 2, 1949, part 14, reel 17, frame 613, NAACP Records, Library of Congress.

36. Quincy Wright, "National Courts and Human Rights: The Fujii Case," *American Journal of International Law* 45, no. 1 (January 1951): 62–82, esp. 72, 77, 78.

37. *In re Drummond Wren*, 4 D.L.R. 674 (1945); Wright, "National Courts and Human Rights."

38. *Mendez v. Westminster*, 64 F. Sup. 544 (1946).

39. "A Joint Resolution," February 14, 1950, reproduced on website of South Carolina Department of Archives and History, accessed May 2020, www .teachingushistory.org/lessons/GenAsmRemovalofWaring.htm.

40. Louis C. Kesselman, "The Fair Employment Practice Commission Movement in Perspective," *Journal of Negro History* 31, no. 1 (January 1946): 42. On Arizona, see "Civil Rights Bills Considered in Arizona and New Mexico," *New York Times*, February 20, 1949, E8. A federal court decision in Texas also ended segregation of students "of Latin extraction." See Guadalupe San Miguel Jr., "The Struggle Between Separate and Unequal Schools: Middle-Class Mexican Americans and the Desegregation Campaign in Texas, 1929–1957," *History of Education Quarterly* 23, no. 3 (Autumn 1983): 343–359.

41. *Briggs et al. v. Elliott et al.*, 98 F. Supp. 529 (1951); *Sweatt v. Painter*, 339 U.S. 629 (1050); *McLaurin v. Oklahoma State Regents*, 339 U.S. 637 (1950); *Henderson v. United States*, 339 U.S. 816 (1950).

42. "Group Reports All Races Basically Alike," *Chicago Daily Tribune*, July 18, 1950. The group was headed by Ashley Montagu. In 1947, congressional opposition to army distribution of the pamphlet *The Races of Mankind*, by Ruth Benedict and Gene Weltfish, was so fierce that the army destroyed all copies of the pamphlet in its possession. See Sec. of War Robert P. Patterson to Walter White, April 24, 1947, in folder 1, box 719, Record Group 407, National Archives and Records Administration, College Park, MD.

43. On the Bricker Amendment, see Duane Tananbaum, *The Bricker Amendment Controversy: A Test of Eisenhower's Political Leadership* (Ithaca, NY: Cornell University Press, 1988). On Bricker, see Richard O. Davies, *Defender of the Old Guard: John Bricker and American Politics* (Columbus: Ohio State University Press, 1993). Bricker was a passionate Cold Warrior.

44. On Walter George, see Anderson, *Eyes off the Prize*, 253. Holman quoted in Natalie Hevener Kaufman and David Whiteman, "Opposition to Human Rights Treaties in the United States Senate: The Legacy of the Bricker Amendment," *Human Rights Quarterly* 10, no. 3 (August 1988): 324. See also Frank E. Holman, *The Story of the "Bricker" Amendment: The First Phase* (New York: Committee for Constitutional Government, 1954). The amendment was championed by the ABA via its Standing Committee on Peace and Law Through the United Nations, but the ABA's own section of International and Comparative Law opposed it. See Glendon Austin Schubert Jr., "Politics and the Constitution: The Bricker Amendment During 1953," *Journal of Politics* 16, no. 2 (May 1954): 261–262; "Bar Leaders Seek

Curb on UN Pacts; Urge That U.S. Association Act Against Covenants That Take Place of Domestic Laws," *New York Times*, February 23, 1952, 14.

45. Harvard University law professor Zachariah Chafee Jr. chastised his ABA colleagues for their fear of international treaties, arguing that the framers of the Constitution "intended the treaty powers of the nation to be wider than its domestic powers, as wide as the unpredictable necessities of international intercourse." The Supreme Court would be a check on any constitutional abuses and would hold invalid "any treaty provision…which infringes a constitutional prohibition." Chafee, "Stop Being Terrified of Treaties: Stop Being Scared of the Constitution," *American Bar Association Journal* 38 (1952): 731, 732. The American Jewish Congress warned that the Bricker Amendment could "cripple…all attempts at International cooperation to protect and safeguard human rights." Anderson, *Eyes off the Prize*, 225. Lael Weinberger argues that the Bricker Amendment was a turning point for the American legal profession in the creation of an anti-internationalist perspective, and that lawyers who supported the Bricker Amendment "shared a basic ideological commitment to limited government powers." See Weinberger, "The Bricker Amendment and the American Legal Profession's Opposition to International Law" (unpublished manuscript, 2017).

46. Which the National Council of Churches supported, of course.

47. "Dulles Bars Pacts of UN on Rights; Fights Treaty Curb; Tells Senators Administration Will Not Sign Two Accords or Press Genocide Convention," *New York Times*, April 7, 1953, 1. Dulles quoted in Mark Phillip Bradley, *The World Reimagined: Americans and Human Rights in the Twentieth Century* (New York: Cambridge University Press, 2016), 113. The NAACP presented its petition "We Charge Genocide" to the UN in 1951. The United States did not sign the Genocide Convention until 1987.

48. Quoted in Patricia Sullivan, *Lift Every Voice: The NAACP and the Making of the Civil Rights Movement* (New York: New Press, 2009), 384.

Chapter Twelve: Grappling with Brown

1. Philip Elman and Norman Silber, "The Solicitor General's Office, Justice Frankfurter, and Civil Rights Litigation, 1946–1960: An Oral History," *Harvard Law Review* 100, no. 4 (1987): 817–852, esp. 840; Bernard Schwartz, "Chief Justice Rehnquist, Justice Jackson, and the Brown Case," *Supreme Court Review* (1988): 245–267 ("God" quote on 267).

2. E. S. Askew, Windsor, NC, to Hon. Fred M. Vinson, February 13, 1951, Coll. No. 2881-z, Southern Historical Collection, University of North Carolina, Chapel Hill (hereafter SHC).

3. The fact that the court delayed ruling on the school cases is more indicative of anxiety on the part of several justices about challenging *Plessy* than of resistance to desegregation per se. In June 1953 the court unanimously upheld a DC statute that barred racial discrimination in restaurants.

4. Harry Ashmore says that as a quid pro quo for not challenging Eisenhower for the Republican nomination in 1952, Warren was promised the first appointment to the Supreme Court. Harry S. Ashmore, *Civil Rights and Wrongs: A Memoir of Race and Politics, 1944–1994* (New York: Pantheon, 1994), 101. The Ninth Circuit ruled racially segregated schools in California unconstitutional in *Mendez v. Westminster*, 161 F. 2nd 744 (9th Cir., 1947); 64 Fed. Supp. 544 (S.D. Cal. 1946).

5. Warren's conference remarks quoted in Michael J. Klarman, *From Jim Crow to Civil Rights: The Supreme Court and the Struggle for Racial Equality* (New York: Oxford University Press), 302.

6. *Plessy v. Ferguson*, 163 U.S. 537 (1896), at 551.

7. Jack Balkin suggests that the justices understood they were effectively annulling *Plessy v. Ferguson* when they issued the *Brown* decision, but did they? That was not accomplished until 1957, when a federal court ruled for the first time in *Simkins v. City of Greensboro*, 149 F. Supp. 562 (M.D. N.C. 1957), aff'd *Greensboro v. Simkins*, 246 F.2d 425 (4th Cir. 1959), that *Plessy* was overturned. On the *Brown* decision see, among others, Jack M. Balkin, ed., *What "Brown v. Board of Education" Should Have Said: The Nation's Top Legal Experts Rewrite the Nation's Landmark Civil Rights Decision* (New York: New York University Press, 2001), 48.

8. *Brown v. Board of Education of Topeka*, 347 U.S. 483 (1954); *Bolling v. Sharp*, 397 U.S. 497 (1954). Warren's desire for the decision was that it be "short, readable by the lay public, nonrhetorical, unemotional, and, above all, nonaccusatory." Quoted in Ashmore, *Civil Rights and Wrongs*, 101, and in Richard Kluger, *Simple Justice: Brown v. Board of Education and Black America's Struggle for Equality* (New York: Knopf, 1975), 711. Because *Brown II* limited relief to "the parties in these cases" rather than allowing for class-action-type lawsuits, it was implemented one suit at a time, with great deliberation and far less speed.

9. Michael J. Klarman, *Unfinished Business: Racial Equality in American History* (New York: Oxford University Press, 2007), 304.

10. The study was carried out and composed by Frankfurter's clerk Alexander Bickel.

11. For a nuanced take on the "originalist" argument, see Michael McConnell, "Originalism and the Desegregation Decisions," 81 *Virginia Law Review* 947, no. 4 (May 1995), 947–1140. For school integration in postwar Washington, see Kate Masur, *An Example for All the Land: Emancipation and the Struggle over Equality in Washington, D.C.* (Chapel Hill: University of North Carolina Press, 2010), 162–177, 188–192.

12. *McCabe v. Atchison, Topeka and Santa Fe Railway*, 235 U.S. 151 (1914); *Buchanan v. Warley*, 245 U.S. 60 (1917).

13. *Missouri ex rel. Gaines v. Canada* 305 U.S. 337 (1938).

14. *Norris v. Alabama* (1935; jury selection); *Smith v. Allwright* (1944; white primary); *Sipuel v. Oklahoma State Regents*, 332 U.S. 631 (1948); *Henderson v. United States* (1950; interstate transportation); *Shelley v. Kramer* (1948; restrictive housing covenants).

15. David A. Strauss, "The Common Law Genius of the Warren Court" (working paper, Chicago Public Law and Legal Theory no. 25, 2002), 22.

16. Jackson draft concurrence, School Segregation Cases, March 15, 1954, 1–2, 7–10, case file: Segregation Cases, box 184, Jackson Papers, quoted in Klarman, *From Jim Crow to Civil Rights*, 305–306.

17. Elman and Silber, "The Solicitor General's Office," 825.

18. Reed quoted in Mark V. Tushnett, *Making Civil Rights Law: Thurgood Marshall and the Supreme Court, 1936–1961* (New York: Oxford University Press, 1994), 211 (first quote); Kluger, *Simple Justice*, 598 (second quote). In *District of Columbia v. John R. Thompson, Co., Inc.*, 73 S. Ct. 1007; 346 U.S. 100 (1953), the Supreme Court upheld an 1873 Act of the Legislative Assembly of the District of Columbia making it a crime to discriminate against a person on grounds of race or color or to refuse service on those grounds.

19. Antimiscegenation laws are the premier example. Although the Supreme Court avoided ruling on miscegenation laws until 1964 (*McLaughlin v. Florida*), lower federal courts upheld two antimiscegenation statutes against attacks based on the Fourteenth Amendment: *Stevens v. United States*, 146 F. 2s 120 (10th Cir. 1944) (marriage of African American to deceased full-blooded Creek Indian void in Oklahoma; statute affects all parties alike), and *State v. Tutty*, 41 Fed. 753 (C.C.S.D.Ga. 1890) (comity does not require recognition of out-of-state marriages that violate a state's public policy).

20. *Brown v. Board of Education*, 347 U.S. 483 (1954); *Brown II*, 349 U.S. 294 (1955).

21. Brief for Appellants at 9, 1952, *Brown*, 34, 23–42, 35. The court embraced a privileged view of education in its decision ("education is perhaps the most important function of state and local governments"). *Brown*, 347 U.S. at 492–493.

22. *Jackson v. State*, 260 Ala. 698 (1954).

23. *Naim v. Naim*, 197 Va. 80; 87 S.E. 2nd, 749 (1955). On *Naim* see: Gregory Michael Dorr, "Principled Expediency: Eugenics, *Naim*, and the Supreme Court," *American Journal of Legal History* 42 (1998): 119–159; Dennis J. Hutchinson, "Unanimity and Desegregation: Decisionmaking in the Supreme Court, 1948–1958," *Georgetown Law Journal* 68 (1979–1980): 2–96, esp. 61–68; Elman and Silber, "The Solicitor General's Office," 845; memorandum from Justice John Marshall Harlan to Other Supreme Court Justices, November 4, 1955, box 11, John Marshall Harlan Papers, Mudd Library, Princeton University, Princeton, NJ.

24. Warren quoted in Ed Cray, *Chief Justice: A Biography of Earl Warren* (New York: Simon and Schuster, 1997), 310, 451. For "bombshell," see memorandum from Justice John Marshall Harlan to Other Supreme Court Justices.

25. Felix Frankfurter to Learned Hand, September 17, 1957, Hand Correspondence, 105-23, Felix Frankfurter Papers, Harvard Law School Library, Historical and Special Collections, Harvard University, Cambridge, MA (hereafter Frankfurter Papers).

26. Hand to Frankfurter, September 13, 1957, Hand Correspondence, 105-23, Frankfurter Papers. Frankfurter argued strenuously against taking on the *Naim* case. His chief concern seems to have been protecting the *Brown* decision. No author (Felix Frankfurter) memorandum to the court, October term, 1955, pt. 2, reel 17, 588, United States Supreme Court Case Files of Opinions and Memoranda, Library of Congress.

27. Frankfurter to Hand, September 17, 1957; Hand to Frankfurter, September 25, 1957. Both in Hand Correspondence, 105-23, Frankfurter Papers. Hand's biographer, Gerald Gunther, interprets Hand's position thusly: "[Hand] thought *Brown* had to be interpreted as announcing a flat, absolute ban on racial discrimination; so read, it compelled the Supreme Court to invalidate miscegenation laws as well." Gerald Gunther, *Learned Hand: The Man and the Judge* (New York: Knopf, 1994), 667.

28. James C. Scott, *Domination and the Arts of Resistance: Hidden Transcripts* (New Haven, CT: Yale University Press, 1992).

29. In his testimony at the trial, Till's uncle Moses Wright identified the ring in the courtroom; he confirmed that it belonged to Till and that the body he identified as Till's had worn the ring. *New York Times*, September 22, 1955, 64. There is some dispute about the timing of the giving of the ring. Mobley says in the 2003 PBS documentary, *The Murder of Emmett Till*, that she gave it to Emmett the day before he left. An article in the *Chicago Defender* from October 1, 1955, has her saying that Emmett wore his father's ring "in the days before the trip."

30. Willie Morris, *Terrains of the Heart and Other Essays on Home* (Oxford, MS: Yoknapatawpha Press, 1981), 8, 71.

31. John Dittmer, *Local People: The Struggle for Civil Rights in Mississippi* (Urbana: University of Illinois Press), 45. The Citizen's Council membership claim was sixty thousand by the end of 1955. Michael J. Klarman, "How *Brown* Changed Race Relations: The Backlash Thesis," *Journal of American History* 81, no. 1 (June 1994): 81–118, esp. 116. Cf. Numan V. Bartley, *The Rise of Massive Resistance: Race and Politics in the South During the 1950s* (Baton Rouge: Louisiana State University Press, 1969), 109–111.

32. Dittmer, *Local People*, 48.

33. On Mississippi, see Dittmer, *Local People*, Chapter 3.

34. On segregated Chicago in the 1940s and 1950s, see Adam P. Green, *Selling the Race: Culture, Community, and Black Chicago, 1940–1955* (Chicago: University of Chicago Press, 2007).

35. William Bradford Huie, "The Shocking Story of Approved Killing in Mississippi," *Look*, January 24, 1956, reproduced on PBS website, accessed May 2020, www.pbs.org/wgbh/americanexperience/features/till-killers-confession/. A white Alabaman, Huie was a prolific and successful writer. He succeeded H. L. Mencken as editor of *American Mercury*. On Huie, see Gene Roberts and Hank Klibanoff, *The Race Beat: The Press, the Civil Rights Struggle, and the Awakening of a Nation* (New York: Knopf, 2006), 101–102.

36. The jury deliberated a mere hour and determined that the body was unidentifiable. *Chicago Daily Tribune*, September 24, 1955, 1.

37. There were no African Americans on the jury because there were no Black registered voters in Tallahatchie County. Mississippi, like a number of other Southern states, limited jury service to men until 1968. Roberts and Klibanoff note that the Till trial brought "unprecedented numbers" of white reporters into the Deep South for the first time to cover a racial story. Roberts and Klibanoff, *The Race Beat*, 86. Cf. Timothy B. Tyson, *The Blood of Emmett Till* (New York: Simon and Schuster, 2017), 131–132.

38. Speech of Roy Wilkins, "The War Against the United States," to the Virginia State Conference of the NAACP, October 7, 1955, coll. #3827, box 7, f. 158, Lenoir Chambers Papers, SHC. At a rally in Detroit, Mississippi NAACP leader Medgar Evers cited public school desegregation and voting rights as the key issues for his state. *Chicago Defender*, October 8, 1955, 4.

39. Dittmer, *Local People*, Chapter 3. The *Chicago Defender* noted that Mississippi had been free of lynching from 1951 until the summer of 1955. *Chicago Defender*, September 10, 1955, 1.

40. At the murder trial of her husband and brother-in-law, Carolyn Bryant testified that Emmett had accosted her physically, grabbing her hands, clutching her waist, and asking for a date. This allowed the defense lawyers to portray Bryant and Milam as defending Carolyn's honor against a dangerous Black man. Sixty years later, Carolyn Bryant Donham denied that any of this had happened. See Tyson, *The Blood of Emmett Till*, 4–7, 165–168.

41. Danielle L. McGuire, *At the Dark End of the Street: Black Women, Rape, and Resistance: A New History of the Civil Rights Movement, from Rosa Parks to Black Power* (New York: Knopf, 2010), 51.

42. All Milam quotes in this passage are from Huie, "The Shocking Story of Approved Killing in Mississippi."

43. The kiss may be seen in the PBS documentary series *Eyes on the Prize: America's Civil Rights Movement*. The *New York Times* described it as a "hearty clinch." *New York Times*, September 24, 1955, 1.

44. The crowd was estimated at between thirty thousand and one hundred thousand. The *New York Amsterdam News*, September 4, 1955, said fifty thousand.

45. William Faulkner, *Chicago Defender*, September 24, 1955, 3. In his use of "children," Faulkner was perhaps following the lead of the NAACP, which announced that Mississippi had "decided to maintain white supremacy by killing children." *Chicago Defender*, September 10, 1955, 1. African American newspapers emphasized the disappointment in the Black community over Eisenhower's lack of action.

46. John Dittmer, *Local People: The Struggle for Civil Rights in Mississippi* (Urbana: University of Illinois Press, 1995), 58.

47. Howell Raines, *My Soul Is Rested: Movement Days in the Deep South Remembered* (New York: Putnam, 1977), 235 (Moore), 299 (Patterson).

Chapter Thirteen: Breaching the Inner Shrine

1. Speech of Roy Wilkins, "The War Against the United States," to the Virginia State Conference of the NAACP, October 7, 1955, coll. #3827, box 7, f. 158, Lenoir Chambers Papers, Southern Historical Collection, University of North Carolina, Chapel Hill (hereafter SHC).

2. Eastland quoted in David R. Colburn and Richard K. Scher, "Race Relations and Florida Gubernatorial Politics Since the Brown Decision," *Florida Historical Quarterly* 55, no. 2 (October 1976): 153–169, esp. 153; Givhan quoted in Melissa Fay Green, *The Temple Bombing* (Reading, MA: Addison-Wesley, 1996), 148.

3. Ethridge, "A Call to the South," in *Nieman Reports* (April 1959): 7–11, esp. 9, in Mark F. Ethridge Papers, folder 154, Coll. No. 3842, SHC; *Jackson Daily News* quote from Stephen J. Whitfield, *A Death in the Delta: The Story of Emmett Till* (Baltimore, MD: Johns Hopkins University Press, 1988), 9.

4. J. Robert Smith, "California Writer Raps Walter White for Taking White Bride," *Los Angeles Sentinel*, n.d. (ca. July 29, 1949), in Part 17: National Staff files, 1940–1955, Reel 24, p. 153, NAACP Records, Library of Congress.

5. Speech of Roy Wilkins, Executive Secretary, NAACP, "The War Against the United States," to the Virginia State Conference of the NAACP, Charlottesville, VA, October 7, 1955, Lenoir Chambers Papers, #3827, box 7, f. 158, SHC; Hoover quoted in Elizabeth Jacoway, *Turn Away Thy Son: Little Rock, the Crisis That Shocked the Nation* (New York: Free Press, 2007), 126.

6. Talmadge quoted in Stephen G. N. Tuck, *Beyond Atlanta: The Struggle for Racial Equality in Georgia, 1940–1980* (Athens: University of Georgia Press, 2001), 77, and in *Ebony*, April 1957, 78; letter, William A. Robinson Jr. to Herman E. Talmadge, May 25, 1954 (copied to Thomas B. Stanley), folder 2, box 100, General Correspondence, Executive Papers, Gov. Thomas B. Stanley (1954–1958), Library of Virginia, Richmond (hereafter Stanley Correspondence).

7. Hodding Carter cited in Tony Badger, "Fatalism, Not Gradualism: Race and the Crisis of Southern Liberalism, 1946–1965," *The Making of Martin Luther King and the Civil Rights Movement*, ed. Brian Ward and Tony Badger (New York: New York University Press, 1996), 67–95, esp. 69; letter signed by thirty-seven to Governor Stanley, June 11, 1954, folder 1, box 100, Stanley Correspondence.

8. Methodist youth in North Carolina took a similar tack when they resolved in August 1954 at the annual Methodist Youth Fellowship that "segregation is

un-Christian" and voted to present resolutions urging support of the *Brown* decision. See *News and Observer* (Raleigh), August 21, 1954. Joe Louis quoted in "Backstage," *Ebony*, August 1954, 14. Of the thirty largest daily newspapers in the South, all were hostile to the *Brown* decision except for a dozen in the border states. See David R. Davies, *The Press and Race: Mississippi Journalists Confront the Movement* (Jackson: University of Mississippi Press, 2001), 9.

9. Quoted in Pete Daniel, *Lost Revolutions: The South in the 1950s* (Chapel Hill: University of North Carolina Press, 2000), 182. Daniel notes that the Baptist periodicals generally supported compliance.

10. The complaint that "the practice of legal segregation on the basis of race weakens our Christian witness at home and abroad and lays a roadblock across the path of our missionaries" is representative of the concerns of those funding foreign missions. *Alabama Baptist*, November 4, 1954, quoted in Joel L. Alvis Jr., *Religion and Race: Southern Presbyterians, 1946–1983* (Tuscaloosa: University of Alabama Press, 1994), 57–58. The governing boards of the National Council of Churches of Christ in the USA (NCC), the World Council of Churches, and the Synagogue Council of America all passed resolutions praising the decision. See Michael B. Friedland, *Lift Up Your Voice Like a Trumpet: White Clergy and the Civil Rights and Anti-War Movements 1954–1973* (Chapel Hill: University of North Carolina Press, 1998), 18–19.

11. Rev. George E. Naff Jr., Coeburn Methodist Church, to Governor Stanley, July 1, 1954, folder 1, box 101, Stanley Correspondence. Michael Friedland points out that "research suggests not only that those in the pews were often considerably more conservative and prejudiced than those who faced them from the altars but also that those who regularly attended services tended to be more prejudiced and intolerant than more sporadic churchgoers." Friedland, *Lift Up Your Voice Like a Trumpet*, 7. Gardiner Shattuck agrees where Episcopalians are concerned. A 1952 study showed that "ordinary Episcopalians were generally more conservative on social matters than the official pronouncements of their denomination suggested." He notes as well that the strongest opposition to desegregation within the Episcopal church came from the most active members. Gardiner H. Shattuck, *Episcopalians and Race: Civil War to Civil Rights* (Lexington: University Press of Kentucky, 2000), 68, 83. "Hand of God" quote from Daniel, *Lost Revolutions*, 184. "Pinkos in the pulpit" from *Citizens' Council*, December 1956. Also cited in David L. Chappell, *A Stone of Hope: Prophetic Religion and the Death of Jim Crow* (Chapel Hill: University of North Carolina Press, 2004), 152.

12. Charles Marsh, *God's Long Summer: Stories of Faith and Civil Rights* (Princeton, NJ: Princeton University Press, 1997), 100–101 (Hudgins); Mark Newman, *Getting Right with God: Southern Baptists and Desegregation, 1945–1995* (Tuscaloosa: University of Alabama Press, 2001), 23 (Storer). Leon Macon, editor of the *Alabama Baptist*, advised distinguishing between "being a Christian and performing a duty. Those who do right under the compulsion of law are performing a duty." *Alabama Baptist*, November 4, 1954, 119. Martin Luther King Jr. objected to this interpretation in his letter from the Birmingham jail, insisting that Christians must embrace the civil rights movement on theological and moral grounds as well as civic ones. King, "Letter from Birmingham City Jail," 1963, in *A Testament of Hope: The Essential Writings of Martin Luther King, Jr.*, ed. James Melvin Washington (San Francisco: HarperSanFrancisco, 1986), 289–302.

13. Shattuck, *Episcopalians and Race*, 79–80; Newman, *Getting Right with God*, 45. This position echoed the one taken by the SBC's Christian Life Commission in 1956. See Friedland, *Lift Up Your Voice Like a Trumpet*, 36; *Alabama Baptist*, February 10, 1955, 120; Ernest Q. Campbell and Thomas Pettigrew, *Christians in Racial Crisis: A Study of Little Rock's Ministry* (Washington, DC: Public Affairs Press, 1959), 100.

14. Rev. James F. Burks, pamphlet, *Integration or Segregation?*, May 30, 1954, folder 1, box 100, General Correspondence, Executive Papers, Stanley Correspondence.

15. The source for the "negro gardener" argument is Samuel A. Cartwright, the influential Louisiana physician and proslavery writer, who argued this point in Samuel A. Cartwright, *Essays, Being Inductions Drawn from the Baconian Philosophy...* (Vidalia, LA, 1843).

16. Ariel [Buckner H. Payne], *The Negro: What Is His Ethnological Status?*, reprinted in John David Smith, *The "Ariel" Controversy: Religion and "the Negro Problem"* (New York: Garland Publications, 1993), 45, 48. See also John David Smith, *An Old Creed for the New South: Proslavery Ideology and Historiography, 1865–1918* (Westport, CT: Greenwood Press, 1985), 43, and George M. Fredrickson, *The Black Image in the White Mind: The Debate on Afro-American Character and Destiny, 1817–1914* (Middletown, CT: Wesleyan University Press, 1971), 188–189, 87–88. For a specific reference to the Antichrist, see Burks, typescript, "Integration or Segregation?," May 30, 1954, folder 1, box 100, Stanley Correspondence, in which the author asserts that "the amalgamation of races is part of the spirit of anti-christ." See also Henry Ansgar Kelly,

"The Metamorphosis of the Eden Serpent During the Middle Ages and Renaissance," *Viator* 2 (1971): 301–328.

17. H. Paul Douglass, *Christian Reconstruction in the South* (Boston: Pilgrim Press, 1909), 114. On Carroll's *The Tempter of Eve* (1902), see Mason Stokes, *The Color of Sex: Whiteness, Heterosexuality, and the Fictions of White Supremacy* (Durham, NC: Duke University Press, 2001), 5. On Carroll's *The Negro as Beast* (1900), see Stokes, *The Color of Sex*, 95–98, and Fredrickson, *The Black Image in the White Mind*, 277. On the longevity of proslavery arguments, including religious arguments, and their applicability in the Jim Crow era, see Smith, *An Old Creed for the New South*, 286.

18. For an example of the sin of Sodom identified as miscegenation, see flyer *God Commands Racial Segregation*, n.d., folder 14, box 1, Citizens' Council/Civil Rights Collection, University of Southern Mississippi, Hattiesburg, Mississippi, which says, "MONGRELIZATION IS THE SIN FOR WHICH SODOM AND GEMORRAH WERE DESTROYED!"

19. D. B. Red, *Race Mixing a Religious Fraud*, n.d. (ca. 1959), box 2, Wm. D. McCain Papers, University of Southern Mississippi, Hattiesburg, Mississippi (hereafter McCain Papers).

20. Carey Daniel, "God the Original Segregationist," cited in Neil R. McMillen, *The Citizens' Council: Organized Resistance to the Second Reconstruction, 1954–1964* (Urbana: University of Illinois Press, 1971), 175.

21. Daniel, "God the Original Segregationist," cited in McMillen, *The Citizens' Council*, 175; Theodore G. Bilbo, *Take Your Choice: Separation or Mongrelization* (Poplarville, MS: Dream House Publishing Company, 1947), 109. In 1958 the American Council of Christian Churches—a group of some fifteen fundamentalist sects—argued that integration "does violence to the true gospel of Jesus Christ." See Numan V. Bartley, *The Rise of Massive Resistance: Race and Politics in the South During the 1950s* (Baton Rouge: Louisiana State University Press, 1969), 298.

22. Rev. James F. Burks, typescript, "Integration or Segregation?" Similar versions of this sermon are reprinted repeatedly, including in *Religious Herald* (May 3, 1956), cited in Newman, *Getting Right with God*, 56. Deuteronomy 32:8: "When the Most High gave the nations their inheritance, when he divided the sons of men, he fixed their bounds"; Acts 17:26: "From one single stock he not only created the whole human race so that they could occupy the entire earth, but he decreed how long each nation should flourish and what the boundaries of its territory should be." Both from Jerusalem Bible (1966).

23. Campbell and Pettigrew, *Christians in Racial Crisis*, 45, 51. Quotes from Newman, *Getting Right with God*, 51, 53, and 56. Sample of pamphlet titles (from box 2, McCain Papers): *Mixed Schools and Mixed Blood* (1956); *Race Mixing a Religious Fraud* (n.d., ca. 1959); *God Gave the Law of Segregation (as Well as the 10 Commandments) to Moses on Mount Sinai* (1960).

24. Letter, Mrs. Jesse L. West to Governor Thomas B. Stanley, June 8, 1954, box 100, Executive Department, Stanley Correspondence.

25. *Citizens' Council*, April 1956, folder 19, box 1, Ed King Collection (MUM00251), Archives and Special Collections, J. D. Williams Library, University of Mississippi.

26. Louttit quoted in Shattuck, *Episcopalians and Race*, 68; Daughters of the American Revolution comment from *Councilor Newsletter*, monthly publication of the Citizens' Councils of Louisiana, May 1958, Miscellaneous Papers, Race Relations #517-381, f. 1, Southern Historical Collection, University of North Carolina, Chapel Hill; *Florida ex rel Hawkins v. Board of Control*, 1 RRLR 89 at 95 (1955), referenced in David L. Chappell, *Inside Agitators: White Southerners in the Civil Rights Movement* (Baltimore, MD: Johns Hopkins University Press, 1994), 91.

27. Harry S. Ashmore, "The Southern Style," *Saturday Review*, May 23, 1959, 16, 46.

Chapter Fourteen: Death Groans from a Dying System

1. David M. O'Brian, *Justice Robert H. Jackson's Unpublished Opinion in Brown v. Board: Conflict, Compromise, and Constitutional Interpretation* (Lawrence: University of Kansas Press, 2017).

2. Martin Luther King Jr., "Facing the Challenge of a New Age," address delivered at NAACP Emancipation Day rally, January 1, 1957, in *The Papers of Martin Luther King, Jr.*, vol. 4, *Symbol of the Movement, January 1957–December 1958*, ed. Clayborn Carson (Berkeley: University of California Press, 2000), 73–74, 78.

3. King, "Facing the Challenge," 77, 78.

4. King, "Facing the Challenge," 83; David J. Garrow, *Bearing the Cross: Martin Luther King, Jr., and the Southern Christian Leadership Conference* (New York: Vintage, 1986), 92.

5. The Mothers' League of Central High School invested the segregationist struggle "with the unassailable twin mantles of Christianity and the sacred authority of southern mothers." Segregationist leader Amos Guthridge quoted

in Elizabeth Jacoway, *Turn Away Thy Son: Little Rock, the Crisis That Shocked the Nation* (New York: Free Press, 2007), 82. See also Elizabeth Gillespie McRae, *Mothers of Massive Resistance: White Women and the Politics of White Supremacy* (New York: Oxford University Press, 2018), 188–197.

6. On Little Rock see Karen Anderson, "The Little Rock School Desegregation Crisis: Moderation and Social Conflict," *Journal of Southern History* 70, no. 3 (August 2004): 603–636; John A. Kirk, *Redefining the Color Line: Black Activism in Little Rock, Arkansas, 1940–1970* (Tallahassee: University of Florida Press, 2002); John A. Kirk, "Massive Resistance and Minimum Compliance: The Origins of the 1957 Little Rock School Crisis and the Failure of School Desegregation in the South," in *Massive Resistance: Southern Opposition to the Second Reconstruction*, ed. Clive Webb (New York: Oxford University Press, 2005), 76–98; Tony A. Freyer, *Little Rock on Trial:* Cooper v. Aaron *and School Desegregation* (Lawrence: University of Kansas Press, 2007); and Jacoway, *Turn Away Thy Son*.

7. The Little Rock banners were so ubiquitous that Billy Wilder worked them into his 1961 film *One, Two, Three*, set in (prewall) Berlin.

8. Mays, August 26, 1950. The World Council of Churches, meeting in Chicago in 1950, "condemned racial prejudice as un-Christian." Quoted in Stetson Kennedy, *Jim Crow Guide to the U.S.A.: The Laws, Customs and Etiquette Governing the Conduct of Nonwhites and Other Minorities as Second-Class Citizens* (London: Lawrence and Wishart, 1959), 198.

9. Martin Luther King Jr., Advice for Living, *Ebony*, March 1958, 92 ("misguided religious views"); February 1958, 84 ("individuals").

10. See Walter Francis White, *A Man Called White: The Autobiography of Walter White* (New York: Viking, 1948), 274, and Beth Bailey and David Farber, *The First Strange Place: The Alchemy of Race and Sex in World War II Hawaii* (New York: Free Press, 1992), 133–166, esp. 150.

11. *Statehood for Hawaii: Hearings Before the Committee and Subcommittee on Territorial and Insular Affairs*, United States Senate, 81st Congress, 2nd sess., May 1–5, 1950, 79; *Chicago Tribune*, September 15, 1952, C1; "No Place for Racism," *New York Times*, July 23, 1950.

12. *Statehood for Hawaii: Hearings*, 68.

13. Moon-Kie Jung, *Reworking Race: The Making of Hawaii's Interracial Labor Movement* (New York: Columbia University Press, 2006), esp. Chapter 2, and Tom Coffman, *Island Edge of America: A Political History of Hawai'i* (Honolulu: University of Hawai'i Press, 2003), 108. Sociologists Nathan Glazer and

Seymore Lipset note that after 1954, the South became the most vehemently anticommunist area.

14. Letter from Joseph C. O'Mahoney, Chairman, to Dean C. Acheson, Secretary of State, April 7, 1950, *Statehood for Hawaii: Hearings*, 50, 487–488. On Hawaiian statehood see Sarah Miller Davenport, *Gateway State: Hawai'i and the Cultural Transformation of Empire* (Princeton, NJ: Princeton University Press, 2019), Chapter 1.

15. The Associated Negro Press reported in 1953, "Southern senators, led by the states of Mississippi and Virginia, have come to regard their fight against admitting Hawaii to statehood as a fight [against] establishing a civil rights law abolishing segregation in America." ANP, "Southerners Against Hawaiian Statehood," *Atlanta Daily World*, March 23, 1953; Enoch P. Waters, "Adventures in Race Relations: A Novel Solution," *Chicago Defender*, May 15, 1954.

16. Peggy Pascoe, "Miscegenation Law, Court Cases, and Ideologies of 'Race' in Twentieth-Century America," *Journal of American History* 83, no. 1 (June 1996): 44–69, esp. 49.

17. Flyer of editorial, "Never Say Die," *Meridian Star*, May 21, 1961, box 1, folder 24, Citizens' Council Pamphlets, University of Mississippi.

18. Reginald Robinson quoted in Adam Fairclough, *Better Day Coming: Blacks and Equality, 1890–2000* (New York: Viking, 2001), 258.

19. Sovereignty Commission, (n.d., ca. June 1964), box 135, f. 1, Johnson Family Papers, University of Mississippi (hereafter Johnson Papers). Another role of the Sovereignty Commission was to channel information to Mississippi's elected officials, especially the state's two US senators, James O. Eastland and John Stennis.

20. Report of Operator #79, April 23–May 9, 1964, box 135, f. 8, Johnson Papers; Neil R. McMillen, *The Citizens' Council: Organized Resistance to the Second Reconstruction, 1954–1964* (Urbana: University of Illinois Press, 1971), 195.

21. Report of Operator #79, Jackson, MS, July 29, 1964, f. 5, Johnson Papers. Scarborough kept a running list of people supposedly engaging in interracial sex.

22. Report, Tom Scarborough (Agent #79), Sunflower County (Ruleville), MS, September 3, 1964, box 136, f. 1, Johnson Papers.

23. Selma's population of twenty-eight thousand in 1960 was evenly divided between whites and Blacks. J. Mills Thornton III, *Dividing Lines: Municipal Politics and the Struggle for Civil Rights in Montgomery, Birmingham, and Selma* (Tuscaloosa: University of Alabama Press, 2002), 382, 380.

24. Thornton, *Dividing Lines*, 393. Selma and surrounding Dallas County were the center of the White Citizens' Council movement in Alabama during these years. Dan T. Carter, *The Politics of Rage: George Wallace, the Origins of the New Conservatism, and the Transformation of American Politics* (Baton Rouge: Louisiana State University Press, 1996 [1995]), 240.

25. Thornton, *Dividing Lines*, 411.

26. King quote from Garrow, *Bearing the Cross*, 372; Thornton, *Dividing Lines*, 433.

27. On SCLC's desire to provoke a confrontation, see Garrow, *Bearing the Cross*, 360. On the ease with which such a provocation could arouse a firm reaction in Selma by Clark, see Thornton, *Dividing Lines*, 476. The extremist Clark was not necessarily representative of Selma whites, however: Selma's police chief Wilson Baker opposed Clark's violence, even to the point of protecting civil rights supporters. See David J. Garrow, *Protest at Selma: Martin Luther King, Jr., and the Voting Rights Act of 1965* (New Haven, CT: Yale University Press, 1978), 46, 72.

28. Adam Fairclough, *To Redeem the Soul of America: The Southern Christian Leadership Conference and Martin Luther King, Jr.* (Athens: University of Georgia Press, 1987), 239; Fairclough, *Better Day Coming*, 291; Carter, *The Politics of Rage*, 242, 245.

29. *U.S. News & World Report*, March 22, 1965, 32–33; Fairclough, *To Redeem the Soul of America*, 247. Cf. Garrow, *Protest at Selma*, 73–80. The *Washington Post* (following the UPI) noted the "praying Negroes" in its story on the Selma march.

30. Quoted in Garrow, *Protest at Selma*, 52, 78; Garrow, *Bearing the Cross*, 399–400. This was not the first time SCLC tried to involve significant numbers of clergy in movement activities. In 1962, King issued a national appeal to clergymen to join him in Albany, Georgia. Some seventy-five responded but stayed only a few days. The visible incorporation of clergy was more successful in the 1963 March on Washington, when SCLC leaders shared the platform with thirty-four clergymen and heads of religious associations. See Michael B. Friedland, *Lift Up Your Voice Like a Trumpet: White Clergy and the Civil Rights and Anti-War Movements 1954–1973* (Chapel Hill: University of North Carolina Press, 1998), 63–64, 88–90.

31. Quoted in Fairclough, *To Redeem the Soul of America*, 250; Sister Thomas Marguerite Flanigan, "Nuns at Selma," *America*, April 3, 1965, 454–456.

32. Garrow, *Protest at Selma*, 103.

33. Organized at a meeting in New Orleans in February 1957, the SCLC was originally named the Southern Leadership Conference. Elected as the group's first president, King immediately sought to align the organization with Christian righteousness: his first organized event was the prayer pilgrimage to Washington. See Garrow, *Bearing the Cross*, 90.

34. Keith D. Miller, *Voice of Deliverance: The Language of Martin Luther King, Jr. and Its Sources* (New York: Free Press, 1992), 174.

35. See, e.g., *Ebony*'s coverage in the May 1965 issue, 46–62, 75–86, which refers repeatedly to the "pilgrimage" and the "pilgrims." For Levison, see Garrow, *Bearing the Cross*, 418. For King, see *Pittsburgh Courier*, April 3, 1965, and James Melvin Washington, *A Testament of Hope: The Essential Writings of Martin Luther King, Jr.* (San Francisco: Harper and Row, 1986), 228.

36. *Ebony*, May 1965, 53. Clergymen and nuns figure prominently in the many pictures that accompany this long article on the march.

37. Clipping, *Memphis Press-Scimitar*, March 21, 1965; speech of Rep. William Dickinson, *Congressional Record*, March 30, 1965, 6,333; sworn affidavit of anonymous Black man, April 12, 1965, read into *Congressional Record*, March 21, 1965, 8,597 (reproduced in *Fiery Cross*, Winter 1965/66. With the cooperation of the governor's office, more than fifteen thousand copies of Dickinson's speech were mailed to Alabamans. Carter, *Politics of Rage*, 260. On Wallace and women workers in the capitol see Carter, *Politics of Rage*, 256.

38. *Time*, April 2, 1965, 21.

39. Cecil H. Atkinson affidavit, November 17, 1965; anonymous affidavit, November 17, 1965; both quoted in *Fiery Cross*, Winter 1965/66. Charles Eagles, *Outside Agitator: Jon Daniels and the Civil Rights Movement in Alabama* (Chapel Hill: University of North Carolina Press, 1993), 48; Mary Stanton, *From Selma to Sorrow: The Life and Death of Viola Liuzzo* (Athens: University of Georgia Press, 1998), 137; *New York Times*, March 30, 1965; Dickinson speech in *Congressional Record*, April 27, 1965, 8,593. See also *Newsweek*, "Kiss and Tell?," May 10, 1965; *U.S. News & World Report*, "What Really Happened on Alabama March?," May 10, 1965; *Time*, "Love on the Lawn?," May 7, 1965. The *Memphis Press-Scimitar*, March 21, 1965, reporting on Dickinson's speech, says the marchers "'left every campsite between Selma and Montgomery littered with whiskey bottles, beer cans and used contraceptives.'"

40. Bob Craig, *Jackson Clarion Ledger*, April 27, 1965.

41. *Newsweek*, May 10, 1965, 40; *U.S. News & World Report*, May 10, 1965. SNCC leader Julian Bond castigated Dickinson for "accusing nuns, priests,

rabbis, and other responsible citizens of misconduct." See *New York Times*, May 5, 1965.

42. Quoted in Joel L. Alvis Jr., *Religion and Race: Southern Presbyterians, 1946–1983* (Tuscaloosa: University of Alabama Press, 1994), 113.

43. And as was the Episcopal church's addition of Jonathan Daniels—shot outside a grocery store in Lowndes County by a white Alabaman scandalized by Daniels's kissing a Black female fellow civil rights worker—to the Calendar of Lesser Feasts and Fasts, which recognizes those who sacrifice their lives "for the faith of Christ." Eagles, *Outside Agitator*, 264, 220.

44. Dickinson, *Congressional Record*, April 27, 1965, 8,596.

Conclusion: The Fall, Without a Whimper, of an Empire

1. Erica L. Coleman, "'Tell the Court I Love My [Indian] Wife': Interrogating Race and Self-Identity in *Loving v. Virginia*," *Souls: A Critical Journal of Black Politics, Culture, and Society* 8, no. 1 (Winter 2006): 67–80.

2. Simeon Booker, "The Couple That Rocked the Courts," *Ebony*, September 1, 1967, 78–86, 80.

3. Booker, "The Couple That Rocked the Courts," 79.

4. Quoted in Sheryll Cashin, *Loving: Interracial Intimacy in America and the Threat to White Supremacy* (Boston: Beacon Press, 2017), 108–109. Mildred already had one daughter by a different man.

5. Nineteen states still had antimiscegenation laws on their books in 1965 (after *McLaughlin v. Florida* [1964]). In 1965, Oklahoma upheld the constitutionality of its antimiscegenation law; Louisiana upheld its a year later. Peggy Pascoe, *What Comes Naturally: Miscegenation Law and the Making of Race in America* (New York: Oxford University Press, 2009), 270.

6. Peter Wallenstein, *Race, Sex, and the Freedom to Marry: Loving v. Virginia* (Lawrence: University of Kansas Press, 2014), 84–85, 97.

7. *Loving v. Virginia*, 388 U.S. 1 (1967), at 7.

8. Geoffrey R. Stone and David A. Strauss, "*Loving v. Virginia*," in *Democracy and Equality: The Enduring Constitutional Vision of the Warren Court* (New York: Oxford University Press, 2019), 119.

9. Although the Warren Court could not possibly have intended to imply a right to same-sex marriage, that is "effectively what *Loving* did." Stone and Strauss, "*Loving v. Virginia*," 115. The lawyers in *McCullough* made this argument, insisting that marriage "is one of the basic civil rights of man." Brief for Appellants, 29, in Pascoe, *What Comes Naturally*, 264. Warren spoke for

eight justices; Justice Potter Stewart wrote a concurring decision reiterating his already-expressed opinion that "it is simply not possible for a state law to be valid under our Constitution which makes the criminality of an act depend upon the race of the actor." Pascoe, *What Comes Naturally*, 283–284.

10. "Genocide" from John Dittmer, *Local People: The Struggle for Civil Rights in Mississippi* (Urbana: University of Illinois Press, 1994), 139; *Loving* quote from clipping, *Southern Courier* (Montgomery, AL), June 17–18, 1967, box 1, folder 2, Ed King Collection (MUM00251), Archives and Special Collections, J. D. Williams Library, University of Mississippi. The *Southern Courier* was an African American paper.

11. "In U.S., 87% Approve of Black-White Marriage vs 4% in 1958," Gallup Minority Rights and Relations poll, Gallup.com, July 25, 2013, https://news .gallup.com/poll/163697/approve-marriage-blacks-whites.aspx; "Nearly 20 Per-cent of Americans Think Interracial Marriage Is 'Morally Wrong,' Poll Finds," *Newsweek*, March 14, 2018, citing new poll by YouGov. Seventeen percent of respondents said interracial marriage was "morally wrong" while 83 percent said it was "morally acceptable." There was a noteworthy divide along party lines on the subject, with 28 percent of Republicans and just 12 percent of Demo-crats replying that interracial marriage was morally wrong. "Intermarriage in the U.S.: 50 Years After *Loving*," Pew Research Center, May 18, 2017, www.pew socialtrends.org/2017/05/18/intermarriage-in-the-u-s-50-years-after-loving-v -virginia/.

12. Tobin Grant, "Opposition to Interracial Marriage Lingers Among Evangelicals," *Christianity Today*, June 24, 2011.

13. Mark Newman, *Getting Right with God: Southern Baptists and Desegre-gation, 1945–1995* (Tuscaloosa: University of Alabama Press, 2001), 33.

14. An analysis of federal data on private school enrollments by the Civil Rights Project at Harvard University found that private religious schools are more racially segregated than public ones. "Study Finds Parochial Schools Seg-regated Along Racial Lines," *New York Times*, June 27, 2002, A18.

15. *Bob Jones University v. United States*, 461 U.S. 574 (1983).

16. Nicholas D. Kristof, "Hate, American Style," *New York Times*, August 30, 2002, A19; World Church of the Creator website.

17. Kathleen Belew, *Bring the War Home: The White Power Movement and Paramilitary America* (Cambridge, MA: Harvard University Press, 2018), 157, 159; Miles quote from 164.

18. *Chicago Tribune*, July 12, 2001.

19. Hannah Arendt, "Reflections on Little Rock," *Dissent*, Winter 1959, 45–56. On this controversy see Werner Sollors, "Of Mules and Mares in a Land of Difference, Or, Quadrupeds All?" *American Quarterly* 42, no. 2 (June 1990): 167–190.

20. Sidney Hook, *New Leader*, April 21, 1958, 203.

21. Sidney Hook, *Dissent*, Spring 1959.

22. David Spitz, "Politics and the Realms of Being," *Dissent*, Winter 1959, 56–64, esp. 63.

23. Carol Anderson, *Eyes off the Prize: The United Nations and the African American Struggle for Human Rights, 1944–1955* (New York: Columbia University Press, 2003), 255.

24. George Chauncey, *Why Marriage? The History Shaping Today's Debate over Gay Equality* (New York: Basic Books, 2004), 60.

25. *Masterpiece Cakeshop v. Colorado Civil Rights Commission*, 138 S. Ct. 1719 (2018); *Newman v. Piggie Park Enterprises*, 390 U.S. 400 (1968).

26. Margaret Halsey, *Color Blind: A White Woman Looks at the Negro* (New York: Simon and Schuster, 1946), 124–125.

Index

Index

Index

Index

Index

Index

Index

Index

Index

Index

Index

Index

JANE DAILEY is an associate professor of history at the University of Chicago. A recipient of fellowships from the American Academy in Berlin, the American Council of Learned Societies, and the Guggenheim Foundation, she is the author or coauthor of several previous books, including *Before Jim Crow* and *Building the American Republic*. She lives in Chicago, Illinois.